Multicultural Counseling
and Psychotherapy

Multicultural Counseling and Psychotherapy

A Lifespan Perspective

Leroy G. Baruth
Appalachian State University

M. Lee Manning
Columbia College of South Carolina

Merrill, an imprint of
Macmillan Publishing Company
New York

Collier Macmillan Canada, Inc.
Toronto

Maxwell Macmillan International Publishing Group
New York   Oxford   Singapore   Sydney

Cover art: Marko Spalatin

Editor: Linda A. Sullivan
Production Editor: Jonathan Lawrence
Art Coordinator: Raydelle Clement
Cover Designer: Russ Maselli
Production Buyer: Pamela D. Bennett

This book was set in Garamond.

Macmillan Publishing Company
866 Third Avenue, New York, NY 10022

Collier Macmillan Canada, Inc.

Library of Congress Cataloging-in-Publication Data
Baruth, Leroy G.
    Multicultural counseling and psychotherapy : a lifespan
perspective / Leroy G. Baruth, M. Lee Manning.
        p.   cm.
    Includes bibliographical references and indexes.
    ISBN 0-675-21225-1
    1. Cross-cultural counseling—United States.   2. Psychotherapy—
United States—Cross-cultural studies.   3. Developmental
psychology—United States—Cross-cultural studies.   I. Manning, M.
Lee.   II. Title.
    [DNLM: 1. Counseling—methods.   2. Culture.   3. Ethnic Groups—
psychology—United States.   4. Psychotherapy—methods.   WM 55
B295m]
BF637.C6B283   1991
158'.3—dc20
DNLM/DLC
for Library of Congress   90-13628
                                                                                   CIP

Printing: 1 2 3 4 5 6 7 8 9   Year: 1 2 3 4

To Carmella

for her modeling of how to appreciate the vast riches found in cultural diversity

To Seana, Kelly, and Katey

who have the opportunity to live in a society where cultural diversity is the norm rather than the exception

—LGB

To Marianne

for her encouragement, support, and patience, and for her respect for cultural diversity and for all people

To Jennifer and Michael

two great children who are growing up in a society increasingly rich in cultural diversity

—MLM

Preface

The United States, a haven for various cultural and ethnic groups for many years, continues to benefit from the rich diversity among its people. The increasing cultural diversity of the U.S. population also has given rise to a more intense need for multicultural counseling. Culturally diverse clients may bring problems to counseling sessions related to a particular lifespan stage or to the frustrations and challenges often facing minority groups struggling to cope in a predominantly Anglo society. Counselors, perhaps not trained in multicultural intervention, may not recognize, or may underestimate, the powerful influence of a client's cultural background and developmental period; thus they may plan inappropriate counseling strategies.

Although few basic counseling strategies are designed for multicultural situations in particular, an understanding of cultural differences is important in using existing strategies to best advantage. Integrating multicultural and lifespan considerations is crucial to counseling effectiveness. Problems associated with multicultural intervention not only arise from situations involving majority-culture professionals counseling minority clients; they also arise when minority counselors intervene with majority-culture clients.

Multicultural Counseling and Psychotherapy: A Lifespan Perspective was written to address these concerns. It provides both majority-culture and minority-culture elementary and secondary school counselors, marriage and family therapists, rehabilitation agency counselors, mental health counselors, counselors in higher education, and counselors in other settings with a multicultural counseling text that explores the lives and potential counseling problems of Native-American, African-American, Asian-American, and Hispanic-American clients at the various stages along the lifespan continuum.

The Lifespan Perspective and Selection of Cultures

The lifespan perspective that provides a framework for the text reflects the current emphasis on lifespan development and stresses the fact that mental health issues and counseling problems differ for children, adolescents, adults, and the elderly. It also recognizes the importance of the prenatal months on an individual's development and calls attention to the often dismal realities of prenatal health care.

Effective multicultural counseling requires that counselors understand the unique problems related to the client's culture as well as the problems unique to the client's developmental period. It takes only a few examples to illustrate the need to consider both culture and development in counseling intervention: The mental health issues of the Native-American child are very different from those of the Asian-American elderly person; similarly, African-American children have unique problems that differ from those of Asian-American children, or even from those of African-American adults.

Our emphasis on four cultural groups—the Native-American, African-American, Asian-American, and Hispanic-American cultures—was determined by two main factors. First, these four groups represent the most populous minority-group cultures in the United States today. Second, these four cultural groups all have significant problems that increasingly will require counseling intervention. All four have been oppressed by years of discrimination and continue to be plagued by negative stereotypes and misconceptions. Moreover, acculturation of younger generations is threatening the continuance of the cherished values, traditions, and customs associated with each of these four cultures.

Organization of the Text

Following the first three chapters, which provide the necessary background for intervening with culturally diverse clients, Part I (Chapters 4 and 5) centers on the child; Part II (Chapters 6 and 7), on the adolescent; Part III (Chapters 8 and 9), on the adult; and Part IV (Chapters 10 and 11), on the elderly. Part V, consisting of Chapter 12 and the Epilogue, explores professional issues in multicultural counseling and points to future directions in the field.

The organization of the text is consistent with our goal to enhance understanding of six broad concepts:

1. The United States is a nation of many different cultural groups and will continue to be enriched by increasing cultural diversity (Chapter 1).

2. Majority-culture counselors can be trained to intervene effectively with minority clients and minority counselors with majority-culture clients; minority counselors can be trained to intervene effectively with minority clients of differing cultural backgrounds (Chapter 2).

3. Knowledge of a client's developmental period and the problems and challenges of each lifespan period contributes to the counselor's expertise (Chapter 3).

4. Knowledge of a client's social, cultural, and ethnic background provides the counselor, regardless of cultural background, with a sound basis for multicultural counseling intervention (Chapters 4, 6, 8, and 10).

5. Counselors and their clients benefit from the selection and implementation of counseling strategies and techniques that are appropriate for specific cultural groups (Chapters 5, 7, 9, and 11).

6. In the coming years, multicultural counselors will be challenged by a number of issues that deserve to be understood and addressed as multicultural counseling continues to gain recognition and respect (Chapter 12).

Special Features and Pedagogical Aids

To clarify and enliven the text and to provoke the reader's thought, several features are included:

- *Highlight boxes,* entitled A FOCUS ON RESEARCH, are placed appropriately within the text to call the reader's attention to recent research on the topic under discussion. Empirical studies and scholarly writings on counseling, development, and multicultural populations are featured.

- *Cultural Comparison Tables* indicate how the Anglo-American child, adolescent, adult, and elderly person differs from culturally different individuals at these lifespan stages. While the tables provide a succinct comparison of general cultural characteristics, readers are reminded of the dangers of cultural stereotyping and are encouraged to consider the individual client's gender, generation, geographic location, and socioeconomic class, as well as intracultural differences.

- *Boxed Vignettes,* entitled UP CLOSE AND PERSONAL, describe individuals from each of the cultures and age groups. Various members of the Lonetree, Johnson, Sukuzi, and Suarez families are introduced, providing a portrait of the child, adolescent, adult, and elderly person within the family, within the culture, and within society at large.

- *Annotated suggested readings* list books and journals that may be of special interest to those wanting to improve multicultural counseling effectiveness.

- An *appendix* following the Epilogue briefly describes the various professional journals in which multicultural issues are sometimes considered.

At various points in the text, the reader is cautioned to keep in mind that each client is unique; that is, individual differences related to gender, generation, geographic location, and socioeconomic class must be accounted for in planning appropriate counseling intervention. Intracultural differences, as evidenced in the many Hispanic and Asian-American subgroups, also must be considered. To avoid stereotyping of cultures, we have made reference to specific populations whenever possible. It is crucial for counselors to recognize that the line between cultural descriptions and cultural stereotypes is very narrow, and that the consequences of stereotypic thinking are potentially damaging to clients of all cultures and at all lifespan stages.

Acknowledgments

We want to thank the following people for their assistance and support: Carolyn Dapo and Susanne Brown for their diligent typing and for their ability to read handwritten material that was often difficult to decipher; John Vassallo and Jane Tuttle, reference librarians, for their patience and their valuable and most appreciated assistance in locating information; Linda Sullivan and Jonathan Lawrence at Merrill, an imprint of Macmillan Publishing; and Ann Mirels, who copyedited the manuscript.

We are particularly grateful to the following individuals who reviewed the manuscript and offered numerous constructive suggestions: Jesus Manuel Casas, University of California—Santa Barbara; Ajit Das, University of Minnesota—Duluth; Farah Ibrahim, University of Connecticut—Storrs; Don Locke, North Carolina State University—Raleigh; John McFadden, University of South Carolina—Columbia; Margery Neeley, Kansas State University—Manhattan; Richard Page, University of Georgia—Athens; Holly Stadler, University of Missouri—Kansas City; Russell Thomas, Memphis State University; and Beatrice Wehrly, Western Illinois University.

Leroy G. Baruth
M. Lee Manning

Contents in Brief

Contents

Overview

Chapters 1, 2, and 3

Chapters 1, 2, and 3 focus attention on the nature of multicultural counseling, the culturally effective counselor, and multicultural human growth and development, respectively. These chapters lay a foundation for intervening with culturally diverse clients along the lifespan continuum.

Chapter 1

Introduction to Multicultural Counseling and Psychotherapy

Questions To Be Explored

1. What are the definitions of culture, race, and ethnicity relative to multicultural counseling?
2. What are the places of origin, population data, and geographical locations of Native-, African-, Asian-, and Hispanic-American people?
3. What intracultural differences should multicultural counselors consider when planning counseling interventions?
4. Why is an understanding of lifespan development crucial for counselors?
5. What lifespan differences affect the outcome of the counseling intervention?
6. What is multicultural counseling and psychotherapy?
7. What is multicultural counseling's status within the counseling profession?
8. What ethical issues should be considered as multicultural counselors plan professional interventions?
9. What cultural factors should be considered when planning individual, group, and family therapy?
10. What challenges confront multicultural counselors in a culturally pluralistic society?

AN INCREASINGLY MULTICULTURAL SOCIETY

The United States has had its doors open to people of diverse cultural, ethnic, and racial origins for many years. Some people entered the country with hopes of realizing the American dream; others came to escape oppressive conditions in their home

countries. Still others were actually brought against their will and expected to conform culturally to the Anglo population. And there were those who first inhabited
the land on which the American nation now exists and who were expected to adopt
the "white man's ways." Through experiences commonly associated with daily living
and working together, it was thought that these people would acculturate or adopt
"American" customs and values and, through a "melting pot," assimilate into mainstream America. For any number of reasons, however, many rejected the "melting
pot ideology" and instead adopted a "salad bowl" model (McCormick, 1984), which
more accurately represents the culturally pluralistic nation. These differing ethnic
groups seek to retain their unique cultural identity and remain true to their heritage.
They want their cultural characteristics and values recognized as different rather than
inferior or wrong.

Clients: Today and the Future

The extent of our multicultural society and the role it plays in shaping people's lives
will continue to become apparent to counseling professionals as growing numbers
of clients from diverse cultures seek mental health services. Undoubtedly, counselors
and psychotherapists will increasingly counsel culturally different clients with differing customs, traditions, values, and perspectives toward life events and the counseling
process. Will the Anglo, middle-class counselor trained to intervene with mainstream
middle-class American clients be able to provide effective counseling services for
such a diversity of clients? The attitudes and skills that counselors bring to the multicultural counseling situation will depend significantly on their knowledge of cultures, their counseling effectiveness with culturally diverse clients, and their willingness to perceive cultural characteristics as "differences" rather than "deficits."

The Client's Lifespan Period

Human development is an ongoing process that starts at birth and continues to death,
with cultural and individual variations existing within each of the lifespan periods:
childhood, adolescence, adulthood, and old age. The problems of children are certainly very different from those of the various adult groups. Culturally perceptive
counselors recognize that while Anglo-American and Native-American children may
share similar developmental characteristics, they may be vastly different in many other
respects. Likewise, although the elderly in all cultures often share characteristics,
elderly Asian-Americans experience problems that differ from those of elderly Native-
Americans or Hispanic-Americans. It is important that counselors understand each
client's cultural background and lifespan period, and the intricate relationships between the two. Although studies in multicultural psychology and human development
have become more sophisticated over the past decade or so, counselors are urged
to draw conclusions and generalizations cautiously; the existing literature in this field
often does not allow for definitive conclusions. There is, however, sufficient evidence
to indicate that cultural differences undoubtedly exist across and within cultures,
between generations, and throughout the lifespan. In this text, we will examine
cultural differences in terms of a lifespan approach and discuss their implications for
counselors and psychotherapists in multicultural settings.

Development and Culture

Counseling and psychotherapy usually are considered two-person relationships, since they normally involve a counselor and a client. It was believed for many years that being empathetic toward the client was sufficient for the counseling relationship to be effective (Ivey, 1986). Recent opinion has suggested that in the empathetic interchange four factors come into play: the therapist, with his or her cultural and historical background, and the client, with his or her cultural and historical background. Rather than counseling relationships being simplistic, each client brings a special cultural and historical background that has powerful implications for the outcome of the session (Ivey, 1986).

UNDERSTANDING DIVERSITY AMONG CLIENTS IN A PLURALISTIC SOCIETY

Present-day counselors are very likely to be middle-class Anglos who received their professional preparation at institutions that provided training for counseling Anglo middle-class American clients. Such training was and is unquestionably appropriate for counselors preparing to work with mainstream Anglo-American clients; however, the possible lack of training and clinical experiences with culturally diverse clients indicates the need for improved understanding of appropriate intervention measures with these clients. A prerequisite to effective multicultural counseling is the professional's understanding of concepts related to the culturally diverse population of the United States. Table 1–1 provides a succinct listing of the key concepts and terms related to culture, race, and ethnicity.

In some cases, the terms *race, culture,* and *ethnicity* have been used interchangeably by professionals, which has resulted in erroneous assumptions. Johnson (1990) warned of this categorical doubletalk and urged that the terms be used in their proper context. With reference to these three terms in this section and throughout the text, readers are advised to keep in mind that they are not synonymous.

Culture

Even readers with only limited awareness of culture and its many dimensions realize that culture has been defined in many ways (Lum, 1986, p. 46):

> the way of life of a society, consisting of prescribed ways of behaving or norms of conduct, beliefs, values, and skills. (Gordon, 1978)

> people's characteristics, behavior, ideas, and values. (Brislin, 1981)

> the sum total of life patterns passed on from generation to generation within a group of people. (Hodge, Struckmann, & Trost, 1975)

> elements of a people's history, tradition, values, and social organization that become meaningful to participants in an encounter. (Green, 1982)

Although considerable debate and controversy continue to rage over an accurate definition (Banks, 1987), culture includes institutions, language, values, religion, ideals, habits of thinking, artistic expressions, and patterns of social and interpersonal

Table 1–1   Concepts and terms related to culture, race, and ethnicity

Culture, Ethnicity, and Related Concepts	Culture
	Ethnic group
	Ethnic minority group
	Stages of ethnicity
	Ethnic diversity
	Cultural assimilation
	Acculturation
	Community culture
Socialization and Related Concepts	Socialization
	Prejudice
	Discrimination
	Race
	Racism
	Ethnocentrism
	Values
	Self-concept
Intercultural Communication and Related Concepts	Communication
	Intercultural communication
	Perception
	Historical bias
	Environmental perception
Power and Related Concepts	Power
	Social protest and resistance
The Movement of Ethnic Groups	Migration
	Immigration

Source: From James A. Banks, *Teaching Strategies for Ethnic Studies*, Fourth Edition. Copyright © 1987 by Allyn and Bacon. Reprinted by permission.

relationships (Lum, 1986). Culture is an essential aspect of all people and consists of the behavior patterns, symbols, institutions, values, and other components of society (Banks, 1987). A FOCUS ON RESEARCH 1–1 concerns the role of culture in counseling and psychotherapy interventions.

Counselors should remember that most clients are multicultural in the sense that they have been influenced by at least five cultures. Rather than living in one culture, people live in five intermingling cultures (Vontress, 1986):

Universal: Humans all over the world are biologically alike; e.g., males and females are capable of producing offspring and of protecting and ensuring the survival of offspring.

Ecological: Humans' location on earth determines how they relate to the natural environment.

National: Humans are characterized by their language, their politics, and their world views.

Regional: Humans tend to settle in a region, thus creating area-specific cultures.

◆ A FOCUS ON RESEARCH 1–1
The Role of Culture in Psychotherapy

Sue and Zane (1987) examined the role of cultural knowledge and culture-specific techniques in the psychotherapeutic treatment of ethnic minority-group clients. Suggestions that counselors recognize and consider cultural differences are not helpful when the advice fails to include treatment procedures and to consider differences and similarities within cultural

Source: Sue, S., & Zane, N. (1987). The role of culture and cultural techniques in psychotherapy. *American Psychologist, 42,* 37–45.

groups. Sue and Zane "examine the principles underlying attempts to develop effective psychotherapy with ethnic-minority groups" (p. 37). Examining four key points and using a case example, the authors maintain that counselors should review current practices. They suggest linking cultural knowledge and cultural-consistent strategies and the processes of credibility and giving. A careful analysis of these processes provides a framework for considering the role of culture and for improving psychotherapeutic practice.

Racio-ethnic: Humans have distinct racial and ethnic differences; however, all people reflect their racial and ethnic background.

According to Vontress, these five cultures constitute socializing forces that influence the way clients perceive their problems, possible solutions, and the counseling process.

Intracultures

Acquiring an objective picture of someone who is culturally different requires a determined attempt to understand that person's culture and how the person relates to it. It is not any more reasonable to group all African-Americans into one cultural group than it is to assume all Anglo-American women are alike. One may assume that a client with black skin shares cultural characteristics with other African-Americans, but intracultural or individual differences must also be recognized in counseling intervention. Intracultural differences might include clients' educational backgrounds, socioeconomic status, acculturation, and their urban and rural backgrounds.

Subcultures

Subcultures are racial, ethnic, regional, economic, or social communities exhibiting characteristic patterns of behavior sufficient to distinguish them from others in the dominant society or culture. Examples of subcultures are the drug culture, the gay culture, the gang culture, and the adolescent culture. Each subculture is a unique social entity that provides its members with a history, social values, and expectations that might not be found elsewhere in the dominant culture. Therefore, meaningful communication between people who appear similar may be hampered due to their very different subcultures and their experiential backgrounds (Porter & Samovar, 1985).

Most cultural groups in fact have characteristics of both the larger culture and a smaller cultural group. Moreover, a client can be a member of several different subcultures, each playing a part in the counseling intervention (Axelson, 1985).

Race

Ashley Montagu (1974) called race "man's most dangerous myth" (p. 3). In fact, it is his belief that the concept of race has been highly destructive in the history of mankind (Banks, 1987). Without doubt, caution is urged when categorizing clients into a particular racial group.

Hernandez (1989) writes that *race* refers to the way a group of people defines itself or is defined by others as being different from other human groups because of assumed innate physical characteristics (Ogbu, 1978). It is based on an anthropological concept used to classify people according to physical characteristics, such as skin and eye color and the shape of the head, eyes, ears, lips, and nose (Bennett, 1986).

Gollnick and Chinn (1990) make several important points concerning race. First, despite the movements of large numbers of people from one geographical region to another and the incidence of intermarriage across racial groups, the concept of race today still has a significant social meaning. Second, race contributes few insights to cultural understanding. Cultural groups defined by nationality, geography, language, and religion seldom correspond with racial categories—at least not to the extent necessary to provide culturally relevant information. Hence, racial identity, in and of itself, does not reveal an individual's nationality, language, or religion. Third, characterizing the population of the United States in government reports based on combinations of race, national origin, and religion documents the confusion regarding race and ethnicity. For example, individuals may be asked to define themselves in terms of categories that are not mutually exclusive; e.g., White, Hispanic, Jewish. An individual could belong to all three of these categories.

Society has generally recognized differences between the races, but classification on this basis addresses only biological differences; it does not explain differences in social behavior (Pedersen, 1988). Anthropologists have experienced difficulty in structuring racial categories because of the wide variety of traits and characteristics shared by people and the extensive differences among groups (Banks, 1987).

Ethnicity

While race technically refers to biological differences, ethnicity describes groups in which members share a cultural heritage from one generation to another (Pedersen, 1988). Ethnicity is defined on the basis of national origin, religion, and/or race (Gordon, 1964). Attributes associated with ethnicity include (a) a group image and sense of identity derived from contemporary cultural patterns (e.g., values, behaviors, beliefs, language) and a sense of history; (b) shared political and economic interests; and (c) membership that is involuntary, although individual identification with the group may be optional (Appleton, 1983; Banks, 1981). The extent to which individuals identify with a particular ethnic group varies considerably; many have two or more identities. When ethnic identification is strong, individuals maintain ethnic group values, beliefs, behaviors, perspectives, language, culture, and ways of thinking (Hernandez, 1989).

Gordon (1969) suggests ethnicity, race, religion, and national origin interact with social class to produce differential patterns of identification and behavior. He continues:

> With a person of the same social class but of a different ethnic group, one shares behavioral similarities but not a sense of peoplehood. With those of the same ethnic group but a different social class, one shares the sense of peoplehood but not of behavioral similarities. The only group which meets both of these criteria are people of the same ethnic and same social class. (p. 53)

Each individual simultaneously has an ethnic identity, a socioeconomic class identity, and a gender identity. Each also constructs a personal reality, which may be influenced and constrained by ethnicity, class, or gender (Grant & Sleeter, 1986). Personal reality represents a complex, dynamic, and unique blend resulting from the interaction of many characteristics (Hernandez, 1989).

Various interpretations of ethnicity are illustrated by the following definitions (Lum, 1986, pp. 42–43):

> loyalty to a distinctive cultural pattern related to common ancestry, nation, religion, and/or race. (Davis, 1978)

> [the sharing of] a unique and social cultural heritage passed on from generation to generation and based on race, religion, and national identity. (Mindel & Habenstein, 1981)

> [social distinction of] a community of people within a larger society . . . primarily on the basis of racial and/or cultural characteristics such as religion, language or tradition. The central factor is the notion of set-apartness with a distinctiveness based on either physical or cultural attributes or both. Ethnicity applies to everyone; people differ in their sense of ethnic identity. (Bennett, 1986)

> [identification] by distinctive patterns of family life, language, recreation, religion, and other customs that differentiate them from others. (Banks, 1987)

Social Class

Social class differences also play a significant role in determining how a person acts, lives, thinks, and relates to others. With respect to minority group clients, differences in values between counselor and client basically represent class differences, since minority group members are often from the lower socioeconomic classes. Differences in values, attitudes, behaviors, and beliefs among the various socioeconomic groups warrant consideration when planning intervention (Atkinson, Morten, & Sue, 1989).

The middle- to upper-class counselor may experience difficulty in appreciating the circumstances and hardships that often surround the client living in poverty. Low wages, unemployment, underemployment, little property ownership, no savings, lack of food reserves, and living from one day to the next easily lead to feelings of helplessness, dependence, and inferiority (Sue, 1981).

Social class differences in some cases may be more pronounced than differences resulting from cultural diversity. For example, as social class differences separate members of the Anglo culture, a lower-class African-American may share more cultural commonalities with lower-class Anglo-Americans than with middle- or upper-class African-Americans.

A person's social class sometimes is thought to be indicative of ambition or motivation to achieve; however, it is a serious mistake to stereotype people on this basis. To those who would contend that the lower classes lack ambition and do not want to work or improve their educational status, it is not unreasonable to suggest that the racism and discrimination they are faced with thwarts their ambition and stymies their efforts to succeed.

Generational Differences

Generational differences within a particular culture result in varying beliefs and values and represent another obstacle to achieving homogeneity within a culture. Older generations may be more prone to retain old-world values and traditions due to the tendency to live within close proximity to people of similar language, traditions, and customs. Through public schooling and a tendency (or a requirement) to adopt middle-class Anglo-American values, younger generations are more likely to accept values different from their elders'.

Several examples illustrate generational differences among people. One example has to do with the ability to speak the English language. While older generations might have lived in cultural enclaves with others speaking their native languages or speaking English with similar levels of fluency, younger generations who can communicate effectively in English are better able to cope in a predominantly English-speaking society. Another example involves the concern of elderly Asian-Americans about the acculturation of younger Asian-Americans; e.g., changing opinions of the extent of which younger generations should visit and care for their elders (Osako & Liu, 1986).

Although acculturation plays a role in generational differences, one's place on the lifespan continuum also plays a significant role. Whether due to wisdom, experience, or the manner in which events are perceived during each lifespan stage, opinions and beliefs change as one matures. Generational differences often lead to interpersonal conflicts that have the potential to create psychological and emotional problems warranting counseling intervention.

Gender

Counselors should also recognize and understand differences resulting from gender, or those characteristics and traits that separate males' and females' lives as well as impart their unique orientations toward problems and solutions. The possibilities for exploring gender differences are endless. Consider, for example, that women who vary from expected norms are often looked on with suspicion or even disdain, or that the beauty of African-American females may be judged according to Anglo criteria, or that women are still being counseled into certain career roles (Cayleff, 1986). It is clear that gender plays a significant role during counseling, but research focusing specifically on culturally diverse females does not consistently allow for generalizations across cultures. In this text, however, we have included research on both cultural diversity and gender issues: Puerto Rican adolescent women and their decisions on whether to choose an abortion; developmental tasks in Mexican-American females; the Hispanic-American woman's changing role; the more assertive stances of Asian-American women; the trend toward African-American women becoming sole bread-winners and heads of households; African-American women and alcoholism and suicide; and women's attitudes and behavior in American, Japanese, and cross-national marriages.

Lifespan

A major premise underlying this text is that clients differ with respect to their lifespan stage. Each lifespan stage (childhood, adolescence, adulthood, old age) has its unique developmental characteristics and counseling problems. The dilemma, however, is compounded when counselors consider that their clients' lifespan differences and cultural characteristics are often closely intertwined. Examples include the previously mentioned elderly Asian-Americans who may exhibit considerable anxiety over the younger generation's acculturation, or the concern of the African-American elderly with health issues, or the machismo so important to Hispanic-American adolescents. An adolescent client and an elderly client of the same culture, race, and ethnic group might very well perceive a problem from totally different perspectives. Problems, values, and beliefs vary so greatly with development that people functioning within the same lifespan stage may actually constitute a subgroup.

Research on human development relative to cultural diversity is admittedly limited, most studies having been directed toward the middle-class Anglo population. The scarcity of literature in this area, however, does not excuse the counselor from making every effort to gain the maximum knowledge of the client's period on the lifespan.

CLIENTS IN A MULTICULTURAL SOCIETY

Glazer and Moynihan (1970) in their book *Beyond the Melting Pot* contend that the melting pot metaphor employed to describe the cultural composition of the United States did not, in fact, provide an accurate description. To substantiate their point, Glazer and Moynihan documented case studies of Jews, Italians, and the Irish of New York City who chose to retain their old-world heritages. Other groups have also failed (or elected not to try) to forsake cherished cultural characteristics in order to become "Americanized." Asians and Hispanics, regardless of the generation, are often reluctant to give up ethnic customs and traditions in favor of "middle-class American habits" that appear to them to be in direct contradiction to beliefs acquired early in life. African-Americans have fought to overcome cultural dominance and discrimination, and, through efforts such as the civil rights movement, have sought to understand and maintain their cultural heritage. In essence, the United States is a nation of many diverse peoples, and, although cultural groups can be described with some accuracy, minority cultures are not monolithic in nature. This need to recognize and respect individual differences and similarities within cultures becomes clear when one considers the generational differences and social-class differences among the Native-, African-, Asian-, and Hispanic-American cultures.

Trends and projections for the future indicate that the present influx and growth of diverse ethnic groups will continue. The following list indicates the breakdown of race and ethnic groups in the United States (U.S. Bureau of the Census, 1980, 1988a; Black population is growing, 1988):

- *Native-Americans*   1.5 m (the various American tribes, Aleuts, and Eskimos).

- *African-Americans*   29.9 m (Africans, West Indians, and Haitians).

- *Asian-Americans and Pacific Islanders*   3.5 m (*Asian*: Chinese, Pilipinos, Japanese, Koreans, Asian Indians, Vietnamese; *Pacific Islander*: Hawaiians, Samoans, Guamanians).

- *Hispanic-Americans*   19.4 m (Mexicans, Puerto Ricans, Cubans, Central and South Americans)

THE CULTURALLY DIFFERENT: ORIGIN, POPULATION, AND GEOGRAPHICAL LOCATIONS

Native-Americans

Banks (1987) contends that scholars do not know exactly when people first came to the Americas. While many archaelogists have concluded that the lack of fossils rules out the possibility of men and women evolving in the Western Hemisphere, some Native-American groups believe that their origins lie in the Americas. Despite their contentions, archaelogists have held to the belief that the ancestors of Native-Americans originally came from Asia (Banks, 1987).

The question of origins aside, it is a fact that the ancestors of the people who are today known as Indians, American-Indians, or Native-Americans have continuously occupied North America for at least 30,000 years (Dorris, 1981). With the coming of the "white man," a crusade was begun of taking their land from them. A somewhat paradoxical situation exists: Rather than emigrating from other lands and being faced with culturally assimilating into the majority culture, Native-Americans were faced with an influx of outsiders to their land, expecting them to relinquish cherished cultural traditions. Although Native-American origins continue to be in dispute, it is well known that these people had a distinct and cherished heritage from the beginnings of their existence (Banks, 1987).

It is difficult to understand why social scientists and the general public view Native-Americans in a collective manner (Trimble & Fleming, 1989). Still, these people have been categorized into one homogeneous group. The Native-American population is reported to be approximately 1.5 million or one-half percent of the total U.S. population (U.S. Bureau of the Census, 1980). Slightly more than half of the present-day Native-American population resides in urban and metropolitan areas. Numerous tribes have as few as five members while some tribes may have only one surviving member (Trimble & Fleming, 1989). Approximately half of the Native Amer-

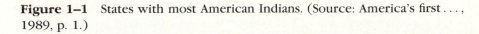

Figure 1–1   States with most American Indians. (Source: America's first ...,
1989, p. 1.)

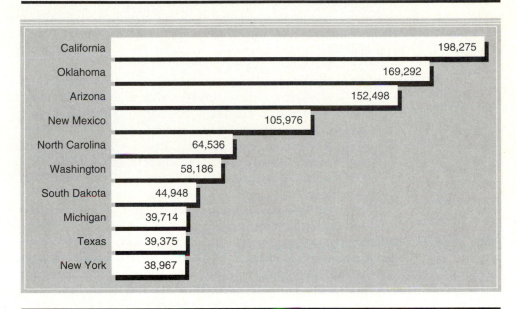

icans in the United States reside on Native-American lands, while the other half live
outside the reservations in urban or other predominantly Anglo geographical areas
(Axelson, 1985). Figure 1–1 indicates those states with the greatest population of
Native-Americans.

Of the federal reservations for Native-Americans, the Navajo Nation Reservation
is the largest and has a population of over 165,000. Other states having reservations
with large land holdings include Oklahoma, South Dakota, Wyoming, Montana, Arizona, and California (U.S. Bureau of the Census, 1988b).

African-Americans

Whether termed African-Americans, Black-Americans, Afro-Americans, blacks,
Negroes, or Colored, most members of this group can trace their origin to an area
in western Africa. The term *African-American* is gaining widespread support as a
replacement for *black* or *Black-American* because it recognizes cultural ties with
Africa. Supporters of the term include Jesse Jackson, Coretta Scott King, former mayors
Andrew Young of Atlanta and Richard Hatcher of Gary, Indiana, Supreme Court Justice
Thurgood Marshall, and Ramona Edelin, president of the National Urban League.
Another argument for the term *African-American* is that it parallels terms describing
other cultures: Asian-American, Native-American, and Hispanic-American (Gill, 1990).

Torn away from their families and cherished cultural traditions, Africans arrived
in America with the earliest European settlers, suffering first the bonds of slavery and

then experiencing all manner of discrimination. Through civil revolts, the civil rights movement of the 1950s and 1960s, and the efforts of such leaders as Dr. Martin Luther King, Jr., the lives of African-Americans have improved significantly. However, they continue to experience covert forms of racism and discrimination that impede their progress in mainstream American society. The lives of most African-Americans have been characterized by a series of struggles and conflicts beginning with their first arrival on American soil (Banks, 1987).

African-Americans presently are the nation's largest ethnic minority group. The latest annual population estimates indicate that African-Americans totaled 29.9 million in 1987 compared with 26.8 million in the 1980 census. In 1985, 16 states had African-American populations in excess of 1 million. Two of these states, New York (2.7 million) and California (2.1 million) had African-American populations of more than 2 million. Ten states and the District of Columbia had between 200,000 and 1,000,000 African-Americans in 1985, and eight additional states had between 50,000 and 200,000 African-Americans (U. S. Bureau of the census, 1989).

The African-American population has been growing faster than the total population; its proportion of the total population increased from 11.8 percent in 1980 to 12.2 percent in 1987 (Black population is growing . . . , 1988). Moreover, in the next few decades African-American population growth will likely continue to outpace Anglo population growth because of the relative youth of the African-American population (U. S. Bureau of the Census, 1986). Table 1–2 indicates the estimated population growth of the African-American people.

About half the African-American population lives in the southern states, with the remainder living in large cities of the East, Midwest, and West. While African-Americans had been moving from the South to the North in large numbers since World War I, the trend reversed during the last half of the 1970s. In fact, 53 percent of African-Americans presently live in the South (Banks, 1987). As previously mentioned, and as Table 1–3 indicates, significant increases in the African-American population are to be expected, considering the age structure of the population.

Counselors working with the elderly will find it particularly interesting that during the period from 1980 to 1985 the population of elderly African-Americans increased by 14.7 percent in the 75–84 age span and by 28.7 percent in the 85+ age span. Moreover, there is indication that such significant increases will continue (U. S. Bureau of the Census, 1986).

Table 1–2 Estimated population changes of African-Americans from 1990 to 2000

Year	Estimated Population (Thousands)
1990	30,934
1995	33,000
2000	34,939

Source: Compiled from U. S. Bureau of the Census, 1988b.

Table 1–3 Age structure of the African-American population: 1985, 1990, 2000

Age	Population (Thousands)		
	1985[1]	1990[2]	2000[2]
5–17	6,898	7,170	7,895
18–64	17,064	18,550	21,353
65–74	1,463	1,608	1,848
75+	675	1,005	1,283

[1]Compiled from U. S. Bureau of the Census, 1986.
[2]Compiled from U. S. Bureau of the Census, 1988b.

Asian-Americans

Risking violation of sacred family traditions and actually breaking a law against emigration from the homeland, many young Asians headed for the promised land of America around the turn of the century. After a rough and hazardous journey, they were greeted with suspicion. Their strange clothing, language, hairstyles, and skin color targeted them as victims of curiosity and racism (Banks, 1987). Asian-Americans often were forced to accept the lowest paid menial jobs and were denied the right of citizenship and the right to ownership of land. Because their opportunities to live and work outside of their cultural community were strictly limited, Asian-Americans often formed their own cultural enclaves, of which Chinatown is an example. Isolated as they were, they continued to speak their native language, maintaining their close-knit families and holding fast to old-world traditions (Banks, 1987). Table 1–4 indicates the top ten countries of origin of Asian-Americans with respect to numbers of immigrants.

Table 1–4 Asian immigrants by country of birth 1961–1986

Country of Birth	Number of Immigrants (Thousands)
Philippines	735.5
China	518.6
Korea	509.6
Vietnam	448.8
India	353.9
Iran	135.6
Laos	127.8
Japan	110.4
Hong Kong	103.8
Thailand	81.6

Source: Compiled from U. S. Bureau of the Census, 1988b.

As previously mentioned, the 3.5 million Asian-Americans and Pacific Islanders in the United States include the following Asian cultures: Chinese, Pilipino, Japanese, Korean, Asian Indian, and Vietnamese. Pacific Islanders refer to the Hawaiian, Samoan, and Guamanian groups. Banks (1987) reports that Asian-Americans have increased in numbers from 1.4 million in 1970 to 3.5 million in 1980, an increase of 141 percent. Of the areas with populations of 250,000 or more, those with the greatest concentrations of Asian-Americans include Buffalo, Chicago, Honolulu County, Los Angeles, New York, and San Francisco (U. S. Bureau of the Census, 1980).

The recent influx of another group of Asian-Americans, the Southeast Asian people, has contributed to the diversity of the Asian cultures. In 1975, as the Vietnam War ended, a wave of 130,000 refugees began arriving in the United States (Divoky, 1988). Three years later, a second wave of 650,000 Indochinese started their journey from rural and poor areas to refugee camps and finally to U.S. towns and cities (New whiz kids, 1987). Originating from such countries as Vietnam, Cambodia, Laos, and Thailand, these people differ from the most populous groups (the Japanese and Chinese); however, it is important to remember that the Southeast Asian groups also differ greatly among themselves (West, 1983).

A discussion of each of the many Asian groups currently living in the United States is beyond the scope of this text. In a study of refugees from Southeast Asia, the following groups were identified: Blue, White, and Striped Hmong; Chinese, Krom, and Mi Khmer Cambodians; Chinese Mien, Thai Dam, and Khmer Laotians; and Lowlander and Highlander Vietnamese. Not only does each group have its own history and culture, but within each exist many stratifications (Kitano, 1989).

Hispanic-Americans

The Hispanic-American culture includes Mexican-Americans, Chicanos, Spanish-Americans, Latin-Americans, Mexicans, Puerto Ricans, Cubans, Guatemalans, and Salvadorans. All are recognized as Hispanics and share many values and goals (Gonzalez, 1989). In some respects, Hispanics constitute members of a single cultural group with a more or less common history and the sharing of language, values, and customs; however, other aspects point to a significant heterogeneous population that should be conceptualized as an aggregate of distinct subcultures (Ruiz, 1981). For example, while Hispanics at large do have much in common, each Hispanic subgroup has its own unique and distinguishing social and cultural practices (Casas & Vasquez, 1989).

The term *Hispanic* is an inclusive designation for all people of Spanish origin and descent. In terms of place of origin, approximately 60 percent are from Mexico, 14 percent from Puerto Rico, 8 percent from Central and South America, 6 percent from Cuba, and 12 percent from other Spanish-speaking countries (U.S. Bureau of the Census, 1988a). This group is a very large, young, rapidly growing, highly diverse group of people. Depending on geographic origins, Hispanics can be Caucasian, Mongoloid, Negroid, or various combinations of the races (Casas & Vasquez, 1989). The 1980 census reported 14.6 million Hispanics living in the United States in 1980, up from 9.1 million in 1970. One of every 16 people in the United States was of Hispanic origin in 1980. From 1980 to 1987, the Hispanic population increased by 34 percent; that is, by about 5 million people (U.S. Bureau of the Census, 1988a). If

Table 1–5 Estimated population changes of Hispanic population by ages

Age	Population (Thousands)		
	1990	1995	2000
5–17	4,825	5,555	6,207
18–64	16,480	18,720	21,011
65–74	707	894	1,041
75+	419	525	678

Source: Compiled from U.S. Bureau of the Census, 1988b.

predicted increases are realized, Hispanics will outnumber African-Americans and people of any other single minority ethnic background. Table 1–5 indicates the estimated population increases for the various Hispanic-American age groups. Recent population data indicate that Hispanics, numbering 19.4 million in 1988, will total nearly 29 million by the year 2000. Already this increasing population is exerting an influence on mainstream American culture in such areas as language, employment, education, and the arts.

Hispanics currently outnumber African-Americans in cities such as New York City, Los Angeles, San Diego, Phoenix, San Francisco, and Denver. In 1988, 55 percent of all Hispanic-Americans resided in two states—Texas and California (U.S. Bureau of the Census, 1988a). Figure 1–2 illustrates the geographical distribution of the Hispanic population in 1988.

Figure 1–2 Geographic distribution of the Hispanic population. (Source: U. S. Bureau of the Census, 1988a.)

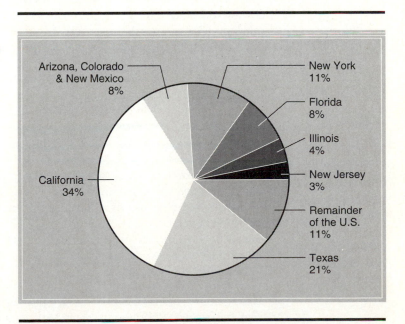

The Selection of Cultures for This Text

For purposes of this text, the decision was made to concentrate on four cultures: the Native-, African-, Asian-, and Hispanic-American cultures. The first factor contributing to our selection of these four groups was the population numbers and, in particular, the estimated growth increases associated with them. To date, all four cultures have shown significant increases and are expected to increase further, either by increased births or by immigration. The numbers are presently of a sufficient proportion that counselors, whether in schools, private practices, mental health institutions, or other settings of service delivery, will likely encounter clients from these cultures. Second, most of the available research data were drawn from these four groups. Third, we believe that these cultural groups have psychological and emotional needs that warrant counseling, yet few counselors have sufficient knowledge of culturally different clients and the expertise to counsel them effectively.

The Current Status of Research

The increased recognition of cultural differences (and their implications for the counseling profession) have led to more and better research on multicultural populations and multicultural counseling processes. Nonetheless, much of the research and scholarly writings presently available must be considered beginning points. Journals publishing research and scholarly opinion are too many to name here; however, a few representative journals that provide information for multicultural counselors are *The Counseling Psychologist, Counseling and Human Development, Journal of Counseling and Development, American Psychologist, Journal of Cross-Cultural Psychology*, and *The Journal of Multicultural Counseling and Development*. Readers interested in information pertaining to children and adolescents might consider *The School Counselor* or *Elementary School Guidance and Counseling*; those counseling the elderly will benefit from selected issues of *The Gerontologist* or *The Journal of Gerontology*. (For a closer look at journals concerned with issues relating to human development and multicultural counseling, the reader is advised to refer to the appendix, "Selected Journals Recommended for Multicultural Counselors.")

Casas (1985), in his reflections on the status of racial/ethnic minority research, states that the need to examine racial/ethnic variables within the counseling process was recognized more than 30 years ago. Although few research studies focused on these variables until the late 1960s, sociopolitical factors such as the civil rights movement and demographic changes resulted in increased attention on cultural differences and the rights of culturally diverse groups. It was Casas's feeling that the overall quality of the research unfortunately did not keep pace with the quantity. He pointed out that the many variables involved in counseling the culturally different may disallow definitive conclusions regarding the impact of racial/ethnic variables on counselor-client relationships.

One of the best discussions of the status of research and writing on multicultural counseling is Ponterotto and Sabnani's (1989) study of "classics" in the field. In researching the literature, these authors found that the *Journal of Multicultural Counseling and Development* published the most articles on multicultural counseling. Among their recommended books are *Counseling American Minorities: A Cross-Cultural Perspective* (1989) by Atkinson, Morten, and Sue; *Counseling the Culturally*

Different (1981) by D. W. Sue; and *Counseling Across Cultures* (1989) by Pedersen, Draguns, Lonner, and Trimble.

COUNSELING AND PSYCHOTHERAPY IN A MULTICULTURAL SOCIETY

Multicultural counseling (sometimes called cross-cultural counseling) and psychotherapy is becoming a major force in counselor training and is recognized and endorsed by leading counselor education accrediting agencies. Both the National Council of Accreditation of Teacher Education (NCATE) and the Council for Accreditation of Counseling and Related Educational Programs (CACREP) have adopted the position that multicultural education should be a part of the educational program from counselors. Lee (1989b) puts it this way:

> It is apparent to me that multicultural counseling is presently the hottest topic in the profession. Every sector of the profession seems to be searching for new ways to intervene successfully into the lives of people from increasingly diverse client populations. This would seem natural because American society in the last several decades has become more pluralistic and projections suggest that ethnic minority groups will have an even greater impact on population demographics in the next century. (p. 2)

A Brief Historical Overview of Multicultural Counseling

The most comprehensive reviews (Atkinson, 1985; Aubrey, 1977) of multicultural counseling substantiate claims of its relatively recent appearance. According to Atkinson (1985), although racial differences in counseling and psychotherapy did receive some attention during the late 1940s, major empirical studies were not undertaken. In the 1950s, several studies promoted cultural orientations toward counseling and psychotherapy. Erikson (1950) made reference to therapeutic situations that extended beyond mainstream America; Abel (1956) also addressed the role of cultural factors among diverse clients; Devereux (1951, 1953) reported in detail on psychotherapy with a "Plains Indian" (Draguns, 1981, p. 15).

By the late 1950s, enthusiasm had waned, but in the mid-1960s, there seemed to be a resurgence of interest in racial and ethnic aspects of minority groups. According to Atkinson, Morten, and Sue (1989), until the mid-1960s counseling and psychotherapy tended to overlook culturally different clients who found themselves at a disadvantage in a predominantly Anglo and middle-class world. Likewise, psychotherapy limited its practice primarily to middle and upper class and neglected the lower classes and minority populations. Events of the 1960s changed and expanded the counseling client base to include, for example, minority groups, Viet Nam War objectors, alienated hippies, those experimenting with drugs, and victims of urban and rural poverty (Aubrey, 1977). By the mid-1970s, the number of studies focusing on effects of race on counseling and psychotherapy had increased (Atkinson, 1985). Issues and concerns included (a) the effects of race on client- and counselor-related variables (Harrison, 1975); (b) the effects of therapist-client racial similarity on counseling and psychotherapy (Sattler, 1977); (c) the effects of black-white pairs (Abramowitz & Murray, 1983); and (d) ethnic similarity in Native-, Asian-, African-, and Hispanic-Americans (Atkinson, 1983).

Draguns (1981) maintained that the origins of cultural orientation in psychotherapy and counseling can be traced to anthropological and ethnographic studies of remote, different cultures and also the more common cultural variations found in modern culturally pluralistic societies such as the United States. Several culturally oriented post-World War II psychiatrists, such as Kiev (1964) and Prince (1976), attempted to document examples of effective counseling and psychotherapy in multicultural situations.

Draguns (1981) documented a progression from the early pioneering studies to Wrenn's (1962) work in which he sought to sensitize counselors to the problem of counselor encapsulation. Wrenn warned against imposing culturally alien goals, values, and practices on culturally different clients.

Although the history of multicultural counseling and psychotherapy has been brief, current research and writing provide a basis for the prediction that the enthusiasm for counseling across cultures will continue into the 1990s and beyond.

Research Directions

Casas and Vasquez (1989) contend that reviews of the literature on multicultural counseling reflect two trends: (1) attempts to identify the particular approach, theory, or philosophy that most effectively facilitates multicultural counseling (Ibrahim, 1985; Ponterotto, 1987; Sue & Zane, 1987); and (2) conceptualizations or modifications of perspectives from which to view interactions between the individual (personality, strength of ethnic identity) and the environment (culture and race, assimilation, social support systems) (Ivey, Ivey, & Simek-Downing, 1986; Katz, 1985; Levine & Padilla, 1980).

Three important features characterize the research to date on multicultural counseling. First, research studies focusing on black and white pairs (client-counselor matchups) far outnumber studies directed toward Native-American, Asian, and Hispanic cultural groups. Second, early research employed either survey or archival research designs. In the former, clients were surveyed to determine their attitudes; in the latter, mental health records were used to examine selected aspects of the counseling process. Third, subjects were drawn from mental health clinics or psychiatric hospitals in most of the early research, whereas in more recent studies numerous multicultural counseling centers have been used (Atkinson, 1985).

A research area that has aroused considerable controversy deals with the impact of race/ethnicity on the effectiveness of counselor-client relationships. Research in this area is often called counselor's race/ethnicity. It explores, for example, minority clients' perceptions of counselors with respect to expertness, trustworthiness, attractiveness, and credibility as a function of counselor-client race/ethnicity match (Casas, 1985).

Ponterotto (1986) analyzed the content of the *Journal of Multicultural Counseling and Development* to determine professional affiliations of the primary authors and the focus of the articles. His findings indicate the progress of the multicultural counseling movement and the direction of contemporary research. Although the contemporary focus continues to be directed toward African-Americans (51 percent), other cultural groups are also being studied: minorities in general, 26 percent; African- and Anglo-American, 4 percent; and whites, Africans, Hispanics, and Asian and Pacific Islanders, 3 percent. Research studies focus on such issues as career and vocational counseling, 23 percent; counseling techniques and strategies, 21 percent; student development and adjustment, 13 percent; and assessment and testing, 11 percent. The developmental level of the clients also provides a clue to the direction of current research: general (or an unspecified developmental group), 33 percent; college students, 28 percent; children, 14 percent; and junior high or high school students, 8 percent (Ponterotto, 1986).

Draguns (1989) suggested that research investigations in multicultural counseling mainly focus on either *etic* or *emic* approaches. While *etic* focuses on similarities and dissimilarities of the cultures being examined, *emic* examines a given culture, itself, rather than making an external comparison of cultures. Choosing the former approach, an investigator might first assume that all human groups display aggressive behavior, then try to establish differences in aggression across cultures. With the latter approach, or the emic, the investigator might consider an indigenous construct, such as the Japanese "amaeru" (which can be translated as "presuming upon another person's benevolence"), and then relate it to a complex pattern of dependence on seeking gratification. The emic approach then, proceeds from within the culture; the etic approach is initiated from the outside on the basis of generic human dimensions (Draguns, 1989). (See Chapter 12 for a discussion of emic and etic approaches to issues affecting multicultural counseling.)

Although current research has contributed significantly to multicultural counseling, the African-American population continues to be the primary target for research efforts. Future research should also include a focus on the Native-American, Asian, and Hispanic cultures, the relationship between culture and counseling, and developmental issues throughout the lifespan.

Definitions and Cultural Dimensions

While some authors distinguish between *counseling* and *psychotherapy,* others elect to use the terms interchangeably. Draguns (1981) stated that "it is obvious that no clear dividing line can be drawn between these two activities" (p. 4). He did suggest, however, that counseling may be construed as an activity that facilitates and fosters personal problem solving, whereas psychotherapy is principally concerned with changing people; e.g., their overt behavior and personalities. More recently, Draguns (1989) again defined counseling broadly "to encompass any and all professional techniques and activities that are undertaken to resolve human problems" (p. 4). Likewise, he maintained his belief that the difference between counseling and psychotherapy is not sharp, and that often the same professional practices are used in both. The goal of the counselor is usually to change a specific activity or behavior, while the goal of the psychotherapist is more global, involving the change and re-organization of people's adaptive resources (Draguns, 1989).

Regardless of whether counseling or psychotherapy is used, both designations describe the systematic process "to assist individuals with problems of life adjustment and interpersonal relations" (Saeki & Borow, 1985, p. 223). Still, however, debate continues in the interest of making definitions perfectly clear. According to Young-Eisendrath (1985), the following three concerns of psychotherapy distinguish it from counseling: (1) a focus on personality change; (2) a consideration of interpersonal relationships (for example, in dreams or irrational thoughts) and the significance of early relationships; and (3) a special use of the symbolic meaning of time.

The definition of *multicultural counseling* is less fraught with controversy. Vontress (1988) defines the term as "counseling in which the counselor and the client(s) are culturally different because of socialization acquired in distinct cultural, subcultural, racioethnic, or socioeconomic environments" (p. 74). An American Psychological Association position paper on cross-cultural counseling competencies (Sue et al., 1982) defines cross-cultural counseling/therapy as "any counseling relationship in which two or more of the participants differ with respect to cultural background, values, and lifestyle" (p. 47). A third definition considers multicultural counseling a situation in which two or more people with different ways of perceiving their social environment are brought together in a helping relationship (Pedersen, 1988). "Multicultural" tends to be preferred over "cross-cultural," "intercultural," or "transcultural," since it is less likely to implicitly suggest the superiority of one culture over another (Pedersen, 1988).

Multicultural counseling includes situations in which (a) both the counselor and client are minority individuals but from different minority groups; (b) the counselor is a minority person but the client is not, or vice versa; and (c) the counselor and client are racially and ethnically similar, yet belong to different cultural groups because of such variables as sex, sexual orientation, socioeconomic factors, religious orientation, or age (Sue et al., 1982).

Draguns (1989) offered the following key points that he felt most proponents of multicultural counseling would agree on:

1. The techniques of the counselor must be modified when counseling the culturally different.

2. The culturally sensitive counselor is prepared to deal with the differences and difficulties that are anticipated during the counseling process as the distance between the cultural backgrounds of the counselor and the client increases.

3. Conceptions of the helping process are cultural, as are modes of self-preparation and communication of distress.

4. Complaints and symptoms differ in their frequency of occurrence in various cultural groups.

5. Cultural norms and expectations of the counselor and client may vary.

Counseling and Culture

In order to understand the close relationship between counseling and culture, counseling must be considered in its cultural context. For example, Draguns (1989) points out that counseling, being a product of twentieth-century Euroamerican civilization, stresses individualism, self-determination, egalitarianism, and social mobility and social change—attributes of the American culture. The counselor's traditional role was to be a "sympathetic but not meddlesome helper" (p. 5). While American counselors considered the client's individuality, they did not give due recognition to his or her cultural background. Counselors often found culturally different clients to be unmotivated and resistant. Without doubt, the culturally different client perceived counseling sessions as baffling, irrelevant, and unhelpful. The current emphasis on multicultural counseling further illustrates that counselors did not recognize the reality of clients being products of differing cultural backgrounds (Draguns, 1989).

Professional Status

Multicultural counseling is a relatively recent phenomenon that has not received accolades in all professional circles. Differing opinions as to the extent to which cultural differences are important in counseling have led some professionals to accept multicultural counseling and others to reject it. There is, however, a general recognition of and respect for cultural differences during counseling intervention. (For a more thorough discussion of whether multicultural counseling belongs in counselor education programs, readers are encouraged to consult the Lloyd (1987), Hood & Arceneaux (1987), and Lee (1989a) articles referenced in Chapter 12.)

Scholarly research on culture and on counseling culturally different clients being published in counseling and psychology journals indicates the steadily rising professional status of multicultural counseling. Advances in multicultural human development research will further enhance the progress of the counseling movement by broadening the knowledge base through which culturally diverse clients on the various stages of the lifespan may be understood.

Growth and Progress

Multicultural counseling is continuing to evolve and is becoming increasingly recognized as a legitimate counseling subspeciality. A FOCUS ON RESEARCH 1–2 highlights an interview with Clemmont Vontress in which he offers his opinion on the progress of multicultural counseling. What directions will multicultural counseling take? Admitting the risky nature of predicting the future of any movement, Vontress offers two other opinions (Jackson, 1987):

1. Multicultural counseling will significantly influence counselor education in general. The effective counselor must have a background in "philosophy, psychology, anthropology, sociology, languages, and the life sciences in general." (p. 23)
2. Different professional factions will promote their own preferences and interests since multicultural counseling has become a recognized professional subspecialty.

A study by Pedersen, Fukuyama, and Heath (1989) sought to predict the course and future of multicultural counseling over the next 10 years. After reviewing the opinions of 53 identified experts in the field of multicultural counseling, the authors concluded that the future of multicultural counseling was bright. The experts predicted increases in all areas of multicultural research. They also expressed consid-

A FOCUS ON RESEARCH 1–2
Multicultural Counseling at the Crossroads

Jackson (1987) presents a dialogue with Clemmont E. Vontress who discusses the genesis, status, and future directions of multicultural counseling. Specific topics of discussion include the death of Dr. Martin Luther King, Jr. and its effects on African-Americans, concentric and interacting cultures, the existentialist foundation of the counseling theories of Vontress, and the politics associated with counseling.

Source: Jackson, M. C. (1987). Cross-cultural counseling at the crossroads: A dialogue with Clemmont E. Vontress. *Journal of Counseling and Development, 66,* 20–23.

Vontress remarks on the past, present, and future:

> The Past—"Like most social and professional movements, there is not a single starting point." (p. 20)

> The Present—"Certainly an established subspecialty of the profession. Hundreds of articles are being written by people in many disciplines about psychotherapeutically helping individuals from culturally diverse backgrounds." (p. 22)

> The Future—"I expect several universities may soon offer master's or even doctoral degree programs in cross-cultural counseling." (p. 23)

erable optimism about improving the quality of current multicultural counseling training and preparation programs. They pointed to positive changes in the area of professional networking and acknowledgment of multicultural issues, despite continued difficulty in transforming ideals and awareness into better services.

Guidelines

Draguns (1989) suggested that multicultural counselors have several resources at their disposal when planning counseling interventions. These include (a) research-based findings on the cross-cultural counseling process; (b) published accounts of personal experiences by other multicultural counselors; (c) personally transmitted accounts; (d) the counselor's own experiences with culturally different clients; and (e) the counselor's professional, cultural, and personal sensitivity.

Based on excerpts from 11 counseling interviews, Axelson (1985) compiled a list of fundamentals for counselors working in multicultural settings. Counselors' understanding of these guidelines contribute to more accurate perceptions of clients, more cooperative working environments, and increased effectiveness of the counseling process.

For the Counselor:

1. self-awareness and comprehension of one's own cultural group history and experiences;
2. self-awareness and comprehension of one's own environmental experiences in mainstream culture;
3. perceptual sensitivity toward one's own personal beliefs and values.

For Understanding the Client:

1. awareness and comprehension of the history and experiences of the cultural group with which the client might identify or is encountering;

2. perceptual awareness and comprehension of the environmental experiences in mainstream culture with which the client might identify or is encountering;

3. perceptual sensitivity toward the client's personal beliefs and values.

For the Counselor in the Counseling Process:

1. careful and active listening, not casual attention; demonstration of a broad repertoire of genuine verbal and nonverbal responses that show the client you understand what he or she is communicating;

2. caring about the client and his or her situation in the same way that you would care about yourself if you were in that situation; encouragement of optimism in seeking a realistic solution;

3. asking for clarification when you don't understand; being patient, optimistic, and mentally alert.

Ethics

Counseling with culturally diverse clients requires more than just knowledge of a client's cultural background. The client's perceptions, expectations, and expression of symptoms also warrant understanding from a cultural context. In fact, these should be understood from both the client's perspective and from that of the majority culture (Ponterotto & Casas, 1987). Ethics comes into play as counselors are faced with understanding (and, subsequently, planning interventions) that all people function from a culturally determined world view that includes values, belief systems, lifestyles, and modes of problem solving and decision making. To address these culturally based aspects of counseling, Ibrahim & Arredondo (1986) suggest that ethical standards focus around counseling preparation, practice, assessment, and research.

What ethical problems might arise in a multicultural counseling setting? Cayleff (1986) lists several multicultural counseling examples in which ethics plays a part: (1) the refusal of a Mexican-American woman with uterine cancer to have a hysterectomy because she fears her husband will leave her, (2) the labeling of culturally different clients as sick or mentally ill when they only vary from Anglo, middle-class norms, (3) stressful and conflicting demands on black women to emulate Anglo standards of appearance and behavior, and (4) paternalistic behavior of counselors to a degree that they withhold vital information from clients so as to act in their "best interests."

The Governing Council of The American Association for Counseling and Development issued its revised *Ethical Standards* (March 1988) and addressed the need for ethical behavior in multicultural situations. Section A (General) Number 10 specifically states that "through awareness of the negative impact of both racial and sexual stereotyping and discrimination, the counselor guards the individual rights and personal dignity of the client in the counseling relationship" (p. 1).

Ethics, without doubt, plays a significant role in multicultural counseling and influences its professional status as well as its growth and progress. While this brief discussion serves only to introduce the importance of ethics in multicultural counseling settings, the question of ethics during professional preparation is addressed in Chapter 2 and ethical issues are addressed in Chapter 12.

Barriers to Effective Multicultural Counseling

Although Chapter 2 discusses the barriers to effective multicultural counseling in considerable detail, at this point let us briefly consider some of the more common ones counselors might encounter when intervening with culturally different clients. They are as follows:

1. erroneous assumptions about cultural assimilation (Arredondo-Dowd & Gonsalves, 1980);
2. differing class and cultural values (Peterson & Nisenholz, 1987);
3. language differences—both cultural or socioeconomic class and nonverbal misunderstandings (Peterson & Nisenholz, 1987; Sue, 1987);
4. stereotypes toward culturally different people (Axelson, 1985);
5. class-bound values and culture-bound values (Sue, 1981);
6. counselor misunderstandings of the culture (Atkinson, Morten, & Sue, 1989);
7. assumptions of cultural bias (Pedersen, 1987);
8. lack of understanding of client's structures of reasoning (Ibrahim, 1985); and
9. lack of cultural relativity among counselors (Ibrahim, 1985).

 A FOCUS ON RESEARCH 1–3
Assumptions of Cultural Bias in Counseling

In Pedersen's (1987) view, counselors have rarely challenged many long-held assumptions. He warns that not examining these assumptions could result in "institutionalized racism, ageism, sexism, and other forms of cultural bias" (p. 16). Some of the assumptions Pedersen cites include the following:

1. All people share a common sense of "normal" behavior.

2. Problems are defined from a framework limited by academic discipline boundaries.

3. Laypersons easily understand the abstractions of counselors.

4. Independence is always valuable and dependence undesirable.

5. Each cause has an effect and each effect has a cause (linear thinking).

6. Counselors are more likely to focus on immediate events than clients discussing their "history."

These frequent assumptions all influence social, economic, and political perceptions.

Source: Pedersen, P. (1987). Ten frequent assumptions of cultural bias in counseling. *Journal of Multicultural Counseling and Development, 15,* 16–24.

This listing of barriers should not be taken to imply that the counselor's challenge is too overwhelming to be tackled. Perceptive counselors can learn about the client's culture, interact with culturally different people, learn appropriate techniques for dealing with culturally diverse clients, and, perhaps most important, examine their own beliefs and opinions concerning people of different cultures. One barrier to effective multicultural counseling, cultural bias, is addressed in A FOCUS ON RESEARCH 1–3.

COUNSELING INTERVENTION: CULTURAL CONSIDERATIONS

Regardless of culture and social class, professionals must often reach difficult decisions concerning whether to use individual, group, or family therapy for their clients. In multicultural situations, such decisions can be particularly difficult as cultural, intracultural, and generational differences are brought into the picture.

Individual/Group Therapy

Selecting counseling techniques becomes intricately complex considering that some cultures might not react favorably to traditional counseling situations. For example, Asian-Americans' commitment to protect the family name and honor at all costs may result in the client being reluctant to reveal significant personal or family information. Similarly, the Hispanic male might be reluctant to disclose events or situations that may reflect negatively upon his family or his manhood. The Western world's tendency to encourage sharing of one's personal feelings runs counter to the Native-American reluctance to allow "outsiders" to intervene in their personal affairs. Minority clients often distrust the Anglo professional, believing that the counselor does not understand the minority perspective.

Marriage and Family

The Western world's tradition of encouraging males and females to share feelings and to communicate openly, freely, and on an equal footing may not be accepted by many Asian-Americans who have long accepted the superiority of the male and his valued role as the family spokesperson. In fact, the likelihood of some minority women assuming significant speaking roles is unlikely during marriage and family counseling sessions. Although younger generations may have acculturated somewhat, the dominance of the male and his control over the family must be understood by mental health professionals who may have intervened predominantly with middle-class Anglo clients.

When planning intervention strategies, the counselor must consider the extent to which the client's cultural traditions affect therapy sessions and their outcome. Specifically, how will the client in multicultural settings respond to the spouse or children being present? Will the wife respond during family therapy, or will she be content to let the husband speak for the family? Such questions can be answered only by considering individual clients, their cultural characteristics, generation, degree of acculturation, and the nature and severity of the problem.

CULTURAL AND LIFESPAN MISUNDERSTANDINGS

The increasing culturally pluralistic nature of the United States populace signifies a vast array of cultural, ethnic, and racial differences deserving of the counselor's respect and appreciation. However, it is also important for counselors to understand that lifespan differences add to the diversity among people and, in many cases, are as important as their unique physical and cultural characteristics. A major premise of this text is that counselors should not only consider a client's cultural differences, but also the client's lifespan period and the characteristics associated with each developmental stage, including potential psychological and emotional problems associated with each stage.

Stereotypes and Prejudices

Lum (1986) defines stereotyping as "the prejudicial attitude of a person or group that superimposes on a total race, sex, or religion a generalization about behavioral characteristics" (p. 135). Stereotypes produce an overly general mental picture of a person or an entire culture. Although a stereotype may hold some validity in a particular case, effective counselors must approach all stereotypes with skepticism and acknowledge that most are accompanied by prejudice, like or dislike, or approval or disapproval of the cultural group (Axelson, 1985). In that stereotypes all too often contribute to racism and ageism, effective multicultural counselors must seek to understand and respond appropriately to others' and their own cultural and age-level beliefs about people.

Axelson (1985) describes the following characteristics of stereotypes:

1. They are *pervasive* in that most people have their own "pet" personality theories about their characteristics of others.
2. They tend to emphasize *differences* when applied to individuals or groups different from oneself but to emphasize *similarities* when applied to individuals or groups similar to oneself.
3. They tend to be *negative* when applied to characteristics of individuals and groups different from oneself or one's own group.
4. They tend to become *habitual* and *routinized* unless challenged.
5. *First impressions* are usually based on stereotypes.
6. *New stereotypes* will supplement or supplant existent stereotypes as conditions and experiences in the culture change.
7. Stereotyping and stereotypes *impair* the ability to assess others accurately and can readily lead to misinterpretations. (p. 374)

Our discussion to this point has concerned stereotypes in general. But what happens when counselors rely on them, or harbor prejudices about culturally different clients? Although several researchers have sought to determine the effects of counselor stereotyping and prejudice, their findings have failed to yield conclusive answers. Harrison (1975), for example, reviewed three studies that all indicated prejudice on the part of Anglo therapists, yet definitive conclusions could not be drawn as to the effects.

Stereotypes and prejudices about a person's lifespan stage also affect perceptions of clients. Do children lack the power to change their lives? Are adolescents rebellious trouble-makers, obsessed with sex? Are adults always preoccupied with progress and material gains? Are the elderly "over the hill," without power or purpose? Such beliefs on the part of the counselor could place the client in a difficult situation. Similarly, if the client subscribes to these beliefs, the therapeutic relationship may be undermined.

Racism

Racism is often defined as the domination of one social or ethnic group by another. That minority groups have suffered its consequences in the United States is clear: African-Americans continue to face discrimination in housing, employment, schooling, and in various other areas despite civil rights legislation; Latino-Americans are still exploited as migrant farmworkers; Asian-Americans were excluded as immigrants into the United States during the early 1900s; and Native-Americans had their land taken from them and were placed on reservations where today, as cited earlier, 50 percent reside (Lum, 1986). Hodge (1975), Davis (1978), and Lum (1986) described racism as

1. the belief that there are well-defined and distinctive races among human beings;
2. the belief that racial mixing lowers biological quality;
3. the belief in the mental and physical superiority of races over others;
4. the belief that racial groups have distinct racial cultures to the extent that some races are naturally prone to criminality, sexual looseness, or dishonest business practices;
5. the belief that certain races have temperamental dispositions, which is a form of stereotyping;
6. the belief that the superior races should rule and dominate inferior races (Lum, 1986, pp. 129–130).

A FOCUS ON RESEARCH 1–4 proposes that racism can be reduced through better understanding of minority cultures.

The range of racial expression includes a variety of forms, as Brislin (1981) describes:

1. *Redneck racism*: People feel that members of another cultural group are inferior or unworthy of decent treatment.
2. *Symbolic racism*: People have negative feelings about a minority group because they perceive it to be a threat to their cultural beliefs and the status quo.
3. *Tokenism*: People harbor negative feelings about a minority, yet are unwilling to openly admit their racial feelings.
4. *Arm's length behavior*: People are friendly to out-group members in some situations, yet hold these same cultural groups at "arm's length" in other situations.
5. *Real likes and dislikes*: People harbor negative feelings about different cultural groups who engage in behavior that they dislike or judge to be unacceptable by their standards.

◢◣ A FOCUS ON RESEARCH 1–4
Understanding Racism through Multicultural Dyadic Encounters

It is Beale's (1986) view that racism continues to exist in America. Indeed, some writers (McConahay, Hardee, & Battes, 1981) contend that it is as prevalent as ever. Others (Battes, 1982; Vontress, 1971) feel that Anglo counselors working with minority clients encounter difficulty because they do not appreciate the similarities and differences between ethnic groups and because of counselor negative experiences and attitudes. For counselors to be effective, an ap-

Source: Beale, A. V. (1986). A cross-cultural dyadic encounter. *Journal of Multicultural Counseling and Development, 14,* 73–76.

proach is needed to help them increase their understanding of differences in backgrounds, values, and lifestyles of minorities. To better understand racism, Beale (1986) suggests the Cross-Cultural Dyadic Approach (CCDA)—"a programmed activity designed to encourage the establishment of an open and honest dialogue between members of different ethnic backgrounds" (p. 74). The activity requires that participants pair up with a member of a different ethnic group and respond to a series of open-ended questions focusing on their interactions with other cultures.

---

6. *The familiar and the unfamiliar:* People simply do not know of others' cultural beliefs and traditions, and so tend to harbor negative feelings due to ignorance and misunderstanding.

Another insidious form of racism that characterizes U.S. society and impedes the social acceptance and economic progress of culturally diverse citizens is *institutional racism.* While the more overt forms of racism can be pinpointed and addressed, institutional racism is more subtle, including policies, practices, and patterns of decision making (Fernandez, 1981). The beliefs of many social scientists and psychologists are derived from research findings that are based largely on European and American cultures. When these beliefs are not subjected to thoughtful reflection, they can lead to cultural bias, including institutional racism (Pedersen, 1987).

Social, economic, educational, and political institutional policies frequently operate to foster discriminatory outcomes or to give preferential treatment to members of one group over members of another. Examples include the following:

1. exclusion from craft unions, professional organizations, and social clubs;
2. seniority systems that result in "last hired, first fired";
3. income differentials;
4. tokenism (minimal desegregation) in fulfilling quota systems;
5. role-casting in media productions and advertising according to racial stereotypes;
6. discriminatory pricing practices in real estate sales and rentals;
7. neglect in the maintenance and repairs of housing owned by absentee slum landlords;
8. inferior municipal services (trash pick-up, police protection, maintenance of streets) in minority group neighborhoods;
9. gerrymandering of legislative voting districts;

10. admission to college based on culturally biased tests;

11. differential educational treatment based on preconceived beliefs of educational potential or intellectual ability;

12. teaching of United States history that includes only white history. (Axelson, 1985, p. 13).

Minorities are undoubtedly affected by these and other examples of institutional racism. Recent years have seen landmark legal decisions in areas such as equal opportunity and desegregation; however, institutional racism continues to elude legislation to eliminate it. Adequately prepared counselors have the responsibility to examine their culturally derived assumptions and to plan professional intervention that recognizes and addresses the effects of institutional racism. A FOCUS ON RESEARCH 1–5 suggests an antiracism training model for Anglo-American counseling professionals.

The Value of Understanding a Client's Developmental Stage

The number of research studies on lifespan development has resulted in a broad spectrum of publications, textbooks, and conference proceedings (Danish, 1981). Counselors who understand the developmental characteristics and unique cultural characteristics of their clients, and the complex relationship between these two dimensions, bring an enhanced perspective to counseling and psychotherapy. The importance of considering human development theories is illustrated in A FOCUS ON RESEARCH 1–6.

As we have already mentioned, a major premise of this text is the importance of recognizing and understanding the client's developmental stage when planning and implementing counseling intervention. Rather than assuming a developmental homogeneity that may not actually exist, counselors benefit from knowing the problems, tasks, and challenges of each developmental period. The decision to use a specific technique should always be based on a sound rationale rather than simply on style, training, or preference. The relevance of human development theories becomes clear

---

◼ A FOCUS ON RESEARCH 1–5
An Antiracism Training Model

Corvin and Wiggins (1989) point out that models developed for multicultural training have not allowed the Anglo trainee to engage in "self-exploration as a member of the White race and examination of one's own racism" (p. 105).

Source: Corvin, S. A., & Wiggins, F. (1989). An antiracism training model for White professionals. *Journal of Multicultural Counseling and Development, 17,* 105–114.

With this thesis firmly established, the authors introduce a multistage model for antiracism training based on characteristics of Anglo identity development. Appropriate training goals are specified and implementation approaches suggested. Use of the model can help counselors become culturally effective by examining their own racism.

A FOCUS ON RESEARCH 1–6
Human Development Theories and Counseling

Young-Eisendrath (1985) discusses counselors' special uses of developmental theories by focusing attention on biological, social, cognitive, moral, affective, and interpersonal process patterns that characterize human life. Clarifying the basis for discussing counselors' special uses of developmental theories, Young-Eisendrath examines three theories employing (1) chronological-age models, (2) life-phase models, and (3) structural models. The relevance of the developmental theories is then related to curative factors of counseling. Topics include ego development, Erikson's eight stages of psychosocial development, Levinson's periods of adulthood, and Sullivan's interpersonal phases. Emphasis is placed on encouraging the client to accept personal responsibility during counseling intervention.

Source: Young-Eisendrath, P. (1985). Making use of human development theories in counseling. *Counseling and Human Development, 17*(5), 1–12.

---

as counselors select technique and counseling strategy based on the client's developmental level and the tasks being worked toward. The counselor having knowledge sufficient to match strategy and developmental levels can formulate appropriate short-term and long-term counseling goals (Young-Eisendrath, 1985).

Critical observers may question the cross-cultural validity of theories of human growth and development. Specifically, for example, are Erikson's (1950) psychosocial stages or Havighurst's (1972) developmental tasks valid only for middle-class Anglo-Americans, or are they valid across culturally diverse populations? Research directed toward lifespan development of multicultural populations has not yielded definitive answers. With regard to minority children's development, for example, research efforts have focused on issues such as cultural conceptions of child development (Gutierrez & Sameroff, 1990); eating habits of obese Mexican-American children (Olvera-Ezzell, Power, & Cousins, 1990); extended family structures among African-American families (Pearson, Hunter, Ensminger, & Kellam, 1990); and social expectations for children among cultures (Rotheram-Borus & Phinney, 1990). As these studies suggest, efforts directed at studying the specific question of whether human growth and development theories are valid cross-culturally do not appear to be at the forefront of interest.

Given this somewhat limited knowledge base, what conclusions, if any, can be reached? Several studies have been conducted indicating that culturally diverse people progress through similar developmental stages and experience similar developmental tasks:

- Werner (1979), in her text on cross-cultural child development, concluded that children from all cultures have the potential for advancing through Piaget's stages of intellectual development.
- Tucker and Huerta (1987) studied developmental tasks in young adult Mexican-American females (age 18–34 years) and concluded that these women experienced the developmental tasks suggested by Havighurst (1972).

- Erikson, in formulating his developmental theories, worked directly with the Oglala Sioux Indians of South Dakota, the Yurok tribes of Northern California, and other minority groups (Elkind, 1984; Maier, 1969).

Although such evidence cannot be considered conclusive, it does suggest that developmental theories are valid cross-culturally, especially in the absence of data indicating otherwise.

A POINT OF DEPARTURE

The development of multicultural counseling from its beginnings to its present status in both counselor education and mental health centers indicates that its growth will continue. Clients will benefit even more with the increasing recognition of lifespan differences. Counselors of the future might very well receive advanced degrees in multicultural counseling, which will contribute even further to the growth of this subspeciality and to the effectiveness of intervention strategies.

Challenges Confronting Multicultural Counselors

Multicultural counselors' expertise in counseling the culturally different and their knowledge of lifespan differences will undoubtedly increase as counseling programs include multicultural counseling competencies in counselor education programs. Multicultural counselors are challenged to understand diversity of all types, understand culturally diverse clients and their backgrounds, develop competency in multicultural counseling, and understand cultural and lifespan issues that affect counseling across cultures and developmental stages. In meeting these challenges, professionals are also responsible to be cognizant of the ethics involved in counseling across cultures.

SUMMARY

The predicted population trends indicate that the United States will continue to be culturally pluralistic. Counselors increasingly will be called upon to counsel culturally diverse clients of all ages along the lifespan continuum. Understanding concepts of culture, race, and ethnicity, as well as lifespan differences, is prerequisite to effective multicultural counseling. A significant challenge is held out to present-day and future multicultural counselors: That is to provide the most effective counseling intervention with clients of various cultures, racial and ethnic backgrounds, and stages on the lifespan.

Suggested Readings

Atkinson, D. R. (1985). A meta-review of research on cross-cultural counseling and psychotherapy. *Journal of Multicultural Counseling and Development, 13,* 138–153. Atkinson reviews the literature on issues such as use of mental health services, client preferences for counselor ethnicity, prejudice and stereotyping, and intervention strategies.

Draguns, J. G. (1989). Dilemmas and choices in cross-cultural counseling: The universal versus the culturally distinctive. In P. B. Pedersen, J. G. Draguns, J. Lonner, & J. E. Trimble (Eds.), *Counseling across cultures* (3rd ed.). Honolulu: University of Hawaii Press. Draguns provides an excellent discussion of counseling the culturally different, examines the evolution of the profession, and explores several dilemmas often encountered in cross-cultural counseling situations.

Ivey, A. E. (1987). Cultural intentionality: The core of effective helping. *Counselor Education and Supervision, 25,* 168–172. Cultural intentionality is proposed as a metagoal of the helping process whereby the cultural awareness is integrated with the uniqueness of each individual.

Johnson, S. D. (1987). Knowing that versus knowing how: Toward achieving expertise through multicultural training for counseling. *The Counseling Psychologist, 15,* 320–331. The question of cultural expertise in multicultural training is examined in terms of ways to make counselor trainees more culturally aware and effective.

Parker, W. M., Valley, M. M., & Geary, C. A. (1986). Acquiring cultural knowledge for counselors in training: A multifaceted approach. *Counselor Education and Supervision, 25,* 61–71. The multifaceted approach demonstrates how counselors in training can acquire cultural knowledge.

Pedersen, P. B., Draguns, J. G., Lonner, J., & Trimble, J. E. (1989). *Counseling across cultures* (3rd ed.). Honolulu: University of Hawaii Press. Generally recognized as the earliest comprehensive text on multicultural counseling, the third edition provides an introduction, general considerations, ethnic and cultural considerations, and research and practical considerations.

Ponterotto, J. G. (1988). Racial consciousness development among White counselor trainees: A stage model. *Journal of Multicultural Counseling and Development, 16,* 146–156. Ponterotto's stage model describes the racial identity and consciousness development process among majority counselor trainees in multicultural settings.

Ponterotto, J. G. (1988). Racial consciousness development among White counselor trainees: A stage model. *Journal of Multicultural Counseling and Development, 16,* 146–156. Ponterotto's stage model describes the racial identity and consciousness development process among majority counselor trainees in multicultural settings.

Saigo, R. H. (1989). The barriers of racism: Righting the wrongs of past and present. *Change, 21*(6), 8–10, 69. In this interesting reading, Saigo discusses racism in terms of both the past and future. In particular, he examines racism directed toward the Asian-American culture.

Chapter 2

The Culturally
Effective Counselor

Questions To Be Explored

1. How does cultural diversity affect the counseling intervention? Why should counselors seek special preparation for counseling culturally different clients?

2. What barriers, myths, assumptions, and stereotypes interfere with effective counseling of culturally different clients?

3. What characteristics describe effective multicultural counselors?

4. What specific beliefs/attitudes, understandings, skills, and ethical concerns should be addressed during professional preparation for multicultural counseling?

5. What are world views, and how can multicultural counselors assess a client's world view?

6. What ethical standards are relevant in multicultural counseling?

7. What four conditions might counselors be subject to in multicultural situations?

8. What sources can counselors explore to enhance their effectiveness in multicultural situations?

INTRODUCTION

American society undoubtedly benefits from the richness of cultural diversity. However, counselors trained in traditional counseling approaches often encounter barriers in working with culturally different clients. Formal preparation and first-hand experiences with culturally diverse groups are essential for multicultural counseling to be effective. In this chapter, we will take a close look at why counselors need multicultural counseling competence, with emphasis on the knowledge, skills, and attitudes they must develop for effective intervention.

CULTURAL DIVERSITY AND THE COUNSELING PROFESSION

The already complex nature of the counseling process is further complicated when the client and counselor come from different cultures. Problems and issues may arise during counseling sessions when, for example, the counselor is middle-class Anglo and the client is lower-class African-American. Generational, intracultural, lifespan, and other individual differences complicate the process to an even greater degree. Planning appropriate interventions must include a consideration of differences in value perspectives and cultural traditions and customs (Pedersen, 1978).

Counselors who are most different from their clients, especially with respect to race and social class, have the greatest difficulty effecting constructive changes; those who are most similar to their clients in these respects have a greater facility for helping appropriately (Pedersen, 1988). Without doubt, counselor insensitivity to the differing viewpoints of clients serves as a barrier to effective counseling. Therefore, efforts to enhance the effectiveness of multicultural interventions have emphasized the need for counselors to assess their clients' and their own value systems (Neimeyer & Fukuyama, 1984).

Minority Counseling Professionals

Although most mental health services are provided by Anglo middle-class counselors, many clients receiving mental health services are non-Anglo and from lower socio-economic levels; they also differ significantly from their counselors with respect to socialization and value assumptions (Pedersen, 1988). Having only Anglo middle-class counselors might result in problems due to differences in value orientations, differing expectations and attitudes toward immediate and extended families, ineffective verbal and nonverbal communication, and to the counselor's lack of understanding of the racism and discrimination that culturally diverse clients so often encounter.

The question may be raised as to whether problems resulting from differing cultural backgrounds can be reduced by carefully matching clients with counselors of similar cultural and socioeconomic backgrounds. Realistically speaking, however, the relatively small number of minority counselors reduces the possibility of counselor-client matchups. Due to this situation, counseling has failed to meet the needs of minority clients and, in some cases, is even counterproductive to their well being (Atkinson, Morten, & Sue, 1989).

Several reasons may account for the relatively small number of minorities entering the counseling profession. First of all, those minority students considering the profession might be dissuaded by the small numbers already in the profession. Where would these students find mentors? Who could guide them appropriately or offer needed support? Second, institutional racism might discourage students wanting to become counselors. Racist admission policies and even more blatant forms of racism might, in fact, lock many minority students out of educational institutions.

According to Young, Chamley, & Withers (1990), faculty members with minority ethnic backgrounds are crucial to the counseling profession because they can serve as role models for minority students. In their study of the underrepresentation of minority faculty members in counselor education programs, these authors concluded that Native-, Asian-, African-, and Hispanic-Americans are seriously underrepresented as both students and faculty in clinical psychology programs and that minority faculty members are more likely to hold nonacademic, nontenured, and part-time appointments than nonminority faculty members. To reduce the problem, they offered several recommendations: (a) encourage bright minority students to continue their studies, (b) offer incentives to attract promising minorities to the counseling field, (c) continue recruitment efforts to attract minority faculty members, and (d) encourage the present pool of minority faculty members to remain in academia.

Barriers to Effective Multicultural Counseling

Barriers to effective communication and counseling have impeded counselors' efforts with clients in multicultural settings (Arredondo-Dowd & Gonsalves, 1980). The effective multicultural counselor must first understand the barriers that thwart counseling efforts, then strive to overcome socioeconomic class differences, value differences, lifespan differences, and stereotypical beliefs.

Assumptions and Realities. Assumptions that are potential barriers to effective multicultural counseling include the following:

1. *"Americanization" or assimilation occurs quickly and naturally. Immigrants are grateful for being in the United States.* Although clients may be grateful, they may also experience grief, depression, and homesickness.

2. *Non-English speakers cannot learn or hold a job because they cannot communicate verbally.* People of all cultures possess common knowledge and life skills; although language is important, people also learn and communicate nonverbally.

3. *Attempting to learn in other than one's native language interferes with the learning process, and thus retards it.* Children pick up a second language quickly; mastery of a second language promotes other learning.

4. *Everyone should "Americanize."* Language and culture are valued by culturally diverse people and American ethnic groups. Effective counselors can develop respect for other cultures.

5. *If someone is hurting and in need of counseling, that person only has to seek it.* Every culture has its unique way of handling personal and family issues. Some minorities are reluctant to seek counseling. The effective counselor is aware of individual differences (Arredondo-Dowd & Gonsalves, 1980).

Differing Class and Cultural Values. According to Draguns (1989), "culture enters the counseling process through the client's cognitions: their expectations, beliefs, and convictions based on their accumulated lifetime of experiences in what is proper, effective, and meaningful" (p. 16). Counselors' class values, partly determined by their own socioeconomic class, influence the effectiveness of multicultural counseling. Pedersen, Fukuyama, and Heath (1989) presented evidence to indicate that professional mental health services are class-bound, and that a dangerous situation develops when the counselor (especially the counselor with a middle- or upper-class background) attributes mental health "disorders" to a client's culture or social structure. Specifically, the values indigenous to a particular socioeconomic class may dramatically result in faulty diagnoses and ineffective counseling. Lower-class clients may be "less time-oriented, may be late for appointments, may be motivated more by immediate concrete reinforcement than by delayed gratification and planning for the future" (Peterson & Nisenholz, 1987, p. 334). The importance of being aware of class- and culture-bound values should be recognized, especially when counselors consider the consequences that could result from misunderstanding those values. For example, an upper-class African-American counselor may experience frustration counseling a lower-class African-American client who is unwilling to change self-destructive behaviors. Likewise, a middle-class Anglo counselor may be unable to relate to a teenage mother of the same culture who is on welfare (Peterson & Nisenholz, 1987).

Cultural differences affecting counseling relationships include the varying amounts of time needed to establish deep personal relationships, some clients' tendency not to disclose personal information with an unfamiliar person, and differing definitions of psychological well being. In fact, some cultures (Native Americans, for example), may consider traditional counseling to be in violation of their basic philosophy of life (Peterson & Nisenholz, 1987; Sue, 1981). Some cultural groups believe that counseling threatens their continued existence. Clients may fear that their minority groups will be indoctrinated in the values and traditions of the majority culture (Pedersen & Marsella, 1982; Peterson & Nisenholz, 1987).

 Language Differences between Counselor and Client. Language or dialectal differences between counselor and client may present formidable barriers to effective counseling relationships. The monolingual nature of Western society may unfairly discriminate against clients from bilingual and lower-class backgrounds. Regardless of the client's native language and cultural background, building rapport during counseling sessions depends significantly on whether participants in the dialogue understand one another (Sue, 1981). Middle- or upper-class African-American professionals may experience difficulty and frustration in trying to understand the street talk of lower-class African-American clients. A Spanish-speaking person of Puerto Rican descent may not understand a Mexican-American migrant worker from California. Peterson & Nisenholz (1987) tell of a Hispanic client who related to a counselor that a relative had "bought the farm." Upon asking the client precisely what happened, the counselor learned that the relative had committed suicide. Such an example documents the importance of counselors exercising caution in communication to avoid assumptions that may affect diagnosis and counseling intervention.

 Stereotyping Culturally Different Clients. Professionals counseling in multicultural situations should scrutinize their own stereotypical beliefs toward culturally different clients. All people use stereotypes at some time, and once they have been ingrained they are difficult to change. Moreover, although stereotypes may be partly true in some respects, most psychologists characterize all stereotypes as inaccurate and usually accompanied by prejudice and dislike (or disapproval) of other cultures (Axelson, 1985).

 Counselor Encapsulation. Wrenn (1962, 1985) described counselor encapsulation as substituting stereotypes for the real world, disregarding cultural variations among clients, and dogmatizing a technique-oriented definition of the counseling process (Pedersen, Fukuyama, & Heath, 1989). The culturally encapsulated counselor may evade reality through ethnocentrism. The individual maintains a cocoon by believing his or her internalized value assumptions are best for society. It is necessary for counselors to become culturally sensitive individuals with new knowledge and skills and also to reorganize old knowledge that no longer applies to present situations. Casas and Vasquez (1989) summarize in this way:

> At this time, given the availability of research, the question is no longer *whether* counselors are personally and professionally encapsulated and biased but *to what degree and in what ways.* Each and every human . . . is encapsulated by the values and beliefs of the society and ethicity that nurtured that individual. (p. 162).

People escape cultural encapsulation through education and training and by rejecting their dependency on a single authority or theory. Rather than being trapped in an inflexible structure that inhibits adaptation to alternative ways of thinking, people can be liberated through multicultural contact and made more capable of coping with constant change (Pedersen, 1988).

 Counselors Understanding Their Own Culture. Counselors need to understand their own culture in order to successfully understand the cultures of others. Ivey, Ivey, and Simek-Downing (1987) devised an exercise in cultural awareness for professionals preparing for counseling in multicultural situations. They suggested that counselors answer the following questions to start them thinking about how their cultural heritage may affect their counseling:

1. *Ethnic heritage.* With what ethnic background do you first identify? First identify your nationality—U.S. citizen, Canadian, Mexican, etc. Beyond this first answer, you may find the words *white, red, black, Polish, Mormon, Jewish,* or others coming to mind. Record these words.

   Then, where did your grandparents come from? Great-grandparents? Can you trace a family history, perhaps with different ethnic, religious, and racial backgrounds? Trace your heritage in list form or in a family tree. Do not forget your heritage from the country within which you live.

2. *Are you monocultural, bicultural, or more?* Review the list you developed and pick out the central cultural, ethnic, religious, or other types of groups that have been involved in your development.

3. *What messages do you receive from each cultural group you have listed?* List the values, behaviors, and expectations that people in your group have emphasized over time. How have you personally internalized these messages? If you are aware of the message, chances are you have made some deviation from the family, ethnic, or religious value. If you are unaware, you may have so internalized the values that you are a "culture-bearer" without knowing it. Becoming aware of obvious but unconscious culture-bearer messages may become the most difficult task of all.

4. *How might your cultural messages affect your counseling and therapeutic work?* This final question is the most important. If you believe in individuality as supreme,

given your family history, you may tend to miss the relational family orientation of many Asians and African-Americans. If you come from a relational orientation, you may have difficulty understanding individualistic WASPs (White Anglo-Saxon Protestants) and label them "cold" and "calculating." As we all have cultural histories, it is easy to believe that our way of being in the world is "the way things are and should be." (Ivey, A. E., Ivey, M. B., & Simek-Downing, L. [1987]. *Counseling and psychotherapy: Integrating skills, theory and practice* [2nd ed.], © 1987, p. 104. Adapted by permission of Prentice-Hall, Inc., Englewood Cliffs, New Jersey.)

Professional counselor preparation should include opportunities to develop racial consciousness. A FOCUS ON RESEARCH 2–1 describes a four-stage model designed for Anglo counselors seeking a better understanding of their racial identities.

Client Reluctance and Resistance. There is evidence (Atkinson, Morten, & Sue, 1989) to support the belief that culturally diverse people prefer to discuss personal, emotional, and other problems with parents, friends, and relatives rather than with professional counselors. The lack of minority counselors in many counseling agencies may contribute to the underutilization of professional services. Native-Americans may feel that counseling services are not responsive to their cultural and individual needs. Other clients, such as Chinese-Americans (and many other Asian-American people), traditionally seek family assistance with personal problems rather than disclosing problems to outsiders. In the Asian-American culture, asking detailed questions about physical and mental illnesses is a social taboo. The culturally effective counselor, recognizing these cultural beliefs, will also want to avoid explicit questions about sexual behavior, such as frequency of intercourse, masturbation, and homosexual relations (Lum, 1986).

 A FOCUS ON RESEARCH 2–1
A Racial Consciousness Development Model

Most research directed toward the multicultural dyad has targeted the minority client. Ponterotto (1988) noted that little research has examined the majority culture's participation, or in this case, the Anglo middle-class counselor. Ponterotto's study sought "to conceptualize and put forth a stage model describing the racial identity and consciousness development process among majority (e.g., Euro-Anglo White) counselor trainees ensconced in a multicultural learning environment (pp. 26–27). He proposed a developmental model wherein counselor trainees acknowledge and accept their own racial identity as well as that of minority individuals. Basing his model on leading theories of African-American racial identities, Ponterotto suggests four stages: (1) pre-exposure, (2) exposure, (3) zealot-defensive, and (4) integration. After exploring these stages, Ponterotto summarized his model as representative of an attempt to conceptualize and describe the process by which Anglo counselors know and accept their racial identity as well as that of minority groups.

Source: Ponterotto, J. G. (1988). Racial consciousness development among white counselor trainees: A stage model. *Journal of Multicultural Counseling and Development, 16,* 146–156.

Atkinson and Gim (1989) studied Chinese-, Japanese-, and Korean-American students to determine their tendency to underutilize mental health services. Their study revealed that more acculturated Asian-American students were more likely than less acculturated students of the same culture to perceive a personal need for professional services.

Differing World Views and Lack of Cultural Relativity. An understanding of the counselor's and the client's world views are key elements in multicultural counseling situations. Over three decades ago, Kluckhohn and Strodtbeck (1961) defined world view through a value-orientation concept derived from existential categories such as "human nature, the relationships of humans to the natural world, time perspectives, activity orientation, and interpersonal relations" (Pedersen, Fukuyama, & Heath, 1989, p. 37). Ibrahim (1985) reported several definitions of world view. For example, a world view consists of the presuppositions and assumptions an individual holds about the makeup of his or her life (Sire, 1976). Or, a world view is how a person perceives his or her relationship to the world (e.g., nature, institutions, and other people) (Sue, 1978c). Counselors should understand both the client's values and their own world views and values to develop appropriate problem-solving strategies (Ibrahim, 1985).

Why should counselors consider "world views," especially in multicultural settings? One's world view is a culturally based variable that influences the essence of the counseling relationship. For example, when the counselor and the client do not share similar world views, communication may not be clear and may result in counselors and psychotherapists making negative judgements about client concerns, behaviors, perceptions, attitudes, and values (Ibrahim, 1985). Furthermore, the counselor's and the client's lack of cultural relativity can result in differing perceptions of problems, which is a barrier to effective multicultural counseling. Effective counselors must (a) be adaptive when faced with difficulties and be able to interact in many multicultural situations, (b) be continually undergoing personal transitions in an attempt to seek new challenges in the different situations, and (c) look at their own culture from the perception of an outsider (Brislin, 1981).

Counselors' Labeling of Women, Multicultural Populations, and the Poor. Culturally different groups, as well as women and the poor, often have been labeled mentally ill when they have only varied from so-called normal patterns of behaving as defined by those believing that Anglo middle-class male beliefs represent the rule of health and desirability (Cayleff, 1986). Some of Cayleff's examples include labeling of women's physiological illnesses as psychogenic and mental health disorders in African-Americans being labeled psychoses more readily than those of Anglo-American clients.

Counselors err if they conclude that such labeling is a new phenomenon or is of small consequence. Cayleff (1986) provided several examples to show how labels have stigmatized people as being mentally ill. African-Americans during the nineteenth century running away to the North were labeled with the disease of "drapetomania." Women's social roles in nineteenth-century America were circumscribed according to the belief that women were biologically weak. Same-sex love relationships continue to be targeted as illness or depravity.

Lack of Understanding of Clients' Structures of Reasoning. There is always the possibility of counselors erroneously assuming that their reasoning patterns are the same as those of clients. In other words, a barrier is created when the counselor fails to understand a client's logic or thinking. Such failure can result in frustration and anxiety for both the counselor and the client. Goals and tasks the counselor feels are appropriate may be antithetical or meaningless for the client (Ibrahim, 1985).

Maruyama (1978) suggested that "difficulty in cross-disciplinary, cross-professional, cross-cultural communication lies not in the fact that the communicating parties use different vocabularies or language to talk about the same thing, but rather they use different structures of reasoning" (p. 23). He called these differences "psychotopology," which may be defined as "a science of structures of reasoning which vary from discipline to discipline, from profession to profession, from culture to culture, and even from individual to individual" (p. 24).

Expecting Culturally Diverse Clients to Conform to Anglo Standards and Expectations. Another common barrier in multicultural counseling is for counselors (perhaps unconsciously) to expect clients to conform to Anglo standards and expectations. For example, as pointed out by Cayleff (1986), expecting black women to emulate white standards of beauty has a demoralizing effect. Or putting pressure on adolescent African-American mothers to undergo sterilization denies them an important source of self-worth and fails to consider the extended kinship network that figures so prominently in childrearing and mothering among African-American women.

Culturally different clients may also be treated differently from Anglo clients. Certain approaches may reflect paternalistic behavior, or the counselor's belief that he or she is acting in the client's best interest. In some cases, the counselor may even withhold or distort information, compromising the client's autonomy and rational decision making based on consent and awarenesses of options and outcomes (Cayleff, 1986).

Another equally serious issue that may threaten the counselor-client relationship involves the cultural dictates surrounding sex roles. Traditional and stereotypical sex roles prohibit strong disagreement between authority figures and clients. Conflicting situations may arise from counseling roles that are often reflected in the power-laden relationships between counselors and clients. Communication and individual decision making by women may be undermined by sex-specific factors. To avoid such situations, the counselor-client relationship must not be paternalistic; it must stress the client's welfare and allows the client to be autonomous (Cayleff, 1986).

UNDERSTANDING CULTURAL DIVERSITY AMONG CLIENTS

Counselors striving to be culturally effective will respond to a variety of issues: the different ways in which cultural backgrounds influence counseling relationships; the need to evaluate their own cultural biases; the ways in which problems and solutions vary among cultures; and the question of whether counseling, itself, is culturally encapsulated (Pedersen, 1988). Will counselors understand, for example, the strong sense of family and community that many African-Americans share? Will they understand the Native-American's love of nature or commitment to sharing, or the Hispanic-American's loyalty to machismo? Such understanding, together with knowledge of development factors during each stage of the lifespan, significantly determines the effectiveness of counseling efforts.

Other relevant counseling issues that have the potential for affecting the outcome of the counseling process and that warrant the counselor's attention include (a) awareness of the sociopolitical forces that influence the minority client; (b) understanding that culture, class, and language factors can act as barriers to effective multicultural counseling; and (c) understanding the importance of world views/cultural identity in the counseling process (Sue, 1981).

Assessing Clients' World Views

While differing world views of counselor and client were previously mentioned as a potential barrier to effective multicultural counseling, here we will discuss how world views are assessed. The broader issue of multicultural testing and assessment will be addressed in Chapter 12.

Lonner and Ibrahim (1989) suggested that assessment in multicultural counseling "is still fairly uncharted territory" (p. 299). They also contend, however, that professionals are unable to diagnose problems without appropriate assessment strategies.

The first step in any counseling or psychotherapy encounter is to understand the client, and the issues, problems, symptoms, and pain that led the client to seek help and relief. As this initial counselor goal is accomplished, meaningful goals for the client and a plan for the counseling intervention should be developed. In multicultural counseling situations, it is necessary to assess the client as a cultural entity prior to the planning and implementation of counseling interventions (Ibrahim & Arredondo, 1986).

There are two specific approaches to assessing a client's world views, beliefs, values, and perspectives. Sue (1978c) proposed an approach based on internal/external locus of responsibility and Ibrahim and Kahn (1984, 1987) proposed the Scale to Assess World Views (SAWV). We will now briefly discuss each of these approaches.

Sue (1978c) defines world view as the manner in which individuals perceive their relationship to the world. As Figure 2–1 illustrates, world view is based on the client's locus of responsibility or the control perceived over his or her life. Sue based one part of his theory on Rotter's (1975) distinction between internal control (IC), in which reinforcement is contingent on a person's own actions, and external control (EC) in which consequences are perceived to result from luck, chance, or fate. Next, Sue added the dimension of internal locus of responsibility (IR), in which success is attributed to a person's skills, resulting in a "person blame," and an external locus of responsibility (ER), in which the sociocultural environment is more powerful than the individual, resulting in "system blame." For example, an IC-IR worldview exemplifies Anglo middle-class cultural perceptions, whereas an EC-IR view reflects the world view of minorities who feel they have little control over the way others define them. The EC-ER view is often prevalent among minorities who blame their problems on an oppressive social system, and the IC-ER view assumes the ability of an individual to achieve personal goals if given a chance (Pedersen, Fukuyama, & Heath, 1989; Sue, 1978c, 1981).

Figure 2–1   Graphic representations of world views. (From Sue, 1978b, p. 422.)

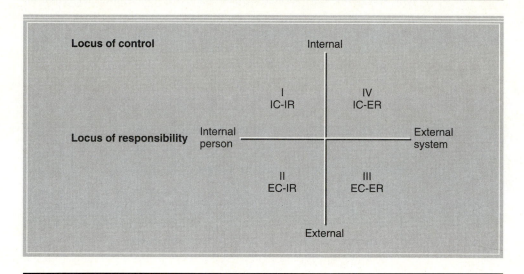

Another means of assessing world view is the Scale to Assess World Views (SAWV). Ibrahim and Kahn (1984, 1987) designed a 45-item Likert-type scale for assessing individual and group world views based on Kluckhohn's (1951, 1956) five existential categories:

Human Nature:	What is the character of human nature?
Relationships:	What is the modality of people's relationships?
Natural Environment:	What is the relationship of people to nature?
Time Orientation:	What is the temporal focus of human life?
Activity Orientation:	What is the modality of human activity (i.e., self expression)?

By using the SAWV, the counselor can better understand the client's values and assumptions and how they relate to his or her cognitive, emotional, and social perceptions and interactions with the world. The SAWV also clarifies the issues and problems the client brings to counseling. Thus, the counselor can formulate approaches and techniques to be used in identifying goals that would be meaningful to a particular cultural group (Ibrahim, 1985; Lonner & Ibrahim, 1989).

CHARACTERISTICS OF CULTURALLY EFFECTIVE COUNSELORS

In a 1978 article, Sue listed several characteristics that distinguish culturally effective counselors:

1. Culturally effective counselors recognize which values and assumptions they hold regarding the desirability or undesirability of human behavior.

2. Culturally effective counselors are those who are aware of the generic characteristics of counseling that cut across many schools of thought.

3. Culturally effective counselors are able to share the world views of their clients without negating their legitimacy.

4. Culturally effective counselors are truly eclectic in their counseling. (Sue, 1978a, p. 451)

Later, in 1981, Sue offered additional characteristics that he felt culturally effective counselors must possess. In this listing, the culturally skilled counselor

1. is one who has moved from being culturally unaware to being aware and sensitive to his/her own cultural baggage.

2. is aware of his/her own values and biases and how they may affect minority clients.

3. will have a good understanding of the sociopolitical system's operation in the United States with respect to its treatment of minorities.

4. is one who is comfortable with differences that exist between the counselor and client in terms of race and belief.

5. is sensitive to circumstances (personal biases, stage of ethnic identity, sociopolitical influences, etc.) that may dictate referral of the minority client to a member of his/her own race/culture.

6. must possess specific knowledge and information about the particular group he/she is working with.

7. must have a clear and explicit knowledge and understanding of the generic characteristics of counseling and therapy.

8. must be able to generate a wide variety of verbal and nonverbal responses.

9. must be able to send and receive both verbal and nonverbal messages accurately and "appropriately." (Sue, 1981, pp. 105–108)

Can cultural sensitivity be taught? Mio (1989) in A FOCUS ON RESEARCH 2–2 briefly explains the "Partners Program," designed to enhance cultural sensitivity.

A FOCUS ON RESEARCH 2–2
Teaching Cultural Sensitivity

Mio (1989) maintains that the American Psychological Association has advocated that cultural sensitivity training be added to clinical psychology training programs. In his view, most professionals would agree that experiential contact with ethnic minority groups is an essential element in the training process. In a 1989 article, Mio describes a "Partners Program" that matched American students with immigrant and refugee students. He concluded that actual one-to-one exchange of ideas with another person enhances one's experience with members of another cultural group above and beyond exchange of factual information. Although Mio recognized that it is not possible to expose individuals to people of all cultures, he felt that the program did provide a groundwork for future involvement leading to enhanced cultural sensitivity.

Source: Mio, J. S. (1989). Experiential involvement as an adjunct to teaching cultural sensitivity. *The Journal of Multicultural Counseling and Development, 17,* 38–46.

Professional Preparation and Training

Rationale

The vast cultural and ethnic differences that characterize the U.S. population provide a sound rationale for including culturally appropriate professional experiences in training counselors. Rather than counselors merely using slightly modified techniques originally planned for Anglo middle-class clients, current thought indicates culturally effective counselors need special professional preparation in counseling culturally different clients.

The Conference Follow-Up Commission of the 1973 APA Vail, Colorado, Conference declared it unethical for those not competent in understanding people of culturally diverse backgrounds to provide services to such groups. It was also declared at the conference that counselors had the professional responsibility to participate in continuing education to be better prepared to work with culturally diverse clients (Axelson, 1985). According to Pedersen (1988) multicultural counseling training programs for mental health professionals are needed for several reasons:

1. Traditional systems of mental health services have a cultural bias favoring dominant social classes that can be counterproductive to an equitable distribution of services.

2. Various cultural groups have discovered indigenous models of coping and treatment that work better for them and may usefully be applied to other groups.

3. Community health services are expensive when they fail; multicultural training might prevent some programs from failing.

4. Training methods that include indigenous people as resource persons directly in training counselors tend to reflect the reality of different cultures.

5. The constructs of healthy and normal that guide the delivery of mental health services are not the same for all cultures and might lead culturally encapsulated counselors to become tools of political, social, or economic systems.

6. Increased interdependence across ethnic and social-cultural boundaries requires direct attention to culture as a part of mental health training.

7. Most therapists come from dominant cultures whereas clients do not. (p. 161)

Exploring Cultural Attitudes

Copeland (1982) maintained that it is clear that if counselor educators prepare counselors to work with culturally diverse groups, programs must be developed that recognize, accept, and emphasize individual needs. The first step toward these goals might include an exploration of multicultural attitudes. A FOCUS ON RESEARCH 2–3 looks at an instrument designed to determine and assess understanding of multicultural attitudes.

Multicultural Counseling Competencies

Table 2–1 lists the attitudes, competencies, and skills which, according to Arredondo-Dowd and Gonsalves (1980), are needed for counselors to be culturally effective.

According to the Education and Training Committee of APA's Division 17 of Counseling Psychology, the culturally competent counselor should have nine competencies:

◄ **A FOCUS ON RESEARCH 2–3**
Exploring Multicultural Attitudes

Neimeyer and Fukuyama (1984) describe the Cultural Attitudes Repertory Technique (CART) as an instrument to determine unique understandings of a person's cultural attitudes and to assess the content and structure of those under-

Source: Neimeyer, G. J., & Fukuyama, M. (1984). Exploring the content and structure of cross-cultural attitudes. *Counselor Education and Supervision, 23,* 214–224.

standings. This instrument can be used as part of a self-exploration exercise to assist counselors in articulating those private dimensions of judgments that may otherwise remain implicit in multicultural interventions. For counselor training, the CART might be beneficial in monitoring changes in attitudes during multicultural experiences.

1. awareness of his or her own cultural characteristics;
2. awareness of how his or her cultural values and biases may affect minority clients;
3. understanding of the American sociopolitical system in relation to minorities;
4. the ability to resolve differences of race and beliefs between the counselor and his or her client;
5. the ability to know when a culturally different client should be referred to a counselor of the client's own race or culture;
6. knowledge and information about the particular group of clients with whom the counselor is working;

Table 2–1   Profile of the culturally effective counselor

Attitudes

1. All persons possess certain intellectual, emotional, linguistic, sociocultural, and physical capabilities and potentials that they bring to counseling and that should be developed and enhanced during the process.
2. Equal opportunities are available to all persons.
3. Cultural discontinuity may affect the self-identity of individuals.
4. Non-English languages are valid, structured systems of communication, with legitimate functions in various social contexts.
5. An individual's culture is the basis for learning to function as a social being.

Competencies	Skills
1. Counseling	1. Teaching
2. Cultural	2. Helping
3. Linguistic	3. Bilingual
4. Pedagogical	4. Life

Source: Arredondo-Dowd and Gonsalves, 1980, p. 659.

7. clear and explicit knowledge and understanding of counseling and therapy;

8. a wide range of verbal and nonverbal response skills;

9. the skill to send and receive both accurate and appropriate verbal and nonverbal messages. (Axelson, 1985, p. 385)

Members of the Education and Training Committee also summarized the beliefs/attitudes, understandings, and skills that culturally effective counselors need:

Beliefs/Attitudes:

1. The culturally skilled counseling psychologist is one who has moved from being culturally unaware to being aware and sensitive to his or her own cultural heritage and to valuing and respecting differences. Culturally skilled counselors have moved from ethnocentrism to valuing and respecting differences. Other cultures are perceived to be just as valuable and legitimate as are their own. A culturally unaware counselor is most likely to impose his or her values onto a minority client.

2. A culturally skilled counseling psychologist is aware of his or her own values and biases and how they may affect minority clients. These psychologists constantly attempt to avoid prejudices, unwarranted labeling, and stereotyping. They try not to hold preconceived notions about their minority clients. As a check upon this process, culturally skilled counseling psychologists monitor their functioning via consultation, supervision, and continual education.

3. A culturally skilled counseling psychologist is one who is comfortable with differences that exist between the counselor and client in terms of race and beliefs. Differences are not seen as being deviant! The culturally skilled counselor does not profess "color blindness" or negate the existence of differences that exist in attitudes/beliefs. The basic concept underlying "color blindness" was the humanity of all people. While its intent was to eliminate bias from counseling, it has served to deny the existence of differences in clients' perceptions of society arising out of membership in different racial groups. The message tends to be "I will like you only if you are the same," instead of "I like you because of and in spite of your differences."

4. The culturally skilled counseling psychologist is sensitive to circumstances (personal biases, stage of ethnic identity, sociopolitical influences, etc.) that may dictate referral of the minority client to a member of his or her own race or culture. A culturally skilled counselor is aware of his or her limitations in cross-cultural counseling and is not threatened by the prospect of referring a client to someone else.

Understandings:

1. The culturally skilled counseling psychologist will have a good understanding of the sociopolitical system's operation in the United States with respect to its treatment of minorities. Understanding the impact and operation of oppression (racism, sexism, etc.), the politics of counseling, and the racist concepts that have permeated the mental health/helping professions is important. Especially valuable for the counselor is an understanding of the role cultural racism plays in the development of identity and world views among minority groups.

2. The culturally skilled counseling psychologist must possess specific knowledge and information about the particular group he or she is working with. This includes an awareness of the history, experiences, cultural values, and lifestyles of various racial/ethnic groups. The greater the depth of knowledge about a cultural group and the more knowledge the counselor has of many groups, the more likely the counselor can be an effective helper. Thus, the culturally skilled counselor is one who continues to explore and learn about issues related to various minority groups.

3. The culturally skilled counseling psychologist must have a clear and explicit knowledge and understanding of the generic characteristics of counseling and therapy. These encompass language factors, culture-bound values, and class-bound values. The counselor should clearly understand the value assumptions (normality and abnormality) inherent in the major schools of counseling and how they may interact with the values of the culturally different. In some cases, the theories or models may limit the potential of those clients from different cultures. Being able to determine those theories that may be relevant across cultures is important.

4. The culturally skilled counseling psychologist is aware of institutional barriers that prevent minorities from using mental health services. Such factors as the location of a mental health agency, the formality or informality of the decor, the language(s) used to advertise their services, the availability of minorities among the different levels, the organizational climate, the hours and days of operation, the offering of the services really needed by the community, etc. are important.

Skills:

1. At the skills level, the culturally skilled counseling psychologist must be able to generate a wide variety of verbal and nonverbal responses. There is mounting evidence to indicate that minority groups may not only define problems differently from their Anglo counterparts, but may also respond differently to counseling/ therapy styles (Atkinson et al., 1978; Berman, 1979; Sue, 1981). Ivey and Authier (1978) state that the wider the repertoire of responses the counselor possesses, the better the helper he or she is likely to be. We can no longer rely on a very narrow and limited number of skills in counseling. We need to practice and be comfortable with a multitude of response modalities.

2. The culturally skilled counseling psychologist must be able to send and receive both verbal and nonverbal messages accurately and appropriately. The key words "send," "receive," "verbal," "nonverbal," "accurately," and "appropriately" are important. These words signify several things about cross-cultural counseling. First, communication is a two-way process. The culturally skilled counselor must not only be able to communicate (send) thoughts and feelings to the client, but also be able to read (receive) messages from the client. Second, cross-cultural counseling effectiveness may be highly correlated with the counselor's ability to recognize and respond not only to verbal but also to nonverbal messages. Third, sending and receiving a message accurately involves consideration of cultural cues operative in the setting. Fourth, accuracy of communication must be tempered by its appropriateness. This is a difficult concept for many to grasp. It deals with communication styles. In many cultures, subtlety and indirectness of communi-

cation are highly prized arts. Likewise, directness and confrontation are prized by other cultures.

3. The culturally skilled counseling psychologist is able to exercise institutional intervention skills on behalf of the client when appropriate. This implies that help-giving may involve out-of-office strategies that discard the intrapsychic counseling model and view the problems/barriers as residing outside of the minority client. (Reprinted from Sue et al., "Position Paper: Cross-cultural Counseling Competencies," from *The Counseling Psychologist, 10* (2), p. 49. Copyright © 1982 by Division 17 of the American Psychological Association. Reprinted by permission of Sage Publishing Co., Inc.)

Ethics

As defined by Axelson (1985), ethics are rules of conduct or moral principles, such as those that guide the practices of professional counselors. Axelson further states that ethical standards are especially important in the counseling profession because of the intense involvement between counselor and client and because of the complexities of the counseling process.

LaFromboise and Foster (1989) in their work "Ethics in Multicultural Counseling" point out that many advocates of the APA's 1986 Accreditation Criterion II ("Cultural and Individual Differences") realize that ethnic infractions will persist until cultural pluralism is reflected in the composition of the faculty providing training and is integrated into the content of courses leading to professional preparation. These advocates of ethical training standards have identified several areas that need to be addressed. First, the demographics of the profession fall short of having a proportion of members that represent the composition of the society at large. In fact, the representation of ethnic minorities in psychology has gradually declined since its peak in the 1970s. Second, surveys of APA-approved programs document the reluctance of graduate programs to train students in cross-cultural factors. Some programs are reluctant to offer even one seminar that focuses on culturally sensitive material, and while accreditation requirements are met by having students work with culturally diverse clients, these students seldom are assigned ethnic minority supervisors. Third, faculty and mentors are considered the prime source of education regarding research ethics, yet few of these faculty teach courses dealing with ethical dilemmas in research. Fourth, a major barrier is that most textbooks take a culturally neutral perspective and fail to address multicultural situations and concerns (LaFromboise & Foster, 1989).

Some ethical standards germane to multicultural counselors in training include the following:

1. *The Ethics of Responding to Individuality.* The "Preamble" of the AACD *Ethical Standards* (1988) states that

    members are dedicated to the enhancement of the worth, dignity, potential, and uniqueness of each individual. (p. 1)

2. *The Ethics of Recognizing Minority/Majority Cultural Experiences and Relations.* Section A (10) of the AACD *Ethical Standards* (1988) states that

the member avoids bringing personal issues into the counseling relationship, especially if the potential for harm is present. Through awareness of the negative impact of both racial and sexual stereotyping and discrimination, the counselor guards the individual rights and personal dignity of the client in the counseling relationship. (p. 1)

3. *The Ethics of Responsible Use of Assessment, Measurement, and Evaluation Techniques and Devices.* AACD *Ethical Standards* (1988) Section C (1) states that

> the member must provide specific orientation or information to the examinee(s) prior to and following the test administration so that the results [are] placed in proper perspective with other relevant factors. In so doing, the member must recognize the effects of socioeconomic, ethnic, and cultural factors on test scores. (p. 2)

4. *The Ethics of Ensuring Multicultural Knowledge and Competence in Counselor Training.* The AACD *Ethical Standards* (1988) in Section H (7) states that

> members must make students aware of the ethical responsibilities and standards of the profession. (p. 4)

Knowledge of the client's constitutional and civil rights and respect for those rights are important in the effective work of multicultural counselors. A counselor's unmet needs or deficiency-motivated needs, such as status, security, companionship, or love, cannot ethically be satisfied through exploitation of the intimate relationship. All individuals have differing degrees of basic psychological needs; however, the professional counselor is aware of his or her own personality dynamics and will not intentionally seek to exploit the counseling relationship (Axelson, 1985).

PROFESSIONAL TRAINING DESIGNS

Copeland (1982) proposed four basic counselor education alternatives that can be introduced into traditional programs to upgrade the competencies of counselors intervening in multicultural situations. It is realistic to expect that all counselors in the 1990s and beyond will work with clients from culturally different backgrounds; thus, Copeland's (1982) suggestions should be considered when reaching decisions concerning counselor education curricula and programs. The four approaches may be used individually or in combination. They are summarized in Table 2–2 in terms of the advantages and disadvantages of each.

Johnson's thesis that multicultural training should not only concentrate on cultural knowledge, but also on what counselors actually can do is explained in A FOCUS ON RESEARCH 2–4.

Pedersen (1990) sought to identify the measures of complexity and balance in the counseling literature and to apply these two constructs to multicultural counseling. *Complexity* involves the identification of multiple perspectives within and between individuals. For example, the professional must be able to perceive a problem from viewpoints of both the counselor and the client. If two different viewpoints are in conflict, a multicultural perspective allows both viewpoints to be right within their own cultural context, rather than demanding one be right and one wrong. The more culturally different the counselor is from the client, however, the more difficult it

Table 2-2 Summary of approaches to incorporate counseling racial minorities into counselor training programs

	Advantages	Disadvantages
Separate course model	1. Assures coverage of topic.	1. Does not require total faculty involvement or commitment.
	2. Does not require total program evaluation.	2. May be viewed as ancillary.
	3. It is easy to employ individuals with expertise in the area. Adjunct or visiting faculty may be hired if there is no one on the faculty to serve as instructor.	3. May not be required of all students.
Area of concentration model	1. Provides more in-depth study.	1. While this method provides training for those students with an interest in the area, it may not reach some students who will be working with minorities.
	2. Offers opportunity for practice with the designated population.	
	3. Provides experience with diverse groups and allows for the study of similarities and differences in approaches.	
Interdisciplinary model	1. Encourages students to take courses in other related disciplines.	1. May not be utilized by all students in the program.
	2. Provides for broad experiences.	
	3. Discourages redundancy of course offerings, which allows for total utilization of university resources.	
Integration model	1. Involves evaluation of total program.	1. Will not work without faculty commitment.
	2. Involves faculty, students, and practicing professionals.	2. Requires considerable time.

Source: Copeland, 1982, p. 192.

<table>
<tr><td>

A FOCUS ON RESEARCH 2–4
Achieving Expertise through Multicultural Training

In an effort to train counselors to be more effective with culturally different populations, Johnson (1987) explored the concept of expertise as both a content issue and an outcome criterion. He first reviewed several studies on intercul-

Source: Johnson, S. D. (1987). Knowing that versus knowing how: Toward achieving expertise through multicultural training for counseling. *The Counseling Psychologist, 15,* 320–331.

tural effectiveness and then proceeded to examine strategies specifically designed for counselors. His main thesis is that since research focuses primarily on counselor trainees' knowledge and intercultural training, intercultural training programs may not be reaching maximum potential until the profession develops instruments to measure "knowing how" as well as "knowing what."

</td></tr>
</table>

will be for the counselor to develop that perspective. With regard to *balance,* Pedersen assumes that it involves the identification of different or even conflicting culturally learned perspectives without necessarily resolving the difference in favor of either viewpoint. Representative examples include (a) the ability to see positive implications in the client's otherwise negative experiences and (b) the ability to avoid simple solutions to complex problems and to acknowledge the constraints of the client's cultural context (Pedersen, 1990). Although Pedersen's work is far too complicated and extensive to explicate in this section, interested readers are referred to the Suggested Readings section of this chapter.

Maintaining that therapist supervision is a topic of increasing concern in therapist training literature, Cook and Helms (1988) concluded that the opportunities for cross-cultural relationships provided by supervisors indicated uncertainty about the supervisor's roles in cross-cultural situations. Overall recommendations included that supervisors acquaint themselves with recent training models designed to promote culturally sensitive attitudes; be aware of the interaction between cultural factors and mental health variables; and learn about the cultural backgrounds and sociopolitical history of the supervisee's racial and ethnic group (Cook & Helms, 1988).

Training and Preparation Issues

Pedersen, Fukuyama, and Heath (1989) identified several issues concerning the counseling profession and multicultural counseling as a subspeciality: (a) counseling professionals are not adequately trained to meet the mental health needs of culturally diverse clients; (b) multicultural groups are underserved, and there is a severe shortage of ethnic minority mental health professionals; (c) current multicultural training programs are described as experimental and are scarce; (d) there is some disagreement concerning how counseling programs can best meet the needs of minorities; and (e) there is concern that multicultural counseling issues are often analyzed from an Anglo middle-class perspective (Pedersen, Fukuyama & Heath, 1989).

Counselor Self-Development

Current counselor education programs use a variety of models to provide training in multicultural counseling. The question remains, however, of how counselors who were trained prior to the emphasis on cultural diversity can most effectively plan a program of self-development. Although any efforts of these counselors to improve their multicultural competence are commendable, culturally diverse clients deserve (and the ethics of the counseling profession call for) counselors who are qualified and competent to intervene in multicultural situations. Counselors planning a program of self-development may take several approaches:

1. The counselor can make a commitment to recognize the value of a client's cultural, ethnic, racial, socioeconomic, lifespan, and all other differences. This commitment can include yet another commitment to improve multicultural counseling effectiveness.

2. The counselor can strive to participate in first-hand social interactions with culturally diverse people, both individually and in groups.

3. The counselor can become familiar with the literature on multicultural counseling including professional publications that focus on cultural diversity and lifespan issues (such as those listed in the appendix); attend seminars offered by counseling organizations; and participate in additional formal coursework.

4. The counselor can use tools, such as the Cultural Attitudes Repertory Technique (CART). Exercises of this type provide opportunities to gain a better understanding of one's own personal values and attitudes and those of others from different backgrounds.

5. The counselor can engage in critical reflection to identify possible racist attitudes and to examine personal behaviors, perceptions, and feelings that might compromise effective and competent multicultural counseling.

As with other professional tasks to be mastered, the success the counselor achieves toward improving multicultural counseling effectiveness depends significantly on the level of enthusiasm and commitment brought to the effort.

Four Conditions of Counseling Culturally Different Clients

For effective multicultural counseling, it is imperative for counselors to understand the goals and counseling processes that are involved. Figure 2–2 indicates the outcomes that may result when counseling a client from another culture (Sue, 1981). In *condition I* (appropriate process, appropriate goals), the client is exposed to a counseling process consistent with his or her values and life experiences. For example, an African-American male student from a ghetto is failing in school and is getting into fights. The counselor is willing to teach the student study and test-taking skills and is willing to give advice and information. In *condition II* (appropriate process, inappropriate goals), the counselor chooses the appropriate strategy, yet the goals of the counseling process are questionable. Continuing the example of the African-American student who fights, the counselor might decide on a strategy to eliminate the tendency to fight. If, however, the African-American student is being harassed and forced to fight because he is a minority member, the counselor's goal of eliminating

Figure 2–2   Processes and goals in multicultural counseling. (From *Counseling the Culturally Different* by D. W. Sue [New York: Wiley], 1981, p. 99.)

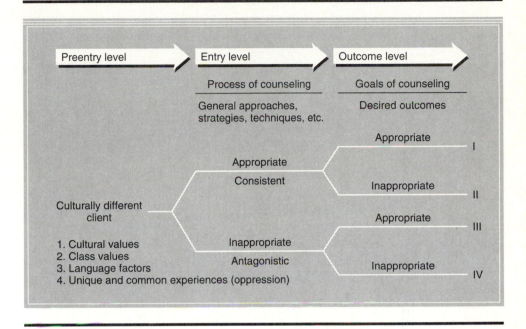

fighting behavior may be inappropriate. In other words, the counselor is imposing his or her own standards and values on the client. *Condition III* (inappropriate process, appropriate goals) exists when the counselor uses inappropriate strategies. For example, the Native-American views people and nature as harmonious; the world is accepted in its present form with no attempt to change it. Such an attitude conflicts with the Anglo's concern with controlling and mastering the physical environment. With this in mind, the reader can readily understand how the counselor's techniques may be viewed as coercive or manipulative. In *condition IV* (inappropriate process, inappropriate goals), the counselor pursues inappropriate goals and fails to understand the client's cultural traditions. Asian-American clients who value restraint of strong feelings and believe that intimate relationships are to be shared only with close friends may cause problems for the counselor who lacks insight. The Asian-American client who seeks vocational counseling may resent counselors who try to learn what motivates their actions and decisions (Sue, 1981).

A POINT OF DEPARTURE

Challenges Confronting Effective Multicultural Counselors

Counselors whose professional training focused mainly on Anglo middle-class adult clients will experience frustration and feelings of inadequacy as the numbers of culturally diverse clients of all ages continue to increase. No longer can counselors expect to intervene with only Anglo clients of a similar social class. Contemporary counselors will increasingly meet clients who have differing values and backgrounds and differing outlooks toward family, friends, and life in general. The counselor might be threatened by his or her lack of ability to understand the client's motives and reasoning, to communicate the objectives and processes of counseling, and to establish an effective counseling relationship. Becoming a culturally effective counselor requires professional education and training, knowledge of cultural diversity, an understanding and respect for others, and an ability to plan and implement intervention appropriate to culture and lifespan level.

SUMMARY

Becoming an effective multicultural counselor has three essential aspects: First, the counselor must have an appreciation for cultural diversity, an understanding of the individual culture, and a sense of empathy with clients. Second, the counselor must have appropriate beliefs/attitudes, understandings, and skills to intervene effectively in multicultural situations. Third, professional preparation, first-hand experiences with culturally diverse groups, and an adherence to ethical standards established by the counseling profession can reduce the barriers to effective multicultural counseling.

Suggested Readings

American school counselor association position paper: Cross/Multicultural counseling. (1989). *Elementary School Guidance and Counseling, 23,* 322–323. This position paper on multicultural counseling defines the term and lists strategies for increasing sensitivity toward culturally diverse people.

Arredondo-Dowd, P. M., & Gonsalves, J. (1980). Preparing culturally effective counselors. *The Personnel and Guidance Journal, 58,* 657–661. The authors propose a counselor training program that emphasizes bilingual-multicultural education. The approach requires specific attitudes, skills, and competencies based on interdisciplinary philosophies of counseling, bilingual education, and multicultural education.

Atkinson, D. R., Morten, G., & Sue, D. W. (1989). *Counseling American minorities: A cross-cultural perspective* (3rd ed.). Dubuque, IA: Wm. C. Brown. Part I of this text, "Why a Cross-Cultural Perspective?," is especially recommended because of its definitions of cross-cultural terms and its overview of minority group counseling.

Ibrahim, F. A. (1985). Effective cross-cultural counseling and psychotherapy: A framework. *The Counseling Psychologist, 13,* 625–638. Ibrahim describes strategies that promote effectiveness during cross-cultural counseling and psychotherapy.

LaFromboise, T. D., & Foster, S. L. (1989). Ethics in multicultural counseling. In P. B. Pedersen, J. G. Draguns, J. Lonner, & J. E. Trimble (Eds.), *Counseling across cultures* (3rd ed.) (pp. 115–136). Honolulu: University of Hawaii Press. LaFromboise and Foster's examination of ethical issues during professional preparation and training is especially recommended. Their chapter also explores several issues that will be discussed in detail in Chapter 12.

Lonner, W. J., & Ibrahim, F. A. (1989). Assessment in cross-cultural counseling. In P. B. Pedersen, J. G. Draguns, J. Lonner, & J. E. Trimble (Eds.), *Counseling across cultures* (3rd ed.) (pp. 299–333). Honolulu: University of Hawaii Press. Lonner and Ibrahim take a general look at assessing multicultural groups and a specific look at assessing world views. The chapter includes a section on standardized assessment.

Parker, W. M. (1988). Becoming an effective multicultural counselor. *Journal of Counseling and Development, 67,* 93. In this interesting personal account, Parker tells of his experiences counseling a young Cuban female college student, his training of African-American peer counselors, and his encounter with a young African-American experiencing difficulties with his doctoral committee. Parker explains how he became aware of his lack of preparation to work with ethnic minority clients and the ways in which he developed multicultural counseling skills.

Pedersen, P. (1987). Ten frequent assumptions of cultural bias in counseling. *Journal of Multicultural Counseling and Development, 15,* 16–24. Pedersen contends that counselors should recognize more clearly what constitutes normal behavior, our emphases on individualism and independence, the fragmentation of academic disciplines, and the dangers of cultural encapsulation.

Pedersen, P. (1988). *A handbook for developing multicultural awareness.* Alexandria, VA: American Association of Counseling and Development. This excellent text examines crucial aspects of counseling the culturally different; for example, awareness, knowledge, and skills.

Pedersen, P. (1990). The constructs of complexity and balance in multicultural counseling theory and practice. *Journal of Counseling and Development, 68,* 550–554. Pedersen applies two traditional counseling constructs, complexity and balance, to multicultural counseling.

Sue, D. W., Bernier, J. E., Durran, A., Feinberg, L., Pedersen, P., Smith, E. J., & Vasquez-Nuttal, E. (1982). Position paper: Cross-cultural counseling competencies. *The Counseling Psychologist, 10*(2), 45–52. This position paper by members of APA's Division 17 (Counseling Education and Training Committee) concludes that the competencies of culturally effective counselors involve beliefs/attitudes, understandings, and skills.

Sue, S., & Zane, N. (1987). The role of culture and cultural techniques in psychotherapy. *American Psychologist, 42,* 37–45. These two authors examine the role of cultural knowledge and culture-specific techniques in the psychotherapeutic treatment of minority-group clients. Their critique provides a meaningful method of viewing the role of culture in psychotherapy practices and training.

Chapter 3

Multicultural Human Growth and Development

Questions To Be Explored

1. Why are the prenatal and infancy stages important in a lifespan approach? What prenatal and infancy issues pertain specifically to culturally different populations?

2. How do historical and contemporary perspectives of infancy, childhood, adolescence, adulthood, and old age differ?

3. Is there a "culture" of each lifespan period? What makes each period unique? What role do cultural differences play during each lifespan stage?

4. What are some issues and questions pertaining to multicultural lifespan development?

5. What are the physical, psychosocial, and intellectual characteristics of clients at each lifespan stage?

6. What special problems and concerns face culturally different clients at each lifespan stage?

7. What are some of the research findings in the multicultural development area? What implications do they have for professionals?

8. What challenges confront multicultural counselors working with clients at the various lifespan stages, and what additional sources of information are available to them?

INTRODUCTION

While most counseling professionals have recognized for some time that understanding cultural differences enhances intervention, the need to take the client's lifespan stage into account has been emphasized only recently. Understanding developmental characteristics and the unique crises, tasks, and problems associated with a particular lifespan period provides counselors with insights into the counseling needs of children, adolescents, adults, and the elderly. This chapter begins with the prenatal and infancy stages and proceeds to examine the developmental characteristics of the four subsequent stages. It underscores the importance of recognizing and understanding lifespan differences.

PRENATAL AND INFANCY STAGES

Crucial Periods. The nine months preceding birth are so obviously significant in lifelong development that their inclusion here does not need explanation. Overall size, health, and weight of an infant are all affected by the pregnant woman's nutritional intake. Smoking and drug and alcohol abuse, as most people know by now, are potentially harmful to a fetus. Improper nutrition may be due either to lack of financial resources or lack of knowledge, the tendency to rely on relatives rather than consult physicians, and language barriers that cause misunderstanding. Drugs, alcohol, the use of oral contraceptives during the early months of pregnancy, and toxins also play a part (Vander Zanden, 1989). For these and other reasons, minority children may begin life at a disadvantage.

Although smoking and alcohol and drug abuse usually may be somewhat controlled by the pregnant woman, maternal malnutrition is more difficult to control. It represents an area that particularly affects minority groups. Malnutrition-related problems such as low birth weight, rickets, physical and neural defects, and low vitality occur most frequently in Native-, African-, Chicano-, and Puerto Rican-American children. Their mothers are more likely to be undernourished than mothers of Anglo-American children (Vander Zanden, 1989). For reasons that may be genetic, environmental, or both, a quarter of all Native-American children born on reservations exhibit fetal alcohol effects (Pregnancy + Alcohol = Problems, 1989).

Hunger and Its Effects. The astounding statistics on hunger indicate that 12 million children and 8 million adults, or about 9 percent of the population, are hungry. Ignorance or indifference may account for their hunger; however, most of these people are victims of an economy that leaves many families below the poverty level and a social welfare system that offers insufficient assistance (Brown, 1987). The results of malnutrition are well known: Mothers with the poorest diets are likely to bear offspring who are premature, weigh the least, have the least vitality, and who die (Werner, 1979).

Cultural Differences. A study of Anglo-, African-, and Southeast Asian-American adolescent women demonstrates that cultural differences affect the unborn baby. One study concluded that Southeast Asian women tend to postpone prenatal care but to abstain from alcohol and tobacco consumption, while Anglo and African adolescent women tend to use both alcohol and tobacco (Swenson, Erickson, Ehlinger, Swaney, & Carlson, 1986).

Is infant behavior universal, or does even infant behavior vary according to culture? Surprising to some observers, research suggests that infants demonstrate culturally specific behaviors. A typical behavior of Western newborns is the Moro reflex.

A FOCUS ON RESEARCH 3–1
Cross-Cultural Perspectives on Infancy

A study by Werner (1988) focuses on two issues: (1) the extent to which information generated by cross-cultural psychologists in the field of infant behavior and development is applicable to developing countries and (2) how relevant this information is to social issues confronting these countries. Werner maintains that studies of infancy have noted a wide range of social factors that affect the rate and quality of infant development; e.g., responsiveness of the care-givers to infant's cues, variations in stimulation the infant receives, routines of infant care, and deliberate teaching of skills valued by the culture. Also noted were a wide range of household characteristics, such as degree of crowding, adult-child ratio, and age mix of children. Researchers must address these variables more systematically, as well as such other factors as demographic constraints, risk factors affecting the survival and quality of life for young children, the changing context of infant care, and the consequences of intervention programs that rely on transfer of Western technology to the developing world.

Source: Werner, E. E. (1988). A cross-cultural perspective on infancy. *Journal of Cross-Cultural Psychology, 19,* 96–113.

To test this reflex, the baby's body is lifted, and the head supported. The head is then released and allowed to drop. Typical newborn Anglo infants extend both arms and legs, cry persistently, and move about in an agitated manner. Conversely, Navajo infants typically respond in a more reduced reflex extension of the limbs. Crying is rare and agitated motion ceases almost immediately. African-American babies appear to be more precocious in gross motor skills, and Asian infants to a lesser degree, than infants of European origin. Asian infants are typically more docile and may tend to stay closer to the parents (Papalia & Olds, 1989). A FOCUS ON RESEARCH 3–1 examines multicultural perspectives on infancy.

CHILDREN

Understanding the unique position of children on the lifespan continuum and the historical and contemporary perspectives surrounding the concept of the childhood years presents professionals with challenging tasks. With physical, psychological, and intellectual characteristics that differ from those of their older counterparts on the lifespan, children have unique physical, psychological, and intellectual traits that must be understood and considered when planning counseling intervention. Although all children progress in the same developmental sequence, it is imperative to recognize the effects of diverse cultural and ethnic backgrounds of young clients.

The Childhood Years: Historical and Contemporary Perspectives

Interest in the unique growth and developmental aspects of children and recognition of the need for special counseling for children have been demonstrated only fairly recently. Lacking social standing and legal rights, children were considered by many as possessions and treated as adults pleased. In essence, the popular mindset was that children were miniature adults. The prevailing opinion of the adult culture was that "children should be seen and not heard." Since society viewed children only as receivers of information, they were denied their rightful place in the world around them (Baruth & Robinson, 1987). For society to accept that children also differed culturally proved equally difficult.

Contemporary perceptions of the childhood years hold that childhood has its own unique culture, which differs significantly from adult culture. Although children differ across cultures, they have their own characteristics that differ substantially from those of adults. Children, by virtue of their developmental characteristics, have their own language patterns, sense of humor, likes and dislikes, and types of social activity and play. Their unique ways of speaking, acting, and perceiving events in their lives indicate that professionals should duly consider the distinct culture of the childhood years.

Counseling professionals who consider children unique and developing individuals rather than "miniature adults" tend to counsel children more effectively. In essence, counselors and psychotherapists intervening with culturally different children should understand (1) the culture of childhood; (2) the physical, psychosocial, and intellectual characteristics of developing children; and (3) the multicultural differences among children.

Multicultural Differences

Werner (1979), in her studies of cross-cultural child development, examined intellectual development extensively and reached several conclusions that have relevance for professionals working with multicultural populations. By far the largest number of studies directed toward testing multicultural dimensions of intellectual development deal with the passage from Piaget's preoperational stage (2 years to 7 years) to the concrete operational stage. In Werner's interpretation, these studies conclude that some children in every culture attain the concrete operational stage, but the question remains as to what extent and at what age. Several factors influencing the onset of Piaget's concrete operational stage include acculturation, the degree of Western-type schooling, ecological-economic demands, maternal styles, socialization values, and sex differences.

It is presently safe to assume that all cultures do not progress at the same rate, and that caution must be exercised in determining at which developmental level children function. Although research and scholarly opinion on child development have made considerable advances during the past half-century, less study has focused on the relationships between culture and development. Table 3–1 examines several issues and questions that need to be addressed for more enhanced understandings of the effects of culture on development.

Developing Children

The current emphasis on child growth and development provides clear proof of the recognition and value currently being placed upon the childhood years. During these

Table 3–1   Cross-cultural child development: Issues and questions

Issues	Questions
Constancies in child behavior and develop-ment	How are children physically, psychologi-cally, and socially alike?
Interactions between processes of develop-ment	How is development affected by physical, cognitive, and social processes?
Effects of ecology and various social systems	How are children affected by ecological, economic, social, and political systems?
Childrearing goals and practices as adaptive to various environments	How do beliefs about children and meth-ods of caring for them fit into the culture?
Changes in behavior of children and care-takers during periods of rapid social change	In what ways and how fast do children and methods of caring for children and their parents change under changing conditions?
Social policies and programs for children	How do various programs affect children? How should programs be designed?

Source: Adapted from Werner, 1979.

years a host of physical, psychosocial, and intellectual changes occur simultaneously: muscles grow and body proportions shift, social interests increasingly move outside the immediate family to a broader community and society, and intellectual problem-solving and reasoning skills enhance in capacity (Gibson, 1978).

Three physical manifestations of childhood are the following: (1) a loss of babylike fat and chubby contours and the rapid growth of legs and arms, resulting in a slimmer appearance; (2) a lengthening of the jaw and an increase in face size as permanent teeth replace baby teeth; and (3) more muscle tissue in boys and more fat in girls (Turner & Helms, 1983).

Children emerge from the socially secure confines of a parent-centered home into a socially expanding world of extended family, with closer and more meaningful friendships and a recognition of peers. As children build their complex social network of friends and significant peers, they also change their self-concepts, their opinions of others, and their perception of the world in relation to themselves. Closely related with physical and psychosocial-emotional development is intellectual development, which opens up vast new worlds of increased thinking ability. No longer confined to the physical or concrete worlds, the child now experiences increased flexibility of thought, the ability to reverse operations, an enhanced memory, and ability to share another's point of view. As always, culturally perceptive counselors need to remember that physical, psychosocial, and intellectual development differ across cultures and that clients should be considered unique (Papalia & Olds, 1989). A FOCUS ON RESEARCH 3–2 examines the particular social expectations of African- and Mexican-American children.

Table 3–2 (pp. 66–67) summarizes children's physical, psychosocial, and intellectual development; however, readers are encouraged to remember that all children differ according to socioeconomic class and age and cultural factors.

A FOCUS ON RESEARCH 3–2
Social Expectations of African- and Mexican-American Children

Rotheram-Borus and Phinney (1990) asked 213 African- and Mexican-American third and sixth graders to respond to eight videotaped scenes of everyday social encounters with same-ethnic unfamiliar peers at school. The goal of the study was to examine the effects of enculturation and acculturation on the social expectations of African- and Mexican-American children and to examine self-esteem of the two groups. Their findings demonstrated clear ethnic differences in the social expectations of African- and Mexican-American school children. Specific findings included the following:

Source: Rotheram-Borus, M. J., & Phinney, J. S. (1990). Patterns of social expectations among Black and Mexican-American children. *Child Development, 61,* 542–556.

1. Mexican-American school children were more group-oriented and more reliant on authority figures for solving problems.

2. African-American school children were more action-oriented and expressive.

3. As other studies also indicated, African-American children were more emotionally expressive and demonstrated more active coping strategies than their Mexican-American counterparts.

4. Both African- and Mexican-American children were deferent to authority. While African-American children apologized more than Mexican-American children, the latter group was more likely to feel bad—a different way of responding to authority.

Self-Concept

Two closely related aspects surface as the social status of children changes: locus of control and self-concept. Children around age 6 or 7 begin to think of themselves in external terms—what they look like, where they live, and what they are doing. This developing self-concept takes two forms: the *real self* and the *ideal self.* The former refers to the child's concept of what he or she is actually like, and the latter refers to what he or she would like to be like (Papalia & Olds, 1987). Thus, children are continually evaluating themselves to determine their degree of self-worth and their sense of adequacy. Positive self-concepts come from development of the sense of industry (Erikson, 1950), when the child feels successful in learning the knowledge, tasks, and technology of his or her society. Likewise, the negative side of this sense of industry, feelings of inferiority and inadequacy, results in anxiety and poor self-concept (Erikson, 1950). Self-concept in Japanese-American children is examined in A FOCUS ON RESEARCH 3–3.

One study (Fu, Korslund, & Hinkle, 1980) of 432 Euro-, African-, and Mexican-American 10-year-old girls used the Self-Concept Self-Report Scale (SC–SR) to investigate the relationship between ethnic and socioeconomic backgrounds and self-concept. Both income levels and ethnic differences exerted varying degrees of influence on the self-concept of the girls. Specifically, as Figure 3–1 illustrates, girls from middle-income homes, with the exception of Mexican-American girls, had higher self-concept ratings than those from lower-income homes. It was concluded that, with

A FOCUS ON RESEARCH 3–3
Self-Concepts of Japanese-American Children

Pang, Mizokawa, Morishima, and Olstad (1985) concluded from their research review that Asian- and Pacific-American children's physical and racial self-concepts appear to be more negative than those of Anglo-American children, and occasionally, those of other groups. To test the hypothesis, this research team designed a study

Source: Pang, V. O., Mizokawa, D. T., Morishima, J. K., & Olstad, R. G. (1985). Self-concepts of Japanese-American children. *Journal of Cross-Cultural Psychology, 16,* 99–109.

that compared self-concepts (especially physical self-concepts) of Japanese-American and Anglo-American children. The study sample was composed of 29 Japanese-American and 47 Anglo-American children. The Japanese-American children were Sansei (third generation) or Yonsei (fourth generation). One significant finding was that the Japanese-American children scored lower than the Anglo-American children on all the physical self-concept scores.

the possible exception of Mexican-Americans, class or income could be assumed to be more important than race in influencing self-concept.

A multicultural comparison study focusing on self-concepts of Native-American and Anglo-American children revealed that the former group referred more to kinship roles, traditional customs and beliefs, and moral worth than the latter. Perhaps equally important as the finding was the caution the authors recommended concerning the methodology of the study. In essence, self-concept instruments may measure attri-

Figure 3–1   Self-esteem, income levels, and ethnic differences. (From *Journal of Psychology, 105,* p. 103, 1980. Reprinted with permission of the Helen Dwight Reid Educational Foundation. Published by Heldref Publications, 4000 Albemarle St., N.W., Washington, D.C. 20016. Copyright © 1980.)

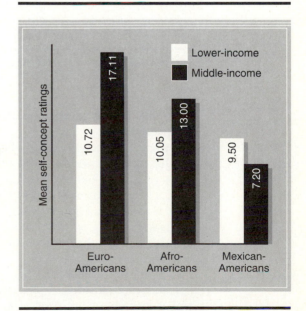

Table 3–2   Developing children: A summary

Physical Development

1. Children are extremely active, often participating in sedentary pursuits such as fingernail biting, hair twirling, and general fidgeting.

2. Children need rest periods; they become easily fatigued as a result of physical and mental exertion.

3. Large-muscle control continues to be superior to small-muscle control, especially in boys.

4. Many children have difficulty focusing on small print, while quite a few may be far-sighted due to the shallow shape of the eye.

5. Children's increasing control of their bodies gives them more confidence in their physical abilities. They may underestimate the difficulty of dangerous pursuits.

6. A growth spurt occurs in most girls and starts in early-maturing boys. On the average, girls between the ages of 11 and 14 are taller and heavier than boys of the same age.

7. Children, especially girls, approaching puberty are almost universally concerned with and curious about sex.

8. Fine motor coordination improves, enhancing both physical skill and self-concept.

9. Physiological changes mark the beginning development of the sexual reproductive system.

10. Structural and skeletal changes, increasingly apparent to growing children, also effect self-concept and other areas of psychosocial development.

Psychosocial Development

1. Children become somewhat more selective in their choice of friends. They are likely to have a more-or-less permanent best friend and may even have an "enemy."

2. Children often like organized games in small groups, but may be overly concerned with rules or get carried away by team spirit.

Source: Adapted from R. F. Bichler and J. Snowman. (1990). *Psychology applied to teaching* (6th ed.). Boston: Houghton Mifflin. Copyright © 1990 by Houghton Mifflin Company. Used with permission.

butes that are not equally important to the cultures being considered. (Rotenberg & Cranwell, 1989).

Locus of control refers to the degree or extent to which a person thinks he or she has control over his or her life. Briefly put, children characterized by internal locus of control believe they can determine what happens to them. On the other hand, children characterized by external locus of control believe that outside forces control their lives (Smart & Smart, 1982). Locus of control has implications for counselors intervening in multicultural settings, since children (as well as adults and the elderly) may feel that racism and discrimination prohibit their taking control of their lives. A FOCUS ON RESEARCH 3–4 examines self-esteem and locus of control in Native-American children.

Multicultural studies help developmental psychologists avoid inappropriate generalizations about universal aspects of children and their social world (Yussen &

Table 3–2 (continued)

Psychosocial Development (continued)

3. Quarrels are still frequent, but words are now more prevalent than physical aggression.
4. Children are increasingly sensitive to the feelings of others.
5. Most place increasing value on their teachers' expectations over those of their friends.
6. The peer group becomes powerful and begins to replace adults as the major source of behavior standards and recognition of achievement.
7. The development of interpersonal reasoning leads to greater understanding.
8. Although behavior disorders are at a peak, most children learn to adapt socially.
9. Conflicts between peer expectations and adult expectations might result in social problems and other difficulties; e.g., juvenile delinquency.

Intellectual Development

1. Generally speaking, children between the ages of 6 and 10 are eager to learn.
2. They like to talk and have much more facility in speaking than in writing.
3. Because of their literal interpretation of rules, primary-grade children may tend to be tattletales.
4. There is a gradual development of the ability to solve problems by generalizing from concrete experiences.
5. There are sex differences in specific abilities and in overall academic performance.
6. Differences in cognitive styles become apparent.
7. Most children are functioning in Piaget's concrete operational stage.
8. Some children near age 12 can deal with abstractions, but some will continue to generalize from concrete experiences.

Santrock, 1982). A knowledge of cultural differences and an understanding of child growth and development are essential for counselors working with culturally different children. In one sense, counselors must be able to think from a child's perspective and to "see" situations from a child's point of view. This will often include recognizing and understanding how a child of a particular age thinks—how the child perceives his or her physical growth and changes, where the child views himself or herself psychosocially, and what level the child is at intellectually.

What do counselors need to remember when intervening with culturally diverse children? First, children are developmentally unique and should not be considered little adults. Second, contrary to some adult thinking, children *do* have problems and may feel helpless to change life situations, may be victims of discrimination (both due to their cultural diversity and their developmental period), and may not have the intellectual capacity to perceive problems and solutions. Third, understanding the relationship between children's development and their cultural diversity improves counseling intervention.

A FOCUS ON RESEARCH 3–4
Self-Esteem and Locus of Control in Native-American Children

From a study designed to assess self-esteem, health locus of control, and health attitudes in Native-American fourth-, fifth-, and sixth-grade students, Lamarine (1987) found that the correlation between self-esteem and health attitudes decreased with age, suggesting that younger children may be the most amenable to interventions directed at improving health attitudes by

increasing self-esteem. Also, some children attempt to enhance self-esteem by adopting socially desirable behaviors, such as those conducive to good health. Lamarine pointed out that the converse may also hold true, as some children may attempt to improve self-esteem by adopting undesirable health practices to gain peer approval. The strongest correlations between self-esteem and health attitudes were noted for Pueblo and Navajo children, respectively. Among Apache children, there was no significant correlation.

Source: Lamarine, R. J. (1987). Self-esteem, health locus of control, and health attitudes among Native-American children. *Journal of School Health, 57,* 371–373.

ADOLESCENTS

The adolescent years have traditionally gone unrecognized as a genuine developmental period on the lifespan. As a result, this group has been plagued with misconceptions, general misunderstandings, and damaging stereotypes. No longer children but not yet adults, adolescents very often experience feelings that tend to lower their self-esteem. Psychosocial and intellectual changes that parallel the more visible physical changes cause adolescents to adopt childlike behaviors at times, and then again, at other times, conform with adult standards. Adolescents often experience identity confusion. Professionals working with adolescent clients need a sound understanding of this lifespan period; they also need to recognize cultural differences that influence adolescent behavior.

The Adolescent Years: Historical and Contemporary Perspectives

While some observers define adolescence in terms of a specific age range, others equate the beginning of adolescence with the onset of puberty and its ending with certain cultural factors. Lefrancois (1981) uses the ages of 11 or 12 to just before or after age 20 with reference to adolescence. Thornburg (1982) offers two age ranges: a traditional range of 13 to 18 and a more contemporary range of 11 to 22.

Contrary to popular belief, the term *adolescence* has not been around very long; in fact, it was hardly accepted before the last century (Demos, 1969). Moreover, proposing the term to suggest a continuation of childhood beyond puberty was even more ludicrous than not recognizing it at all.

Multicultural Differences

Adolescents vary from culture to culture, just as children do. What might be normal behavior in one culture might be considered inappropriate in another. For example, many Anglo-American adolescents feel a strong need to act in accordance with peer pressure, while the Asian-American adolescent is apt to feel that loyalty to parents takes precedence over any peer pressure that may be experienced. Simarly, the sense of "machismo" that so strongly influences the behavior of many Hispanic-Americans is less important to both Anglo-Americans and to Asian-Americans.

Developing Adolescents

Table 3–3 provides a summary of the physical, psychosocial, and intellectual development of adolescents. Specific cultures are not considered, since "adolescence" is associated with different ages and developmental levels across cultures. Moreover, in some cultures the term is not recognized at all. Therefore, readers are reminded that Table 3–3 presents adolescent development in general terms; it is taken to span ages 11 or 12 to age 18.

The Adolescent Identity

Who am I? What am I to be? The main task of adolescence is to build a reasonably stable identity. Identity refers to a person's sense of placement within the world; in other words, it is the meaning that one attaches to oneself in the broader context of life (Vander Zanden, 1989). Friendships can play vital roles in determining the adolescent identity. A FOCUS ON RESEARCH 3–5 looks at friendship patterns of African- and Anglo-American early adolescents.

Multicultural adolescents often develop individual and cultural identities under difficult circumstances, involving racism, discrimination, and injustice. The "culture of poverty" image may influence the Native-American's identity; similarly, African-Americans, hearing repeatedly that their culture is "inferior," may develop negative identities. As A FOCUS ON RESEARCH 3–6 indicates, Mendelberg (1986) feels that being considered in derogatory terms may result in identity confusion.

Self-Concept Development

The significance of self-concept during all periods of the lifespan cannot be overstated. The adolescent's degree of self-worth can have long-lasting effects on identity formation, social development, and academic achievement. Self-perception is vital in determining whether the adolescent will become alienated from parents, peers, and society, or whether he or she will become a sociable person, capable of sustaining satisfactory relationships.

While self-concept begins to develop at birth and continues developing until death, the real crisis in identity occurs during adolescence. Coming through this crisis with the emergence of a strong, healthy, and independent self-concept allows the

Table 3–3   Developing adolescents: A summary

Physical Development

1. There is likely to be a certain amount of adolescent awkwardness—probably due as much to self-consciousness as to sudden growth—and a great deal of concern about appearance.
2. Although this age period is marked by general good health, the diet and sleeping habits of many adolescents are poor.
3. Most adolescents reach physical maturity and virtually all attain puberty.
4. Sexual development and reproductive capabilities often result in confusion regarding sexual relationships.
5. Rapidly developing sexual capabilities also leads to increased sexual activity, with attendant high rates of illegitimate births and sexually transmitted diseases.

Psychosocial Development

1. The peer group becomes the general source of rules of behavior.
2. The desire to conform reaches a peak during these years.
3. Adolescents are greatly concerned about what others think of them.
4. A sense of *sturm und drang* (storm and stress) may be experienced.
5. Parents are likely to influence long-range plans, while peers are likely to influence immediate status.
6. Girls seem to experience greater anxiety about friendships than boys.
7. Toward the end of these years, girls may be more likely than boys to experience emotional disorders.
8. The most common emotional disorder during adolescence is depression.
9. If depression is severe, suicide may be contemplated.

Intellectual Development

1. This is a transition period between the concrete operational stage and formal thought. Although they may be capable of engaging in formal thought, adolescents may not use the capability.
2. This is a transition period between obeying all rules without question and considering extenuating circumstances and intentionality.
3. Between the ages of 12 and 16, political thinking becomes more abstract, liberal, and informed.
4. Beginning formal thinkers may engage in unrestrained theorizing. They may be threatened by awareness of possibilities and be subject to adolescent egocentrism.

Source: Adapted from R. F. Biehler and J. Snowman. (1990). *Psychology applied to teaching* (6th ed.). Boston: Houghton Mifflin. Copyright © 1990 by Houghton Mifflin Company. Used with permission.

A FOCUS ON RESEARCH 3–5
Friendship Patterns in Early Adolescence

DuBois and Hirsch (1990) investigated friendship patterns, both school and nonschool, of 292 black and white young adolescents who attended an integrated junior high school. Their review of the literature revealed that among children and adolescents (a) own-race friendship choices are more common than other-race choices, (b) racial cleavage in friendship patterns increases between the elementary and secondary school years, and (c) the increased separation of the black and white peer groups and the conflicts between the groups serve to make interracial friendships increasingly rare during adolescence.

Source: DuBois, D. L., & Hirsch, B. J. (1990). School and neighborhood friendship patterns of Blacks and Whites in early adolescence. *Child Development, 61,* 524–536.

DuBois and Hirsch concluded that there may be important differences in the peer friendship networks of black and whites during early adolescence:

1. More than 80 percent of both blacks and whites reported having an other-race school friend.

2. Fewer students, yet still more than half, reported having an other-race school friend with whom they were close.

3. A smaller group reported having a close other-race school friend who was frequently seen outside of school.

4. Blacks were almost twice as likely as whites to report having a close other-race school friend who was frequently seen outside of school.

A FOCUS ON RESEARCH 3–6
Identity Conflicts in Mexican-American Youths

A study by Mendelberg focused on 20 Mexican-American adolescents (age 16 to 18) whose families had origins in rural Texas but who had later settled in an industrial mid-sized city in the Midwest. Attempts were made to clarify subjects' reactions to distortions of Mexican-American characteristics as frequently appear in the mass media; e.g., the "wetback"; or the comical, lazy,

Source: Mendelberg, H. E. (1986). Identity conflict in Mexican-American adolescents. *Adolescence, 21,* 215–224.

somewhat obtuse Mexican. Mendelberg reported that (1) identification with members of outside groups appeared to be blocked for minority members, and identification with their own group was difficult; (2) symptoms, such as self-hate, self-blame, and aggression against self and significant others were evident; and (3) the number of ideal images that could be explained by the Mexican-American's migrant origin was limited.

adolescent to progress further and face the challenges of the adult world. Adolescents who are unable to develop a positive self-concept may withdraw from others or develop a negative identity. Vontress (1971) contends that successful mastery of the developmental tasks that lead to a healthy self-concept is even more difficult for minority group members. Failure can result in academic problems, loneliness, and isolation. Bradley and Stewart suggested that the self-concept of African-Americans might be enhanced by (1) rediscovering the history of the African- and Anglo-American relationship and its essential human character, (2) identifying the overt and covert effects of past and present relationships, (3) joining hands with the oppressed, (4) identifying with those committed to helping, and (5) acting as facilitators to effect the union of the committed and the oppressed (Bradley & Stewart, 1982). How do African names affect the self-concepts of African-American adolescents? A FOCUS ON RESEARCH 3–7 looks at a study that sought to examine the self-concept of African-American adolescents with and without African names.

Mboya (1986) explored self-concepts of African-American tenth graders and found significant relationships between self-concept and academic achievement, suggesting the importance of successful school experiences. While some studies have shown that African-American adolescents generally have poorer self-concepts than their Anglo counterparts (Proshansky & Newton, 1968), other more recent studies have contradicted the earlier ones (Rosenberg, 1979; Simmons, Brown, Bush, & Blyth, 1978). One multicultural study included an attempt to determine the self-esteem of

---

A FOCUS ON RESEARCH 3–7
Do African Names Affect the Self-Concept of African-American Adolescents?

An ongoing effort among many African-Americans has consisted of devising and implementing strategies to improve their self-concept and to help them take pride in their ethnic group membership. During the 1960s and 1970s, many African parents gave their children African names in an attempt to enhance their self-concept. Terrell, Terrell, and Taylor (1988) explored the self-concepts of African adolescents with and without African names. A total of 77 African male youths 15 to 18 years of age and their parents participated in the study. Thirty-seven of the youths had African names, and 40

did not. Admitting somewhat confusing findings, the researchers concluded that adolescents with African names had significantly healthier self-concepts than the youths without African names. The researchers did urge caution in drawing conclusions, since the entire sample lived in the South, attended a predominantly African-American high school, and all had been given their names at birth. However, indications were strong that names do enhance self-concept. Terrell et al. pointed out that other research shows that adolescents with desirable names have higher levels of achievement. However, they suggested that additional research must explore the relationship between names and achievement levels before definitive judgments can be made.

Source: Terrell, F., Terrell, S. L., & Taylor, J. (1988). The self-concept of Black adolescents with and without African names. *Psychology in the Schools, 25,* 65–76.

A FOCUS ON RESEARCH 3–8
Self-Esteem and Delinquent Behavior in Three Ethnic Groups

Leung and Drasgow (1986) designed a study to examine a theory of self-esteem and delinquent behavior in three ethnic groups (Anglo-Americans, African-Americans, and Hispanic-Americans) living in the United States. The authors concluded that Anglo-Americans and African-

Americans were similar with regard to self-esteem, while Hispanic-Americans had somewhat lower self-esteem than either Anglo- or African-Americans. A slightly higher frequency of delinquent behavior was reported for Anglo-Americans than for African-Americans or Hispanic-Americans. Apparently the lower self-esteem of the Hispanics did not cause them to be more delinquent than the groups with higher self-esteem as one might have supposed.

Source: Leung, K., & Drasgow, F. (1986). Relationship between self-esteem and delinquent behavior in three ethnic groups. *Journal of Cross-Cultural Psychology, 17,* 151–166.

adolescents in the United States, Australia, and Ireland (Offer, Ostriv, & Howard, 1977). It was found that American adolescents had the highest self-esteem, followed by Australian, and then Irish adolescents. A related investigation comparing those findings with self-esteem of Native-American adolescents indicated that the Native-Americans had significantly lower self-esteem than the overall group of Americans and Australians, but significantly higher self-esteem than the Irish adolescents (Agrawal, 1978). Still another study (Carter, 1968) did not find any differences in feelings of self-worth of Mexican-Americans and Anglo-American adolescents. Once again, although the results are interesting, they must be considered with caution, since the instruments used to measure self-concept were constructed and validated in the United States and may have little multicultural validity (Lloyd, 1985).

A FOCUS ON RESEARCH 3–8 concerns the relationship between self-esteem and delinquent behavior.

At-Risk Adolescents

While suicide, accidents, and homicides account for most adolescent deaths, many adolescents are at risk due to eating disorders, drug abuse, and sexually transmitted diseases. Common eating disorders include anorexia nervosa and bulimia, which are evidenced by a distorted body perception and a preoccupation with food. Drug abuse may involve alcohol, tobacco, and marijuana, which may lead to use of still more powerful drugs. Venereal diseases, or sexually transmitted diseases (STDs), are becoming increasingly serious problems, with particular implications for adolescents. Three out of four cases of STD involve young people from 15 to 24 years of age. Chlamydia, gonorrhea, syphillis, herpes simplex, and acquired immune deficiency syndrome (more commonly referred to as AIDS) are a few of the STDs that take a considerable toll on adolescents (Papalia & Olds, 1989).

Another problem resulting from an increase in sexual activity is adolescent pregnancy and its consequences. The teenage birth rate in the United States is the highest in the world. A survey of single women in their twenties concluded that 1 out of 3 sexually active Anglo women and 7 out of 10 sexually active African-American women had had at least one pregnancy, and the younger the woman was at first intercourse, the more likely she was to have become pregnant (Tanfer & Horn, 1985). Many unmarried teenagers choose to terminate their pregnancies through abortion; in fact, teenage abortion accounts for one-third of all the abortions performed in this country. A FOCUS ON RESEARCH 3–9 examines adolescent pregnancy among Puerto Ricans.

It takes special commitment and expertise to intervene with multicultural adolescents. Not only may they experience frustrations due to being between childhood and adulthood, but also from being a minority in a predominantly Anglo society. At a time when development of positive self-concept and identity is crucial, adolescents often find themselves caught between their parents' admonitions and peer pressure to experiment with tobacco and drugs and to engage in casual sex. In fact, being culturally different has the potential for making the difficult adolescent years even harder. The Native-American adolescent valuing noninterference with others (Richardson, 1981) and the Asian-American adolescent believing errant behavior brings shame and disgrace upon the family (Sue, 1981) can encounter problems with identity formation. Understanding the complex relationship between development and cultural diversity provides counselors with clearer insights into counseling Native-, African-, Asian-, and Hispanic-American adolescents.

 A FOCUS ON RESEARCH 3–9
Adolescent Pregnancy and Abortion among Puerto Rican Teenagers

Pregnant teenagers in the United States tend to carry the baby to term, rather than abort the pregnancy. Ortiz & Nuttall (1987) studied 43 Puerto Rican adolescents to determine the influence of family relationships and support, religion, and education on their decision to carry full-term or to abort. Specifically, the researchers sought to discover which factors exerted the most influence on the young person's decision to carry or to abort. They concluded that (1) girls in the carry group were more significantly influenced and supported by family and friends than those in the abort group; (2) fathers were the least influential in both the carry and the abort group, while mothers were the most influential in the carry group and sisters the most influential in the abort group; (3) brothers, boyfriends, and best friends were more influential in the carry group than in the abort group; (4) girls in the abort group reported being more religious than did those in the carry group; and (5) girls in the abort group who had received strong support from family and friends reported a higher degree of satisfaction with their decision than did those in the carry group.

Source: Ortiz, C. G., & Nuttall, E. V. (1987). Adolescent pregnancy: Effects of family support, education, and religion on the decision to carry or terminate among Puerto Rican teenagers. *Adolescence, 22,* 897–917.

ADULTS

Too often thought to be "grown and not developing," adults do, in fact, continue to experience physical, psychosocial, and intellectual developmental changes. Tasks facing counselors of adult clients include a commitment to consider adulthood as a unique developmental period between adolescence and the elderly years, and to take multicultural differences among adults into account.

The Adulthood Years: Historical and Contemporary Perspectives

The term "adulthood" only recently has begun to receive attention and respect as a valid period on the lifespan. Lacking the concreteness of "childhood" or "adolescence," adulthood found use as a catch-all term to encompass all developmental changes in human beings beginning with some specific chronological age—whether 18, 21, or some other age (Graubard, 1976). Not until the 1970s did an interest appear in the adulthood years specifically, which caused some researchers to consider them a largely unexplored phase of the human cycle (Barnett & Baruch, 1978). Once thought to be homogeneous, fully developed "products," adults are now recognized as diverse and continually changing and developing.

Adult Development

As we have already pointed out, to assume that adults do not continue to experience both visible and invisible developmental changes demonstrates a lack of knowledge of human development. From the time of conception, humans experience many developmental changes, both desirable and undesirable, that continue until death. Considerable individuality is associated with these developmental changes; some adults experience them without psychological turmoil, while others require counseling intervention.

The adult developmental stages basically can be divided into three arbitrary age ranges: early, middle, and late. The young adult category ranges from 20 to 40 years of age. During these years, young adults make decisions regarding marriage and careers that will affect the rest of their lives (Rogers, 1982). The middle-age adult is approximately 40 to 65 years of age. (The late adult stage arbitrarily begins at 65 and will be discussed in the next section.) Middle age brings with it an aging physical appearance, the development of a distinct adult intelligence, and changes in personality. Although the transition from the young adult years to the middle-aged years may go virtually unnoticed, counselors can still benefit from determining the stage clients think they are at. Transitions are culture-based, which means that middle age in one culture may not coincide with the previously suggested age range of 40 to 65 that is often considered appropriate for the Western world (Papalia & Olds, 1989). Table 3–4 examines the physical, psychosocial, and intellectual characteristics of developing adults.

Table 3–4   Adult development: A summary

Physical Development

1. The adult body is continually aging and changing, often unnoticed.

2. Body changes, such as decreased height and increased weight (especially around the waist and hips), can have negative effects on self-esteem.

3. The effects of aging on skin and hair represent two of the most noticeable changes as adults grow older.

4. The senses become less keen as the adult ages.

5. The various body systems deteriorate; however, proper nutrition and exercise contribute significantly to either restoring or lengthening the life of these systems.

6. Although most young and middle-aged adults are in reasonably good health, the physique, body systems, and senses have all begun the degenerative process.

Psychosocial Development

1. Often not easily recognized, psychosocial changes still can have serious consequences for developing adults.

2. Young and middle-aged adults have age-level developmental tasks to meet for satisfactory developmental progress.

3. Culturally different adults in the United States may not develop according to "Western" theories.

4. Young adults must successfully resolve the intimacy-versus-isolation stage by forming strong emotional bonds with others. Likewise, middle-aged adults facing the productivity-versus-stagnation stage must continue to make a contribution to others and to society in general.

5. Aging is sometimes accompanied by personality changes, such as becoming more introspective or assuming characteristics of the opposite sex.

Intellectual Development

1. The ability and desire to create and be creative do not terminate with the end of youth; creativity continues into adulthood and later.

2. Adult intelligence is unique and distinctive from other developmental periods; it is characterized by maturity and practicality.

3. Intellectual functioning during adulthood allows for accepting contradictions, imperfections, and compromise.

4. Intelligence and intellectual functioning are influenced significantly by steadily accumulating life experiences.

5. Moral development and intellectual functioning are so closely related that distinguishing between the two is virtually impossible.

6. The experiences adults acquire over time play a major role in their moral reasoning and decision making.

7. The various areas of adult functioning are closely interrelated, each exerting an effect on the others.

Sources: Data compiled from Papalia and Olds, 1989; Rogers, 1982; and Whitbourne, 1986.

Concerns and Tasks of Adulthood

Early Adulthood and Middle Adulthood

Adult concerns differ with each substage (early, middle, late) and also with culture and socioeconomic status. Problems associated with specific cultures might include high unemployment rates among African-, Hispanic-, and Native-Americans; alcoholism among Native-Americans; acculturation (and attendant rejection of old-world values) of Asian-Americans; the portrayal of African-American males as violent and prone to drug use; and the emerging role of African-American females as family heads.

Havighurst compiled a list of developmental tasks that he maintained were age-level appropriate for both early adulthood and middle-adulthood. Success or failure in these tasks determined future happiness or unhappiness. Tasks during early adulthood include selecting a mate, learning to live with a partner, starting a family, rearing children, managing a home, and getting started in an occupation. The middle adult years includes tasks such as assisting teenage children to become responsible adults, assuming social and civic responsibility, performing satisfactorily in one's chosen occupation, developing leisure time activities, relating to one's spouse as an individual, accepting the physiological changes of middle age, and adjusting to aging parents (Havighurst, 1972).

Recognizing the role of cultural and socioeconomic factors in mastering these developmental tasks, Havighurst acknowledged that they are extremely important. A person in one culture might be encouraged to seek financial independence; in another culture, financial dependence might be the norm. While a successful middle-aged Anglo-American might be established and performing satisfactorily in an occupation, the unemployed middle-aged Native-, African- or Hispanic-American with few marketable skills might still be seeking gainful employment. Similarly, socioeconomic differences affect one's leisure activities, one's degree of social and civic responsibility, and one's ability to manage a home.

Although Havighurst's developmental theories undoubtedly contribute to our knowledge of adults, many questions still remain as to the complex interaction of development, culture, and socioeconomic class in a nation of increasing diversity. A FOCUS ON RESEARCH 3–10 describes a study of developmental tasks in young-adult Mexican-American females.

Development changes during the substages of the adult period are as distinctive as the previously discussed child and adolescent developmental changes; hence, the need for specific counseling strategies planned for early, middle, and late adulthood. Intervening with culturally diverse adults requires an understanding of the physical and psychosocial effects of growing older, the different tasks and crises among cultures, and the complex relationship between an individual's development and culture.

THE ELDERLY

What does it means to be elderly? What does it means to be an elderly minority person living in a culture that emphasizes youth? Myths and stereotypes surrounding the elderly have long cast them in an undesirable light. They are often misunderstood,

A FOCUS ON RESEARCH 3–10
Developmental Tasks in Young Adult Mexican-American Females

Questions continue to focus on whether tasks for middle-class Anglo-Americans are valid for other cultural and ethnic groups residing in the United States. Tucker and Huerta (1987) interviewed young Mexican-American females from 18 to 34 years of age. The interviews revealed six tasks that provide a better understanding of the developmental patterns of these young Hispanics: (1) establishing a stable relationship, (2) obtaining education for a career, (3) establishing independence, (4) starting a family or rearing children, (5) maintaining friendships, and (6) participating in civic or community activi-

ties. The writers concluded that young Mexican-American women have developmental tasks similar to those described by Havighurst, yet variations were found to exist as a function of age, marital status, education level, and parenthood factors. For example, (a) married women, women with children, and women from 25 to 34 years of age placed a lower priority on their own education than unmarried, divorced, or childless women; (b) women educated above the baccalaureate level placed a lower emphasis on maintaining friendships than those with less education; (c) married or divorced women with children considered having and rearing a family more important than did unmarried women; and (d) women with children were less interested in participating in civic and community activities than those without children.

Source: Tucker, B., & Huerta, C. (1987). A study of developmental tasks as perceived by young adult Mexican-American females. *Lifelong Learning: An Omnibus of Practice and Research, 10*(4), 4–7.

and perhaps more often, neglected. Undoubtedly, the elderly, culturally different client may present difficult problems for the counselor: Planning appropriate intervention requires an understanding of the declining capacity of the body to function properly and the health problems and concerns that often plague the culturally diverse elderly.

The Elderly Years: Historical and Contemporary Perspectives

Beliefs about the elderly, up until the last several decades, were based partly on myth and partly on misinformation. Disturbingly, even less was known about the culturally diverse elderly.

How do different cultures view the elderly? It is a well-known fact that the Anglo culture favors youthfulness at the expense of the elderly, who often experience discrimination and prejudice. The elderly may be edged out of family life by children who perceive them as sick, ugly, and parasitic. They may be considered incapable of thinking clearly, learning new things, enjoying sex, contributing to the community, and holding responsible jobs (Butler, 1987; Gatz, 1989; Santrock, 1989). The elderly in many other cultures, however, do not suffer the neglect and abuse that the Anglo elderly often suffer. For example, in the Chinese and Japanese cultures, the elderly are accorded a higher status than the elderly in the United States. Elderly Asians are more integrated into their families and fewer single elderly adults live alone. Seats are reserved for them, their food preferences are catered to, and they are bowed to as a sign of respect (Santrock, 1989).

The last several decades have witnessed a new interest in the elderly years, with more attention focused on the minority elderly. Gerontology, or the study of aging, has come into its own, and there is increasing awareness that being elderly differs across cultures. These enhanced perspectives will help shed light on the particular needs of this lifespan period and clear up some of the misconceptions surrounding it.

Myths and Stereotypes Surrounding the Elderly

Even in our contemporary society, elderly people are often described in negative terms: "fading fast," "over the hill," "out to pasture," "down the drain," "finished," "out of date," "old crock," "fogy," "geezer," and "biddy" (Butler, 1975). Although more recent appellations are somewhat kinder (e.g., "older Americans," "golden-agers," "senior citizens"), we seem somewhat confused as to how to describe the elderly, especially those who are culturally different. Table 3–5 lists a few of the more common myths pertaining to this age group.

A relationship between the degree of industrialization of a society and percep-tions of aging has been demonstrated. For example, in a highly industrialized society, such as the United States, perceptions of aging are often negative. In fact, attitudes toward the elderly are more favorable in primitive societies, with positive attitudes declining with increasing industrialization and modernization (Tein-Hyatt, 1986–1987). How does self-perception in the elderly vary across cultures? A FOCUS ON RESEARCH 3–11 describes a multicultural study focusing on this question.

The Developing Elderly

Such changes in physical appearance as graying hair, balding, and wrinkling skin are usually the first indications of growing older; however, many other less visible changes occur as people age. Table 3–6 (p. 82) summarizes the physical, psychosocial, and intellectual changes occurring in the elderly.

Health Problems and Concerns of the Culturally Diverse Elderly

The health status of the elderly is commonly misperceived. Most people over 65 do not have to limit any major activities for health reasons, and not until age 85 does more than half the total population report such limitations. Even those 85 and over are usually able to take care of their own basic needs. Thus, the stereotype of the elderly as helpless is not based on reality (Papalia & Olds, 1989). This is not meant to imply, however, that health problems of the elderly do not warrant special atten-

Table 3–5   Common myths about the elderly

MYTH: The myth of aging itself

FACT: It is clear that there are great differences in the rates of physiological, psychological, and social aging among individuals and cultures.

MYTH: The myth of nonproductivity

FACT: In the absence of diseases and social adversities, old people tend to remain productive and actively involved in life.

MYTH: The myth of disengagement

FACT: Evidence does not exist to support the theory that a separation between the person and society is necessarily a part of the aging process.

MYTH: The myth of inflexibility

FACT: The ability to change and adapt has little to do with one's age; it has more to do with one's lifelong character.

MYTH: The myth of senility

FACT: The notion that senility is an inevitable outcome of aging, or that the elderly are always forgetful and confused ignores research suggesting that these conditions are treatable and reversible.

MYTH: The myth of serenity

FACT: Rather than living in a fairyland of peace and serenity, older people experience stress, depression, anxiety, and psychosomatic illnesses. Depression is particularly evidenced late in life; in fact, 25 percent of all suicides are people over 65 years of age.

Source: Adapted from Butler, 1974, pp. 6–12.

tion. A FOCUS ON RESEARCH 3–12 looks at one contemporary health problem that also affects the elderly, with additional age-related complications.

How do minority cultures' health issues differ from those of the majority culture? Is one group healthier than another? Research focusing on the mortality and morbidity patterns of Chinese elderly in America reveal that (1) Chinese-Americans are relatively healthier than Anglo-Americans, (2) age-specific death rates for all causes of death are lower for Chinese than for the majority Anglo population, (3) sex differences within each ethnic group appear to be consistent with the widely observed higher death rate for males than females, and (4) higher rates of suicide are associated with elderly Chinese women as compared to elderly Anglo women (Yu, 1986).

What reasons can be offered for one culture being healthier? A FOCUS ON RESEARCH 3–13 describes a multicultural study comparing the health status of Japanese-Americans and Anglo-Americans residing in Hawaii.

A FOCUS ON RESEARCH 3–11
Self-Perceptions of Aging among Anglo-Americans, Chinese-Americans, and Chinese in Taiwan

Tein-Hyatt (1986–1987) used interviews to explore the differences in self-perceptions of aging among Anglo-Americans, Chinese-Americans, and Chinese living in Taiwan. Findings included the following:

1. Anglo-Americans had the most positive self-perceptions of aging; Chinese-Americans, the next; Chinese in Taiwan, the least.

2. Although there were varying degrees of satisfaction with current life situations, all three groups revealed positive perceptions of aging.

3. Self-rated physical health and self-perceived reverence for the elderly were two correlates of self-perception of aging for Anglo-Americans.

4. For Chinese-Americans, mental health and self-perceived reverence for the elderly were two crucial factors associated with self-perceptions of aging.

5. For Chinese in Taiwan, mental health and service utilization were two correlates of self-perception of aging.

Source: Tein-Hyatt, J. L. (1986–1987). Self-perceptions of aging across cultures: Myth or reality? *International Journal of Aging and Human Development, 24*, 129–146.

The need to consider the cultural aspects of health is becoming increasingly clear. Keeping in mind individual differences as well as differing environmental conditions, we will now summarize health problems facing the culturally diverse elderly.

Native-Americans. The average life expectancy for Native Americans is only 65 years, eight years less than that of Anglos. The major health problems of elderly Native-Americans are tuberculosis, diabetes, liver and kidney disease, high blood pressure, pneumonia, and malnutrition. The majority of Native-American elderly rarely see a physician, primarily because they often live in isolated areas and lack transportation. Other reasons relate to a longstanding reliance on ritual folk healing and a different cultural understanding of disease.

African-Americans. African-American elderly are more likely to be sick and disabled and more likely to see themselves as being in poor health than the Anglo elderly. They have higher rates of chronic disease, functional impairment, and risk factors, such as high blood pressure. Between the ages of 65 and 75, the mortality rate of African-Americans is higher than that of Anglos. African-Americans over 75 years of age have lower mortality rates but more poverty and illness.

Asian-Americans. Certain types of cancers, hypertension, and tuberculosis are major health concerns of Asian/Pacific Islander elderly. Asian/Pacific Islander elderly are less likely to use formal health care services, such as those reimbursed under Med-

Table 3–6   The developing elderly: A summary

Physical Development

1. Changes in physical appearance and in the skeletomuscular systems are usually the first signs or indicators of growing older.

2. Aging of the skeletomuscular system can be both physically painful and damaging to the self-concept.

3. Although perhaps only they suspect these changes, the elderly usually experience (a) a decline in sensory functioning (vision, hearing, taste, and smell) and (b) a deterioration of the body systems and their ability to function.

4. Regular exercise and proper nutrition can help deteriorating body systems so that elderly individuals may live longer and more satisfying lives.

5. Although sexuality in the elderly is clouded with myths and misconceptions, sexual interest does not decline with age; many elderly people enjoy satisfying sexual activity, often into their eighties.

Psychosocial Development

1. Psychosocial changes may not be as easily recognized in the elderly as in children or adults, yet the consequences have equal potential for affecting the total functioning of the elderly person.

2. The last period of life has unique developmental tasks, such as adjusting to declining health and to the death of a spouse.

3. Ego integrity versus despair must be successfully resolved in meeting the crises associated with the elderly.

4. "Grand schemes" of lifespan development theories must be thoughtfully applied when considering elderly clients from minority cultures.

5. The elderly sometimes experience personality changes, becoming more rigid, less adaptive, more dogmatic, and less tolerant. Many do not experience such changes.

6. The self-concept of the elderly appears to be fairly positive, especially with respect to individuals living above their anticipated socioeconomic levels.

Intellectual Development

1. Intellectual functioning in the elderly continues to be clouded with uncertainty and controversy; whether or not intelligence declines depends on one's definition of intelligence.

2. Although memory loss may be experienced as one grows older, some people retain sound memory throughout their lives. Loss of recent memory is a more common occurrence than loss of more distant memory.

3. The elderly may experience learning problems or attitudinal problems associated with new situations for accomplishing tasks.

4. Although many early studies of elderly creativity have been refuted, considerable controversy continues to surround the issue of whether creativity declines in the elderly.

5. Considerable research on whether problem-solving abilities decline is inconclusive, although some researchers have assumed a decline and proposed reasons for the demise.

Sources: Data compiled from Cox, 1984; Kart, 1985; and Papalia and Olds, 1989.

A FOCUS ON RESEARCH 3–12
Elderly and AIDS—Forgotten Patients

In his lecture at the annual meeting of the American Society on Aging, James D. Waltner maintained that many elderly people do not consider themselves at risk of contracting AIDS; however, "the elderly are sexual, sometimes have more than one partner, [and sometimes] have sexual relationships with the same sex" (Elderly and AIDS, p. 17). Statistics indicate that approximately 10 percent of people with AIDS are over 49 years old. Since further age breakdowns are not available, little attention has been focused on the special problems associated with the elderly.

To complicate the problem, service providers to the elderly have not been educated adequately, and symptoms can often be dismissed as due to other ailments. Teaching safety precaution to an age group unused to discussing sexuality poses additional problems. Related problems facing elderly people with AIDS include emotional isolation, lack of a support network, family tensions, and dealing with children or grandchildren.

Source: Elderly and AIDS—Forgotten patients? (1988, June/July). *Modern Maturity*, p. 17.

---

icare. Primary reasons for not using such health care services include cultural and language differences, a reliance on folk medicine, and a distrust of Western medicine.

Hispanic-Americans. Of those 65 years of age and over living in the community rather than in nursing homes, 85 percent report at least one chronic ailment. Forty-five percent report some limitation in performing day-to-day activities. Hispanic elderly spend more days per year in bed because of illness (AARP, 1986).

A FOCUS ON RESEARCH 3–13
A Cross-Cultural Health Study: Japanese and Caucasian Elders in Hawaii

Peterson, Rose, and McGee (1985) investigated and compared the health status of Japanese elderly and Caucasian elderly populations. The authors proposed at the outset that minority status, especially that of the Hawaiian Japanese, might be advantageous due to ethnic membership and to culturally related factors of family support and socioeconomic level. The population examined included 1,098 Japanese and 873 Caucasians, all over 60 years of age. Findings included the following:

1. Younger subjects, those with higher family incomes, and those with steady jobs were healthier. Better health also was associated with Japanese ethnicity.

2. Ethnocultural support in health maintenance of the elderly has theoretical relevance for the role of culture in health.

Source: Peterson, M. R., Rose, C. L., & McGee, R. I. (1985). A cross-cultural health study of Japanese and Caucasian elders in America. *International Journal of Aging and Human Development, 21*, 267–279.

Health and culture are also intertwined in other ways that have implications for counselors. Is the widely held belief that Asian young people take care of the elderly still valid? Liu (1986) compared elderly Asian-Americans with the general American population and concluded that economic realities and structural factors of the ethnic community have left many elderly Asian-Americans living alone or with nonrelatives.

A POINT OF DEPARTURE

Challenges Confronting Multicultural Counselors

Many of today's counselors who received their training prior to the current emphasis on multicultural counseling and lifespan development might not realize the insight to be gained from an understanding of multicultural differences and a lifespan perspective. Multicultural counselors working with clients at the four lifespan stages face several challenges that have potential for improving the counseling intervention and enhancing the client-counselor relationship:

1. understanding the historical and contemporary perspectives of each lifespan stage;
2. understanding the importance of human growth and development in the counseling process;
3. understanding that culturally diverse clients differ both within and across cultures; and
4. understanding the complex relationship between counseling, culture, and human growth and development.

SUMMARY

Counseling culturally and developmentally different clients requires knowledge of clients' cultural backgrounds and their physical, psychosocial, and intellectual characteristics. While some human needs cross developmental levels and cultural boundaries, other concerns, problems, and tasks differ according to lifespan stage and cultural background. Understanding the client's individual needs and the complex relationship between culture, development, and counseling provides a solid framework for counseling intervention.

Suggested Readings

Child Development. (1990). *61*(2). The April 1990 issue of *Child Development* is devoted entirely to the development of minority children. Minority groups addressed include African-, Asian-, Hispanic-, and Native-Americans.

Ivey, A. E. (1986). *Developmental theory*. San Francisco, CA: Jossey-Bass. Ivey suggests that one can apply developmental theory directly to therapeutic and counseling practice. Readers will find Chapter 8, "Development Over the Life Span," particularly helpful in this regard, especially the sections on cultural and sexual differences.

Ivey, A. E., & Gonsalves, O. F. (1988). Developmental therapy: Integrating developmental processes into clinical practice. *Journal of Counseling and Development, 66*, 406–413. Ivey and Gonsalves suggest that the facilitation of development may be a primary goal of counseling and therapy. Differing from lifespan developmental psychology, developmental therapy supplements lifespan theories and can provide specific suggestions for clinical-counseling interventions.

Kart, G. S. (1985). *The realities of aging: An introduction to gerontology*. Boston, MA: Allyn and Bacon. Kart's text comprehensively examines gerontology, with a particular look at the lives of the minority elderly.

Lloyd, M. A. (1985). *Adolescence*. New York, NY: Harper & Row. This text includes such multicultural topics as cognitive development, family organization, identity development, moral reasoning, and peer group functions across cultures.

Munroe, R. L., & Munroe, R. H. (1975). *Cross-cultural human development*. Monterey, CA: Brooks/Cole. Munroe and Munroe consider the lifespan from a multicultural perspective and look specifically at lesser-known cultures.

Santrock, J. W. (1989). *Life-span development* (3rd ed.). Dubuque, IA: W. C. Brown. In his lifespan human growth and development text, Santrock includes numerous multicultural references to point out differences between Anglos and those of other cultures.

Spencer, M. B. (1990). Development of minority children: An introduction. *Child Development, 61*, 267–269. Spencer provides the introduction to this special issue (April 1990) focusing on the development of minority children. Issues addressed include what being minority means over the lifespan, the current status of research, societal meanings of minority, and children as resources.

Super, C. M. (1981). Cross-cultural research on infancy. In H. C. Triandis & A. Heron (Eds.), *Handbook of cross-cultural psychology: Developmental psychology* (Vol. 1, pp. 17–53). Boston, MA: Allyn and Bacon. In his comprehensive examination of cross-cultural research, Super argues for a variety of research perspectives and methodologies in studying non-Western cultures.

Triandis, H. C., & Heron, A. (1981). *Handbook of cross-cultural psychology: Developmental psychology*. (Vol. 4). Boston, MA: Allyn and Bacon. This text examines cross-cultural developmental psychology by focusing on research on infancy, bilingual development, language development, schooling and cognitive skills, Piaget's theories, and personality theories.

Werner, E. E. (1979). *Cross-cultural child development: A view from the planet Earth*. Monterey, CA: Brooks/Cole. A prerequisite to any study of cross-cultural development, this interesting text utilizes first-hand examples to show how child development differs in several cultures.

Young-Eisendrath, P. (1985). Making use of human development theories in counseling. *Counseling and Human Development, 17*(5), 1–12. Young-Eisendrath defines counseling, describes the various categories of human development theories, and shows the relevance of developmental theories to the counseling process.

Part I

Understanding and Counseling the Child

Part I consists of two chapters, one on understanding the childhood years and the other on counseling culturally diverse children. Specifically, Chapter 4 provides readers with a cultural portrait of Native-American, African-American, Asian-American, and Hispanic-American children. Chapter 5 then directs the reader's attention to appropriate strategies for professional intervention with children of these cultures.

Chapter 4

Social and Cultural Aspects of Childhood

Questions To Be Explored

1. How has the perception of the childhood years changed? What societal and cultural influences have changed the concept of childhood? Why is understanding past and present perceptions of childhood important?

2. How do the various perceptions of childhood differ?

3. What needs do children across cultures share? What are some of the similarities and differences of children of different cultures?

4. What stereotypes, prejudices, and assumptions surround children, cultural diversity, and development?

5. What should the multicultural counselor know and understand about the childhood years in the Native-American, African-American, Asian-American, and Hispanic-American cultures?

6. What unique challenges confront multicultural counselors working with children?

7. What sources of information are available for multicultural counselors working with children?

INTRODUCTION

The childhood years in the various cultures and societies have failed to receive recognition commensurate with their importance and have been overlooked or short-changed as a vital period in lifespan development (Aries, 1962). The social and cultural influences on the childhood years have suffered yet greater neglect, with the apparent assumption that childhood traits and characteristics were unworthy of serious debate; that is, they were considered unimportant as determinants of the kind of person the child was becoming. Only recently have the childhood years been recognized as a unique growth period with special traits and characteristics significant in lifespan development. And only recently has it become clear that these years are influenced significantly by the society and culture in which the child lives. Thus, understanding children's cultural and ethnic backgrounds contributes to a more accurate and complete picture of the client as an individual. This chapter examines children and the childhood years and provides descriptions of children in the Native-American, African-American, Asian-American, and Hispanic-American cultures.

THE CHILDHOOD YEARS: HISTORICAL AND CULTURAL INFLUENCES

The acceptance of childhood as both a concept and a growth period worthy of consideration, with specific psychological characteristics, has been a recent phenomenon in some cultures. Kessen (1979) refers to the theme of the child as a cultural invention and takes the position that history provides evidence of the shifting nature of childhood. The literature indicates that for many years children were considered miniature adults—not-so-important individuals. A clear-cut distinction between the childhood and adulthood years was not established.

An objective assessment of one's feelings towards children and the childhood years clarifies the value one places on this developmental period. Ask yourself the following questions:

- Do you consider childhood a special time, or merely a period children must "pass through"?
- Do you see children as unique individuals, or as a group growing and developing at the same rate?
- Do you recognize children as having special needs and considerations?
- Do your actions indicate that you treat children in accordance with their individual needs?
- Do you think of childhood and children in stereotypical terms?
- Do you recognize that cultural differences play a significant role in children's lives and the counseling intervention?

A more enlightened philosophy considers the childhood years as a unique developmental period in an individual's life. Spanning the period from infancy to adolescence, or roughly the ages from 2 to 12 years of age, the childhood years will never be matched again in the development of the individual. Understanding children's development assists counselors in assessing the child's total development and provides guidelines for appropriate counseling intervention (Baruth & Robinson, 1987).

The child's ethnic group membership, social class, minority group status, and culture all contribute significantly to the "person" into whom the child is developing. A three-fold task for multicultural counselors includes understanding the childhood developmental period, understanding the cultural influences on the developing child, and understanding the often complicated relationship between childhood and culture. Such understanding is a prerequisite to proper assessment and diagnosis and to the selection of counseling strategies. After first considering some stereotypes and prejudices toward children, we will then examine cross-cultural needs that may hold true for the more industrialized nations and, finally, focus attention on the childhood years and experiences of the four cultural groups with which this text is primarily concerned.

Stereotyping, Prejudice, and Assumptions

Toward Children. Children have their own unique and individual characteristics, needs, and goals. Too often, however, they are not considered in the positive light they deserve. Whether because of prejudice toward their age or because their developmental period is not understood, children are often treated as second-class citizens. Frequently, they are described as "kids" or "brats"—terms with negative connotations (Cook, 1983). Hearing children described in derogatory terms has the potential for affecting the professional's attitudes toward them and toward counseling intervention with them.

Toward Cultural Diversity. Rather than judging children as individuals, counselors very often base their perceptions on cultural beliefs thought to be true of adults. A popular stereotype is that modern Western individuals have lost certain unique qualities characteristic of people living in simpler cultures. As this stereotype has it, Western cultures are self-oriented, highly competitive, and constantly pushing for achievement, while non-Western cultures have remained more group-oriented, cooperative, and accepting of life's events. People perpetuating this stereotype tend to group all non-Westerners together, ignoring individual differences among non-Western groups (Munroe & Munroe, 1975). Likewise, African-American learners are often stereotyped as lazy and uneducated, while Asian-Americans are considered highly motivated, educated, and often gifted in mathematics and science. Working actively to combat stereotypes requires recognizing and understanding them, at the same time striving to see the individual "person" within the culture.

Toward Development. Professionals working with children in multicultural settings should be aware of stereotypes pertaining to child growth and development. For example, misunderstanding may result from the assumption that children in all cultures go through one-word and two-word phases in their language development. As another example, Erik Erikson's psychosocial stages and Piaget's intellectual stages may characterize only modern people, yet these models may be universally applied. To add to the confusion and the need for careful decision making, some developmental theories hold more cross-cultural promise than others; for example, the lower stages in Erikson's theories (e.g., basic trust) and in Piaget's theories (e.g., sensorimotor intelligence) describe developmental characteristics holding the greatest cross-cultural promise (Munroe & Munroe, 1975).

The perils of cross-cultural developmental assumptions are evident in a study of Southeast Asian children. It was observed that these youngsters did not play pat-a-cake, did not pick up raisins, and did not dress themselves at the standard ages. It would be a mistake to assume that these children were delayed developmentally. Considering the cultural factors involved, children in Southeast Asia simply do not play the game of pat-a-cake, raisins look like medicine that they are taught to avoid, and they are not expected to dress themselves as early as Western children (Munroe & Munroe, 1975).

Children: Cross-Cultural Needs

In considering the cross-cultural needs of children, it is necessary to question which assumptions are valid for which cultures, to take individual differences into account within the culture, to remember that it is important for all children to develop a positive racial identity, and to recognize the stereotypes that plague children of all cultures.

Human Needs. Maslow (1964) proposed a hierarchy of needs that may be cross-culturally valid for children. In Maslow's hierarchy, higher needs do not become a focus until lower ones have been at least partially satisfied. The first or lowest level includes physiological needs; e.g., air, water, food, and rest. The second level includes safety and (physical) security needs—shelter from the weather, protection against predators, and so on. At the third level, the needs begin to take on more "social" qualities—the need for acceptance, for intimacy, and for affection. Esteem needs, at the fourth level, bear on evaluation and self-evaluation. Included here is a need to be appreciated by others. At the highest level of the hierarchy are self-actualization needs. Everyone has an intrinsic desire to become all that he or she is capable of being. While all children have increasingly higher level needs, cultural factors play a large part in determining the extent to which needs are met.

Positive Racial Identities. In addition to the basic human needs proposed by Maslow, James P. Comer, a prominent African-American psychiatrist and co-author of *Black Child Care*, proposes that children of all cultures have the need to establish a positive racial identity. Comer suggests that children of all racial groups should be able to develop positive feelings about themselves and their cultural group. Negative or ambivalent feelings may result in adverse social and psychological consequences (Comer, 1988).

Determining whether childrens' unique needs are being met is a major step toward understanding children. In the Native-American, African-American, Asian-American, and Hispanic-American cultures, this understanding requires knowledge of both the respective culture and the childhood years in that culture. In developing a cultural portrait, it is important to consider individual differences, and other variables existing within cultures, such as socioeconomic level, family structure, and geographic location. The following sections synopsize the childhood years in the four cultures.

NATIVE-AMERICAN CHILDREN

Societal and Cultural Description

It is crucial for professionals intervening with Native-American children to understand the history of the United States from the standpoint of the Native-American culture, and also from the child's perspective (Banks, 1987). The assumption that Native-Americans belong to one homogeneous tribe is far from the truth. The federal government recognizes 478 Native-American tribes; in addition, there are 52 identifiable tribes that are Native-American but not recognized by the federal government (Lazarus, 1982).

Although physical and cultural diversity have long characterized Native-Americans, certain similarities with respect to values and beliefs allow for a broad-based description of the Native-American child. As mentioned previously, caution must be exercised when developing such a portrait, since considerable intracultural variation is to be expected. Particularly relevant is the child's location (on or off the reservation), the child's school (predominantly Native-American or Anglo-American), and the socioeconomic class of the parents. The term *Indian* suggests stereotypical physical appearance, when, in fact, height, hair texture, facial features, and skin colors vary widely. This diversity also extends to personality traits, cultural practices, and lifestyles (Banks, 1987).

The values and beliefs of Native-Americans are often at variance with those of Anglo-Americans. While the Anglo-American child is taught that individuals are free to do as they please as long as their actions remain within the law, the Native-American child is taught that actions must be in harmony with nature. (Interestingly, Anglo-Americans are now coming, too, to value the land, much as the Native-Americans, through heightened awareness of environmental crises.) Native-Americans also prize self-sufficiency and learning gained from the natural world. Children are taught to respect and protect the aged who provide wisdom and acquaint the young with traditions, customs, and legends (Axelson, 1985). Elderly Native-Americans teach younger family members crafts and cultural morals (Edwards & Edwards, 1989). Other distinct cultural values are also reflected in interpersonal relationships. For example, children are accorded the same degree of respect as adults, cooperation and harmony are encouraged, and individuals are judged by their contribution to the group. Native-Americans have an unhurried lifestyle that is present-time oriented. A deep respect for tradition is evident (Lazarus, 1982).

Concern for the welfare of Native-American children resulted in the passage of the Indian Child Welfare Act of 1980. This legislation was enacted to reaffirm tribal jurisdiction over child welfare matters, reestablish tribal authority to accept or reject jurisdiction over Native-American children living off reservations, require state courts and public welfare agencies to follow specific procedural requirements, specify that preference be given to a child's extended family when making substitute care and adoptive placements, provide for intergovernmental agreements for child care services, and authorize grants for comprehensive child and family service programs operated by tribes and off-reservation organizations. Through this act and other legislation, Native-American children's rights to their tribal and cultural heritage are being protected better than in the past, and the role of parents and tribes in protecting their rights has been strengthened (Plantz, Hubbell, Barrett, & Dobrec, 1989).

The criteria for evaluating achievement differ from one culture to another; therefore caution must be exercised in making cross-cultural comparisons. Munroe and Munroe (1975) warn of the difficulty involved in comparing levels of achievement across cultures. Cultural conflicts contribute significantly to the academic failure of many Native-American children who function at the average-to-superior range until the fourth grade. Then, their academic achievement typically declines each year, so that by the tenth grade, they are doing below-average work (Sanders, 1987).

A FOCUS ON RESEARCH 4–1
Fifth-Grade Navajo Children: A Profile

Tempest (1987) interviewed 222 Navajo fifth graders of average age 11 years, 2 months to develop a profile of a reservation student and to assess his or her overall strengths and needs. The profile revealed that 88 percent of the children had transportation, 75 percent had a television set, 83 percent had electricity, and 79 percent came from families earning incomes.

Source: Tempest, P. (1987). The physical, environmental, and intellectual profile of the fifth grade Navajo. *Journal of American Indian Education, 26*(3), 29–40.

Other findings were that the parents of 77 percent were not divorced, 92 percent of the children were not parentally rejected, 59 percent of the families were free from alcoholism, and 93 percent of the children had not experienced the death of a family member. Ninety-eight students were considered to be achievers and 62 underachievers. Reasons for underachievement included having to learn a second language, a high prevalence of ear disease, and Fetal Alcohol Syndrome contributing to learning disabilities.

Native-American tribes, organizations, and communities play vital roles in improving educational opportunities for Native-American children. More than 100 tribes operate Head Start programs serving 16,548 Native-American children. Many public schools, Bureau of Indian Affairs schools, and tribal schools also strive to provide special education and culture-related learning designed to assist the development and early education of Native-American children (Walker, 1988). A FOCUS ON RESEARCH 4–1 presents a profile of the Native-American fifth-grade learner.

Language

Native-American languages can be divided into about a dozen stocks, and each stock divided again into languages as distinct as English from Russian. Most classifications of Native-Americans into nations, tribes, or peoples have been linguistic rather than political. The fact that Native-Americans continue to speak about 2,200 different languages adds to their difficulties in school. This broad and diversified language background, albeit personal and sacred to the Native-American, has not contributed to the Anglo-American definition of school success. Moreover, widescale differences exist in the Native-American's ability to speak English (Wax, 1971).

Nonverbal communication of Native-American children adds another dimension that must be considered in the counseling intervention. In the last decade, anthropologists, counselors, sociologists, and teachers have begun to awaken to the urgent need to understand "silent languages." Gestures, body movements, and general social behavior all provide valuable information about the client (Jensen, 1985). Native-American children speak more softly than do Anglo children, and at a slower rate. They also tend to avoid such direct interaction between speaker and listener as expressed by signs such as head-nods and "uh huh" (Sanders, 1987).

Families

The immediate and extended families of Native-American children contribute to the child's cultural identity and play a significant role in overall development. Grandparents retain official and symbolic leadership in family communities. They monitor children's behavior and have a voice in childrearing practices (Lum, 1986). The Native-American family considers children to be gifts, worthy of sharing with others, while the Anglo perception holds that children constitute private property to be disciplined as deemed necessary (Richardson, 1981). In essence, children have fewer rules to obey in the Native-American culture, whereas Anglo children have more rules with strict consequences for disobedience. Native-American parents train their children to be self-sufficient very early on. Also, contrary to the individualism prized in the Anglo-American society, the Native-American family places more emphasis on group welfare (Axelson, 1985). This group-welfare emphasis is reflected in the high rate of school-absenteeism. Any crisis in the home results in absences from school until the crisis has been resolved and the family situation returned to normal (Sanders, 1987). A FOCUS ON RESEARCH 4–2 provides a description of family life as experienced by children.

Native-American childrearing practices and differing cultural family expectations for behavior sometimes result in confusion and frustration for Native-American children growing up in an Anglo society. They may demonstrate feelings of isolation, rejection, and anxiety which can result in alienation, poor self-image, and withdrawal (Sanders, 1987). Such feelings undoubtedly affect achievement aspirations of Native-American children and can cause them to question the worth of their family life.

 **A FOCUS ON RESEARCH 4–2**
Native-American Families

An understanding and appreciation of Native-American family strengths, weaknesses, attitudes, and values contribute to professionals' knowledge of children in the Native-American culture. In their research designed to study characteristics of Native-American families, Light and Martin (1986) surveyed 32 Native-American women, age 35, on the average, with four children. Using the Family Inventory of Resources for Management (FIRM), they selected items for which "most of the time" applied:

Source: Light, H. K., & Martin, R. E. (1986). American Indian families. *Journal of American Indian Education, 26*(1), 1–5.

1. Fifty-five percent reported their relatives do and say things to make them feel appreciated.

2. Seventy-five percent reported they tried to keep in touch with their relatives as much as possible.

3. Sixty-three percent reported family members respect one another.

4. Seventy-seven percent reported decisions being discussed with other family members so as to demonstrate respect toward one another.

5. Sixty-eight percent reported the family tried to look at the bright side of issues regardless of circumstances.

UP CLOSE AND PERSONAL 4—1
Bill Lonetree—A Native-American Child

Bill Lonetree, an 8-year-old Native-American child, lives with his mother, father, 10-year-old sister, 15-year-old brother, and his elderly grandmother. The Lonetree family home is in a small community several miles from the reservation. Although the family's financial status is not poverty level, money often poses a problem. For many years, Bill's ancestors lived on the reservation, but his grandparents moved to an Anglo-American community in an attempt to better their deterioriating financial status. After his grandfather died, his grandmother moved in with Bill's parents.

Bill, a quiet and often reflective child, is a third grader at the local Anglo-American school. Although he generally likes his school and has several Native-American friends, he experiences difficulty in making Anglo friends. While the Anglo-Americans do, in fact, have much in common with Bill, their differences make "an understanding of one another" difficult.

Bill's schoolwork is below average. In home and neighborhood situations, he appears to be relatively bright and thoughtful. His Anglo-American teacher, who recently began teaching at the school, encourages Bill to try harder, to listen attentively, and to be more proactive in his learning. In her attempts to motivate Bill, she sometimes tells him of her learning experiences in high school and college, and encourages him to prepare for similar experiences that he can someday enjoy. She hopes that Bill will "speak up" and give her some indications that he is at least listening to her. Bill's parents think

he is trying hard in school, although he is not performing at the level they would like. They hope his grades will not decline further at about sixth grade, as was the case with Bill's older brother.

When Bill is asked about his academic problems, he responds that he's trying, but admits he doesn't always understand what the teacher is saying. Admittedly, reading the textbooks and other materials proves difficult for him. Understanding (and speaking) two languages is often confusing.

In Bill's family, there is a sense of mutual respect and appreciation for one another. His grandmother, although elderly and unable to make a financial contribution, is close to Bill. He has tremendous respect for her and listens attentively when she tells him of the rich heritage of the Native-American culture. Also, he feels a sense of loyalty to her. On the days when she is ill, Bill stays home from school to watch over her and assist her with her needs.

In many ways, Bill is a typical third grader. He is looking for a sense of self-worth (although perhaps not the same "self-worth" his teacher considers important) and he desires friendships. However, his poor self-concept makes it hard for him to find new friends and develop self-worth. He sometimes feels he is "caught in the middle" of his Native-American home and his Anglo-American school. Conforming to Native-American cultural expectations at home and Anglo-American expectations at school often seems to be too much for Bill to handle.

Unique Challenges Confronting Native-American Children

Several obstacles that may hinder counseling interventions for Native-American children are not a factor for their Anglo-American counterparts. First, centuries of injustice have resulted in significant feelings of suspicion and distrust of Anglo-American professionals and institutions (Lum, 1986). Second, communication problems may

Table 4–1   Cultural comparison: Native-American and Anglo-American children

Native-American Children	Anglo-American Children
Honor their elders	Have a less reverential attitude toward elders
Learn through legends	Learn from books and schoolwork
Share—everything belongs to others	Stress ownership rather than sharing
Put immediate and extended family first	Think of themselves first
Tend to be humble and cooperative	Tend to be competitive
Appear to be carefree—unconcerned with time	Are more structured—constantly aware of time
Have few rules to obey	Have rules for every contingency

Source: Adapted from Richardson, E. H. (1981). Cultural and historical perspectives in counseling American Indians. In D. W. Sue, *Counseling the culturally different* (pp. 216–255). New York: John Wiley.

result in an inability to understand, trust, and develop rapport (Vontress, 1976b). Such problems include Native-American nonverbal communication habits, which may hinder counseling efforts. The Native-American child who may appear to be unemotional or detached may only be painfully shy and overly sensitive to strangers due to language problems and mistrust of Anglo-Americans.

A cultural comparison of Native-American and Anglo-American children is presented in Table 4–1. UP CLOSE AND PERSONAL 4–1 looks at a particular Native-American child.

AFRICAN-AMERICAN CHILDREN

Societal and Cultural Description

Describing African-American children requires an understanding of the intracultural differences in their culture. Lower, middle, and higher socioeconomic groups live differently; likewise, significant differences characterize urban and rural African-Americans.

African-American children interact with two cultures on a daily basis: the African-American culture of the home/neighborhood and the Anglo-American culture of the schools and other social institutions. It is important for counselors to remember that African-American children are sometimes told by other children (or perhaps adults) that the African-American race and culture are inferior. Such thinking is an outgrowth of the culturally deficient model, in which the culturally different are considered inferior and deprived of "culture." African-American children should be afforded the opportunity of growing up in a society in which minority cultures are considered "different" rather than "deficient," and in which the advantages of being bicultural and the value of cultural differences are recognized (Baratz & Baratz, 1970).

Governmental social programs such as Headstart and Follow-Through undoubtedly have improved the lives of many Arican-American children. However, the National Urban League reports that millions of African-American children continue to live in a desolate world where physical survival alone is a triumph, where fear and hopelessness reign, and where the future holds few promises (Edelman, 1989). The National Black Child Development Institute (1986) and the Children's Defense Fund (1987) described the plight of the black child in more specific terms:

- Nearly one of every two black children lives in poverty.
- Almost two-thirds of young black children live in homes relying on public assistance.
- Black children generally receive poorer health care than Anglo children.
- Nationally, the school dropout rate for black youth is almost 28 percent, approaching 50 percent in some regions of the country. (Clark-Johnson, 1988)

To make matters worse, AIDS poses a new and grave threat to black babies and children. Black children constitute more than half of all reported cases of AIDS in children younger than age 13 (Edelman, 1989).

Self-concept may be the most influential factor in the development of the child. The African-American child's self-concept influences not only academic achievement but also many other social and psychological aspects of his or her development. Axelson (1985) describes self-concept factors in terms of what children think of themselves, what others think them to be, and what views of others the children adopt. For example, the African-American child may tend to accept others' views, either negative or positive, of him or her and the African-American culture. Lee and Lindsey (1985) consider racism and oppression by the predominantly Anglo society as hindering the development of the African-American child's positive self-concept. According to Axelson (1985), research through the 1960s concluded that "self-hatred" existed in much of the African-American community; however, the black power movement engendered pride in African-American identity, resulting in considerable gains relative to African-American self-concept. Other gains may be attributed to African-American parents fostering positive self-concept development in their children. Such ego-bolsters as "You're just as good as anyone else" lessen the anxiety that many black children experience when they engage in social comparison with Anglo children (Hale-Benson, 1986).

Although the economic and social injustices long imposed upon African-Americans certainly had the potential for damaging self-concept, Smith (1981) cautions that the accomplishments and developments of African-Americans indicate that widespread negative self-concept of African-Americans may be an overexaggeration. In his view, to believe that many African-American children have negative self-concepts because of their embittered history and present struggles in a predominantly Anglo society is an error with potentially serious consequences.

The African-American child's achievement (which is closely related to self-concept) must also be considered objectively rather than relying on traditional stereotypes of achievement expectations. While some African-American pupils lag behind Anglo-American pupils on standardized tests, the debate rages over where the responsibility for lower academic performance lies (Pinkney, 1975). There is a tendency among many to "blame the victims" rather than to examine the underlying causes of the problem. Moreover, school officials often find it convenient to blame the child's "disadvantaged" or "culturally deprived" home. Some African-American educators are now calling for effective schools where teachers have an objective understanding of African-American children and similar expectations for both African-American and Anglo-American children (Boykin, 1982). A FOCUS ON RESEARCH 4-3 presents one suggestion for how to deal with the plight of young African-American males early in the school years.

Language

First of all, it must be noted that the degree to which children speak "Black English" varies considerably as a function of socioeconomic class, geographic location, and the level of acculturation of both the child and the parents. Children of educated and socially mobile urban African-American parents may not speak the dialect of children of rural parents who may be less fortunate socioeconomically. Second, many African-American children are faced with a problem: Their language is "worthy" at home, yet being "different" makes it unworthy in school. Hall (1981) summarizes the situation as follows:

> [African-American children] come to school equipped with a rich and different dialect ideally suited to the multiple needs of the Black culture, only to be told that [their language is] a degraded, substandard form of English. (p. 32)

The linguistic patterns of African-American children play a significant role in their school achievement and their social and psychological development. Although the child may not experience communication difficulties at home or in the neighborhood, problems may result when speech patterns vary considerably between home/neighborhood and school settings. Children's language skills are crucial in their education, and much of what is being measured as "intelligence" and "achievement" are actually language and communication skills (Hale-Benson, 1986), or perhaps, more accurately, linguistic intelligence.

A FOCUS ON RESEARCH 4–3
Educating Young African-American Males

In the view of Holland (1987), the inability of urban public schools to effectively address the problems of African-American male children must be remedied. That these boys often come from poor, single-parent, female-headed households lacking positive role models is commonly cited as a reason for their academic and social failings. In any case, the widespread "blame-the-victim" syndrome does little to help the situation. Not having positive male role models in schools clearly contributes to the social and academic problems of inner-city African-American males. Holland suggests one answer is to create all-male classes in kindergarten through the third grade and have these classes taught by African-American male teachers. Women, Holland contends, cannot provide realistic examples for survival outside the home and school.

Source: Holland, S. H. (1987). Positive primary education for young Black males. *The Education Digest, 53*(3), 56–58.

African-American children are likely to face several problems in a predominantly Anglo-American society that places emphasis on standard English. First, the dialect of African-American children, albeit an excellent means of communication in the African-American culture, is apt to result in communication difficulties and other problems generally associated with not being understood by the majority culture. Second, when children hear negative statements about their dialect, and are urged to change to a more "standard" form of English, their self-esteem may be damaged.

What position should counselors and other professionals working with African-American children take? Rather than imply that black dialect is "wrong," "inferior," or "substandard," they should attempt to understand the role the dialect plays for people who have experienced a history of injustices and struggle for survival. Counselors should not expect African-American children to change their dialect during counseling sessions or to abandon it in all situations in favor of the language of the school; however, both African-American children and their educators should understand the frustrations and problems that might result from speaking differently among people predominantly speaking standard English.

African-Americans have communication habits that are culturally based. For example, although it may seem odd to Anglo-Americans, it is not necessary to nod one's head or to make little noises to indicate that one is listening to a speaker; similarly, active listening does not require always looking the speaker in the eye (LaFrance & Mayo, 1978).

Families

African-American children grow up in homes that may be very different from Anglo-American homes. In the African-American culture, there is an extensive reliance on family kinship networks, which include blood relatives and close friends called kinsmen (Lum, 1986). Also, young African-American children are often taken into the households of their elderly grandparents. These arrangements reflect a sense of corporate responsibility; that is, children belong to an extended family clan, not merely to the parents. Consequently, uncles, aunts, cousins, and grandparents all exert considerable authority in the family and are responsible for the care and rearing of children and for teaching them appropriate skills and values (Lum, 1986). These strong kinship bonds probably originated from the African ethos of survival of the tribe and the oneness of being. African-Americans sometimes refer to each other as "sister," "brother," "cousin," "blood brother," or "homeboy" to imply a familial closeness when actual kinship does not exist (Hale-Benson, 1986).

An important cultural heritage of the African-American family is a de-emphasis on rigid sex-linked roles. Both men and women are likely to assume household responsibilities, care for children, and work outside the home. Children learn early that both parents are important as providers. This often reflects the economic reality that survival depends on the combined income of husband and wife (Smith, 1981).

Many African-American parents stress to their children the importance of exceeding Anglo children's achievement; to fall short would reflect unfavorably on the group. In fact, evidence indicates achievement orientation to be very strong in African-American families. According to one poll, 75 percent of African-American children said that their mother wanted them to be one of the best students in the class. Also, maternal warmth in lower income families (e.g., use of reinforcement, consultation with the child, and sensitivity to the child's feelings) appears to be conducive to intellectual achievement (Hale-Benson, 1986).

Religion is another important aspect of African-American life; however, research on the role religion plays in the development of the African-American child is scant. More attention has been focused on religion with respect to the civil rights movement, economic leadership, and the quest for equal opportunities. It is clear, though, that children perceive the church as a hub of social life, the provider of a peer group, and a source of leadership in the community. Church is not limited to Sunday morning services; rather, children perceive it to be an integral aspect of African-American family life (Hale-Benson, 1986).

Unique Challenges Confronting African-American Children

African-American children growing up in a predominantly Anglo society face difficult problems that impede their overall development into adulthood. It is important to note at the outset that these problems result from their culture being different from mainstream American culture, and from years of discrimination and misunderstanding with respect to both their culture and their developmental period. Language barriers, lower academic achievement, and poor self-esteem are a few of the problems many of these children are confronted with. Such being the case, it is also imperative that counselors and other professionals consider individual differences rather than perpetuate a stereotypical image of the African-American child. All African-American children are not struggling and problem-laden. Counselors need to take individuality among African-American children into account, and to recognize that motivation and determination are powerful determinants of success, even in the face of hardship.

A cultural comparison of African-American and Anglo-American children is presented in Table 4–2. UP CLOSE AND PERSONAL 4–2 centers on Carl, an African-American child.

Table 4–2   Cultural comparison: African-American and Anglo-American children

African-American Children	Anglo-American Children
Accept others' views of their culture	Question others' views of their culture
Score lower on cognitive tests	Score higher on cognitive tests
"Worthy" dialect at home; "unworthy" at school	"Worthy" language—both home and school
Do not always maintain eye contact in communicating	Look speaker in the eye
Seek support from larger families/"kinship networks"	Seek support from smaller, more immediate family
Reared by parents and extended family	Reared by immediate family
Exhibit cultural pride	Exhibit individual pride

Sources: Data compiled from Axelson, 1985; Boykin, 1982; Hale-Benson, 1986; Hall, 1981; Pinkney, 1975.

> ### ◆ UP CLOSE AND PERSONAL 4–2
> ### Carl Johnson—An African-American Child
>
> Five-year-old Carl lives with his mother, father, one older brother, and two younger sisters in a lower middle-class neighborhood in a large city. His grandmother, several aunts and uncles, and six or seven cousins live in the immediate neighborhood. William, his father, has completed 11 years of schooling and works in a local manufacturing plant. His mother, Cynthia, has had a similar formal education. She works as a hospital aide.
>
> Carl spends considerable time with his grandmother. In fact, he considers his grandmother and aunts and uncles as "parents away from home." He visits them often and plays with his cousins and other children in the neighborhood. The closeness of the family has its advantages. When Carl is ill and unable to attend kindergarten, he stays with his grandmother or other relatives; hence, his parents do not have to miss work.
>
> Carl's neighborhood is predominantly African-American, although several Puerto Rican and Cuban families have recently rented houses in the area. Carl already realizes that people of different ethnic groups have different customs and lifestyles. He attends the neighborhood integrated school with a racial composition that is approximately 50 percent African-American, 30 percent Anglo-American, and 20 percent Hispanic-American. His teachers, however, are predominantly middle-class African-Americans. Although Carl tries in school, his readiness scores and his performance on kindergarten objectives place him below average. His teachers assume his problems stem from a poor home environment, and they blame Carl and his parents for the difficulties. Carl's self-esteem is low; sometimes he blames himself for not doing as well as the other children. Although his dialect works well with his parents and in the neighborhood, it is not viewed favorably at school. Sometimes, he does not understand his teachers or textbooks. The teachers frequently "correct" Carl because, they say, students will need "correct English" when they enter the real world.
>
> Carl is in a cross-cultural bind. Is one culture wrong and one right? Is his culture somehow inferior?

ASIAN-AMERICAN CHILDREN

Societal and Cultural Description

Asian-Americans consist of the Chinese, Pilipino, Japanese, Asian Indian, Korean, Indochinese, Hawaiian, Samoan, and Guamanian populations, composing one of the most diverse and interesting ethnic groups in the United States. Because of their achievements in the classroom and in business, Asian-Americans are often called the "model minority" (Banks, 1987). Teachers often consider Asian children to be ideal students—studious, high-achieving and well behaved (Huang, 1976; Yee, 1988). These children are expected to excel in American society, yet retain the values and traditions of their Asian-American culture.

Questioning the tendency to stereotype all Asian-Americans as being model minority "whiz kids," and "problem-free," Hartman and Askounis (1989) caution professionals to consider the tremendous cultural diversity among Asian-Americans—the distinct subgroups and their various languages, religions, and customs. Moreover, individual differences must be considered with respect to how successfully Asian-Americans conform to the expectations of Anglo society. The model minority stereotype is examined in A FOCUS ON RESEARCH 4–4.

The many diverse nationalities composing the Asian-American culture make a general description difficult. There is wide variation in physical characteristics, as well as differing attitudes, values, and ethnic institutions (Banks, 1987). Japanese-Americans have been described as quiet, reticent, or aloof (Padilla, 1981). As compared to Anglo-Americans, Asian-American children may be more dependent, conforming, obedient to authority, and willing to place family welfare over individual wishes (Sue, 1981). Yao (1988) describes Asian-American children in this way:

> Not all of them are superior students who have no problems in school. Some have learning problems; some lack motivation, proficiency in English, or financial resources; and some have parents who do not understand the American school system, because of cultural differences, language barriers, or their own single-minded quest for survival. (p. 223)

The more recent influxes of Southeast Asians to the United States include people from Vietnam, Cambodia, Thailand, and Laos. However, people often refer to any Southeast Asian child as Vietnamese without realizing that such labeling may be

---

◆ A FOCUS ON RESEARCH 4–4
■ The "Model Minority" Goes to School

Without doubt, the significant increase of Asian-American children challenges educators to deal with language problems, cultural differences, and stereotypes. The total enrollment of Asians and Pacific Islanders in the San Diego school district doubled between 1982 and 1986. Studies have shown that Asian-American students earn higher grades and that high-school juniors and seniors outperform virtually all groups, including Anglo learners. Their academic achievement and their success in earning scholarships to prestigious universities and music conservatories have earned them the reputation of being a model minority. But, according to Divoky (1988),

too often we forget that those whose roots are in Asia are not necessarily alike; a recently arrived Hmong refugee has virtually nothing in common with an affluent Japanese-American student whose parents were born and raised in the Midwest. (p. 220)

The stereotype of Asian-American students being polite and hard-working results in problems. First of all, teachers expect more from them academically, often overlooking their problems. Secondly, insofar as they expect Asian students to be docile and passive, teachers tend to treat them more harshly when they do misbehave. Finally, their reputation as good students may result in hostility from other students.

Source: Divoky, D. (1988). The model minority goes to school. *Phi Delta Kappan, 70,* 219–222.

offensive to certain nationalities. Bitter feelings exist among various ethnic groups. "Children may not know one another's language. They may not be of the same religion; their parents may have been opposing enemies; or they may harbor feelings of superiority, inferiority, or resentment toward one another" (West, 1983, pp. 85–86).

The social customs and values of Southeast Asians are often quite different from those of Anglo-Americans. As described by West (1983), physical contact between members of the same sex is permissible, but not acceptable between members of the opposite sex. Self-effacement is encouraged and saving face is very important. Children wait to be asked by the teacher to participate in activities, not wanting to draw attention to themselves. Should the teacher put a child's name on the board for misbehaving, the child would quite likely be extremely distressed. Children are often considered to be shy when, in reality, they have been socialized to listen more than speak, and to speak in a soft voice. Southeast Asian children are also taught to be modest in dress, manner, and behavior. Teachers in Southeast Asia are accorded a higher status than teachers in the United States, and are always treated with great respect; the informal relationship between American teachers and students may be confusing to Southeast Asian children and appalling to their families. Finally, cultural backgrounds and values cause Southeast Asian children to expect considerable structure and organization.

West (1983) tells the story of a teacher who felt that she was not "reaching" a Vietnamese student. Although the student was not disruptive, he was not participating fully in class. When the teacher requested a parent-teacher conference, the father came to school full of disgrace and feeling his son had done something terrible. The teacher repeatedly explained that she liked the student and was only trying to improve communication. The father struck the child and ordered him to kneel and apologize. The boy immediately obeyed, only to be joined by the teacher who informed him and his father that no one in America had to kneel to anyone.

Language

Without doubt, the considerable emphasis placed on education and the promise that education holds for successful students has contributed to the academic success of many Asian-American children. Language difficulties, however, do exist and must be overcome. In one school district in California, the number of Asian-American children with limited English skills grew from 8 percent to 42 percent in just seven years (Divoky, 1988). Census documents report that two of every five Asians and Pacific Islanders aged 5 and over speak a language other than English at home: The proportion was highest for Laotians, Cambodians, and Hmongs at about 95 percent and lowest for Japanese at about 44 percent. For Pacific Islanders, the documents report 88 percent for Tongans and 10 percent for Hawaiians (Asian and Pacific Islander data: '80 census still producing riches, 1988). Japanese-Americans and Chinese-Americans of both sexes scored lower than Anglo-Americans on the verbal sections of an achievement test. Language difficulties may be traced to the fact that Asian-Americans often come from bilingual backgrounds. Furthermore, cultural traditions and customs often restrict or impede verbal communication; e.g., many Asian-American families encourage one-way communication in which parents speak to children, but not vice versa (First, 1988).

If several factors relative to the Asian-American child's language are kept in mind, stereotypical thinking may be avoided. First, it must be remembered that many Asian-American students are communicating in the equivalent of a second language. Although English may be the predominant language, these children may still continue to hear their parents' native language at home. Second, the Asian-American child should not be viewed as a clumsy, inarticulate child who is good with numbers but poor with words. Such a perception might result in rigid expectations (Atkinson, Morten, & Sue, 1989). Third, although many Asian-American children have proven to be quite successful academically, children deserve individual consideration of their unique strengths and weaknesses. Fourth, generational differences and socioeconomic factors warrant consideration; second- and third-generation learners with educated and successful parents probably will have fewer language problems than first-generation learners of lower socioeconomic status.

Families

Family allegiance and respect for parents and family significantly affect the achievement and behavior of the developing Asian-American child. In the traditional family, ancestors and elders are viewed with great reverence and respect and elders are involved actively with childrearing. The family is patriarchial; children are taught that the father is the head of the family, with absolute authority. The primary duty of the son is to be a good son; his obligations to be a good husband or father come second to his duty as a son. The female is subservient to males. She is primarily the childbearer and nuturing caretaker, responsible for domestic chores (Sue, 1981).

There is a sense of mutual obligation in the Asian-American family. Children obey their parents and elders; in exchange, the parents and elders are responsible for the support, upbringing, and education of the children. Both parents and children demonstrate respect for elders of the household; in return, ancestral spirits are believed to protect the family. The interdependency of the family members is meant to keep the family intact (Lum, 1986). This family structure, so arranged to minimize conflicts, spells out specific roles for each member, and each has the responsibility not to interfere with the peace, harmony, and unity of the family (Sue, 1989). Because of cultural differences, counselors and other professionals often experience difficulty working with Asian-American families. A FOCUS ON RESEARCH 4–5 addresses some of the problems surrounding Asian immigrant parents.

Inherent in the childrearing techniques of Asian-American families is the powerful message not to bring embarrassment and shame to the family. The inculcation of guilt and shame are the principal techniques used to control the behavior of family members. Parents emphasize their children's obligation to the family and their responsibility to meet family expectations. If a child acts contrary to the family's wishes, he or she is considered to be selfish, inconsiderate, and ungrateful. Aberrant behavior is usually hiddent from outsiders and handled within the family. On the other hand, outstanding achievement is a source of great pride. It, too, reflects not only on the child but on the entire family unit.

◆ A FOCUS ON RESEARCH 4–5
Working Effectively with Asian Immigrant Parents

Yao (1988) reports that more than 1.2 million Asians have legally immigrated to the United States since 1981. Defying cultural stereotypes, these recent Asian immigrants are diverse in terms of race, religion, language, national background, and economic status. Although the importance of schools working closely with parents has been well documented, the schools must employ special strategies to accommodate the unique cultural characteristics of Asian immigrant parents. Yao points to several factors in devising appropriate strategies:

1. Asian parents are often depicted as quiet, submissive, and cooperative.

2. Asian parents' lack of knowledge about American society and customs results in insecurities and confusion.

3. Asian parents' problems with language hamper their communication with teachers and other school officials.

4. Asian parents often set high goals for their children. Pressure from parents can be detrimental to the children's emotional and social development.

Yao not only provides an excellent description of Asian parents, but also offers specific recommendations for educators working with Asian immigrant children.

Source: Yao, E. L. (1988). Working effectively with Asian immigrants. *Phi Delta Kappan, 70*, 223–225.

Unique Challenges Confronting Asian-American Children

First, a major challenge confronting the Asian-American child is the language barrier. Understanding the spoken word is one thing; being understood when speaking is quite another and is often a source of difficulty for Asian-Americans attempting to

Table 4–3   Cultural comparison: Asian-American and Anglo-American children

Asian-American Children	Anglo-American Children
Tend to be quiet, reticent, aloof	Tend to be more talkative and outgoing
Tend to be dependent, conforming, obedient	Tend to be independent; have a do-my-own-thing attitude
Place family welfare over individual desires	Satisfy individual desires first
Have a bilingual background	Have a monolingual background—not as many problems
Show respect and reverence toward elders	Have a less reverential attitude toward elders
Reared by parents and extended family	Reared by immediate family
Controlled by strong family structure	Free to do their own thing
Bring shame on the family by not conforming to expectations	Exhibit signs of "independence" by breaking with family tradition

Soures: Data compiled from Sue, 1981, 1989; Sue and Sue, 1983.

speak English. They may experience considerable anxiety with interpersonal communication (Lum, 1986). Second, reconciling loyalties to two different cultural traditions is another challenge for the Asian-American child. The pluralistic society requires the child to maintain his or her ethnic identity while meeting differing cultural expectations of home and school (Sue, 1981). Third, Asian-American children are faced with pressures from peers that may conflict with basic family values and traditions. Fourth, the "model minority" stereotype presents a significant dilemma for these children. Not all of them fit the mold, and even those who do have trouble meeting unrealistic expectations.

Table 4–3 lists several differences between Asian-American and Anglo-American children. UP CLOSE AND PERSONAL 4–3 introduces Mina, an Asian-American child.

◆ UP CLOSE AND PERSONAL 4–3
Mina Sukuzi—An Asian-American Child

Mina, a 10-year-old Japanese girl, lives with her parents, older sister, younger brother, and elderly grandfather. Although her community is predominantly Asian-American, the immediate area in which she lives is as diverse as her culture; she has many opportunities to meet both Asian-American and Anglo-American children.

Mina lives in a close-knit family. Her father works two jobs and her mother one; together, they provide a comfortable standard of living. Mina's grandfather does not work outside the home, but he takes an active part in childrearing and has other household responsibilities. The whole family looks to him for advice in making everyday decisions. In essence, the family is an interdependent unit working toward common goals and toward solving their own problems. Each member accepts his or her own specific role and is committed not to disappoint other family members. Mina does not question the dominance of her father's authority. Neither does she question that her younger brother seems to have more important roles and privileges than she has.

Mina has demonstrated above-average academic achievement. She plays the piano, works part-time at the school library, and is a member of the School Honor Society. Her family views education as an avenue to success and has always insisted that Mina excel in whatever she does. Although her teacher is concerned that Mina is a little quiet and aloof, she also appreciates Mina's obedience and fine academic work. Mina doesn't think she is too quiet, but she realizes that her commitment to fulfill family expectations does, indeed, influence her interpersonal conduct and social standing. She feels pressured to excel, both in personal conduct and academics. To do otherwise would bring shame and disappointment to her family.

Although Mina wants very much to please the members of her family, their high expectations have given rise to several problems. English does not come easy for Mina; it requires considerable work. Also, her Anglo-American peers and some of her Asian-American friends think she is somewhat aloof—a bit of a goody-goody, in fact. Mina feels that her academic success has caused some of her fellow students to reject her. Of course, she wants friends and to be accepted by her peers; however, family expectations must come first. Meanwhile, Mina continues to work diligently to fulfill her family obligations and to maintain her excellent academic standing. At the same time, she is trying to develop her own identity.

HISPANIC-AMERICAN CHILDREN

Societal and Cultural Description

The Hispanic-American culture consists of the populations of Cuba, Mexico, Puerto Rico, and other Central and South American countries. As with the Asian-American culture, a general cultural description is difficult due to the marked diversity of the various subcultures. In some aspects, Hispanics constitute members of a single cultural group with a fairly common history and the sharing of language, values, and customs, while other aspects point to a significant heterogeneous population that should be conceptualized as an aggregate of distinct subcultures (Ruiz, 1981). Moreover, there is also diversity resulting from individual differences, generational differences, and socioeconomic levels within the Hispanic cultural group. In considering the social and cultural characteristics of Hispanic-American children, this intracultural diversity must be kept in mind in order to avoid the pitfalls of stereotyping.

The Hispanic-American child in many cases will live in poverty. Some reports contend that 38.7 percent of all Hispanic children live at the poverty level, with 71 percent living in homes in which the head of the household is female (Colburn & Melillo, 1987; Valero-Figueira, 1988). Those children who are not members of an elite group tend to avoid any competition or activity that would set them apart from their group. To stand out among one's peers is to place oneself in great jeopardy and is to be avoided at all costs (Hall, 1981).

Another cultural influence on children is the notion of *machismo*. This term may be translated as a strong sense of masculine pride, and is used flatteringly among Hispanic-Americans. Both Hispanic-American boys and girls learn early on that machismo refers to manhood—to the courage to fight, to the manly traits of honor and dignity, to keeping one's word, and to protecting one's name. More subtly, machismo also refers to dignity in personal conduct, respect for others, love for the family, and affection for children (Ruiz, 1981). The term also implies a clear-cut distinction between the sexes, whereby the male enjoy rights and privileges denied women—a fact that children often learn early in life (Vontress, 1976b).

A third Hispanic characteristic with particular relevance to multicultural counselors is the distrust many Hispanic-American children feel toward Anglo-Americans. Vontress (1976b) contended that some cultures, such as the Mexican-American, often teach children to regard Anglo-Americans with fear and hostility. Children being taught such attitudes have difficulty believing that Anglo-American counselors have their best interests at heart (Vontress, 1976b). As A FOCUS ON RESEARCH 4–6 documents, Hispanic children newly arrived in the United States often come from less-than-desirable backgrounds and have problems requiring counseling intervention.

Before discussing language and families, it must be mentioned again that the tremendous cultural diversity among Hispanic-Americans warrants consideration. For example, Mexican-Americans and Cuban-Americans may be very different with respect to culture-based values. In fact, each of the numerous ethnic subgroups adheres to unique and distinguishing cultural and social practices. Acculturation rates, socioeconomic factors, educational levels, and region of residency must also be taken into account.

A FOCUS ON RESEARCH 4–6
Immigrant Children in California

Olsen (1988) describes the effects of today's unprecedented racial and ethnic diversity in California classrooms. With reference to Southeast Asian and Hispanic learners, Olsen points to "children of war," "undocumented chil-

Source: Olsen, L. (1988). Crossing the schoolhouse border: Immigrant children in California. *Phi Delta Kappan, 70,* 211–218.

dren," language and academic needs, and the difficulties these children experience in a strange educational system. Personal stories of children's experiences in war-torn countries and their dangerous voyages to the United States are recounted in this study. The reader gains an appreciation of the problems these children meet in the schools and the challenges educators face.

Language

The Hispanic-American child encouraged to speak Spanish at home and English at school may experience dual cultural identification which could lead to chronic anxiety (Padilla, 1981). Which language should be considered the "mother tongue"? One survey of language preferences among Hispanic-Americans clearly revealed that the majority (68.9 percent) identified Spanish as the primary language. While children want to be true to their parents' language, they are pressured to consider English as the primary factor contributing to their school success (Ruiz, 1981).

Nonverbal language, as in other cultures, is important in the Hispanic-American culture and should be understood by professionals of all cultures. Hispanic-Americans tend to stand close while communicating and to touch one another; eye contact may be avoided (Padilla, 1981).

Families

Family lifestyles and activities in the Hispanic-American culture play a large part in determining what the developing child will be like as an adult. Ethnic awareness in children is perpetuated by family gatherings and communities celebrating cultural holidays. Puerto Rican-Americans have a deep sense of commitment to the family. Those who achieve success use their resources to assist family members who may be in need (Lum, 1986). A FOCUS ON RESEARCH 4–7 examines the influence of the mother on academic achievement.

The father in the Latino-American family is clearly head of the household. Children learn early that their father's authority goes unchallenged, that he often makes decisions without consulting their mother, and that he expects to be obeyed when he gives commands. Male dominance extends to sons, who have more and earlier independence than daughters. Sex roles tend to be rigidly circumscribed, and the elderly are accorded respect and reverence (Lum, 1986).

Professionals working with Hispanic-American children and their families need to understand the traditional clearly-defined sex roles. They should also be aware

A FOCUS ON RESEARCH 4–7
Academic Achievement in Black, White, and Hispanic Children

Stevenson, Chen, and Uttal investigated school achievement among African-, Anglo-, and Hispanic-American elementary school children. One area of interest was the degree to which the children and their mothers valued education. Interviews were conducted with approximately 1,000 mothers and their children. In addition, achievement tests in reading and mathematics were administered to approximately 3,000 first-, third-, and fifth-grade children. Interviews revealed several interesting findings:

1. Minority mothers and children placed greater emphasis on the value of education than Anglo mothers and children.

2. Minority mothers were more positive about education; hopes for their children's academic success were high.

3. Mothers of minority children and teachers in minority schools believed more strongly than Anglo mothers and teachers in the value of homework, competency testing, and a longer school day as a means of improving education.

Source: Stevenson, H. W., Chen, C., & Uttal, D. H. (1990). Beliefs and achievement: A study of Black, White and Hispanic children. *Child Development, 61*, 508–523.

that changes are taking place. Hispanic women are increasingly exerting their influence; indeed, in many cases, they are beginning to seek equality with males. As women continue to redefine their roles in the Hispanic and Anglo societies, children, too, will experience changes.

As with Native-American and the African-American families, the extended family and kinship network of Hispanic and Chicanos is widely recognized. Parents often arrange for godparents or "companion parents" for their children. These "parents" also have a right to give advice and are expected to be responsive to the child's needs (Fitzpatrick, 1987).

Unique Challenges Confronting Hispanic-American Children

Adherence to cultural traditions, acceptance of the cultural notion of machismo and an allegiance to Spanish as the "mother tongue" have created several challenges for Hispanic-Americans. Despite a significant degree of acculturation, many Hispanic-American children are confused with respect to cultural identity. In addition, language problems continue to plague Hispanic-American children; their tendency to speak their parents' native language at home and in the community while speaking English at school may prolong communication problems.

A cultural comparison of Hispanic-American and Anglo-American children is presented in Table 4–4. UP CLOSE AND PERSONAL 4–4 provides a portrait of Ramon, a Hispanic-American child.

◆ UP CLOSE AND PERSONAL 4—4
◆ Ramon Suarez—A Hispanic-American Child

Ramon, an 8-year-old Puerto Rican boy, lives with his parents, a younger brother, an older sister, and an older brother in a dilapidated apartment building. Ramon's grandfather, Rafael, lives on the same floor of the building. Another brother, the eldest of the children, is married and lives with his wife across the street. The community is predominantly Hispanic-American and quite diverse. Ramon's Puerto Rican cultural traditions are very different, for example, from those of the Mexican-Americans in the neighborhood.

Ramon's father is without doubt the head of the family. Although his mother has begun to receive more respect as an individual and valued family member, Ramon's father continues to make nearly all the decisions concerning the household. The immediate family and extended relatives function as a unit, with Ramon's grandfather having a considerable influence in family matters. Ramon likes the arrangement. His brother nearby continues to visit nearly every day, and his grandfather, in the same building, spends considerable time with him telling stories of when he lived in Puerto Rico.

Despite a relatively tranquil home life, Ramon is troubled at school, and his Anglo-American teachers are at a loss for appropriate solutions. Ramon's parents acknowledge his academic problems; however, their limited knowledge of the American school system and their lack of command of the English language make it hard for them to assist the school professionals. Ramon's teachers consider him unmotivated and uninterested in schoolwork. The school counselor, however, thinks Ramon's troubles can be traced to specific causes. For example, one of Ramon's fights involved two other Hispanic-American boys. The three of them were trying to "impress" their friends. Ramon admitted that he wanted his peers to think he could defend himself like his father and older brothers. Ramon's language problem stems from his home, where Spanish continues to be the primary language. In fact, Ramon speaks Spanish at home and in the neighborhood and English only at school. He has problems understanding the teacher and reading the textbooks. Although his counselor has spoken to Ramon on several occasions, a persistent problem continues to handicap the counseling situation: Ramon does not trust the counselor. He has learned from his family and friends that Anglo-American professionals cannot always be trusted and must be viewed with suspicion.

Still another problem is that Ramon never wants to stand out among his peers. He once confided to the counselor that "making good" might be costly in terms of peer approval. Reconciling himself to mediocre school work while demonstrating machismo was Ramon's chosen path.

Ramon will continue to have problems as long as English is spoken at school and Spanish at home. His Anglo-American teachers tell him machismo is unimportant, but his friends disagree. Meanwhile, Ramon's self-concept and academic achievement suffer as he struggles to reconcile the differences of two cultures.

Table 4–4   Cultural comparison: Hispanic-American
and Anglo-American children

Hispanic-American Children	Anglo-American Children
Do not want to be singled out for being different or excelling	Want recognition for skills and abilities
Value *machismo;* clearly distinct sex roles	Value equal rights and responsibilities
Tend to distrust Anglo-American professionals	Tend to trust Anglo-American professionals
Value Spanish as their native language	Regard English as the language of "worth"
Stand close; touch; avoid eye contact	Respect distance; avoid touch; maintain eye contact
Respect extended family/"kinship networks" and companion parents	Exhibit loyalty to the immediate family
Prefer a personal approach in relationships	Favor a more impersonal style

Sources: Data compiled from Hall, 1981; Padilla, 1981; Vontress, 1976b.

A POINT OF DEPARTURE

Challenges Confronting Multicultural Counselors of Children

The childhood years and cultural differences have been neglected or misunderstood for many years. Considered of "lesser importance" as individuals, children have failed to receive the serious consideration they deserve. Likewise, cultural differences have gone unrecognized and the role of culture in counseling often has been misunderstood or underestimated. The multicultural counselor must not only understand childhood development, but also the dynamics of cultural diversity and the complex relationship between culture and development.

Challenges for multicultural counselors working with children include (1) understanding childhood as a unique lifespan period with special characteristics, needs, and problems and (2) understanding that objectivity must be maintained to avoid unwarranted comparison between the client's culture or perception of childhood and the counselor's culture or perception of childhood.

SUMMARY

Two topics we have explored in this chapter are critical to effective multicultural counseling: First, counselors' understanding of children and the childhood years and, second, their knowledge of cultural diversity among children. Native-American, African-American, Asian-American, and Hispanic-American children have different cultural, social, familial, and language backgrounds and deserve to be understood and accepted as individual and culturally unique. Multicultural counselors are challenged to examine long-held attitudes toward children and cultural diversity that significantly influence the counseling process.

Suggested Readings

Edelman, M. W. (1989). Black children in America. In J. Dewart (Ed.), *The state of Black America* (pp. 63–76). New York: African-American children in America, focusing on poverty, child care, health and nutrition, and education.

First, J. M. (1988). Immigrant students in U.S. public schools: Challenges with solutions. *Phi Delta Kappan, 70,* 205–210. First maintains that most immigrant families are profoundly committed to their children's education and contends that this caring and determination should not be wasted.

Hale-Benson, J. E. (1986). *Black children: Their roots, culture, and learning styles* (rev. ed.). Baltimore, MD: Johns Hopkins. This excellent resource on African-American children includes discussions on African backgrounds, culture, and childrearing. The question of how culture shapes cognition is explored.

Hartman, J. S., & Askounis, A. C. (1989). Asian-American students: Are they really a "model minority"? *The School Counselor, 37,* 109–111. Questioning the "model minority" and "whiz kid" stereotypes, Hartman and Askounis examine Asian-Americans' language, family, customs, and religion. Concrete suggestions for counseling these learners are offered.

Kellogg, J. B. (1988). Forces of change. *Phi Delta Kappan, 70,* 199–204. Kellogg provides an excellent discussion of the life experiences, skills, and problems of immigrant children, who often pose problems for educators.

Plantz, M. C., Hubbell, R., Barrett, B. J., & Dobrec, A. (1989). Indian child welfare: A status report. *Children Today, 18*(1), 24–29. These authors conducted the first systematic national examination of the effects of the Indian Child Welfare Act (P.L. 95–608) enacted by Congress in 1978.

Rotenberg, K. J., & Cranwell, F. R. (1989). Self-concepts in American Indian and White children. *The Journal of Cross-Cultural Psychology, 20,* 39–53. In this cross-cultural study of self-concept, the authors urge that caution be exercised in making comparisons.

Teaching Exceptional Children. (1988). *20.* G. Clark-Johnson, Black children (pp. 46–47); E. Valero-Figueira, Hispanic children (pp. 47–49); L. Y. Yee, Asian children (pp. 49–50); J. L. Walker, Young American Indian children (pp. 50–51). In a special section of this September 1988 issue, the authors explore family community involvement, assessment bias, at-risk populations, and service delivery.

Werner, E. E. (1979). *Cross-cultural child development: A view from planet Earth.* Monterey: Brooks/Cole. As the title implies, Werner looks at child development in selected cultures and points out differences among children resulting from cultural practices.

Chapter 5

Counseling the Child

Questions To Be Explored

1. What differences during counseling intervention (for example, with respect to self-disclosure, attitude toward the counseling process, and time orientation) can counselors expect when working with multicultural children?

2. How can counselors detect stress in children?

3. What are some of the developmental aspects of children in the Native-American, African-American, Asian-American, and Hispanic-American cultures that may present problems for the counselor?

4. How can counselors plan and implement counseling intervention with multicultural children?

5. How can counselors accommodate cultural differences in selecting individual, group, and family therapy?

6. How can counselors meet the unique challenges often encountered when working with culturally diverse children?

7. What additional sources of information are available for professionals counseling culturally diverse children?

INTRODUCTION

As pointed out in the previous chapter, interest in the childhood years as a unique and important developmental period has grown only recently. Interest in the multicultural aspects of child development is an even more recent occurrence. Increasing numbers of culturally diverse children, the recognition of the importance of the childhood years, and the realization that multicultural differences warrant consideration in counseling interventions have contributed to this long-overdue interest. This chapter examines the years between birth and age 12; explores counseling strategies for children in the Native-American, African-American, Asian-American, and Hispanic-American cultures; and discusses the role of counselors working with these children.

With regard to counseling services for children, especially culturally diverse children, typical attitudes are reflected in such statements as the following: "Children don't have any problems—what do they have to worry about?" "Multicultural differences don't count for very much." Or, "The child will have to adjust to the counselor's culture and strategies." The notion that real problems do not exist for children has contributed to their being one of the last groups afforded counseling services for psychological, social, emotional, and educational concerns. A poor understanding of child development and a lack of understanding of the multicultural dimensions of children's lives have created a less-than-desirable environment for preventive and developmental counseling with children. This century has brought changes and will, it is hoped, foster even greater interest in children and their cultural diversity. A FOCUS ON RESEARCH 5–1 is concerned with children's mental health issues and points out some disturbing statistics.

Counselors intervening with culturally diverse children should be prepared to suggest to parents and family members appropriate resources or agencies that could provide additional assistance. Of course, counselors should be aware of available services in their own geographical areas. These might include councils on child abuse and neglect, health departments, Boy's Clubs, the YMCA and YWCA, and Big Brothers and Big Sisters, to name but a few of the most well known.

A FOCUS ON RESEARCH 5–1
Children's Mental Health Issues

Despite considerable justification for scholarly interest and policy considerations regarding mental health services for children, both have been neglected issues. Inouye (1988) commented on the paucity of research to support the development of cost-effective treatment and prevention strategies. The senator from Hawaii pointed to some startling statistics in calling for needed changes in the way professionals conceptualize, finance, and provide care for children: Twelve to 15 percent of children under 18, or approximately 7.5 to 9.5 million children in the United States, have mental health problems sufficiently severe to warrant treatment. Nearly 80 percent of this group, however, either receive inappropriate mental health services or no treatment at all. After examining several governmental mental health programs, such as the Community Mental Health Center Act, the Mental Health Systems Act, and the various Alcohol, Drug Abuse, and Mental Health block grants, Inouye stated that "we must stop treating our children like miniature adults; instead we must recognize their special needs" (p. 816). Obviously, the complex requirements of children can only be met through child-centered mental health care systems.

Source: Inouye, D. K. (1988). Children's mental health issues. *American Psychologist, 43* 813–816.

DIFFERENCES IN COUNSELING CULTURALLY DIVERSE CHILDREN

Cross-cultural, intracultural, ethnic, and racial differences must be considered in counseling children in multicultural situations. In Chapter 4 we suggested that designing counseling intervention with regard for cultural and ethnic factors enhances counseling effectiveness for all cultures. In Chapter 3 and again in this chapter, we suggest that developmental theory also plays an important role in understanding the various client populations.

What implications do cultural differences and developmental characteristics have for counselors? First, because of children's limited concept of time, it might be difficult for them to receive maximum benefit from the standard once-a-week session. The counselor might want to schedule sessions for at least twice a week in order for children to experience carry-over between the sessions. Second, counseling effectiveness may be hampered by difficulties in communication resulting from language differences and differences in nonverbal behavior styles. Third, children are still in the process of developing a sense of self and a cultural identity. The counselor and child may benefit greatly from experiential activities that enable the child to explore the culture and immediate environment in a concrete fashion. —play therapy?

Typical Concerns and Stresses of the Childhood Years

What problems might children bring to counseling sessions? To what extent are these concerns related to developmental issues or cultural heritage? These are not easy questions, especially when one considers the developmental variation in children and the tremendous diversity among the various cultures. Table 5–1 lists some of the life events that may necessitate counseling intervention with children, along with corresponding stress values. Again, individual differences and cultural factors must be considered in planning appropriate counseling strategies.

Although the stress scale of Table 5–1 provides a comprehensive list of factors that may lead to stress, counselors working with culturally diverse children should also consider stress resulting from racism (both individual and institutional), discrimination, and prejudice. A FOCUS ON RESEARCH 5–2 (p. 120) concerns stress experienced by African-American children, although such stress may be experienced by children of all cultures.

Stressful situations or concerns caused by life events may vary with culture. For example, a Hispanic-American boy not living up to the machismo expectations of his peers might experience stress, whereas a Native-American boy in the same situation might not be concerned. For African-American children, stress may be more prevalent than for the Anglo population: nearly half live in poverty, two-thirds live in homes relying on public assistance, and many receive poorer health care than the Anglo-American populations (Clark-Johnson, 1988). While the Native-American child may talk to counselors about academic difficulties, Asian-American children may refrain from doing so for fear of not living up to the idealized image of the superintellect. Symptoms of children who are experiencing stress due to childhood or developmental concerns are listed in Table 5–2 (p. 121).

Table 5–1   Stress scale for children

Life Event	Value
Death of a parent	100
Parent's new relationship (new siblings involved)	90
Divorce of parents	73
Parent's new relationship	70
Separation of parents	65
Parent's jail term	63
Death of a close family member (e.g., grandparent)	63
Personal injury or illness	53
Parent's remarriage	50
Suspension or expulsion from school	47
Parent's reconciliation	45
Summer vacation	45
Parent or sibling illness	44
Mother's pregnancy	40
Anxiety over sex	39
Birth of a new baby (or adoption)	39
New school or new classroom teacher	39
Money problems at home	38
Death (or moving away) of a close friend	37
Death of a valued pet	37
Change in school work	36
More quarrels with parents (or parents quarreling more)	35

Scoring: Total those items that have occurred during the past 12 months. A score exceeding 300 points may indicate the child is vulnerable to stress-related problems.

Source: From S. Reed, *Instructor, 94*, 1984, p. 29. Reprinted by permission of Scholastic Inc.

The tremendous cultural and developmental differences in children call for each child to be considered as an individual. Children generally require counseling strategies different from those used with adults; however, it is a serious error to group children of all cultures together without regard for individual differences.

We will now look at children in the four cultures and offer suggestions for effective multicultural counseling.

Table 5–1   (continued)

Life Event	Value
Change in school responsibilities	29
Siblings going away to school	29
Family arguments with grandparents	29
Winning school or community awards	28
Mother going to work or stopping work	26
School beginning or ending	26
Changes in family's living standard	25
Changes in personal habits (bedtime, homework)	24
Trouble with parents—lack of communication, hostility	23
Change in school hours, schedules, or courses	23
Family's moving	20
A new school—high school	20
New sports, hobbies, family recreation activities	20
Change in church activities—more involvement or less	19
Change in social activities—new friends, loss of old ones, peer pressures, teasing	18
Changes in sleeping habits (giving up naps)	16
Change in number of family get-togethers	15
Change in eating habits—going on or off diet, new way of family cooking	15
Vacation, other than summer	13
Christmas	12
Breaking home, school, or community rules	11

NATIVE-AMERICAN CHILDREN

What are the effects of the many cherished values, traditions, and customs of the Native-American culture on the mental health of the children of that culture? Sometimes counseling intervention may be warranted due to strict adherence to these cultural traditions; sometimes problems may arise in acculturating to the dominant

A FOCUS ON RESEARCH 5–2
What Counselors Should Know about African-American Children's Stress

A life period of rapid transitions, childhood is the time for learning to adjust to the demands and expectations of parents, the rules and regulations of school, and the customs and laws of society. The childhood years may be particularly stressful for African-American children. Stress signals sent out by these children are frequently misunderstood or ignored by parents, teachers, counselors, and others in a position to lend assistance. Although writing specifically about African-American children, Grant and Grant (1982) offer several strategies applicable to children of all cultures:

1. Learn to recognize the early signs of excessive stress.

2. Be positive and remain calm in counseling troubled children.

3. Be sensitive to individual and cultural differences.

4. Pay attention to dramatic changes in behavior.

5. Help children understand that they are not alone.

6. Encourage children to communicate what they feel.

7. Don't give up.

Source: Grant, A. F., & Grant, A. (1982). Children under stress: What every counselor should know. *Journal of Non-White Concerns, 11,* 17–23.

culture. Counselors also may be faced with problems requiring an understanding of developmental differences related to the childhood years. Some of the more common problems in counseling Native-American children include the following:

1. failure of the child to develop a strong cultural identity and a positive self-concept;

2. adverse effects on the child of misperceptions about Native-Americans and the childhood years;

3. the child's distrust of Anglo-American professionals;

4. the child's poor English skills and confusion with regard to language;

5. the child's nonverbal communication style, which may result in misunderstandings;

6. the child's inability to reconcile Native-American cultural values and Anglo-American values;

7. the adverse effects on the child of discrimination;

8. the child's lower academic achievement after the fourth grade;

9. the child's increasing socialization from a parent-centered to a peer-centered world;

10. the child's physical, psychosocial, and intellectual differences.

Table 5–2   Warning signs of childhood stress

Bed-wetting

Boasts of superiority

Complaints of feeling afraid or upset without being able to identify the source

Complaints of neck or back pains

Complaints of pounding heart

Complaints of stomach upset, queasiness, or vomiting

Compulsive cleanliness

Compulsive ear tugging, hair pulling, or eyebrow plucking

Cruel behavior toward people or pets

Decline in school achievement

Defiance

Demand for constant perfection

Depression

Dirtying pants

Dislike of school

Downgrading of self

Easily startled by unexpected sounds

Explosive crying

Extreme nervousness

Extreme worry

Frequent daydreaming and retreat from reality

Frequent urination or diarrhea

Headaches

Hyperactivity or excessive tension or alertness

Increased number of minor spills, falls, and other accidents

Irritability

Listlessness or lack of enthusiasm

Loss of interest in activities usually approached with vigor

Lying

Nightmares or night terrors

Nervous laughter

Nervous tics, twitches, or muscle spasms

Obvious attention-seeking

Overeating

Poor concentration

Poor eating or sleeping

Use of alcohol, drugs, cigarettes

Psychosomatic illnesses

Stealing

Stuttering

Teeth-grinding (sometimes during sleep)

Thumb-sucking

Uncontrollable urge to run and hide, social withdrawal

Unusual difficulty in getting along with friends; shyness

Unusual jealousy of close friends or siblings

Unusual sexual behavior, such as spying or exhibitionism

Source: Excerpt from *Childhood Stress* by Barbara Kuczen, copyright © 1982, 1987 by Barbara Kuczen. Used by permission of Dell Books, a division of Bantam, Doubleday, Dell Publishing Group, Inc.

Cultural Differences

Cultural differences between Native-American children and their peers of other cultures may lead to misunderstandings and the need for counseling. While cultural differences should be valued and respected, in reality this is often not the case. Native-American children may perceive differing cultural characteristics as "right" or "wrong"; they may be inclined to regard discrimination toward their culture as an indication of the culture's inferiority. Such misunderstanding can complicate the counseling process by posing additional barriers.

What specific cultural characteristics have the potential for being misunderstood? According to Lum (1986), the Native-American child's short-term orientation, tendency to avoid self-disclosure, reflective and passive temperament, and loyalty to both immediate and extended family may be misunderstood to a degree that serious problems result; for example lowered self-esteem, a feeling of not being valued, or a feeling of general inferiority. The child in a school, whether on or off the reservation, that is predominantly staffed with Anglo-Americans may have teachers who do not understand the long-cherished Native-American cultural traditions of sharing material goods rather than owning, learning through legends, and living freely, unencumbered by formal rules. While Native-American children may act in a culturally appropriate manner, professionals lacking adequate knowledge of their culture may make false assumptions. For example, a humble and cooperative attitude and speaking in a lowered voice when angry may be misinterpreted by both professionals and peers (Richardson, 1981).

Language

The Native-American child's difficulty with the English language and the misunderstandings resulting from his or her nonverbal communication style may require counseling intervention. Communication problems also may exist between the counselor and client. As mentioned in Chapter 4, Native-American languages can be divided into about a dozen stocks; however, many variations (perhaps as many as 2,200 different languages) exist between tribes and nations (Wax, 1971). The many variations among Native-American languages and the differences between "reservation language" and "school language" may create academic difficulties. Furthermore, nonverbal communication characteristics may also lead to problems. Some Native-American mannerisms include the inclination to speak more softly and at a slower rate than Anglos and to interject less frequently with encouraging communicational signs (Sanders, 1987).

Family Issues

Children growing up in poverty and in a predominantly Anglo-American society experience family-related problems. First, parents may not understand that their children are having academic difficulties in school or that they may want to drop out altogether. A second issue, related both to school and family, concerns the child's cultural mannerisms being perceived by teachers as indicative of laziness or ignorance. A third issue, especially for Native-American families living off the reservaton, is the differences that arise between children and their parents as a result of the children's acculturaton to Anglo-American society. Yet another problem may stem from parents' failure to provide definitive role models. Since many Native-American parents grew up out of their own homes and were educated in boarding schools, they sometimes do not understand parenting roles and expectations. The therapist may need to serve as a parental role model, especially since some parents may be confused as to how to conduct a household efficiently and to educate their children in a bicultural world (Ho, 1987).

Developmental and Other Concerns

Developmental differences may also contribute to the problems of Native-American children. Differences in size and growth rates may result from cultural factors, genetics, environment, and socioeconomic status. Although it has been long understood that differences are normal, problems can arise when an individual perceives his or her development, size, and appearance as abnormal. Hair texture, facial features, and skin colors of Native-American children may be looked upon as "inferior" or "wrong" rather than "different." Differences in height and weight can also affect perceptions of self-worth as children compare their sizes to peers, both of the same and of different cultures. With respect to social development, the Native-American child may wonder, Why don't the white kids like me? Do they not like "me" or is it my culture? The Native-American child may also feel inferior in the intellectual domain. Academic difficulties may cause these children to conclude that Native Americans simply are not as smart as Anglos. Sometimes they may give up trying to improve their academic performance, reasoning that such efforts would be futile. Any of these physical, social, and intellectual factors, real or perceived, hold the potential for necessitating counseling intervention.

Other problems that plague Native-American children include a failure to develop a positive cultural identity, the belief that Anglos cannot be trusted, the acceptance of stereotypes and myths that have stigmatized their culture, the injustices their culture has experienced, a failure to develop a sense of worth to family and society, and the belief that children in general are not very important members of society (Lum, 1986). Whether negative feelings are actually warranted is not the pressing issue; the child who is experiencing such feelings is a likely candidate for counseling intervention.

Counseling Considerations

Counselors working with Native-American children should first recognize the possibility of a certain degree of ignorance on their part concerning the Native-American culture. This recognition might open the door to communication and enhance openness and trust (Richardson, 1981). Well-informed, objective, and appropriate counseling requires an objective perception of Native-American children and their many cultural and individual variations. According to Youngman and Sadongei (1983), the following stereotypical description of Native-American children should not be allowed to interfere with counseling effectiveness:

> All Indian children are slow learners, shy, lack positive identification, are thieves by nature, are undependable, and are potential alcoholics. Indian children who do not care to fit in the mold are labeled as incorrigible, hyperactive, brain-damaged, and rude. (p. 74)

Behavior that may appear bizarre to the counselor might be the cultural norm for the Native-American child. First, Native-American children may appear to pilfer objects from teachers, peers, or the counselor. When confronted, they will usually admit taking the objects; however, they are likely to be both surprised and hurt if the act is referred to as "stealing". These children have been taught that people of rank and importance share. The counselor could tell the child that sharing with one's family is acceptable, but that one should ask before "borrowing" objects outside the home. Second, freedom in the Native-American culture extends to the childhood years. Children are allowed considerable involvement in decision making and are usually given choices. Counselors working with Native-American children may want to provide the child with opportunities to make decisions during counseling sessions (Youngman & Sadongei, 1983).

Although mental health clinics and public agencies have created many specialized programs for children, perhaps elementary school counselors represent the largest single group of counselors working with Native-American children. These counselors should consider the non-Native-American's perceptions of the Native-American people and culture, the strengths and contributions of the culture, the special needs and problems of young Native-Americans, and the barriers that stymie communication between Native-Americans and their counselors. To promote counseling effectiveness, counselors may want to improve their understanding of the Native-American child's perceptions, values, and cultural heritage. They may also aid counseling effectiveness by learning to communicate verbally and nonverbally in a manner that is acceptable to the child and by learning about Native-American art, dress, and life (Herring, 1989a).

Individual/Group Therapy

Believing that patience is the key to counseling Native-Americans, Youngman and Sadongei (1983) and Edwards and Edwards (1989) offer several suggestions for counselors working with Native-American children. First, eye contact, which is valued in the Anglo-American society, may be considered rude or discourteous by some Native-American children (depending on the tribe) who may be taught to see without looking directly at someone. Second, counselors should exercise caution in placing children in situations where self-praise is required, since speaking of one's accomplishments may be considered to be in poor taste. Especially in group sessions, considerable strain is placed on a child who is asked to talk about his or her strengths. The child may resort to telling unbelievable stories, or may refuse to speak altogether. Praise must always come from someone else. Third, it is important that clients receive positive reinforcement during group therapy; however, it may be more appropriate to provide reinforcement in individual situations. Being praised in front of one's peers in the initial stages of group therapy may be embarrassing and culturally inappropriate when working with Native-Americans. Once group cohesion is developed, group members may provide positive support to one another (Edwards & Edwards, 1989).

Group therapy appears to be a logical mode of delivery for Native-American children because their culture places more value on group contributions than on individual successes and accomplishments. As with other cultures, many topics are appropriate for group counseling with children: developmental concerns, such crises as death and divorce, developing friendships, or improving study skills (Mitchum, 1989).

A FOCUS ON RESEARCH 5–3
Counseling Native-American Children

Herring describes the dismal circumstances of many Native-American children and suggests that guidance and counseling are the best vehicles for helping these children. Counselors can be instrumental in reducing the ethnic and cultural limitations imposed by geographical and residential patterns that often limit the Native-American child's opportunities. Herring's suggestions include the following:

Source: Herring, R. D. (1989b). Counseling Native-American children: Implications for elementary school counselors. *Elementary School Guidance and Counseling, 23,* 272–281.

1. Counseling intervention should be highly individualized.
2. Assessment should have minimal socioeconomic or cultural bias.
3. Counselors should recognize learning styles and life purposes.
4. The child's culture should not be devalued.
5. Methodologies should place high value on self-worth.
6. The school counselor should help the school staff become sensitive to needs of Native-Americans.

Native-American children are taught early that nonverbal communication plays an important role in their lives. A significant factor will be the counselor's own nonverbal communication style and his or her own personality. For example, communication will break down and the client may wish to leave if the counselor gives the impression of being busy or preoccupied. Native-American children will place value on time spent listening and talking rather than on the number of counseling sessions (Youngman & Sadongei, 1983). A FOCUS ON RESEARCH 5–3 presents several suggestions for counseling Native-American children.

Family Therapy

Since extended families are a major source of support for the Native-American people, counselors should plan intervention strategies that involve the entire family. The usefulness of involving the entire family in any type of treatment situation has been long recognized by the Native-American people. More recently, writers of other cultures focusing on the Native-American family and experience have also recognized its possibilities (Everett, Proctor, & Cartmell, 1989; Lewis & Ho, 1975).

Prior to counseling Native-American children in family situations, the counselor needs to understand the nature of family and children in the culture. Suggestions include (a) acquiring an understanding of the reason for the contact; (b) establishing rapport; (c) responding appropriately to the family's mistrust, which will be particularly high during the first encounter; (d) realizing that the family might perceive the counselor as meddling in their family affairs; (e) being sensitive and avoiding uncertainty about counseling procedures; and (f) if the contact has been initiated by the counselor, explaining openly and clearly to the family who he or she is, what his or her role is with the agency or the school, and the reason for the session (Ho, 1987).

avoids self disclosure

UP CLOSE AND PERSONAL 5–1
Counseling Bill Lonetree

non-verbal congue

self-esteem

language

Eight-year-old Bill, introduced in Chapter 4, was recommended for counseling by his Anglo-American teacher who reported that Bill did not listen, showed little emotion, and appeared anxious or stressed at times. The counselor, an Anglo-American, has met with Bill weekly for about four weeks, and Bill is just beginning to open up to him. Bill was suspicious at first, but slowly and reluctantly he has begun to confide that the teacher urges him to try harder, to listen attentively, and to take a more active role in the learning process. Bill does not understand the teacher's suggestions: He *is* listening and he *does* try; however, he admits to a lack of interest in the future. The counselor noticed that Bill tended to look away as he spoke, although he appeared to listen attentively. The counselor also observed that Bill seemed nervous when he spoke about his schoolwork. Bill admitted that he wanted to do well in school, but that school was not like home. Things were different in school—the language, for example. Besides, he had no Anglo-American friends. The counselor reached several conclusions: (1) Bill's comments indicate that some of his problems might stem from the teacher, who neither understands the Native-American culture nor recognizes the differences between Bill's home life and school life; (2) Bill is experiencing stress due to his lack of school progress; and (3) Bill should be counseled in individual sessions several times and then participate in a group session with other Native-American children.

Group sessions with Native-American families may involve participation of extended family members, members of the clan or tribe, or significant others. These sessions may need to be informal and may require longer periods of time to develop relationships and achieve desired goals. The work accomplished, however, will include the knowledge and support of a group of significant people (Edwards & Edwards, 1989).

AFRICAN-AMERICAN CHILDREN

The richness and diversity of the African-American culture have long gone unrecognized. African-Americans have been subjected to ridicule, shunned, and generally misunderstood. Counselors of other cultures, without proper knowledge of the African-American culture, have often tried to "conform" the African-American to be more in line with middle-class Anglo-Americans. Some of the potential problems in counseling African-American children include the following:

1. the child's failure to develop a strong African-American identity and a positive self-concept;
2. adverse effects of stereotypes, prejudices, injustices, and racism (overt and covert) against African-American children and the childhood years in general;

3. adverse effects of inappropriate value judgments based on differences;
4. the child's academic problems, due either to the child's lack of educational experiences or the school's inability to build on experiences;
5. the child's inability to overcome society's perception of African-American children as "behavior problems";
6. the child's language problems and different nonverbal communication style;
7. the child's different home life and cultural concept of "family";
8. the child's physical, psychosocial, and intellectual differences;
9. the child's health and nutritional problems, associated with lower income families;
10. the child's increasing desire to move from a parent-centered world to a peer-centered world.

Cultural Differences

Cultural factors that may create a need for counseling intervention can be grouped into two broad categories: (1) a home life different from that of the dominant culture and (2) academic problems stemming from cultural background or the school's failure to respond to the learners' cultural differences. Although these two aspects will be examined separately, it should be remembered that they are closely related. Also, as with other cultures, African-American children vary among themselves; they will demonstrate many individual differences.

The home lives of African-American children often puzzle their counselors. The family organizational structure is such that family members are always welcome in one another's home. Also, African-American families have a sense of corporate responsibility to extended family members; e.g., aunts, uncles, cousins. A counselor who visited a child in the home remarked that "there just seemed to be too many people in that house.... I felt as if we [counselor and client] had no privacy at all" (Smith, 1981, p. 170).

In some instances, African-American children experience academic problems due to lack of appropriate educational experiences. Sometimes, however, it is the school's failure to build on the child's personal and cultural experiences that leads to problems. Children need to achieve success in school, yet African-American students often leave educational institutions with that need unmet due to racism and discrimination. Students not experiencing school success often do not believe they can function adequately in a predominantly Anglo-American society (Lee & Lindsey, 1985).

Language

Language problems of African-American children fall into two major categories: (1) problems associated with English and (2) problems associated with nonverbal communication. The black vernacular constitutes a crucial aspect of African-American culture and plays a significant role in children's self-concept development, in their

culture and from other cultures), and in learning appropriate masculine or feminine social roles.

Counselors may experience difficulty relating to the circumstances and hardships affecting children living in poverty. Consider the following clinical description of a 12-year-old:

> Jimmy Jones is a 12-year-old Black male student who was referred by Mrs. Peterson because of apathy, indifference, and inattentiveness to classroom activities.... Other teachers have also reported that Jimmy "does not pay attention," "daydreams often" and "frequently falls asleep" during class.... There is a strong possibility that Jimmy is harboring repressed rage that needs to be ventilated and dealt with. His inability to directly express his anger had led him to adopt passive aggressive means of expressing hostility, i.e., inattentiveness, daydreaming, falling asleep. It is recommended that Jimmy be seen for intensive counseling to discover the basis of the anger. (cited in Sue, 1981, p. 35)

After getting to know Jimmy, the counselor realized that the problem resulted from a home of extreme poverty where the boy experienced hunger, lack of sleep, and overcrowding.

Counseling Considerations

Counselors intervening with African-American children are often at a loss in choosing appropriate strategies (Smith et al., 1974) Prior to making any counseling decisions involving these children, professionals must assess their abilities objectively. Often, African-American children are assessed using instruments primarily designed for Anglo-Americans, which could result in a culturally biased picture. If the counseling professional views the child in an unfavorable light, the child's self-perception may be affected. According to Isen (1983),

> children try to live up or down to the expectations held by others who are important to them. They see their own abilities through the eyes of their parents, siblings, teachers, and peers. Although some Black children are able to adjust and fall into the mainstream of the educational system, many are not. Those who do not are generally considered the "troubled population" characterized by underachievement, low academic motivation, low self-esteem, and inappropriate behaviors. (p. 49)

Examples of tests either designed specifically (or which are appropriate) for African-American children include the following:

The Black Intelligence Test of Cultural Homogeneity (BITCH)—A test to identify early indicators of intelligence in black children. Included are items on black American folklore, history, life experiences, and dialect.

Themes of Black Awareness (TOBA)—A 40-item sentence-completion instrument that elicits thematic material relative to an individual's level of black awareness.

Themes Concerning Black (TCB)—An instrument to measure various aspects of the black person's personality.

Multicultural Pluralistic Assessment (SOMPA)—A test to be used with culturally diverse children 5 to 11 years of age. Based on the assumption that the American society is pluralistic, both culturally and structurally, this assessment tool includes an interview with parents, a medical examination, and a Wechsler IQ test.

Counselors must be extremely sensitive to how their statements during counseling sessions will be perceived by children of diverse cultural backgrounds. Consider the following case presented by Smith et al. (1974): Ricky, a third-grade African-American boy, was one of 32 African-, Puerto Rican- and Anglo-American students squeezed into a small third-floor room. His Anglo-American teacher perceived him to be a troublemaker. According to the teacher, Ricky couldn't behave, had learning disabilities, and couldn't appreciate anything. The teacher sent Ricky to the counselor, whereupon the following dialogue ensued:

Counselor: Hi, Ricky. How's it been going today? Have you had a good morning?

Ricky: Yes.

Counselor: Did your teacher send you down? What's the problem **this** time?

Ricky: Nothing.

Counselor: Come on now, Ricky. I know she must have sent you for something. Why don't you tell me about it?

Ricky: [silence]

Counselor: Ricky, I thought you and I could talk. You think about what you want to tell me.

Ricky: My teacher told me to come down here and tell you what I did this morning. But I didn't do nothin'. Everytime I git out my seat she holler at me and I don't be doin' nothin'. We wuz workin' on our readin' and she know I can't read the directions that tell you wha' to do. I raised my hand, but she never came to my desk. So I went to ask somebody what it mean and she saw me and start hollerin' and told me to git in my seat. Then BB took my scissors and when I try to get 'em back, she start hollerin' at **me**. My other scissors got stole and my momma bought me some more and told me I bet' not lose these 'cause she can't 'ford to be buyin' me scissors every week. She beat me if I lose 'em. BB wouldn't give 'em back. So I hit him and we start fightin'. Then the teacher sent me down here.

Counselor: Ricky, your temper always gets you in trouble. You know you can't have everything your way all the time. You should try to control your actions. You've got to do as your teacher tells you. When you disrupt the class, you make her very upset. This isn't what you want, is it?

Ricky: [silence]

Counselor: Now, I want you to try much harder to be a nice boy. I know you can do it. Now, you know that I don't punish students when they have misbehaved. But I have a suggestion for you: you may sit in my outer office if you like until you feel you're ready to go back to your classroom. When you get back why not tell your teacher that you're sorry and that you'll try to do better.

Ricky: I'm ready to go back to my classroom now. (pp. 249–250)

Smith et al. maintain that Ricky was completely misunderstood. Neither the teacher nor the counselor understood Ricky's culture, his language, or Ricky himself. The teacher concluded that Ricky was a troublemaker based on his behavior alone, and referred him to the counselor to ease her frustration. The counselor also failed to respond to Ricky's needs as he assumed the role of teacher advocate rather than

Table 5–3   The counselor and the black student

Student Development Facilitator	
Counselor Function	Implementation
1. Personal-Social Growth	
Facilitating the development of positive Black self-identity	Conduct self-awareness groups emphasizing self-appreciation through cultural heritage: use culturally specific curriculum materials and aesthetic dimensions to cultivate self-pride from a Black perspective in group interactions
Facilitating the development of positive interpersonal relations and responsible behavior	Explore the nature and importance of positive interpersonal relationships in growth groups: incorporate traditional Afro-American notions of community into group interactions to develop greater interpersonal respect, particularly between young Black men and women
	Conduct social behavior guidance groups: facilitate collective explorations of pragmatic strategies for enhancing behavioral repertoires for optimal school success while maintaining culturally-learned response styles
2. Academic Achievement	
Facilitating the development of positive attitudes toward academic achievement	Conduct motivation groups: develop group guidance activities focusing on inherent Black potential which incorporate historical and contemporary references to the educational experiences of influential Afro-Americans

Source: Lee, 1982, p. 96.

attempting to help Ricky. Both professionals ignored Ricky's cultural background and unique circumstances. Thus, Ricky's counseling needs were not met.

Situations like Ricky's are not uncommon. Some specific guidelines for elementary school counselors working with children like Ricky include being open and honest, seeking to respect and appreciate cultural differences, participating in activities of the African-American community, rejecting prejudice and racism, asking questions about the African-American culture, and holding high expectations for African-American children (Locke, 1989). Table 5–3 lists counselor functions and implementation strategies pertaining to African-American children.

Individual/Group Therapy

Larrabee (1986) advocates an affirmation approach to counseling African-American males. He presents the following dialogue of a therapist counseling a 14-year-old boy using individual therapy:

Counselor: Hi, you must be Joe _____; I'm Mr. (Ms.) _____.

Table 5–3   (continued)

Student Development Facilitator	
Counselor Function	**Implementation**
Facilitating the development of academic skills and competencies	Conduct guidance workshops in the following areas: 1–academic planning 2–study skills and time management 3–testwiseness 4–remediation
3. Career Development	
Facilitating the vocational choice and career development process	Develop relevant guidance and training experience related to the world of work: 1–conduct information forums on nonstereo-typed jobs and careers 2–sponsor "Career Days" and invite Black career role models to explain their perceptions and experiences in the world of work 3–develop internship and co-op experiences with Black businesses and professionals 4–conduct workshops on the mechanics of the world of work—i.e., how to look for, apply and interview for a job 5–conduct workshops on the rules of work— i.e., proper attire, behavior and attitude in the work setting 6–conduct workshops on survival issues—i.e., money and its management, tax concerns, social security, etc.

Come on in and have a seat. We don't know each other, but the assistant principal told me that he wanted you to come to see me. Now that you're here, I'd like to get acquainted and find out the reason he thought you should come in.

Joe: [He is quiet as he looks over the office with a somewhat sullen expression.] Look, I don't know what all this is about.

Counselor: If there is no real reason why you're here, what would you like to talk about?

Joe: [pause] I don't want to talk about nothin'.... You know, he just said I had to come. I figure, it's better than sittin' in math.

Counselor: Because the assistant principal insisted, you decided it would be better than math class.

Joe: Sure, I hate Ms. _____ anyway.

Counselor: One of the advantages of being here is not having to deal with Ms. _____. What are some other good reasons for talking a bit with me today?

Joe: [laughing] I can get that S.O.B., Mr. _____, off my back.

Counselor: So you can dump Mr. _____'s pressure and avoid Ms. _____ then by coming in and getting to know me a little bit.

Joe: Yeah, I guess . . . He's always on me about somethin'.

Counselor: What seems to bug him the most?

Joe: Oh, he thinks I bust ass too much.

Counselor: Then, it bothers you that he thinks you fight too much.

Joe: Nope, he's buttin' in where he don't belong sendin' me to see you when he already settles it.

Counselor: It just bugs you that he dealt with you on the fighting and then sent you to me too.

Counselor: It seems like one of the advantages of us getting together is to get Mr. _____ off your back. You know it might just help me out, too. Because I don't usually get involved in stuff like fighting. I think talking with you would help me understand kids who get in fights better. If you decided to come in to talk a few times about your experiences with fighting it might keep the assistant principal off your case and kind of educate me about some of the things that go on with kids who fight. What do you think about that?

Joe: Well, I don't know . . . but maybe it'd be okay if I get out of math.

Counselor: Okay, let's see what we can work out. I have time during this period on Wednesdays. How many times would you want to miss math on Wednesdays?

Joe: Hey, I'll cut every day if you want.

Counselor: [chuckling] I can't handle that. What would you think about this time on Wednesdays for about the next month? Is it a deal?

Joe: Ya got a deal! Shake? (pp. 31–33)

Larrabee contends that the affirmation approach works effectively with reluctant clients. It is clear that such an approach must be continued in future sessions if positive results are to occur.

Groups often provide a more natural setting for working with children than individual counseling. Children function as members of groups in their daily activities; e.g. in the family, in the classroom, and in the peer group. Group counseling has been advocated as an effective method of counseling several children simultaneously. An even more important advantage is that children can learn appropriate behaviors and new ways of relating more easily through interaction and feedback in a safe situation with their peers (Thompson & Rudolph, 1988).

Considering the number of African-American students experiencing problems within the educational system, greater emphasis should be given to group approaches. As an added benefit, such approaches reflect the communal nature of the African-American experience. Also, the dynamics of socialization among African-American people emphasize cooperation and group cohesiveness (Lee, 1982). Continuing this line of thought, A FOCUS ON RESEARCH 5–5 looks at minority family outreach.

◤ A FOCUS ON RESEARCH 5–5
◣ **School Counselors and School Psychologists:
Partners in Minority Family Outreach**

School counselors and psychologists can bridge the gap between minority families and schools by serving as a link between families and schools and by increasing the level of minority participation in school matters. Cole, Thomas, and Lee (1988) present a comprehensive consultation model for promoting family and community involvement in the education process of

minority youth. They examine outreach issues and describe the roles of counselors and psychologists in both community and family situations. The authors maintain that "in most instances, education in minority communities has been conducted by professionals whose cultural realities were fostered in a different environment" (p. 114). To remedy this situation, they recommend appropriate professional development and offer suggestions for a comprehensive teamwork approach.

Source: Cole, S. M., Thomas, A. R., & Lee, C. C. (1988). School counselor and school psychologist: Partners in minority family outreach. *Journal of Multicultural Counseling and Development, 16,* 110–116.

Family Therapy

Relying extensively on Satir's (1967) work on family therapy, Thompson and Rudolph (1988) contend that counseling children in family therapy settings can be particularly useful. First, all family members are part of a family homeostasis in which all must balance forces to achieve unity and working order. Second, family relationships can be redefined during the session as each family member adds input. The close-knit nature of the African-American family (both immediate and extended) also might contribute to the effectiveness of family therapy.

What status and what role will the African-American child be accorded during family therapy? In essence, how will the African-American child be perceived by the family and the counselor? Three factors are particularly relevant in answering these questions. First, African-American families generally accord equal status to sons and daughters. Second, there are clear responsibilities assigned to siblings on the basis of age. Third, the firstborn, regardless of sex, receives special preparation for the leadership role in the child group. Also, being victims of racism and discrimination, some African-American parents feel determined to create a more favorable environment for their children. They expect their children to earn greater rewards than they were able to achieve (Ho, 1987).

Therapists meeting with African-American children and their families in group sessions can benefit from several specific techniques. First, as a matter of procedure, the therapist should arrange to meet with the child, the family, and the school officials to clarify issues and facilitate change. Second, a key to success in engaging the family is communicating respect and openly acknowledging the family's strengths. Third, the therapist should avoid jargon and relate to the family in a direct but supportive manner. Fourth, assuming familiarity with adult family members before asking their permission should be avoided. The therapist who uses first names prematurely may

---

◣ UP CLOSE AND PERSONAL 5–2
Counseling Carl Johnson

What concerns and needs will 5-year-old Carl bring to the counselor? Carl's kindergarten teacher referred him to the counselor because she felt Carl was not achieving at the level for 5-year-olds. After talking with Carl, the Anglo-American counselor felt that although his readiness scores and kindergarten objectives were below average, he indeed had been putting forth considerable effort. The counselor concluded that Carl's poor self-concept was adversely affecting his schoolwork. Carl believed that he could not do the work the teachers expected. The counselor also pointed to Carl's dialect as another factor contributing to his problems. The dialect worked well at home, but did not seem to be acceptable at school. Although his teachers were middle-class African-American, they encouraged Carl to give up the neighborhood language for a "school lan-

guage." Although Carl does not want to change, he does recognize that his dialect is quite different from the language he hears at school.

Also apparent to the counselor was Carl's confusion regarding his cultural identity. Carl wonders why so many people encourage him to change his "ways," especially since his family speaks and acts the same way at home and in the community. The counselor summed up the assessment: If Carl could improve his self-concept and establish a strong cultural identity, his overall school achievement might improve and he might show an increased interest in school. The counselor decided to try to help Carl understand that his dialect was a natural aspect of his culture and to talk to Carl's teachers to obtain information that might help his intervention with Carl.

---

offend adult family members who may view this as showing disrespect in front of their children (Hines & Boyd-Franklin, 1982).

ASIAN-AMERICAN CHILDREN

As emphasized in Chapter 4, tremendous intracultural diversity characterizes the Asian-American culture. Although the generic term *Asian-American* is used extensively in the literature, in the following discussion we will attempt to refer to specific populations whenever possible.

While it is true that Asian-Americans continue to experience injustices and discrimination lingering from previous decades, it is also true that today's young Asian-Americans, largely those with Chinese, Korean, and Indochinese backgrounds, are often achieving remarkable academic success. This success has been at least partially responsible for the "model minority" stereotype, which places unrealistic expectations on many of the children of this culture (Sue, 1981). Counseling intervention will be most effective when counselors avoid the tendency to accept stereotypes, to understand the much-valued Asian cultural heritage, and to understand the frustrations of the culture as well as the accomplishments.

Several problems that counselors might encounter in intervening with Asian-American children include the following:

1. failure of the child to develop a strong Asian-American cultural identity and a positive self-concept;

2. the belief that Asian-American children constitute a "model minority"—all intellectually superior, hard-working, and academically successful, with superior skills in math;

3. the child's different cultural characteristics;

4. the child's inability to reconcile loyalties to conflicting Asian- and Anglo-American cultures;

5. pressures on the child to excel in Anglo-American society, yet maintain old-world Asian values;

6. the child's language difficulties, which may hamper academic achievement and socialization;

7. the adverse effects on the child of overt or covert racism, injustices, discrimination, and years of oppression;

8. the child's physical, psychosocial, and intellectual differences;

9. the child's increasing tendency to move from a parent-centered world to a peer-centered world.

Cultural Differences

Several cultural characteristics of Asian-American children may cause stress and problems for them in a predominantly Anglo society. The tendency of many Asian-American children to be quiet, aloof, dependent, obedient, and conforming may conflict with the reality of many Anglo-American schools. Problems result when the behavior of these children is assessed in terms of Anglo-American cultural values. For example, while the Anglo-American child might admit all mistakes to the counselor, the Asian-American may lack trust in the Anglo-American counselor and may tend to hide aberrant behaviors, or feel a personal sense of responsibility for solving one's own problems (Yao, 1985).

Choosing between conflicting cultural demands can lead to confused identities for young Asian-American clients. Peer pressure tends to be more intense for Asian-Americans; hence, they are often inclined to make "adjustments" to their tradition to conform to peer expectations. In coming to grips with changing loyalties, these children face the displeasure of older "more loyal" family members (Yao, 1985).

Language

The problems Asian-Americans have with English and their different communication styles may create various academic and psychological problems. Newly arrived Japanese children, having been taught the cultural demeanor of quietness and aloofness, often are misunderstood as they reluctantly participate in verbally oriented activities in American schools (Kitano, 1981).

Hawaiians and some of the other Pacific Islander cultures use extensive nonverbal communication. This may put them at a disadvantage in school, since such language lacks the precision required to communicate the kind of factual information associated with formal education. Hawaiian children tend to understand gestures, facial expressions, body language, and other nonverbal cues more readily than spoken English. If they are unable to speak English well or understand it, these children may become bored, confused, inattentive, and disruptive (Omizo & Omizo, 1989).

Rapport between counselor and child also may be difficult to establish because of language problems. The children may have to be urged to speak if they are used to one-way communication in which the adult speaks and the child listens. Moreover, speaking English in school and continuing to hear and speak the native language at home presents yet another problem (Sue, 1981).

The notion that all Asian-American children have superior intellects and are high-achievers diffuses attention toward genuine language problems and places an undue burden on these children. Although attempts to alleviate the situation have met with legal success (Gollnick & Chinn, 1990), the language problem is far from remedied. A class-action suit in 1974 on behalf of 1,800 Chinese-American children claimed that the San Francisco Board of Education failed to provide programs designed to meet the linguistic needs of non-English-speaking students. This failure constituted a violation of Title VI of the Civil Rights Act of 1964 and the Equal Protection Clause of the Fourteenth Amendment. Essentially, it was claimed that children not able to understand the language used for instruction were deprived of an equal education. In the *Lau v. Nichols* decision, the Supreme Court stated that simply providing the means and materials of education did not guarantee equal treatment. Although the Court did not mandate bilingual education for non-English-speaking students, it did stipulate that special language programs were necessary. Even with this legal mandate, Asian-Americans may not always receive appropriate services due to lack of tolerance for, or insensitivity to, language or dialectical differences (Gollnick & Chinn, 1990). This lack of commitment to providing appropriate language instruction (whether it be in the child's native language or in English as a second language) has resulted in language difficulties for many Asian-American children.

Family Issues

Some Asian traditions involving family relationships may result in problems requiring counseling intervention. For example, sons are considered to be of more value than daughters; older siblings receive better treatment than younger ones and command more respect; and parents have high academic expectations for their children, even though the children may have problems with English (Shon & Ja, 1982). As the children become more Americanized; that is, as they become more vocal, express their opinions more freely, and become more independent, the parent-child relationship may suffer (Yao, 1985).

The loyalty of Hawaiian children to family traditions and customs may hamper counseling effectiveness. For example, children are taught early not to discuss situations that could bring shame to the family; not to display signs of anger, depression, or guilt outside the family; and to seek advice from family elders rather than outsiders.

Hawaiian children may find it very hard to disclose personal information to strangers; they even may be severely reprimanded by their parents for being referred for counseling (Omizo & Omizo, 1989).

Developmental and Other Concerns

Poor self-concepts, family conflicts resulting from moving toward a peer-centered world (and away from the parent-centered world), and physical differences of Asian-American children due to cultural genetics all may warrant the need for counseling intervention. First, a poor self-concept resulting from language problems may weaken a child's ability to cope with everyday problems in a predominantly English-speaking society. Second, during these years in which there is a normal pulling back from emotional dependence on the family, considerable conflict may result from parents who are unwilling to accept contemporary Western viewpoints on child-family allegiances. Third, the somewhat smaller physical size of the Asian-American population may create problems for children when being smaller causes children to feel inadequate in other ways.

Counseling Considerations

With particular reference to Chinese-Americans, Sue and Sue (1983) suggested that Asian-American children are conflicted with respect to their cultural background and the Western values advocated in school and in the media. The Anglo emphasis on spontaneity, assertiveness, and independence often conficts with Asian-American values. The adjustment needs of Asian immigrant children are examined in A FOCUS ON RESEARCH 5–6.

 A FOCUS ON RESEARCH 5–6
Adjustment Needs of Asian Immigrant Children

Yao (1985) maintains that the recent influx of Asian people to the United States calls for an enhanced understanding of the adjustment needs of the children of this culture. She identifies several issues relative to the lifestyle changes these children must make:

1. Many refugee children face separation from their parents during their resettlement.

2. The patriarchial role of the husband/father

often alters employment patterns, economic needs, and educational pursuits of family members.

3. Many Indochinese women have become heads of households and family protectors after husbands have been killed or left behind in their homelands.

4. The Asian-American children's traditional place in the family is challenged by the American culture that does not advocate valuing boys over girls, authority by sibling age, unquestioning obedience, or maintaining the family's honor at all costs.

Source: Yao, E. L. (1985). Adjustment needs of Asian immigrant children. *Elementary School Guidance and Counseling, 19,* 222–227.

Asian immigrants are not accustomed to seeing counseling professionals. Counselors are few in their native lands, and there is also a cultural reluctance to admit to a need for help in handling personal problems. Children are taught that problems are to be kept within the confines of the family to avoid bringing shame and embarrassment to the family. As a result, children are not only unfamiliar with counseling procedures, but are also uncomfortable in sharing inner feelings with strangers with whom trust has not been established. The counselor who is aware of these cultural factors is more likely to develop rapport with these children. Problems associated with involving parents are often diminished when parents are enrolled in language programs, are familiarized with the Anglo-American educational system, and are taught parenting skills of the new country (Yao, 1985).

To help counselors work effectively with their Asian-American clients, Hartman and Askounis (1989) suggest the following:

1. Determine individual strengths and weaknesses.

2. Be aware of the client's degree of acculturation.

3. Understand Asian-Americans' difficulty in being self-disclosing and open. For them, restraint is a sign of emotional maturity, admitting problems is thought to reflect negatively on the entire family, and having emotional difficulties may shame the entire family.

4. Understand that confrontational, emotionally intense approaches may cause additional problems and turmoil for Asian-American clients.

5. Learn about individuals and their respective cultures. Ask about the culture, develop ethnic sensitivity, and avoid stereotypical labels.

Hawaiian children experience many social, economic, and educational inequities that may warrant the intervention of elementary school counselors. These children may feel inferior, incompetent, and helpless in school situations. They may experience social and health problems or problems resulting from conflicting values and language differences (Omizo & Omizo, 1989). A FOCUS ON RESEARCH 5–7 offers suggestions for counseling Hawaiian children.

Individual/Group Therapy

What strategies are most appropriate for working with Asian-American and Pacific Islander children? Understanding the reserved demeanor of these children and developing an enthusiasm for their cultural heritage enhance the relationship between client and counselor. To promote cultural understanding, the child should be encouraged to share his or her background, values, needs, and problems (Grambs, 1981).

Counselors working with Asian-American children are cautioned not to misinterpret reticence as apathy. During the session, Asian-Americans may remain silent for quite some time, briefly verbalize a problem, and wait for the counselor to take the initiative in the relationship (Lum, 1986). The counselor should understand that such behavior in relating and responding is culturally based.

A FOCUS ON RESEARCH 5–7
Counseling Hawaiian Children

Prior to counseling Hawaiian children, Omizo and Omizo (1989) feel that counselors should understand issues relating to four major areas: group orientation, concepts of time, communication and learning, and appropriate behavior. They provide a comprehensive list of suggestions for counselors, a few of which are as follows:

1. Counseling activities should include group formats, since the group is important to Hawaiian children.

Source: Omizo, M. M., & Omizo, S. A. (1989). Counseling Hawaiian children. *Elementary School Guidance and Counseling, 23,* 282–288.

2. Individual competition should be minimized. Children should not be recognized or punished in front of the group.

3. Counseling activities should focus on the present time.

4. Participation of parents and elders in the communities should be sought whenever possible.

5. Direct counseling approaches work best.

6. The counselor should take the role of a mentor, since Hawaiians may be reluctant to seek professional help.

7. Counselors should gain an understanding of the Hawaiian child's nonverbal skills.

In examining counseling techniques used with Asian-Americans, Kitano (1981) concluded that counseling sessions with Japanese-American clients should be more formal and less confrontal than sessions with Anglo-Americans. Also, group therapy sessions should be used less often with Japanese-American children. These children may be reluctant to disclose personal problems that could reflect negatively on the family. The child who might disclose problems and concerns in individual sessions may not risk peers knowing personal or family problems.

Family Therapy

The Asian-American family's cohesiveness and loyalty to the welfare of the family unit should not rule out family therapy altogether. Realistically speaking, however, Asian-American children may have to be encouraged to disclose significant information. Also, the child in the family therapy situation will probably be reluctant to speak, since the father is generally expected to be the spokesperson. Furthermore, the child's disclosure of a significant problem might reflect poorly upon the father's ability to manage his house and family.

Elementary school counselors may want to involve parents and families in certain situations. A few essentials to consider include (a) reviewing the parents' background, (b) being aware of cultural differences, (c) developing a sense of trust, (d) respecting the "pride and shame" aspect, (e) recognizing the family's face-saving needs, and (f) finding out how the parents feel about school (Morrow, 1989).

◆ UP CLOSE AND PERSONAL 5–3
Counseling Mina Sukuzi

Mina's teacher had asked her on several occasions whether she wanted to see the counselor, and although the teacher thought Mina had several concerns, Mina was always a little hesitant. Finally, the teacher took the initiative to arrange an appointment.

During the first and second sessions, the counselor found that Mina was hesitant to reveal her problems. She trusted her teachers; they had shown a great deal of interest in her and her schoolwork, but the counselor—well, Mina couldn't imagine what to talk about.

Mina lived in a close-knit family in which her father reigned supreme. He made all the decisions and Mina was afraid to ask him whether she could participate in the extracurricular activities her peers enjoyed. After her schoolwork and her piano practice, there was little time left; however, she did regard her peers (especially the Anglo-Americans) with a sense of envy. Why couldn't she do some of the things they did? When would her father change? Couldn't he see that living in America required some change of ways? She worked very hard to live up to his high expectations for her, but her few friends did not have to meet such expectations. They enjoyed play a lot more than work. Mina thought that the exceptional demands of her family might be costing her friends.

Mina's other concern, which she was slow to admit, was her developing body. Was she developing too slowly, perhaps? Were all the changes normal? Luckily, her counselor was a woman; but even so, it took Mina to the eighth session to admit her concerns. Now Mina feels fortunate that she has the counselor to answer her questions, since no one at home is willing to discuss such matters.

The counselor tried diligently to establish a trusting counseling relationship and proceeded slowly so as not to confront Mina "head-on." Finally, the counselor determined that Mina's problems could be attributed primarily to the pressure placed on her to excel in all endeavors, her perceived rejection by her peers, and her developing body. Since Mina probably would not disclose information in a group setting, the counselor decided to schedule several more individual sessions with her.

HISPANIC-AMERICAN CHILDREN

Just as with Asian-Americans, the tremendous intracultural diversity among Hispanic-Americans complicates discussions of individuals in this culture and disallows broad generalizations about the culture as a whole. Hence, any discussion of the Spanish-speaking people, whenever possible, should refer to a specific population.

The stereotypes that plague Spanish-speaking children not only cause problems that may lead to counseling intervention, they may also reduce the effectiveness of counseling. The belief that Hispanic-Americans are all prone to violence, troublemakers, and problem students does not allow for an objective consideration of a culture that is rich in tradition, customs, and diversity. Some of the problems that counselors might encounter in intervening with Hispanic-American children include the following:

1. failure of the child to develop a strong cultural identity and a positive self-concept;
2. adverse effects of stereotypes;
3. the child's distrust of and hostility toward Anglo-American professionals;
4. conflicts between "home language" and "school language"; the child's belief that speaking English is disloyal to the "native tongue";
5. the child's inability to reconcile loyalties to conflicting Hispanic- and Anglo-American cultures;
6. the child's different cultural expectations—rigid sex roles; boys being "manly" and girls being "retiring and reserved";
7. the adverse effects of racism, injustices, and discrimination;
8. the child's physical, psychosocial, and intellectual differences;
9. the child's socialization to a peer-centered world.

Cultural Differences

Several characteristics of the Spanish-speaking cultures are at variance with traditional Anglo-American values and may be misunderstood in counseling sessions. One such characteristic is the Hispanic's tendency to avoid being set off from peers, as may result, for example, from competing with them. Another characteristic is the expectation of specific sex-role behavior, although this appears, in general, to have diminished somewhat in the acculturative process. A third characteristic, much distorted and misunderstood, is *machismo*. Among Hispanics, the term connotes physical strength, sexual attractiveness, virtue, and potency. When applied by non-Hispanics to Hispanic males, however, it refers to physical aggression, sexual promiscuity, and dominance of women (Ruiz, 1981).

The Hispanic's strict allegiance to family loyalty also can be misunderstood by majority cultures. Commitment to the extended family, the elderly, and even to brothers and sisters may be interpreted by the counselor as overdependence. Continuing to live in the same neighborhood should be understood objectively as cultural loyalty rather than an inability to function on one's own (Lum, 1986).

Again, it should be remembered that the vast diversity among Hispanic-American children warrants special attention to individual populations. Cuban children, for example, "tend to be outgoing, warm, expressive, talented, versatile, and resourceful. . . . eager to learn, and they respect authority and accept graciously any corrections and suggestions for their improvement" (Klovekorn, Madera, and Nardone, 1974, p. 256).

Language

Spanish-speaking children experience several problems that can be traced to the culture's allegiance to the "mother tongue." Spanish is spoken at home; English, at school. Substituting English for Spanish may be perceived as being disloyal to the culture. Children trying to juggle two languages may experience chronic anxiety. The child, however, may have no way out if English is required at school and if the family is unable to speak English well enough to cope in today's society (Padilla, 1981).

The problems associated with language can have several damaging effects. Not believing their language is "good enough" to use outside the home can cause children to doubt their own worth. Also, academic achievement and intelligence test scores can suffer if the child cannot understand the English-speaking teacher or read the textbook and other materials written in English (Maes & Rinaldi, 1974). A third problem is that Spanish-speaking groups may lack the English vocabulary to give adequate expression to their feelings (Klovekorn et al., 1974).

Family Issues

In what family issues might Hispanic-American children find themselves involved? How can family situations lead to counseling intervention? While the family expects allegiance to such values as familism, spirituality, personalism, and hierarchical social arrangements, the children may have experienced some degree of acculturation; hence, they may be inclined to question traditional values. In Hispanic-American families, males have a greater authority than females. Cousins are sometimes as close as brothers and sisters. Household chores are assigned to children early on, and they are expected to get along with other children and care for younger brothers and sisters (Ho, 1987). For the Hispanic-American child growing up in a predominantly Anglo society, family expectations may seem increasingly unreasonable, especially as peers come to play a more central role in the child's life.

Developmental and Other Concerns

Developing children are likely to have difficulty in successfully coping if they are burdened with language problems, poor self-concepts, and oppression. Psychosocial development may be retarded if peers consider Hispanic-American children as inferior "illegals" or as troublemakers.

What other potential problems deserve the counselor's attention? The relatively low socioeconomic status of many Hispanic-American families often results in a lack of personal resources (Valero-Figueira, 1988). Growing up in conditions of poverty with the head of the household out of work negatively affects all aspects of development. Also, reconciling family loyalties with individual desires during a time of transition from a parent-centered world to a peer-centered world can result in problems for the developing child.

Counseling Considerations

Counseling Hispanic-American children requires knowledge of individual Hispanic cultures whenever possible. Although Hispanics may be considered a single cultural group due to their similarities in language, values, and traditions, this culture also represents an aggregate of heterogeneous subcultures, each possessing a recognizable pattern of unique traits (Ruiz & Padilla, 1977).

Understanding two important cultural characteristics of Hispanic-Americans is prerequisite to effective counseling. First, many children in the Hispanic-American culture distrust and are hostile toward Anglo-American professionals to some degree, which may result in a hesitancy to disclose personal information. Second, it is imperative not to "misread" the Hispanic's nonverbal behavior patterns; e.g., avoiding eye contact, standing close while speaking, and touching (Padilla, 1981).

In counseling Cuban-American children, the counselor should be aware that Cuban-American families are usually concerned about their children's academic progress and are often cooperative because they tend to value the teacher's position and role. The counselor should ease into discussions of problem areas, since Cuban families may be apprehensive and uncertain about the counseling process (Klovekorn et al., 1974).

Individual/Group Therapy

What should the counselor consider when planning intervention with Hispanic-American children? Professionals will want to assist these children in coping with changing demands on them. Klovekorn et al. (1974) use the example of Maria to illustrate the approach of one counselor. Maria, a non-English-speaking second-grader, attended a school in which 60 percent of the children were African-American, 35 percent were of Spanish origin, and 5 percent were from other cultures. Maria was referred to the counselor because she would not speak. First, the counselor, who was bilingual, sought to gain Maria's confidence and to learn the cause of the problem. The problem was simple yet complicated: When Maria tried in Spanish to ask Alicia, the girl sitting next to her, what the teacher wanted her to do, Alicia replied that she could not tell her in Spanish because she would be punished if she spoke Spanish. Again, the language problem surfaced. Only English was spoken in the classroom and Spanish would not be recognized. The counselor, concluding there was little Maria could do to alleviate the situation, met with Maria's teacher in the hope of convincing the teacher that non-English-speaking children should be permitted to express themselves freely in the language that was natural for them. Also, the counselor explained that Maria could both improve academically and socially through interaction with classmates.

In counseling Chicano-American children, Maes & Rinaldi (1974) point out four counseling priorities they believe to be most important: (1) language and cognitive development, (2) expansion of career-choice options, (3) personal respect and pride in the Chicano culture, and (4) personal value exploration. Although these authors caution that value should not be placed on one priority at the expense of another, they maintain that counselors' respecting and conveying an appreciation for a child's cultural heritage can have a positive impact on children and their developing identities and self-concepts.

What should be required of counselors working with Hispanic-American children? Although referring specifically to counselors of Chicano-American children, the following three requirements apply to counselors of other Spanish-speaking cultures: (1) the ability to speak both English and Spanish fluently (highly desirable); (2) first-hand experience with and an understanding of the culture; and (3) helping characteristics, such as empathy, warmth, positive regard, congruence, and authenticity (Maes & Rinaldi, 1974).

Hispanic - Grp therapy

Group therapy has helped Hispanic clients work toward solving personal problems and expanding personal awareness. School counselors often perceive group counseling as particularly effective for furthering Hispanic-American children's skills in expressing their feelings in English, stimulating self-respect and pride in Hispanic culture, and clarifying personal values (Padilla, 1981).

Family Therapy

The belief that a dysfunction within the family affects all family members in some manner especially holds true for Hispanic-American families. Including all children in family therapy, not just the child with the problem, is imperative for effective family counseling. The complex relationships surrounding the immediate and extended Hispanic families contribute to the effectiveness of family counseling (Thompson & Rudolph, 1988).

The cultural concept of familism is so important that Hispanics are taught early to sacrifice self-interest in the effort to help other family members and the family unit as a whole. Satir's theory focusing on the "feeling good" component of each individual and the entire family should greatly appeal to Hispanic-American clients (Ho, 1987).

◆ UP CLOSE AND PERSONAL 5–4
Counseling Ramon Suarez

Eight year-old Ramon was referred to the Anglo school counselor by his teacher, who was concerned about Ramon's academic achievement, language problems, and self-concept. "I don't know what to do with Ramon," Mr. Perkins complained, "I encourage him, yet he just doesn't seem interested." After reading the referral sheet and speaking with Ramon, the counselor concluded that the child did, indeed, have problems: low-income family, poor grades, weak self-concept, and language difficulties. Plus, Ramon gave every indication of not trusting the counselor or the teacher!

The counselor, realizing he had to begin slowly, encouraged Ramon to speak and to trust him. In early sessions, the counselor chose to emphasize Ramon and his cultural background: his family, his language, and his life. Ramon hesitatingly began to trust and to speak—much to the counselor's surprise, in mixed English and Spanish. The counselor learned that Ramon came from a traditional Puerto Rican family where Spanish was spoken in the home. The counselor also saw evidence of Ramon's reading difficulties and behavior problems.

The counselor decided that he had to work to improve Ramon's self-concept and arrange appropriate English instruction and remedial tutoring to help him catch up academically. The counselor recognized that he would have to proceed cautiously to convince Ramon that he could still maintain his cultural identity and respect without getting into fights with other children. Finally, the counselor decided to arrange a conference with Ramon's parents who possibly could help the boy if they knew exactly what to do. Although little could be done about Spanish being spoken in the home, the counselor would explain to the parents the conflict Ramon experienced due to the dual language situation.

To enhance the effectiveness of family counseling with Hispanic-Americans, the counselor should (a) respect the family's hierarchical structure by interviewing parents first and children second; (b) communicate in Spanish with the parents and in English with the children to delineate blurred generational boundaries; (c) use the polite form of the pronoun "you" with adults to indicate respect, reserving the familiar form for use with children (Falicov, 1982); and (d) recognize that Hispanics are taught to be cooperative and "other-centered" in interpersonal relationships (Ho, 1987).

A POINT OF DEPARTURE

Challenges Confronting Multicultural Counselors of Children

Counselors planning to work with culturally diverse children face several challenges. First, the childhood years on the lifespan, which historically have received little attention, must be perceived as a critical developmental period for forming individual and cultural identities. Second, in every cultural group, there will be intracultural differences—generational, socioeconomic, and geographical differences. The counselor who strives to understand differing cultures and subcultures will be more likely to plan effective multicultural counseling.

SUMMARY

Counseling culturally diverse children can be a rewarding experience if counselors understand children's developmental levels and cultural backgrounds. The multicultural child's lack of trust, especially of Anglo-American counselors, presents a barrier that can usually be dealt with by caring counselors who are ready to spend the time required to learn the reasons for the distrust and then to exhibit the patience needed to establish rapport. With the proper formal training, knowledge, skills, and attitudes, the counselor can intervene effectively, taking into account both the child's cultural background and developmental level.

Suggested Readings

Disasa, J. (1988). African children's attitude toward learning. *Journal of Multicultural Counseling and Development, 16,* 16–23. This interesting reading provides considerable insight into African children's societal role, their parents' role, and the children's attitudes toward education.

Elementary School Guidance and Counseling. (April 1989 [Special issue]). Counselors working with children will benefit from this special issue on multicultural children. Several readings on counseling elementary-age children in the various cultural groups are included. The issue also includes an excellent bibliography and a position statement on multicultural counseling.

Herring, R. D. (1989b). Counseling Native-American children: Implications for elementary school counselors. *Elementary School Guidance and Counseling, 23,* 272–281. Maintaining that Native-American children face cultural and ethnic barriers, Herring looks at the present condition of Native-American learners and suggests implications for elementary school counselors.

Lazarus, P. J. (1982). Counseling the Native-American child: A question of values. *Elementary School Guidance and Counseling, 17,* 83–88. Lazarus looks specifically at the values of Native-American children as they pertain to the provision of elementary school counseling services.

Lee, C. C., & Lindsey, C. R. (1985). Black consciousness development: A group counseling model for Black elementary school students. *Elementary School Guidance and Counseling, 19,* 228–236. These authors relate African-American children's experiences, provide background information on the culture, and offer a practical counseling model.

Omizo, M. M., & Omizo, S. A. (1989). Counseling Hawaiian children. *Elementary School Guidance and Counseling, 23,* 282–288. Omizo and Omizo describe the problems Hawaiian children may experience, examine cultural differences in values, and offer an extensive list of recommendations for elementary school counselors.

Thompson, C. L., & Rudolph, L. B. (1988). *Counseling children* (2nd ed.). Pacific Grove, CA: Brooks/Cole. This comprehensive counseling text focuses on the counseling process, the various types of therapy, and group/family counseling—an excellent resource for counselors of children.

Part II

Understanding and Counseling the Adolescent

The main thrust of Part II is toward enhancing the reader's understanding of culturally diverse adolescents and their developmental period. To achieve this end, Chapter 6 examines adolescents' cultural characteristics, language, and families. Chapter 7 explores the counseling strategies that may be most appropriate for culturally diverse clients at this developmental stage.

Chapter 6

Social and Cultural Aspects of Adolescence

Questions To Be Explored

1. What is the nature of the developmental period of adolescence?
2. What evidence suggests an adolescent "subculture"?
3. What historical and cultural factors affect adolescence?
4. What adolescent and cultural stereotypes must counselors recognize?
5. What are the adolescent years like in the Native-American, African-American, Asian-American, and Hispanic-American cultures?
6. What challenges confront multicultural counselors working with adolescents?
7. What are additional sources of information for counselors working with culturally diverse adolescents?

INTRODUCTION

Adolescence, both as a term and a recognized concept, is relatively new and clouded with obscurities. Lack of agreement on when adolescence begins and ends has contributed to the confusion surrounding this lifespan period. Without doubt, however, before the last two decades of the nineteenth century, adolescence was barely even recognized as a legitimate developmental period between childhood and adulthood. This chapter explores the concept of adolescence, examines its social and cultural aspects, and focuses attention on the adolescent years in the Native-American, African-American, Asian-American, and Hispanic-American cultures.

The Adolescent Years: Historical and Cultural Influences

A Product of Modern Times

The relatively recent appearance of adolescence as an accepted period of development is attested to by Bakan (1971):

> The idea of adolescence as an intermediary period starting at puberty and extending to
> some period in the life cycle unmarked by any conspicuous physical change but socially
> defined as "manhood" or "womanhood" is a product of modern times. (p. 979)

Although contemporary cultures generally agree that adolescence begins at age
12 and ends at age 18, being considered a child in some situations and an adult in
others contributed to a problem of confused identity in which an individual may
question whether behavior should be childlike or adultlike. Difficulties may also arise
when adolescents consider themselves to be grown while parents, teachers, counselors, and other authority figures consider them to be children.

The Role of Culture

Although several factors contribute to this developmental period being a difficult
time of life, the young person's culture will, of course, play a significant role in
determining the extent of the difficulty. For example, Western society may allow for
a longer childhood than, for example, Asian and Hispanic cultures, which may require
individuals to enter the employment market earlier to assist with family finances, or
which may expect them to play a more active role in household responsibilities at
an earlier age.

Being an adolescent member of a minority group in the United States can be
very trying, especially when mainstream values of individualism and materialism
conflict with cultural values taught in the home. For example, consider the dilemma
of Mexican-American adolescents whose culture stresses family ties and dependency,
living in the present, and honor, as opposed to the values needed for success in a
society emphasizing independence and achievement, deferred gratification, and util-
itarian ethics (Lloyd, 1985).

Is There an Adolescent Subculture?

The behavior of adolescents raises the question of whether this group of individuals
should be considered a unique subculture. Many adolescents demonstrate behavior
patterns that not only distinguish them from adults, but that also seem to reject adult
culture (Lefrancois, 1981).

A complex relationship exists between adolescents' development, their cultural
backgrounds, and their subculture. For instance, the Asian-American adolescent often
experiences difficulty conforming to subcultural expectations which may be contrary
to the family's expectations. The Anglo-American tends to value materialistic possessions, while the Asian-American places a greater emphasis on spiritual values. Yet, in
all cultures, feeling "liked" or feeling accepted by one's peer group is fundamental
to the development of a positive identity and self-image. And adolescents of all cultural
backgrounds experience frustration as some people perceive them as children, while
others consider them adults.

Some observers of adolescent behavior have questioned whether an adolescent subculture actually exists. Although differences in adolescent and adult behavior and lifestyles are readily discernible, the wide variability in adolescents' attitudes and experiences due to sex, age, class, and individual differences indicates that it is probably inaccurate to speak of a specific youth subculture, except in superficial terms. Nonetheless, adolescents' preferences with respect to dress, manner of speech, and music do not allow the idea of an adolescent subculture to be totally dismissed (Lloyd, 1985).

Adolescent Problems and Alienation

Some adolescents experience problems that may result in delinquent or other undesirable behavior. Most of these behaviors involve such infractions of the law as underage drinking, smoking pot, stealing, or vandalism. At the same time, however, youths are responsible for a significant number of more serious offenses such as arson and burglary. Less than 10 percent of the offenders are ever arrested and taken to juvenile court (Gold & Petronio, 1980). Other adolescent problems include depression due to school failure, anxiety, antisocial behavior, teenage pregnancy, and poor peer relations. Along the same lines, adolescent suicide has quadrupled in the last thirty years. Adolescent males are more likely to commit suicide and females are more likely to threaten such behavior (Santrock, 1990). It is clear that adolescents from minority cultures are apt to experience problems that could lead to depression and ultimately to suicide given their limited opportunities and the discrimination they are faced with.

The issue of adolescent alienation has become a major problem for contemporary society. Adolescent alienation stems from the inability to self-regulate and control one's life activities in the contexts of work, family, education, and the community. Alienation may be demonstrated by any number of antisocial behaviors, or by depression or even suicide. It is important to examine the relationship of adolescent alienation to the significant problems or issues that involve adolescents. For example, strained relationships between youths and their parents seem to be linked to adolescent alienation. Likewise, drug abuse, alcohol abuse, and teenage sexual activity might suggest a pattern of behavior leading to alienation (Schiamberg, 1986). Although the issue of adolescent alienation has not been definitively settled, one can conclude that culturally diverse adolescents might experience alienation or the conditions leading to alienation. Rejection by the peer group or the perception that one's cultural background is inferior can result in feelings of isolation and powerlessness to effect change in a majority-culture society.

NATIVE-AMERICAN ADOLESCENTS

Societal and Cultural Description

Although both "Indian" and "adolescent" tend to evoke stereotypic images, the Native-American culture and the developmental period are highly diversified. While there is significant physical and cultural variance within the Native-American population, differences in individuals during the adolescent years are even more marked. Not all Native-Americans are slow learners, shy, undependable, or rebellious. Although some common characteristics emerge when studying Native-American adolescents, one must be careful not to oversimplify or to ignore intracultural and individual differences.

Societal and cultural beliefs and traditions of the Native-American people particularly influence the developing adolescent and his or her evolving identity. Adolescents living in Native-American families and attending Anglo-American schools experience cultural confusion and often question allegiance to a cultural identity (Sanders, 1987). This can be particularly serious for adolescents wanting to retain their rich cultural heritage, and at the same time be accepted in the Anglo-American mainstream.

Although some acculturation undoubtedly has occurred, several Native-American cultural characteristics contributing to the adolescent's evolving identity include tendencies toward passive temperaments, noninterference, and sharing. These cultural characteristics have the potential for affecting identity development, especially when the adolescent is surrounded by Anglo-American adolescents and teachers who might expect conformity to their cultural values.

Patience and Passive Temperaments. Native-American adolescents are taught to be patient, to control emotions, and to avoid passionate outbursts over small matters. Such attributes as poise under duress, self-containment, and aloofness often conflict with the Anglo-American tendencies toward impatience and competitiveness. The result is that the Native-American is often considered lazy, uncaring, and inactive (Lewis & Ho, 1989). Patience and poise are demonstrated in the Native-Americans' tendency to lower their voices when angry, unlike Anglo-American adolescents who tend to become strident in expressing their anger (Kostelnik, Stein, Whiren, & Soderman, 1988).

Noninterference with Others. Noninterference with others and a deep respect for the rights and dignity of individuals constitute a basic premise of Native-American culture (Banks, 1987). Adolescents are taught early to respect the rights and privileges of other individuals and the responsibility of working together toward common goals in harmony with nature.

Sharing. Sharing, representing a genuine and routine way of life for Native-Americans, does not equate with the Anglo-American custom of accumulating private property or savings. The Anglo-American's "worth" and social status are often measured in terms of amount of material possessions, while the Native-American considers a person's ability and willingness to share to be most worthy (Lewis and Ho, 1989).

The problem of high school dropouts is not unique to Native-Americans; however, among this cultural group, the dropout rate is high, regardless of region or tribal affiliation. Low self-esteem, directly related to group identity, is considered by some to be a major cause of the low school achievement records of Native-American

---

A FOCUS ON RESEARCH 6–1
Native-American High School Dropouts

Coladarci (1983) sought to determine the factors contributing to the high-school dropout rate (over 60 percent) of Native-American students who constituted roughly 90 percent of the student body in a Montana high school. Working from school records, a list was compiled of 224 students who had dropped out of school over the past three years. A questionnaire was administered in the form of an interview, so students would not be required to read. Findings indicated that (a) over a third of the dropouts reported an uneven application of school rules; (b) teacher-student relationships were often poor (e.g., teachers did not provide sufficient assistance); (c) students sometimes disagreed with teachers; and (d) students perceived the content of the schooling as not important to what they wanted to do in life.

Source: Coladarci, T. (1983). High-school dropouts among Native-Americans. *Journal of American Indian Education,* *23,* 15–21.

---

adolescents (Sanders, 1987). A FOCUS ON RESEARCH 6–1 examines reasons for the dropout problem.

Factors undoubtedly contributing to the high dropout rate include growing feelings of isolation, cultural conflicts between Native-American adolescents and Anglo-American teachers, cultural and individual rejection, and anxiety resulting from differences in cultural values (Sanders, 1987). A FOCUS ON RESEARCH 6–2 examines cultural conflicts between Native-American adolescents and their teachers.

Language

Native-Americans, like adolescents of other cultures, need the security and psychological safety provided by a common language. However, some Native-American adolescents speak only their Native-American language, some speak only English, and others are bilingual. Both self-concepts and individual and cultural identities are being formed during the adolescent's transition from the family-centered world to a wider social world. No longer is communication limited to that with elders, parents, and siblings. The Native-American adolescent's ability to reach out to a wider world depends greatly on his or her ability to speak and understand the language of the majority and other cultures (Youngman & Sadongei, 1983).

Attending a school staffed with Anglo-American teachers and facing the problems associated with not being understood may affect the adolescent's perceived ability to cope successfully in a predominantly Anglo-American world. Language problems also might contribute to the adolescent's tendency to decline in academic achievement, especially since lack of cognitive and academic skills do not appear to be major factors (Sanders, 1987). A FOCUS ON RESEARCH 6–3 describes a study designed to determine specific problems Native-Americans experience with English.

A FOCUS ON RESEARCH 6–2
Cultural Conflicts of Native-American Adolescents

After reviewing the literature on cultural clashes between Anglo- and Native-American students in predominantly Anglo schools, Sanders (1987) describes how conflict contributed to negative self-concepts and examines the learner's failure to achieve academically. A comparison is offered below.

Sanders suggests that teachers exert a major influence on students' success or failure and that educators should be aware of cultural diversity and conflicts. They should accommodate the goals of education while allowing Native-American students to preserve their values and feelings of self-worth.

Native-American Adolescents	Anglo-American Adolescents
Speak softly, at a slower rate	Louder and faster speech
Avoid direct confrontation	Address listener directly, often by name
Interject less	Interrupt frequently
Use fewer "encouraging signs"	Use verbal encouragement
Do not respond as quickly	Respond immediately
Rely on nonverbal communication to a greater extent	Prize verbal skills
Cooperate	Compete
Consider group needs more important	Consider personal goals more important
Work toward immediate goals	Plan for future
Encourage sharing	Need to acquire personal possessions
Value privacy and noninterference	Need to exert control
Exhibit patience—let others go first	Tend to be aggressive and impatient

Source: Sanders, D. (1987). Cultural conflicts: An important factor in the academic failures of American Indian students. *Journal of Multicultural Counseling and Development, 15,* 81–90.

Another language problem results when adolescents must decide which language to speak. Native-Americans consider their language to be a crucial aspect of their culture and a cherished gift that should be used whenever possible (Richardson, 1981). However, this regard for their native language conflicts with the Anglo-American opinion that English is the Native-American's means to success (or, at least, the Anglo definition of success) and should be the predominant language.

Families

Native-American adolescents place a high priority on immediate and extended family relationships. Although the adolescent's developing social consciousness results in a gradual transition from a family-centered to a more peer-centered environment, the traditional Native-American respect and commitment to the family continues (Lum, 1986). Young people seek social acceptance and approval from older members of the family as well as from the younger family members. Unlike the Anglo-American culture that emphasizes youth and the self, the Native-American places family before self and has a great respect for elders and their wisdom. Wisdom is to be gained through interaction with the older people, whose task it is to acquaint the young with traditions, customs, legends, and myths of the culture. All members of a family care for the old and accept death as a natural fact of life (Axelson, 1985).

Early training received by Native-American adolescents continues to have an impact during the adolescent years. Although the loyalty to and dependence upon the immediate and surrounding family continue to be valued, adolescents grow increasingly independent and confident of their abilities to deal with the world outside the family. Their early training, however, might contribute to their confusion. For example, some cultures might have difficulty understanding the Native-American's belief that great wealth and materialistic possessions should not be accumulated at the expense of sharing with one's fellow human beings. Likewise, self-gain cannot be at the expense of family or tribal members, or at the expense of harming any aspect of the natural world.

Unique Challenges Confronting Native-American Adolescents

The Native-American adolescent is in a unique and often difficult situation. Not only must the cultural values of the Native-American and the Anglo-American cultures be reconciled, but the usual problems of adolescence as a developmental period on the lifespan continuum must also be dealt with.

Educational and societal dilemmas as well as cultural conflicts during these crucial developmental years often result in feelings of frustration, hopelessness, alienation, and loss of confidence. Teachers having little or no experience with Native-

---

◤ A FOCUS ON RESEARCH 6–3
Recommendations for Working with Native-Americans with English Problems

Maintaining that few studies examine the language problems of Native-Americans, Fletcher (1983) designed a survey to determine the specific problems American Indians experience in learning English, which is required for survival in a modern technological world. Recommendations from the study suggested that Native-Americans need practice with (a) minimally contrasting vowel pairs and contrasting consonant pairs and (b) selected phonemes (which do not exist in some Indian languages), irregular pronoun forms, selected verb tenses, third-person singular pronouns, prepositions, and basic vocabulary.

Source: Fletcher, J. D. (1983). What problems do American Indians have with English? *Journal of American Indian Education, 23*, 1–12.

Table 6–1 Cultural comparison: Native-American and Anglo-American adolescents

Native-American Adolescents	Anglo-American Adolescents
Avoid eye contact	Indicate listening by looking speaker directly in the eye
Regard dance as a religious expression	Regard dance as primarily an art form
"I will share with you."	"I have mine. You get yours."
Put family first	Are more peer-centered
Question which culture to identify with	Are secure in their cultural identification
Show great respect for elders	View elders as having lost touch with "the real world"
Are willing to wait; patient	Demand more immediate need gratification
Lower their voices to make a point	Raise their voices to make a point

Source: Adapted from Richardson, E. H. (1981). Cultural and historical perspectives in counseling American Indians. In D. W. Sue, *Counseling the Culturally Different* (pp. 225–227). New York: John Wiley.

American cultural characteristics may judge these adolescents to be shy, retiring, or unmotivated. The adolescent's frequent steady decline in academic achievement may contribute to even greater feelings of hopelessness and frustration (Sanders, 1987).

Three specific issues with particular relevance for Native-American adolescents are the following: (1) whether Native-American or Anglo-American values (or some "cultural combination") should provide the basis for the adolescent's developing identity; (2) whether proficiency in both the Native-American language *and* English should be encouraged; and (3) whether harmony with family and nature can be maintained while surviving in the Anglo-American world. Survival in the majority culture often requires Native-Americans to question the priorities of their own culture. Table 6–1 provides a cultural comparison of Native-American and Anglo-American adolescents. UP CLOSE AND PERSONAL 6–1 introduces Carl Lonetree.

AFRICAN-AMERICAN ADOLESCENTS

Societal and Cultural Description

Being both an adolescent and an African-American in a predominantly Anglo society can carry both a cultural and a developmental stigma. African-American adolescents are often portrayed as school dropouts, drug abusers, and lawbreakers. It is imperative that counselors recognize the considerable individual differences among African-American adolescents, rather than automatically stereotyping them. Negative stereotypes used to describe the African-American culture and the adolescent lifespan period lower the self-esteem of these adolescents; they must be given a fair opportunity to develop positive cultural and individual identities.

◆ UP CLOSE AND PERSONAL 6–1
Carl Lonetree — A Native-American Adolescent

Carl, Bill's 15-year-old brother, lives with his parents, sister, and, of course, Bill. The elderly grandmother continues to live with the Lonetree family. They still live several miles from the reservation and continue to have some financial difficulty.

Carl, in the middle of his adolescent years, has problems Bill has yet to experience. Although Carl was a relatively small child, his growth spurt began at about age 12, accompanied by considerable physical and psychosocial change. He thinks about these changes and does not always understand what is happening. He wonders whether all the changes are normal. Sometimes he admits to feelings of confusion. How can I be a child, an adolescent, *and* an adult? Carl asks himself.

Carl is in the eighth grade for the second time. Although he thought he was trying last year, the schoolwork was more difficult and he experienced language problems. In fact, language may be his greatest problem. He thinks his "choice of language" will depend on where he lives when he grows up. He will speak the Native-American language if he returns to the reservation; he will speak English if he lives in the local community. Meanwhile, he speaks the Native-American language with his grandmother (and sometimes with his father) and speaks English at school.

Carl is thinking of joining the Indian League organization when he turns sixteen. The group is concerned with the civil rights of Native-Americans and generally promotes their interests. Carl's dad thinks he will still be too young, and that finishing school and speaking English might be best for Carl. Secretly, Carl knows that he will not join if his grandmother opposes the idea. Disappointing his grandmother would not be worth joining the group. And, after all, she has always given him good advice in the past.

Carl has experienced a few problems at school. His teachers continue to write notes on his report cards referring to his lack of interest. Carl thinks he is interested and motivated, but the issue is not worth confronting the teachers. Also, he has tried to make friends with some of the Anglo-American adolescents, but has not experienced a great deal of success.

Carl wonders about the future. Will he return to the reservation? Will he be able to speak the Native-American language, English, or both? Will he ever pass the eighth grade? Will he have Anglo friends? These questions continue to plague Carl.

African-Americans often face overt and blatant racism that has been handed down for generations. In fact, the reality of their social situation has even led African-Americans, themselves, to resort to racial aspersions (Smith, 1981). Undoubtedly, this self-defeating pattern of behavior lowers adolescent aspirations and undermines efforts toward achieving desired goals.

If counselors understand the African-American culture, they will appreciate the predicament of many African-American adolescents. These adolescents want to retain the cultural heritage with which they feel comfortable; however, they may also feel that some acculturation must take place for economic and psychological survival. A balance must be struck whereby African-American adolescents can retain their African heritage, and at the same time achieve success in contemporary multicultural or pluralistic society.

Language

Language constitutes another distinctive cultural characteristic. Appreciation of one's own language, along with the development of communication skills sufficient for understanding and being understood, significantly influences a person's self-concept. Emphasis should be placed on understanding and accepting the value the client places on his or her language rather than subscribing to a language-deficit belief in which some languages are judged to be "unworthy" and destined for extinction.

The dialect of African-Americans, sometimes called Black English, is used in varying degrees depending on the individual person and the situation. Its widespread use among African-Americans at all socioeconomic levels continues to arouse concern among people not understanding the language, its background, and the African-American culture. Although some of these concerns result from a lack of knowledge and appreciation of the language, some educators question whether the contrast between Black English and standard English may possibly result in severe consequences for African-American students (Weber, 1985). A FOCUS ON RESEARCH 6–4 poses the question of whether the dialect impedes learning progress in science and mathematics.

The grammatical structure of African-American speech patterns frequently leads listeners to conclude that a genuine structural pattern does not exist. Linguists acquainted with the various vernaculars and African-American dialects realize the fallacy

---

A FOCUS ON RESEARCH 6–4
Is Black English Standing in the Way of Learning?

In her publication *Twice as Less,* Eleanor Wilson Orr, co-founder of a private high school in Washington, DC, asks the question: Does Black English stand between African-American students and success in mathematics and science? Long thought to inhibit African-Americans' learning to read, Black English is now thought to inhibit them in learning mathematics. Orr's book proved to be both controversial and timely. As she pointed out, African-American students are being classified as "learning disabled" in disproportionately high numbers.

Source: Heys, S. (1988, February 14). Is Black English standing in the way of learning? *The State Newspaper* (Columbia, SC) 1B, 6.

Possibly related to this is the fact that studies have shown that Black English is continuing to evolve away from standard English despite earlier predictions that television, radio, and movies would serve as a homogenizing influence on language in the United States.

Orr contends that the lack of prepositions, conjunctions, and relative pronouns in Black English does not allow speakers to communicate effectively in mathematics and science. Although solutions to this problem are not readily apparent, Orr does recommend that teachers be educated as to the differences between Black English and standard English that lead to misunderstandings.

of such thinking. In a classic and comprehensive study of the African-American's English dialect, Dillard (1972) contends that the African-American speaker saying "Mary hat" and "he book" does, indeed, have as much knowledge of the possessive case as the speaker saying "Mary's hat" and "his book."

Many Anglo-Americans have sought to "change" or even eliminate the African-American dialect. Some, no doubt with good intentions, have sought to "help" African-Americans by teaching them standard English. The African-American dialect, however, has withstood attempts to eradicate it; it persists as an integral aspect of the African-American culture. Why has this dialect proven so durable? First, it provides a vehicle for expressing the uniqueness of the African-American culture. Second, it binds African-Americans together and reaches across the barriers of education and social position (Weber, 1985). What position should counselors and other professionals working with African-American adolescents take? Rather than perceiving the dialect as wrong or substandard, the counselor should help these adolescents understand that Black English is a unique and valuable aspect of their culture. As they develop into adulthood and into an ever-widening social world, they must also be made to realize the implications of using a language that is not wholeheartedly accepted by the majority culture. During this crucial time of moving away from the safe confines of family and home, adolescents will benefit from speaking a language that is accepted and understood outside the predominantly African-American community. Feeling and being understood in their own community, but being rejected by the prevailing culture has the potential for damaging self-concepts and retarding development.

Families

Counselors intervening with African-American adolescents need to understand the African-American family from a historical perspective rather than allowing misconceptions and stereotypes to cloud their perception. First, throughout centuries of cultural oppression and repression, the African-American family has developed, perhaps through necessity rather than choice, a network of "significant others" who have close ties and are willing to assist. The family plays a critical role in determining the adolescent's capacity and readiness to develop a sense of self and an identity (Conger, 1977). A second aspect of African-American family life is the large number of people often living in the same household. In the extended network, visiting is encouraged. Relatives are welcome to stay, often for long periods of time.

Considerable concern has been expressed for the adolescent's identity formation, especially in African-American households and in father-absent homes. Disturbing numbers of African-American families live in poverty and, increasingly, families are headed by females. Evidence indicates, however, that African-American adolescents might not be as detrimentally affected by female-headed households as once believed. Generally, the fathers and the extended family and kinship network continue to play a role in their lives (Bell-Scott & McKenry, 1986). The physical presence or absence of adult males in the home also says little about the availability of other male models. Adolescent males living in female-headed households often identify male role models in their extended families, in their neighborhoods, in their classrooms, and even from instruction from their mothers (Rubin, 1977).

Understanding African-American family customs contributes to effective counseling intervention. Also, both Anglo-American counselors and counselors from other cultures will benefit from an objective understanding of the developmental period of adolescence. It should be recognized that all African-American adolescents do not experience role confusion. They are not all poverty-stricken or uneducated. Nor do they all suffer from living in single-parent households. African-American adolescents must be perceived in a more objective light.

Unique Challenges Confronting African-American Adolescents

Several challenges facing African-American adolescents will significantly influence their identity development and their transition into adulthood. First, they must accept the challenge of combating the racism and discrimination that have plagued their culture for decades. A related challenge is for adolescents to reject stereotypes of their culture and developmental period. Buying into misperceptions and stereotypes precludes an objective examination of one's personal abilities, and, without doubt, may retard the development of a cultural identity and a strong self-concept. A third challenge is to develop an identity that embodies the African-American culture; the adolescent; and individual abilities, skills, and characteristics. To do otherwise results in role confusion and a loss of potential.

African-American adolescents also are challenged to appreciate the value of education in their lives. Many of them believe that time in school is wasted time—especially those attending poorly staffed, dilapidated schools. Adolescents living in

Table 6–2 Cultural comparison: African-American and Anglo-American adolescents

African-American Adolescents	Anglo-American Adolescents
Do not perceive themselves in need of change; that is, their cultural values and characteristics	Perceives African-Americans as needing to change their cultural values and characteristics
Usually (but not always) do not do as well academically	Usually (but not always) do better academically
Have strong extended family and kinship network	Rely on immediate family
Are subject to stereotypes regarding both their race and developmental period	Are subject to stereotypes regarding only their developmental period
Face overt and blatant racism	Rarely face racism
Value Black English as a part of their culture	Value standard English—the language of the majority
Are usually subject to more authoritarian childrearing styles	Are usually subject to less authoritarian childrearing styles

Sources: Data compiled from Axelson, 1985; Boykin, 1982; Hall, 1981; Pinkney, 1975.

poor neighborhoods often perceive little reward from working for academic achievement and may underestimate their opportunities (Jaynes & Williams, 1989). It is imperative for these students to understand individual potential and the benefits of education.

Table 6–2 provides a cultural comparison of African-American and Anglo-American adolescents. UP CLOSE AND PERSONAL 6–2 focuses on Tyrone, an African-American adolescent.

UP CLOSE AND PERSONAL 6–2
Tyrone Johnson—An African-American Adolescent

Tyrone Johnson, a 16-year-old ninth-grade African-American adolescent, lives with his parents, younger brother, and two younger sisters. Since most of Tyrone's relatives also live in the lower middle-class neighborhood, he enjoys the extended family network. Tyrone feels free to visit his relatives in their homes and they often spend time at his house. When Tyrone cannot attend school because of illness, he usually goes to the home of his adolescent cousins.

Tyrone has experienced several "identity crises." He has questioned his success in developing from childhood to adulthood and he has also questioned the significance of being African-American in a predominantly Anglo-American world. Although he has learned a great deal about his cultural heritage and is proud of being an African-American, he also realizes that racism and discrimination will very likely limit his opportunities. Also, being adolescent has not been easy. While his parents and siblings view him as "not yet grown," his peers think he is ready for adult activities. Should he listen to his family, or should he go along with his friends?

Another problem confronting Tyrone is his education. Quite frankly, he is not sure he will graduate from high school. His grades in elementary school were below average, but his grades are even lower now, and this is his second year in the ninth grade. He thinks he could do the work, but his recent academic record discourages him and he admits to a changing world of many interests. He does not have many behavior problems with his teachers (except perhaps talking with his friends too much at times), yet he feels his teachers are not too interested in him. Also, although he has both African-American and Anglo-American teachers, he doubts if any of them really understand what it's like being an African-American adolescent in a large school. His parents talk to him often about the importance of school and encourage him to do his best work, but neither parent is able to help him much with homework.

Tyrone continues to speak his dialect. He communicates well with his parents, his extended family, and his friends. In fact, he is proud of his Black English, even though his teachers don't like it. Language puzzles Tyrone though. The Anglo-American teachers "don't sound right," he says. It appears, though, that he will have to be the one to change.

Although Tyrone has not confided in his friends, he has several concerns. What will he do if he can't improve his grades? Since the teachers insist that he speak a more standard form of English, can he still maintain his cultural heritage? Will he be able to accommodate his parents' insistence for academic achievement, his own motivation, and the expectations of his peers? Sometimes, Tyrone actually wishes the adolescent years would end so he could begin his adult life.

ASIAN-AMERICAN ADOLESCENTS

Societal and Cultural Description

As mentioned in Chapter 1, Asian-Americans have been victims of appalling forms of discrimination. Finding their new environment hostile and threatening, the early immigrants voluntarily and in some instances, involuntarily, isolated themselves from the larger society (Banks, 1987). Often they were forced to accept the lowest paid menial jobs and were denied the right of citizenship and to ownership of land. Without opportunity to live and work in Anglo communities, Asian-Americans often formed their own cultural enclaves, such as Chinatown. In these isolated enclaves, they continued to speak only their native language, maintaining their old-world traditions (Sue, 1981).

Asian-American adolescents, much like African-American adolescents, must overcome a stereotype that has the potential for affecting their identity formation, self-concept, and the manner in which others perceive them. The enviable academic success of many Asian-Americans has led to a perception that all Asian-Americans are bound to succeed in all their pursuits. To make this assumption on the basis of culture alone, however, does not have any greater validity than assuming that all African-Americans are incapable of high academic achievement or that all Native-Americans live on reservations. The generational differences between adolescents and their parents (and grandparents) also influence identity formation. More will be said about this later.

The contemporary image of Asian-Americans as a highly successful minority continues to prevail. Young Asian-Americans, largely from Chinese, Korean, and Indochinese backgrounds, have outpaced their Anglo-American counterparts in several academic areas. These young people are reported to spend more time on homework, take more advanced high-school courses, and graduate with more credits. In addition, a higher percentage of these young people complete high school and college than do Anglo-American students. Also notable is the low rate of juvenile delinquency reported for this cultural group. A FOCUS ON RESEARCH 6–5 examines the reasons for Asian-American adolescents having higher grade-point averages and SAT scores. Actually, the high expectations for Asian-American adolescents often work to their disadvantage. For example, expectations based on stereotypes mask individuality. Not all Asian-American adolescents excel; indeed, many have academic problems serious enough to warrant their dropping out of school.

The importance of identity formation and personality development during the adolescent years must be considered from a cultural perspective. The beliefs and values of the family play an important role in shaping the emerging adult. Studies of personality development suggest that Asian-Americans adopt a more practical approach to life and problems than do Anglo-Americans; for example, ideas are evaluated more on pragmatic than on theoretical grounds. Another personality trait is the tendency to prefer concrete, well-structured, and predictable situations over ambiguous situations (Sue & Kirk, 1972, 1973). Although some acculturation has occurred, cultural emphasis continues to be placed on restraint in exhibiting strong

---

A FOCUS ON RESEARCH 6–5
Why Asian-American High School Students Succeed

Reglin and Adams (1990) report "an inordinate number of success stories coming from Asian-American students, especially in the areas of math and science" (p. 143). Using a 15–item questionnaire, these authors attempted to determine whether cultural differences between families of Asian-American high school students and non-Asian-American high school students contribute to the Asian-American's greater success in high school. Although detailed findings were reported for each item, Reglin and Adams came to several general conclusions:

1. Asian-American students are influenced more by their parents' desire for them to do well than their non-Asian counterparts.

2. Asian-American students in the study did not start dating until their late teens and had little interest in rock music, television, or athletics.

3. Asian-American students valued their leisure time more, and spent considerable time doing homework.

4. With respect to their future careers, Asian-American students indicated they would rather be scientists than athletes.

In general, the study suggested that cultural differences were contributing factors to Asian-American students' greater academic success in high school.

Source: Reglin, G. L., & Adams, D. R. (1990). Why Asian-American high school students have higher grade point averages and SAT scores than other high school students. *The High School Journal, 73,* 143–149.

---

emotions, unquestioning obedience to family authority, submergence of individuality in the interest of family welfare, and avoidance of outspokenness for fear of retaliation from society at large (Lum, 1986).

Language

It is crucial to effective multicultural counseling that the counselor realize the problems Asian-Americans have with English and understand their unique forms of nonverbal communication. Without doubt, the language barriers and problems confronting Asian-American adolescents make educational attainments even more significant. Although many Asian-American parents encourage the use of English, many adolescents still live in homes where the native language continues to be the primary language (Sue, 1981).

In many cases, additional coursework is recommended to remediate language deficiencies of Asian-American students. Some of them have such difficulty in understanding English and in making themselves understood that considerable extra study is required for them just to be minimally competent. Moreover, the direct teaching of English language skills to correct deficiencies indicates a failure to understand the

Asian-American's difficulty with English and has resulted in remedial programs being generally ineffective (Sue, 1981).

Some of the nonverbal behavior patterns demonstrated by Asian-Americans are distinctly different from those of other cultures. For example, the forward and backward leaning of the body indicates feelings. A backward lean indicates a degree of discomfort with the conversation and a withdrawal from it, while a forward lean lets the speaker know the listener is interested, concerned, and flexible. Japanese-American females express anxiety through increased vocalization, whereas Japanese-American males express anxiety through silence (Bond & Shirashi, 1974). Also, Japanese-Americans often communicate nonverbally through gestures: (a) rubbing or scratching the back of the head or neck indicates shame or discomfort; (b) hand-waving back and forth on front of the face means "no"; and (c) holding up the index finger to the temple area indicates jealousy or anger (Ishii, 1973).

Families

Adolescents learn early that the traditional Asian-American family considers the father to be the head of the household. Each family member recognizes and respects rigidly defined roles and accepts that the father is without doubt the authority figure. The father-son relationship is held in the highest esteem. The wife is subordinate to the husband and is expected to act as a servant to her in-laws. Although the majority-culture emphasis on equality has no doubt exerted some influence on traditional customs, the Asian-American family has been conservative and slow to change (Axelson, 1985).

The son, a prized and valuable family member, receives greater privileges and responsibilities than the daughter. The son is obligated to respect and obey his father; in turn, the father assists the son with his education and his marriage and provides him with an inheritance. By virtue of the fact that she is married to his father, the son owes his mother the same respect and obedience he owes his father. Ideally, the son does not harbor any complaints against this arrangement; after all, his turn will come when others will have to submit to his authority. Also, being a son means having a greater voice in family decisions and enjoying freedoms that daughters do not enjoy. Understandably, in this culture, adolescent males are given more freedom than adolescent females (Axelson, 1985).

Although daughters are less favored than sons, being a daughter does not carry with it a son's obligations. The daughter's role in the family is to perform domestic duties and to be subservient to males. Her ties with her family are severed when she marries into another family. She is expected to become an obedient helper of her mother-in-law and to bear children, especially male heirs (Sue, 1989).

Children and adolescents are taught early that elders are to be respected, held in high esteem, and treated with great respect due to their wisdom. Even after the son marries, he seeks the advice of elders. The oldest family member is especially revered, cared for, and looked to for advice in family matters (Sue, 1989).

Rigidly defined family roles are so arranged as to eliminate or minimize family conflicts. The welfare and integrity of the family is of great importance, and family members often suppress their individual needs for the sake of the family and its reputation. Family problems are approached discreetly, with much care and effort expended to avoid offending any family member. Any feelings that might disrupt the harmony of the family are kept in check. This lack of emotional display has translated into the Anglo-American image of the "inscrutable Oriental" (Sue, 1989).

Respect for family values and expectations without doubt influences the behavior of the adolescents. If adolescents demonstrate disrespect or any form of undesirable behavior, it reflects poorly on the entire family. The Chinese-American family serves as a source of emotional security, personal identity, and as a reference point for individual members. In turn, the family exerts control over interpersonal conduct, social relations—even over the choice of a career or marriage partner. The Japanese-American family functions similarly, with its strong emphasis on filial piety, respect and obligation, harmony, and group cooperation. There are also strong family-centered values and extended kinship relationships among Filipino-Americans (Lum, 1986). Although acculturation has contributed to increasing individualism, such cultural characteristics as avoidance of shame, indirect communication, self-effacement, and modesty appear to be maintained in recent generations. Adolescent behavior will continue to be strongly influenced by old-world family expectations.

Unique Challenges Confronting Asian-American Adolescents

Living in the predominant Anglo-American culture and continuing to meet the expectations of their respective Asian-American cultures, adolescents will probably experience problems that may warrant counseling intervention. Being loyal to Asian-American family expectations may result in conflicts, especially during this time of pressure to conform to Anglo standards and to make the transition into a wider social world.

One of the authors of this text recently taught a Japanese-American student whose achievement record outpaced all others in the class. Her language problems often exacted a burdensome toll: She studied far longer, more conscientiously, sought more assistance, relied heavily on her Japanese-American dictionary, and usually requested additional time for in-class assignments. However, with all her language difficulties, her persistence and determination overcame her deficiencies in English.

The Anglo-American emphasis on individualism presents challenges for the adolescent seeking to satisfy the demands of contemporary society and still remain loyal to Asian-American family traditions. The Asian-American female adolescent, in particular, experiencing the cultural conflict between traditional values and the more contemporary Anglo-American values may question her role in life. Will females continue to be relegated to second-class status in the Asian-American family? Should they seek more equitable standing, as exists in the Anglo-American family? Female Asian-Americans are often forced to make additional cultural compromises to achieve success in the majority culture.

Asian-American and Anglo-American adolescents are compared in Table 6–3. UP CLOSE AND PERSONAL 6–3 introduces Rieko, an Asian-American adolescent.

Table 6–3 Cultural comparison: Asian-American and Anglo-American adolescents

Asian-American Adolescents	Anglo-American Adolescents
Sons are of more "value" than daughters	Sons and daughters are of equal "value"
Are influenced by both Asian-American and Anglo-American cultures in identity formation	Are influenced by only the Anglo-American culture in identity formation
Exhibit extreme loyalty to the family, especially to the father and older generations	Exhibit loyalty to immediate family members, yet place great emphasis on individualism
Regard family as "first"; peers, second	Often reject family values for peer values
Do better academically	Do not do as well academically
Lean forward to indicate attention and interest	Use eye contact and encouraging sounds to express understanding and interest

Sources: Data compiled from Axelson, 1985; Lum, 1986; Sue, 1989.

HISPANIC-AMERICAN ADOLESCENTS

Societal and Cultural Description

Several precautionary remarks are in order before discussing the Hispanic-American culture. First, the considerable intracultural diversity of Hispanics makes it difficult to generalize across subgroups. Also, further diversification results from varying levels of acculturation, socioeconomic class, proficiency with English, and with region of residency within the United States. Such diversity must be recognized in order to avoid the errors that can result from stereotypical interpretations.

Hispanics are the fastest growing ethnic group in the United States. By the year 2000, Hispanics from 15 to 24 years of age will constitute 14 percent of the total U.S. youth population. Some states, such as California and Texas, will have even higher percentages. The adolescent years frequently can be times of personal turmoil. Consider, for example, the physical and emotional changes associated with developing from childhood into adolescence; the increased freedoms and responsibilities encountered when leaving the structural confines of the elementary school; and other problems associated with drugs, sex, pregnancy, a desire to conform to group standards, and increasing poverty (Closing the gap for U.S. Hispanic youth, 1988).

Forces that influence the lives of Hispanic-American adolescents include the social and psychological changes accompanying adolescence as well as the cultural customs and traditions considered sacred to the culture. These two forces, along with Hispanics' tendency to speak only Spanish or to live in predominantly bilingual areas, provide significant challenges to both adolescents and their counselors.

Several Hispanic-American cultural characteristics illustrate that Anglo-American standards are inappropriate when intervening with Hispanic-Americans. First, Anglo-

UP CLOSE AND PERSONAL 6–3
Rieko Sukuzi — An Asian-American Adolescent

Rieko, a 16-year-old Japanese-American, lives with her parents, younger sister, Mina, and her younger brother. Her elderly grandfather continues to live with them. Rieko enjoys the closeness of her family and particularly seeks the advice of her grandfather, who is always available to listen to her concerns.

Rieko is in the tenth grade and is doing above average work, but her studies take up most of her time. She is not sure why she has to study so much more than the Anglo-American students, but she suspects that her language problem is the reason. She hasn't discussed this with her family, however, because they continually emphasize the value of education. Also, she doesn't want them to know that her English is not as good as the Anglo-American students'. Rieko does pride herself, however, on being able to speak Japanese, too. In fact, she and her grandfather sometimes speak in his native tongue. She enjoys speaking the language that makes her grandfather proud.

Excelling not only in schoolwork, Rieko also has learned the responsibilities of running the household. She can cook, clean, sew, and shop for groceries. Since her mother is responsible for these tasks, Rieko was encouraged to learn them too. She is aware, though, that her younger brother is not being taught how to care for the household. She accepts the fact that girls must assume more responsibility despite having fewer privileges, but she sometimes envies her Anglo-American girlfriends who have considerably more freedom. What will it be like when she finishes high school and college (if the family can afford to send her) and enters a predominantly Anglo-American world? Secretly, she wonders whether she will be drawn away from her Asian-American culture.

Sometimes, but not often, Rieko worries about her situation. Will she be more accepted by the Anglo-Americans next semester? Are they a little "standoffish" because of her culture, because of her grades, or because she always tries to satisfy the teacher? If it is her grades and behavior, there isn't much she can do. She would never disappoint her family. Will her English improve? She has been working on it a lot lately, but there is just so much time for schoolwork and household chores. Then, too, she does want some time to spend with her grandfather. Right now, though, these problems do not seem overwhelming to Rieko. She has always persisted, and besides she knows that her family is there to support her.

Americans often believe that equality within the family and self-advancement are in keeping with the ideals of freedom, democracy, and progress. In contrast, Mexican-Americans value placing one's family above self (Madsen, 1973). Second, *machismo* plays a much more significant role in Spanish-speaking cultures than in the Anglo-American culture. The adolescent male must adhere to the machismo expectations of the culture or risk the loss of respect for himself and his manhood, which is culturally unacceptable (Fitzpatrick, 1987).

According to Mirandé (1986), the concern with negative, deviant, or pathological dimensions of Spanish-speaking adolescents is sometimes not warranted. Emphasis has been placed on such issues as delinquency and gangs, drinking and drug abuse, school failures, and dropouts rather than on the more average adolescent behavior in the culture. This is not to suggest that the negative aspects be ignored, but that they receive an objective and cautious interpretation.

A cultural description of Spanish-speaking peoples must include an understanding of certain attributes that play a significant role (in varying degrees, depending on the individual subgroup) in the Hispanic-American culture (Christensen, 1989). Some of these attributes are as follows:

Spanish Term	Meaning
afecto	literally, "affect"; refers to warmth and demonstrativeness
dignidad	dignity—one may oppose another person, but should never take away his or her dignity
machismo	a strong sense of masculine pride; sometimes taken by non-Hispanics to imply an innate inferiority of women
respeto	respect for authority, family, and tradition

Data pertaining to the level of educational achievement of Hispanic-American students indicate that, by the senior year, only 31 percent of Hispanic-American high school students are enrolled in college preparatory courses. Even worse, Hispanic-Americans have one of the highest dropout rates of any minority group. Of the Hispanic students graduating from high school, only about 10 to 15 percent are academically qualified to enter state universities in California (Closing the education gap for Hispanics, 1987).

The issue has been raised as to whether Anglo-American teachers harbor biases against Hispanic-American students and their culture. So (1987) felt that Anglo-American teachers first label these students either "good" or "bad," and then give differential treatment to them. The students are inclined to accept the teacher's evaluation and respond accordingly. Thus, a student with a "bad" label will avoid talking to the teacher. The student's motivation may suffer and his or her academic expectations may be lowered. A FOCUS ON RESEARCH 6–6 further examines So's research on the labeling of Hispanic students.

The poverty issue continues to plague the Hispanic population and will have its effects on developing adolescents. According to Fitzpatrick (1987), second-generation Puerto Ricans have experienced substantial improvement in socioeconomic status; however, poverty continues to be widespread. Another factor contributing to the poor financial status of Hispanic-Americans is the increase in the number of female-headed households. Furthermore, the unemployment rate of Puerto Rican males is twice as high as the Anglo-American rate.

Language

Spanish-speaking adolescents have much in common with other cultural minorities. Like other minorities, language poses a problem outside the immediate neighborhood. Many Hispanics tend to retain their native tongue rather than make the transition to English. Not perceiving a need to develop proficiency, some Spanish-speaking people continue to risk survival in a bilingual world. In the southwestern United

A FOCUS ON RESEARCH 6–6
The Labeling of Hispanic Students

Convinced that Anglo-American teachers labeled Hispanic-American students as "good" or "bad," So (1987) designed a cross-cultural study to determine whether Hispanic-American teachers harbored biased feelings toward students of their own culture. Questions for consideration included the following: (1) Do Hispanic-American teachers make better teachers for Hispanic-American students? (2) What is the impact of labeling on those students who have received "good" labels? (3) Would Hispanic- and Anglo-American teachers treat "good" Hispanic-American students the same as "good"

Anglo-American students were treated? Findings indicated that

1. Anglo-American teachers demonstrated a more positive treatment of Anglo-Americans than of Hispanic-American students;

2. once the label of "going to college" was assigned to a Hispanic-American student, then Anglo-American teachers treated this student in the same manner as college-going Anglo-American students were treated; and

3. Hispanic-American students received a more positive treatment from Hispanic-American teachers than they received from Anglo-American teachers.

Source: So, A. Y. (1987). Hispanic teachers and the labeling of Hispanic students. *The High School Journal, 71*, 5–8.

States, many Hispanic-American people live in Spanish-speaking communities isolated from the English-speaking community. In fact, children often enter the English-speaking world for the first time when they begin their public school education. Then, to make matters worse, these children are often threatened in school environments with punishment for speaking Spanish (Vontress, 1976b). Olsen (1988) relates the story of Socorro:

> I just sat in my classes and didn't understand anything. . . . Sometimes I would try to look like I knew what was going on; sometimes I would just try to think about a happy time when I didn't feel stupid. My teachers never called on me or talked to me. I think they either forgot I was there or else wished I wasn't. I waited and waited, thinking someday I will know English. (p. 216)

Anyone trying to survive in a society speaking a different language can attest to the problems encountered. However, language problems during the adolescence years have the potential for negatively affecting both individual self-concept and developing cultural identities.

Families

The counselor's understanding of the family's role in the Hispanic-American culture is a prerequisite to understanding and counseling the adolescent client. A deep feeling for family, both immediate and extended, permeates the culture and often becomes the basis for individual and group decisions (Fitzpatrick, 1987).

The Hispanic-American family is like families of other minority cultures in some respects and different in others. As in the Asian-American and African-American families, the extended kinship network plays a vital role; also, as in the Asian-American family, the natural superiority of the male is a basic tenet. The "extended family" concept plays a major role in each family member's life. Grandparents and other family members may live in the same household. Or they may live nearby in separate households and visit frequently. With respect to the dominance of the male, in the Puerto Rican family, the man exercises the authority in the family and makes decisions without consulting his wife. It follows that he expects to be obeyed when he gives commands (Fitzpatrick, 1987). A third feature, in common with Native-American and Asian-American families, is the emphasis on cooperativeness and placing the needs of the family ahead of individual concerns. This should not be construed to imply that the family impedes individual achievement and advancement. One must be careful to distinguish between being cooperative and respectful and being docile and dependent (Mirandé, 1986).

Any discussion of Hispanic families must consider the effects of acculturation and recognize that second- and third-generation Hispanics have experienced change. Increasingly, women are demanding more active and equal roles and are heading households.

Unique Challenges Confronting Hispanic-American Adolescents

Counselors working in multicultural situations need to be aware of several challenges confronting Hispanic-American adolescents. First, they are often stereotyped as being gang members and involved with drugs. Second, these adolescents must try to reconcile the different family structures of the Hispanic-American and Anglo-American cultures. Third, they must recognize the need to speak the language of the majority

Table 6–4   Cultural comparison: Hispanic-American and Anglo-American adolescents

Hispanic-American Adolescents	Anglo-American Adolescents
Exhibit strong commitment to family and godparents, including extended family	Exhibit strong commitment to immediate family
Are dedicated to *machismo*—pride in manhood	Emphasize *machismo* to a lesser degree; tend to disavow male dominance
Either continue to speak Spanish only, or both Spanish and English	Speak English only—the "appropriate" language
Tend to exhibit lower academic achievement	Tend to exhibit higher academic achievement
Have strong commitment to *dignidad, machismo,* and *respeto*	Do not incorporate these values into daily life to such a great degree
Are reputed to be delinquent or violent	Tend to be labeled "mischievous" or "rebellious," rather than delinquent

Sources: Data compiled from Fitzpatrick, 1987; Mirandé, 1986; Sue, 1981; Sue and Sue, 1983.

culture. Although wanting to maintain an allegiance to the mother tongue is natural, learning English increases the adolescent's chances of success in a predominantly Anglo-American world. Fourth, the large numbers of adolescent Hispanic-American mothers have little chance of escaping the cycle of poverty (Closing the gap for U.S. Hispanic youth, 1988).

What remedies can possibly improve the lives of Hispanic-American youth? Counseling, flexible work/study programs, mentoring, involvement with the Job Training Partnership Act's Private Industry Councils, and nontraditional learning programs such as ESL programs all hold promise (Closing the gap for U.S. Hispanic youth, 1988).

In Table 6–4 the cultural characteristics of Hispanic-Americans and Anglo-Americans are compared. Carlos Suarez is the featured adolescent in UP CLOSE AND PERSONAL 6–4.

◢ UP CLOSE AND PERSONAL 6–4
Carlos Suarez — A Hispanic-American Adolescent

Sixteen-year-old Carlos and his family live in a predominantly Hispanic-American neighborhood. Although Carlos is experiencing the changes of adolescence, he still enjoys being with his brother, 8-year-old Ramon. His Hispanic-American friends and peers in the community and school are becoming increasingly important. However, he continues to have a close relationship with his immediate family, his grandfather Rafael, and his married brother, who lives across the street. The Suarez family has financial problems because the father, a laborer, has been unemployed for several weeks. Carlos does not feel too bad about the situation though, since many of his friends also have fathers without jobs.

Carlos is faced with several difficult situations. Although he has never been arrested, he does have several friends who have been involved in delinquent behavior, either in school or the neighborhood. Because he lacks Anglo-American friends at school, he spends quite a bit of time with several Hispanic-American youths in the neighborhood. Although his parents and grandfather do not like these boys, Carlos needs friends, and he is not sure what other friends he can make. Also, although he

doesn't always agree with these friends, he does enjoy spending time with them. They all speak Spanish and share Hispanic-American values. Besides, they accept him for who he is, not questioning his cultural habits.

Carlos wonders which language he will eventually speak. He now speaks English in his classroom because his teachers say he should, but he speaks Spanish in the neighborhood. In fact, he nearly always speaks Spanish with his grandfather. He would not, however, qualify as bilingual. His teachers insist that English is important, yet Carlos feels a commitment to the native language of his parents and friends.

Carlos is also experiencing academic problems, which is hurting his self-esteem and making him dislike school. He admits that his language difficulties might be contributing to his poor academic achievement. Of course, he wants to do better. But then again, if he improves significantly, he might "stand out" among his Hispanic-American peers, which could hurt his friendships. Trying to deal with schoolwork, maintain his friendships, and continue to satisfy his parents and family are proving to be harder and harder for Carlos.

A POINT OF DEPARTURE

Challenges Confronting Multicultural Counselors of Adolescents

Counselors working with adolescents in multicultural situations face several challenges. First, they must understand adolescence as a recently recognized lifespan stage. Second, developmental changes specifically associated with adolescence (the forming identity, the budding self-concept, and the transition to adulthood) have only recently been examined in an adolescent context. Thus, the available information on which to base counseling decisions and efforts is sometimes hard to come by. A third challenge is for multicultural counselors to accept the professional responsibility to intervene from an adolescent perspective.

Understanding multicultural adolescent clients in term of their values, aspirations, families, language difficulties, and other personal and social concerns is beneficial to both client and counselor. Counselors professionally trained in traditional counseling techniques with adults can prepare themselves for working with culturally diverse adolescents through conscientious study of the professional literature on adolescent development and cultural diversity, carefully assimilating this knowledge base, and looking for implications for successful professional intervention in specific cases.

SUMMARY

Adolescence has been recognized as a legitimate developmental period of the lifespan only over the past hundred years. It deserves to be understood as a complex time of age-appropriate developmental task acquisition and identity formation. It also deserves to be understood in the context of cultural heritage, which must be considered as counseling decisions are reached. No longer can the needs and problems of clients be considered only in light of the counselor's own cultural and lifespan period. Although the commitment to acquire knowledge of the adolescent developmental period and each client's cultural characteristics is a task of some magnitude, the original training and experiences acquired in counselor education programs provide a sound foundation for the acquisition of new knowledge and skills.

Suggested Readings

Atwater, E. (1988). *Adolescence* (2nd ed.). Englewood Cliffs, NJ: Prentice-Hall. Atwater examines many aspects of adolescence: development, the family, self-concept and identity formation, and the various problems adolescents experience.

Closing the gap for U.S. Hispanic youth. (1988). Report from the 1988 Aspen Institute Conference on Hispanic Americans and the Business Community. Washington, DC: The Hispanic Policy Development Project. This objective report examines public and private strategies for improving Hispanic youths' lot in life. Relevant background information is provided, with suggestions for improvement based on the idea that there is "no quick fix."

Fitzpatrick, J. P. (1987). *Puerto Rican Americans* (2nd ed.). Englewood Cliffs, NJ: Prentice-Hall. In this excellent text on mainland Puerto Ricans, Fitzpatrick looks at their migration, their island background, and their families.

Leigh, G. K., & Peterson, G. W. (1986). *Adolescents in families.* Cincinnati, OH: South-Western. This edited book provides useful information on adolescents and their families, particularly Chapter 17, "Black Adolescents and Their Families," and Chapter 18, "Adolescence and Chicano Families."

Reglin, G. L., & Adams, D. R. (1990). Why Asian-American high school students have higher grade point averages and SAT scores than other high school students. *The High School Journal, 73,* 143–149. Reglin and Adams draw several conclusions from a questionnaire to determine the study and living habits of Asian-American adolescents.

Chapter 7

Counseling the Adolescent

Questions To Be Explored

1. What are the typical stresses and concerns of the adolescent years? To what extent does stress vary according to cultural groups?

2. What are the problems and concerns of adolescents in the Native-American, African-American, Asian-American, and Hispanic-American cultures?

3. What issues concerning generational differences and family relationships might adolescents bring to counseling sessions?

4. What cultural and individual differences can counselors expect when counseling culturally diverse adolescents?

5. What strategies should counselors consider when counseling culturally diverse adolescents?

6. What unique challenges confront counselors working with culturally diverse adolescents?

7. Should individual, group, or family therapy be employed when counseling culturally diverse adolescents? To what extent should the decision on counseling modality depend on the specific culture?

INTRODUCTION

The physical, psychosocial, and intellectual changes occurring during adolescence can result in great emotional upheaval. Physically, adolescents are experiencing significant glandular changes, with the onset of puberty marking a radical change in their physical development. Socially, adolescents are leaving the world of childhood, in which adults are perceived as always being right and as always having the answers.

For children, questions of right and wrong are often one-dimensional and simple. Cognitively, adolescents begin to think and to understand their world differently. They have usually entered Piaget's formal operations stage and are developing higher levels of thinking ability. During this period, adolescents come to realize that adults do not always have the correct answers and that, with respect to issues and problems, grey areas almost always overlay the black and white (Baruth & Robinson, 1987).

DIFFERENCES IN COUNSELING CULTURALLY DIVERSE ADOLESCENTS

As with children, adolescents are still dependent on the adult world, although not to the degree that the young child is dependent. Adult control of adolescents varies culturally, but it is evident to all adolescents that adults still exert significant control over much of their lives. Since the concept of adolescence varies across cultures, rights and responsibilities of adolescents also vary; what one culture expects or allows may be taboo in another culture. It follows that the counselor cannot consider all adolescents to be alike. Specifically, counseling the Asian-American adolescent requires an understanding of old-world cultural expectations for adolescents and also of the differing expectations for males and females. As another example, counselors who suggest that Hispanic-American clients become more competitive exhibit a gross ignorance of culture-based behavior; e.g., being reluctant to stand out in the company of peers.

Uncertainty about life's mysteries and their own ability to cope with the world independently often causes adolescents to waver between a search for independence and the safety of dependence. Caught in this conflict, adolescents' behavior may often seem erratic; they may be contemptuous and rebellious one moment and affectionate and conforming the next. Uncertainties continue to increase as some adolescents experience problems resulting from differing parental and peer expectations for them at this stage in life.

At the core of personal development at this stage are increased interpersonal, decision-making, problem-solving, and conflict-resolution skills, yet counselors in multicultural situations often experience frustration when counseling adolescents who are having difficulties in these areas. Ohlsen (1983) states that "although adolescents often pretend to be confident and spurn significant adults' desires to protect them from needless risks, they can admit in a counseling group that they are not very confident and that they need to practice skills required to cope with peers as well as adults" (p. 155). The adolescent's false bravado and outward confidence often challenge the counselor's expertise and patience. Moreover, youths who are referred to the counselor by a teacher, parent, principal, or other authority figure often project the authority of those who force them to be in "counseling" onto the counselor. Even youths who have chosen, themselves, to seek counseling may find it difficult to share their suspected deficits with adults they are desperately trying to impress with their ability to be independent and self-assured (Ohlsen, 1983).

Counseling adolescents requires considerable insight and skill. Ohlsen (1983) offered the following advice for enhancing the counselor-client relationship:

1. Counselors need to protect and project their role as counselor as uniquely different from that of other adults in the adolescent's life; e.g., they must keep confidences, be sensitive and sympathetic yet honest, and work cooperatively with the client in providing feedback and openly seeking feedback from the client.

2. Counselors should encourage self-referral whenever possible.

3. Counselors must remember that cultural differences play a significant role in the counseling process. Both developmental characteristics and unique cultural characteristics must be understood and considered when planning counseling strategies.

Counselors intervening with culturally diverse adolescents will want to make use of as many sources of assistance as possible. These might include health departments, urban leagues, hospitals with comprehensive health programs, and other organizations geared toward helping adolescents. Counselors should maintain an up-to-date file of such organizations, especially service groups for culturally diverse populations.

Typical Concerns and Stresses of the Adolescent Years

The concerns and stresses of culturally diverse adolescents may have several sources. First, the developmental period, itself, can be a source of problems—developing an identity, sometimes being independent and other times dependent, being an adult in some ways and only an older child in others. Also, a general lack of understanding of the lifespan period may result in confusion. Erikson (1950) postulated that the most critical task of adolescence is resolving the crisis of personal identity. This crisis might be even more traumatic for culturally different adolescents who must forge their identity in a predominantly Anglo society. The Asian-American girl may experience stress when choosing between striving to meet her parent's expectations for academic achievement and her Anglo peers' quite different expectations. Also, the adverse emotional impact of not doing well in schoolwork, a parent losing a job, perceived unattractive appearance, or a parent with alcohol problems also may be traumatic to adolescents (Basch & Kersch, 1986).

Some stressful situations apply across cultures; the death of a parent, for example, while other stressful situations might be more indigeneous to a particular culture, such as the Hispanic-American adolescent's need to uphold the honor of the family name, should it be threatened. Therefore, an understanding and genuine acceptance of an adolescent's unique cultural background and differences contribute significantly to the effectiveness of counseling intervention. Many stress-provoking situations and life events for children also apply to adolescents. Therefore, readers are encouraged to review Tables 5–1 and 5–2 listing childrens' stressful events and symptoms of stress, respectively.

A FOCUS ON RESEARCH 7–1 focuses on family-related stressors. Although the list provided by McCubbin and Patterson (1986) pertains specifically to stress in adolescents, multicultural counselors still must decide which factors are culturally relevant and also determine additional factors that might pertain to a specific client.

◆ **A FOCUS ON RESEARCH 7–1**
Family-Related Stressors

McCubbin and Patterson (1986) examined adolescent stress from a family perspective. The changes occurring during the adolescent years, the increasing complexities of teenagers' lives, and the challenges and decisions they must face all have the potential for leading to stress. Some stress-provoking situations involving family relationships include

1. increased arguments about getting jobs done at home;

Source: McCubbin, H. J., & Patterson, J. M. (1986). Adolescent stress, coping, and adaptation: A normative family perspective. In G. K. Leigh, & G. W. Peterson (Eds.), *Adolescents in families* (pp. 256–276). Cincinnati, OH: South-Western.

2. pressures to get "good" grades or to do well in school sports;

3. increased adolescent resistance to participating in family activities;

4. increased arguments over the use of the car or over curfews;

5. increased arguments over the selection of friends or activities;

6. the hospitalization of family members;

7. serious illnesses of grandparents;

8. the death of a close relative;

9. financial problems; and

10. beginning junior high or senior high school.

NATIVE-AMERICAN ADOLESCENTS

Understanding the heritage and unique cultural characteristics of Native-Americans, and being aware of the years of oppression and discrimination they have suffered are prerequisites to appropriate counseling intervention. Some of the problems in counseling Native-American adolescents include the following:

1. the adolescent's failure to develop a positive individual and Native-American identity;

2. misperceptions and stereotypical images of Native-American and adolescents that may result in the adolescent's poor self-image;

3. communication problems: English as a second language; nonverbal communication being misunderstood; differences in "reservation" or "tribal" languages and "school" languages;

4. conflict between loyalty to family and elders and a desire to conform to peer standards;

5. the adverse effects of being misunderstood by Anglo-American teachers;

6. the adolescent's poor academic achievement;

7. the adolescent's poor self-concept;

8. drug or alcohol addiction;

9. the adverse effects of racism and discrimination;

10. generational conflict caused by parents' allegiance to Native-American values and the adolescent's acculturation.

Cultural Differences

The Native-American adolescent's unique cultural characteristics may seem strange to those of other cultures, especially to Anglo-American peers and professionals. Too often, lack of understanding of the Native-American's culture leads to professional decisions based on Anglo-American cultural standards. Professionals may expect all adolescents to "earn and own," to raise their voices to show emotion, to consider long-term options, and to think of themselves first and foremost. They may not understand the Native-American need to be in harmony with nature or to de-emphasize the acquisition of material wealth. Hence, Native-American adolescents may be considered lazy, unambitious, or unmotivated.

Although problems can result from significant others having negative feelings toward the Native-American culture, even greater problems result when the adolescents, themselves, feel that they are culturally or individually inferior. What can counselors do to help adolescents develop positive feelings about their age and culture? A prerequisite to planning professional intervention is to use culturally appropriate counseling strategies rather than attempt to fit Native-Americans into an Anglo-American mold. The counselor can also help these adolescents realize that both their developmental period and their culture are worthy of respect.

Language Problems

Language problems of Native-American adolescents pose significant barriers to counseling relationships and may lead to considerable misunderstandings between counselor and client. In counseling, the heavy reliance placed on verbal interaction to build rapport cannot be overestimated. Communicational breakdowns can lead to lack of confidence and trust between client and counselor, further hindering the counseling process.

Because trained Native-American counselors are scarce, the adolescent experiencing difficulties will probably meet with an Anglo-American counselor (Dauphinais, LaFromboise, & Rowe, 1980). This may actually make the Native-American adolescent language situation worse. The counselor's inability to speak the Native-American client's language or inability to understand his or her nonverbal cues may contribute to the client's problems with identity formation, feelings of cultural worthlessness, and poor self-concept.

Generational Differences and Other Family Issues

To what extent do generational differences affect Native-American adolescents and their families? As Thurman, Martin, and Martin (1985) remark,

> although some members of the older American Indian population have retained their identity with former Indian ways and received stability from them, the young American Indian finds it difficult to adhere to such values and customs in many instances. (pp. 177–178)

Older generations continuing to maintain strict allegiance to Native-American values may be troubled by the acculturation of the younger generations. Acculturation may result in a pulling back from the cultural traditions of sharing and noncompetitiveness and a movement toward ownership and competitive attitudes. The extent of acculturation that occurs depends on the younger generation Native-Americans' ability to use the English language effectively and their ability to become assimilated into a predominantly Anglo-American society (Attneave, 1982).

Value clashes often begin early in Native-American families due to pressure placed on youth to assume a share of the group responsibility in the family. Simultaneously, the family instills the sense that each person is innately an individual whose potential is to be fostered yet not forced. While the parent continues to appreciate traditional cultural values, some tension can be reduced if there is also a realization of the pressure on youth to conform to dominant cultural expectations (Attneave, 1982).

Developmental and Other Concerns

Living somewhere between childhood and adulthood, Native-American adolescents move intermittently between the former developmental stage and the latter. Problems can arise when adolescents and families do not agree on appropriate ages for certain activities, or when one culture allows or encourages activities that another culture frowns upon. No longer content within the safe confines of the home and the family, the adolescent meets new tasks and challenges in which the ability to cope or succeed must be demonstrated. Successful development of a positive identity may result in the adolescent feeling worthy of respect and capable of becoming a contributing member of the community and overall society.

Dauphinais et al. (1980) surveyed eleventh- and twelfth-grade Native-American adolescents in four categories to determine problems that they thought were worthy of counseling: Native-American students attending Bureau of Indian Affairs boarding schools, those attending rural high schools, those attending metropolitan high schools, and non-Native-American students in rural and metropolitan high schools. Table 7–1 indicates the percentage of adolescents listing various problem areas.

Some of the problems and concerns during the adolescent years can be of sufficient magnitude to result in suicide attempts. A FOCUS ON RESEARCH 7–2 discusses adolescent suicide among the Cherokees.

Counseling Considerations

As previously stated, since there are relatively few Native-American counselors, most Native-Americans will likely be counseled by an Anglo-American, or perhaps by another minority counselor (Dauphinais et al., 1980). The non-Native-American counselor planning intervention with Native-American adolescents should consider the following questions: What unique Native-American cultural and developmental characteristics are important to know about? How can counselors develop trust, rapport, and genuine respect for adolescents with this cultural background? Will individual, family, or group therapy work best? We will now explore the significance of these questions and provide specific suggestions for counseling Native-Americans.

Table 7–1 Problems of Native American students in four categories

Problems	Indian			Non-Indian
	Board	Rural	Metro	
A personal problem	24	40	28	32
Problem about my future	16	36	36	56
Problem about money	22	34	16	12
Problem about being depressed or not caring	20	14	32	10
Problem making a decision	18	22	24	34
Problem keeping grades up	12	24	22	28
Problem with parents or family members	6	20	10	20
What one's life work might be	16	16	20	18
Problem with teacher or school personnel	14	12	16	20
Class scheduling problem	8	8	16	18
Whether to stay in school or not	16	16	8	6
Problem about sex	0	10	4	16
Social conflicts	8	10	6	6
Problem about getting married	4	6	8	6
Problem getting along with friends	6	8	4	4
Problem getting in contact with family	6	6	6	4
Problem with beer or liquor	4	8	0	2
Problem with drugs or glue	2	0	0	2
Problem related to BIA	6	0	2	—
Feelings about being an Indian	0	6	4	—
Problem about having time to study	0	4	6	—

Source: Dauphinais et al., 1980.

A FOCUS ON RESEARCH 7–2
Attempted Suicides among Adolescent Cherokee Indians

The American Indian population has a suicide rate nearly twice that of the national average. Some reservations have rates at least five or six times higher than the national average, especially among younger age groups. The authors used a questionnaire to determine a profile of

Source: Thurman, P. J., Martin, D., & Martin, M. (1985). An assessment of attempted suicides among adolescent Cherokee Indians. *Journal of Multicultural Counseling and Development, 13,* 176–182.

the adolescent Cherokee suicide attempter. Overdoses of medication and body cuts were the most common methods of attempted suicide. Reasons for the attempted suicides included respondents considering themselves to be failures, problems with sexuality, broken relationships with boyfriends or girlfriends, the loss of a loved one, family disruptions, cultural pressures, and lack of opportunity because of race.

Although differences among the various tribes do not allow for the establishment of concrete rules for counseling Native-Americans (Youngman & Sadongei, 1983), the counselor's understanding of the culture's unique characteristics is prerequisite to effective counseling. A review of the literature on counseling Native-American young people (Lazarus, 1982; Thompson & Rudoph, 1988) highlights several aspects of the culture that are important for counselors to remember:

1. Young people are respected to the same degree as are adults.

2. Cooperation and harmony are valued.

3. Generosity and sharing are important, and individuals are judged on their contributions.

4. Competition may be encouraged as long as it does not hurt anyone.

5. The Native-American lives in the present, with little concern for planning for tomorrow.

6. Native-Americans may consider some behaviors strange or rude; e.g., loud talking and reprimands.

7. Ancient legends and cultural traditions are important.

8. Peace and politeness are essential; confrontation is rude.

The Native-American's attitude toward silence differs significantly from that of Anglo adolescents. The Native-American does not feel a need to fill time with meaningless speech, just to avoid silence. Also, the adolescent not looking the speaker in the eye should be understood as culturally appropriate (Dauphinais et al., 1980).

Perceived trust is the most important variable in how Native-Americans decide whether a counselor should be viewed as a helper (Dauphinais et al., 1980). The Native-American's general distrust of Anglo-Americans and the adolescent's more individual distrust of the Anglo-American professional may pose hurdles. Responsibility for developing trust will rest primarily with the counselor, since the Native-American adolescent will not be familiar with the counseling process, especially with an Anglo-American professional. Once trust in the counselor and the counseling process is established, rapport and mutual respect likely will follow.

The first meeting with the Native-American adolescent should be designed to build trust. Effective listening and empathic responding are helpful in this regard. Counselors able to show genuine appreciation for the Native-American culture and its values and traditions likely will reduce adolescents' distrust. During this first session, it is important that counselors work diligently to accommodate the Native-American time orientation and fatalistic view of life rather than imposing Anglo standards (Lum, 1986).

Individual/Group Therapy

In counseling adolescents, as in counseling other populations, the theoretical orientation of the counselor plays a large part in shaping the counseling sessions. Once the adolescent has been referred or has initiated a self-referral, the counselor can decide whether individual or group therapy will be the most effective approach. Group counseling approaches are often the preferred mode of treatment, since most adolescents find it easier to speak freely in a group setting. They believe that their peers will understand and accept their deficiencies more readily than adults (Ohlsen, 1983). Indications are that group therapy may work particularly well with Native-American adolescents. Activity groups are especially enjoyed by these youngsters; they have proven helpful in boarding school situations where group members can discuss mutual interests and concerns and can enjoy associating with one another (Edwards & Edwards, 1989).

Counseling adolescents in individual or group situations does have drawbacks, however. Clients may, indeed, change their behavior, but upon returning to the family, they often are confronted with relatives unwilling to accept the changes. Thus, they may be forced back to old behaviors (Peterson & Nisenholz, 1987). It is important to remember, too, that in some cases group therapy might result in Native-American adolescents being somewhat reserved due to their lack of trust or tendency toward noninterference with others. Their soft speech and suspicion of strangers might also impede the counseling process in a group situation.

Family Therapy

Practical and immediate solutions to problems during family therapy may be more relevant than future-oriented philosophical goals. Reflecting Native-American values, group decisions will take precedence over individual decisions during family counseling sessions. Whenever possible, the therapist should involve all family members, even extended family members, in selecting therapy goals. This process of involving all family members can often be so therapeutic in and of itself that further counseling intervention might be unnecessary. Ho (1987) related the cases of Phillip and Debbie. In Phillip's case, there was misunderstanding regarding the extended family:

> Phillip, a 15-year-old probationer, was brought to the attention of a court-related worker when she received a complaint that Phillip was running around from house to house visiting female friends without parental supervision. When the worker inquired about Phillip's family background, she discovered that he had several aunts and cousins. When the worker called all Phillip's aunts and cousins together for a family conference, she discovered that all his cousins were young females. The worker later learned that Phillip's behavior was very natural in the extended family system.[1]

In the case of adolescent Debbie, it was necessary to mobilize a social support network to assist her:

> Although a "good" student in the past, Debbie, the teenage daughter of the Tiger family, has been missing school recently. When the parents were informed of this, they displayed no surprise, but expressed willingness to cooperate with the school official in getting

---

[1]M. K. Ho, *Family Therapy With Ethnic Minorities,* p. 97, copyright © 1987 by Sage Publications, Inc. Reprinted by permission of Sage Publications, Inc.

Debbie back to school regularly. The school social worker, who served as a family therapist, happened to live in the same neighborhood as the Tigers, and she volunteered to transport Debbie back and forth to school. Through this consistent relationship, the therapist became a trusted friend of the Tiger family. To express the family's gratitude and friendship, Mrs. Tiger provided the therapist with a regular supply of home-grown vegetables. Through this informal exchange, the therapist learned that the Tigers were totally shut off from the community, with Mr. Tiger labeled as "crazy" and "not to be trusted." Mr. Tiger did not have a regular job. On his days off, "he managed to get drunk," according to Mrs. Tiger. Although Mrs. Tiger was willing to get some therapy for their family problems, Mr. Tiger insisted that he would not have any of "that stuff" (therapy). After learning that the Tigers were religious individuals who attended church regularly, the therapist referred the Tigers to a minister for consultation. The minister, although a non-Indian, was highly respected by the Indians who also attended the same church but belonged to different tribes. Through such extended interaction with other Indians, Mrs. Tiger became more relaxed and paid attention to Debbie, who managed to attend school regularly without the family therapist's assistance.[2]

 UP CLOSE AND PERSONAL 7–1
Counseling Carl Lonetree

Carl, age 15, was referred to the school guidance counselor by his teacher for poor academic achievement. On the referral slip, the teacher's notation read "poor grades, lack of interest, and unmotivated." During Carl's first session, he demonstrated some apprehensiveness and distrust of the Anglo counselor. The counselor and Carl discussed Carl's development and his Native-American culture. Carl was somewhat hesitant to share information ("you can't trust people in this school"), and he made vague references to the counselor "doing something to him."

During the first session, the counselor sought to lessen Carl's anxiety and develop rapport. Carl's poor language skills made conversation a bit difficult, but the counselor worked to overcome this barrier. The counselor noticed that Carl paused a lot in his speech. It was as if he couldn't find anything to say. Yet, silent periods didn't seem to bother Carl.

After talking at length with Carl, the counselor came to two conclusions. First, Carl's academic problems were the result of poor language skills and, second, Carl's teacher did not understand the mannerisms of Native-Americans. The teacher failed to recognize that Carl was, indeed, interested in school and motivated to learn.

The counselor decided to do three things: First, he would offer to assist Carl's teacher in understanding Carl's behavior. Then, since many of Carl's academic problems stemmed from his language problem, he would recommend Carl for special language classes. Finally, he would follow up on Carl's progress in individual sessions. The prospect of Carl speaking up in group therapy sessions seemed unlikely, unless all the other members of the group had similar academic and language problems. However, after Carl's language problem improved, he could be considered for group therapy.

---

[2]Ibid., pp. 100–101.

AFRICAN-AMERICAN ADOLESCENTS

The counselor's perception of African-American adolescents is influenced to a large extent by the effort the counselor expends toward understanding the culture, the development period, and the individual within the culture. This perception is also influenced by the degree to which the counselor understands the racism and discrimination that have exacted significant tolls on individual and collective progress of African-Americans over a long period of time. Specific problems that African-American adolescents may bring with them to counseling include the following:

1. the adolescent's failure to develop positive self-concept and strong African-American identity;

2. adverse effects of stereotypes toward African-Americans and adolescents;

3. the poor academic achievement of the adolescent;

4. language problems, both verbal and nonverbal, due in part to Black English being accepted in the home and community, yet deemed inappropriate at school;

5. the absence of the father in the home;

6. adverse effects of the culture being perceived as inferior or in need of change;

7. the adolescent's cultural and social-class differences;

8. the adolescent's developmental differences, for example in height, weight, and coordination;

9. the problems associated with increasing socialization of the adolescent outside the African-American community;

10. the adverse effects of racism, prejudice, and discrimination.

Cultural Differences

African-American adolescents' cultural differences, developmental changes commonly associated with their lifespan period, and stereotypical images that plague both the culture and the developmental period can lead to mental health problems. Adolescence is a critical time for developing identities and positive self-concepts. It is a time for building confidence with which to grow personally and socially. However, during this critical time, African-American adolescents often become increasingly aware that their differences are neither understood nor accepted by many people. Furthermore, their future may be limited by racism, discrimination, and misunderstandings.

What African-American cultural characteristics or facts pertaining to the culture may lead these adolescents to be misunderstood? First, the African-American commitment to extended families often translates to "too many people living in one house." Second, the African-American's tendency to interrupt speakers in an encouraging manner may be considered rude by those who do not understand the intent. Third, the academic difficulties African-American adolescents experience are often attributed to lack of motivation or intelligence. Fourth, African-American adolescent males have a 53 percent unemployment rate—one of the highest in the nation (McNatt, 1984; Warfield & Marion, 1985). This is more likely the result of the failure of society to meet their needs rather than that of a culturally based character trait.

Often, the majority culture views the African-American as needing to "improve" or "change," but the minority culture may not perceive a need for change (Boykin, 1982; Hall, 1981). Recent decades of heightened African-American consciousness have resulted in many African-Americans wanting to hold onto valued cultural traditions and take pride in their cultural backgrounds. Although placing positive values on one's cultural background can contribute to a strong cultural identity, it may also result in counseling needs due to other cultures' lack of acceptance and understanding.

Language Problems

Whether adolescents perceive themselves as contributors to society and as worthwhile members of a culture depends significantly on their ability to communicate in the language of the society. No longer satisfied to live within the psychologically safe confines of home and the family, the adolescent ventures into a world of peers and friendships. The success experienced in the wider social world depends significantly on how well the adolescent can communicate with people outside the home and immediate community.

Perceptive counselors recognize that language differences, both verbal and nonverbal, play a critical role in overall development and in counseling relationships. Some clients hesitate to talk with counselors because they feel their speech will be evaluated negatively. Such a situation might lead clients to respond only briefly to the counselor's inquiries, sometimes giving the impression that they are uncooperative and sullen (Smith, 1981).

Nonverbal behavior, an equally important (or perhaps even more important) aspect of the language issue, also warrants the counselor's attention. According to Smith (1981), the cultural tendency of African-Americans to look away or to do something else while conversing often concerns Anglo-American counselors who interpret such behavior as indicative of "sullenness, lack of interest, or fear" (p. 155). Smith cites the incident of a African-American female adolescent who was sent to the principal's office for her "insolent behavior." The adolescent explained,

> Mrs. X asked all of us to come over to the side of the pool so that she could show us how to do the backstroke. I went over with the rest of the girls. Then Mrs. X started yelling at me because she said that I wasn't paying attention to her because she said that I wasn't looking directly at her. I told her I was paying attention to her (throughout the conversation, the student kept her head down, averting the principal's eyes) and then she said that she wanted me to face her and look her squarely in the eye like the rest of the girls (who were all white). So I did. The next thing I knew she was telling me to get out of the pool—that she didn't like the way I was looking at her. So that's why I am here. (p. 155)

This incident illustrates how important it is that professionals working in multicultural situations understand cultural differences to avoid misinterpreting nonverbal behaviors.

Generational Differences and Other Family Issues

Research focusing on generational differences among African-American adolescents and their elders is not as prevalent as similar research on other cultures. Although reaching firm conclusions remains difficult, several factors contribute to an argument that generational differences exist. First, the development of a positive black identity resulting from such social changes as the integration of America's schools probably have resulted in generational differences. Also, the Civil Rights Act, the equal rights movement in general, and the push toward African-American pride and awareness have strengthened the cultural identity of younger African-Americans (and, without doubt, some older cultural members, too). The popular song of several years ago, "Say it Loud; I'm Black and Proud," is just one example of an effort to encourage cultural pride and assertive action (Smith, 1981). The development of positive black identities probably has been greater, however, among younger African-Americans who were brought into the mainstream of American life through integration into America's educational systems. While younger generations have enjoyed more equal opportunities, older African-Americans may have continued to experience discrimination in employment, social life, educational opportunities, and religious life.

The boundaries in a family can become so blurred that, in some cases, there is no clear division of responsibility or source of authority. One example of such a situation is the three-generational system, in which a grandmother plays a role. Another example is the parental child system, in which parental power is allocated to a child, male or female, particularly if there are many children in the family or if both parents work. Such a family structure can result in adolescents displaying their stress through delinquency, sexual impulsiveness, or inappropriate handling of younger children when the demands of the household conflict with their age-appropriate need to be with peers (Hines & Boyd-Franklin, 1982).

Developmental and Other Concerns

Whether African-American adolescents satisfactorily meet the various developmental crises has implications that extend into the adulthood years. Rather than forming positive identities, African-American adolescents may experience role confusion due to the stereotypes and prejudices involving both their developmental period and their culture. According to Smith (1981), developing a strong cultural identity requires self-identity:

> Black people need to affirm the essence of their Blackness and to use their Blackness as a means of examining their mental health. What I am talking about here is the necessity of "self-identity." (p. 170)

Related developmental issues include self-concept and personality development. Mastering such developmental tasks as getting along with peers, progressing toward personal independence, and learning culturally appropriate masculine and feminine social roles that lead to a healthy self-concept may be difficult for any individual, but mastery becomes especially difficult for members of a minority group, whether the reason be race, color, culture, or physical handicap. Adolescents can experience many problems as they seek to develop a healthy self-concept (Bradley & Stewart, 1982). Another issue that may lead to the need for counseling concerns the learning of survival behaviors and the loss of security of close friends as adolescents tend to widen their social circles (Smith, 1981).

Counseling Considerations

As previously mentioned, language differences and communicational barriers can be a factor in determining the success of counseling intervention. In fact, a counselor's ability to communicate is considered to be more important than his or her similarity to the client's racial membership group (Smith, 1981). What, then, must counselors of African-American adolescents recognize to ensure effective communication? First, some African-Americans resent counselors' attempts to use slang in order to show understanding. Smith (1981) tells of one client who stated, "I knew that I didn't ever want to see that counselor again when he started talking about how 'I hope you don't think I'm trying to rip you off.' He was just trying too hard, and I didn't trust him" (p. 169). Second, counselors who are unfamiliar with the directness of some African-Americans may find their style of communication offensive and interpret directness as hostility. On the other hand, some clients, particularly males, may use the "playing-it-cool syndrome," in which the client tries very hard to act worldly, unconcerned, and "together." Other minority clients may be hesitant to speak altogether for fear that their speech will be evaluated negatively. Ho (1987) points out that African-Americans are often labeled by therapists as nonverbal and incapable of dealing with feelings. In fact, African-Americans often deal with anxiety by becoming either passive or aggressive—either they say nothing or become loud, threatening, and abusive. Their passive or aggressive behavior during therapy may be a manifestation of their frustration and displaced anger toward the therapist, particularly the Anglo therapist. Consider the following dialogue with Jessie:

Client: Well, you're the one who wanted to talk, so talk.

Counselor: Yes, the absence list showed you weren't in school for three days. Didn't we have an agreement that when things weren't going right for you, we'd talk, rather than you cutting out?

Client: All this same White counselor talk. You Whites always coming down on us and jiving us.

Counselor: Jessie, I thought we were going to talk about what happened during the three days of absence.

Client: This whole damn system of yours—it's hooked us all into money.

Counselor: Would you cut out all that crap about the system and talk about what's been going on with you the last three days? You know we can talk about what you can do for you, but that other thing is out there and not in here.

Client: Uh? Tell me more, ha!

Counselor: Jessie, I know you believe unfair things happen to you, but I want you to talk about what's been happening to you the last few days and try to forget that other for now.

Client: Uh? Well, uh, see. Our check didn't come in and we had the bills and I had to get us some quick bread and . . . . (Axelson, 1985, pp. 400–401)

What type of counselors do African-American adolescents prefer? Do age, sex, and type of problem make a difference? A FOCUS ON RESEARCH 7–3 looks at one research study to determine African-American preference for counselors. Other research on counselor preference indicated the following top five concerns: amount of education, similar attitudes and values, similar personality, same ethnicity, and age (counselor should be older than client) (Atkinson, Furlong, & Poston, 1986). While African-Americans tend to prefer African-American therapists over Anglo therapists, they also prefer competent therapists over less competent therapists. Competent skills and techniques needed for counseling African-Americans include the consideration of family and community life from an African-American perspective (Ho, 1987).

A FOCUS ON RESEARCH 7–3
African-American Student Preferences for Counselors

Relationships between client and counselor are of prime importance to the outcome of counseling. Martin and Thomas (1982) reviewed the available research on counselor performance and offered conclusions on whether males and females disclosed more or less with counselors of each sex. The two researchers then conducted a study to determine preferences of African-American college students for African-American counselors of varying age and sex and with respect to the type of problem. Fifty-seven male and 122 female students were asked to indicate their counselor preferences for educational, personal, and vocational problems. The results were somewhat unclear; however,

the authors came to the following general conclusions:

1. There are preferences on the part of some students; however, these preferences may vary with the age and the sex of the counselor and the type of problem.

2. Females tended to select female counselors for most problems, occasionally selecting a male counselor.

3. Counseling services should allow for a choice of counselors and attempt to match clients to counselors on the basis of the preference of clients.

4. Female counselors should be employed to accommodate the trend toward female preferences toward counselors of their own sex and male preferences for female counselors for certain types of problems.

Source: Martin, D. O., & Thomas, M. B. (1982). Black student preferences for counselors: The influence of age, sex, and type of problem. *Journal of Non-White Concerns in Personnel and Guidance, 4*, 143–153.

African-American counselors should be available in areas having large African populations. When an African-American high school student goes to a counselor, particularly an Anglo counselor, and is reluctant to reveal information, the student may be experiencing inner conflicts with racial identity and may be choosing not to participate in a multiracial relationship. Since having only Anglo counselors might have a detrimental impact on African-American adolescents, it is important for African-American adolescents to experience feelings of acceptance and openness in multiracial counselor-client relationships (McFadden, 1976).

School guidance services designed to effectively address the career development needs of African-American adolescents should be characterized by advocacy, proactive services, and outreach. Advocacy activities include in-school action to address policies and procedures that may negatively affect educational opportunities. These may involve undue suspension and expulsion, alienation of parents from schools, and placement of students based solely on scores (Perry & Locke, 1985). Counseling services have been also identified as a key nonacademic factor that contributes positively to the success of minorities, internationals, and nontraditional students enrolled in higher education (Walter & Miles, 1982).

Concerns that African-American adolescents bring to counseling sessions include (a) establishing a meaningful personal identity, (b) academic performance, (c) interpersonal relations, (d) autonomy, (e) sexual and aggressive feelings, and (f) long-term career plans (Gibbs, 1973). A FOCUS ON RESEARCH 7–4 examines how African-American students perceive counseling appropriateness.

 A FOCUS ON RESEARCH 7–4
African-American Students' Perceptions of Counseling Appropriateness

Counseling centers have become integral units on most college and university campuses, and their services have contributed to the growth, development, and success of students. A review of the literature revealed that students make use of counseling services for personal, academic, and vocational reasons. Walter and Miles designed an exploratory survey to determine African-American students' perceptions of counseling appropriateness. Thirty-seven students, all members of the African Student Association lo-

cated in a large state university, participated in the survey. The researchers offered several findings:

1. As problems become more personal and more threatening, the willingness to seek counseling diminishes. There is an almost self-defeating effect that appears to counteract the interpersonal relationship mission of the counseling center in regard to helping the minority student.

2. Counseling centers, in order to be more effective and more widely used by minorities, must promote their services and eliminate an implicit credibility gap.

Source: Walter, J., & Miles, J. H. (1982). African students' perceptions of counseling appropriateness: A preliminary study. *Journal of Non-White Concerns in Personnel and Guidance, 4*, 133–142.

Individual/Group Therapy

A primary task for multicultural counselors during initial counseling intervention will be to determine the appropriateness of individual and group therapy. Although the basic and most common form of counseling is individual, a more recent phenomenon has been expanded work with groups. A decision on which technique to use requires a basic understanding of intervention strategies and a careful consideration of the individual's culture and developmental period.

Reaching a decision concerning the appropriate intervention mode requires consideration of several questions: Is the African-American adolescent more likely to disclose personal information during individual or group sessions? In individual and group therapy, how effective is counseling if the family is not involved? Although adolescents tend to prefer group therapy sessions because their age-level peers may have similar problems (Ohlsen, 1983), will African-American adolescents speak of personal matters in the presence of adolescents from other cultures? Answering these questions requires getting to know the individual adolescent and the nature of the problem.

To what extent do adolescents' counseling needs result from problems associated with the adolescent years and from racism or perceived racism harbored by the majority society? Consider Marcia, a high school senior, who faces doubts and perceptions of discrimination:

Client: Oh, I can blame it (shyness, feelings of dispair) on a lot of things, parents, family environment, but I have to start looking on it as my mistake. I try so hard to look back and see how I overcame my shyness. I think it had a lot to do with being poor and my color.

Counselor: Oh?

Client: I kept entering beauty pageants, plays, and things. I didn't think I was convincing enough. I always sounded shy and scared, so I kept entering pageants. I won one in my sophomore year. I don't know how, but I did. That was giving me what I needed. I got fourth place in the county contest last summer. Something in me told me I should have won first. The thing that hurt me the most was they didn't even put me in the newspaper.

Counselor: I wonder why that was?

Client: I think I was just lucky that year . . . things were going more for Blacks then . . . a Black had never won any place before.

Counselor: You know, I'm real surprised that you would think that was the reason.

Client: Since I won, they don't have the county pageant anymore and various people say it's because you're Black. It's something they have to deal with here in this city . . . no matter how great you are, or beautiful, or how well you can speak, or anything else.

Counselor: Do you really believe it was stopped because of your race? I just don't have that impression.

Client: Oh . . . I just feel when I graduate I'll have to get out of this town to get anywhere—or any other small town like this one. I really don't want to stay here and go to [the community college]. If I can get the money, I want to go away to [state university]. I also thought about attending a Black college (Axelson, 1985, pp. 403–405).

Whether or not the county pageant was discontinued because an African-American won cannot be determined; however, the client feels that it was, and expresses her opinion to the counselor. Although the effects of centuries of racism and discrimination on African-Americans may be difficult for Anglo counselors to comprehend, they must not be discounted when working with African-American adolescents. In the transition from a family-centered world to a wider social world, adolescents readily perceive discrimination in their daily lives. Conscientious attempts to gain firsthand knowledge of the African-American culture provides a foundation for understanding how African-American adolescents think and perceive life events.

Family Therapy

As with individual and group therapy, a fundamental step is to consider whether the adolescent will disclose personal information during family counseling sessions. Another point to be considered is the extent to which the family can assist during and after the counseling session. As with Native-Americans, there may be a better chance of family members helping to facilitate change when African-American clients are involved.

Since African-American adolescents may not have learned a rigid distinction between male and female sex roles in childrearing and household responsibilities, therapists should seek the father's participation in family counseling. Hines and Boyd-Franklin (1982) maintained that involving fathers may be difficult for low-income African-Americans, since the father (who may be working two jobs) may not be able to leave work for therapy. The father, however, may be willing to come to an evening session or to take time off for one or two sessions that are focused on solving a specific problem. Therapists may have to become creative in their telephone contacts and letters to keep fathers abreast of family therapy. Even the father's limited involvement in family therapy can decrease the potential for sabotage of counseling efforts and may promote the attainment of the therapist's and family's goals. Since fathers sometimes do not live in the home, or may be only minimally involved, therapists often assume that the household lacks a "male model." The therapist involving the father (or a male from the extended family living in the home) should recognize that a male model does actually exist (Hines & Boyd-Franklin, 1982).

ASIAN-AMERICAN ADOLESCENTS

Asian-American adolescents face several problems: the "model minority" stereotype, often used to describe the culture (The new whiz kids, 1987); myriad language problems (Sue, 1981); elders' expecting younger generations to retain old-world traditions rather than assimilate into Anglo society (Kalish & Moriwaki, 1973); and racism and discrimination, involving both the culture and the developmental period.

UP CLOSE AND PERSONAL 7–2
Counseling Tyrone Johnson

Tyrone Johnson, age 16, was recommended by his teacher for a district-wide school dropout prevention program. A requirement for enrolling in the "at-risk" program was at least one session (one part of an overall assessment) with a community agency counselor. After the initial visit, the counselor used established guidelines to decide whether additional sessions were warranted. Tyrone was brought from his school to the 35-year-old Anglo counselor who met with students individually at the agency. Tyrone's previous worst behavior was too much talking with his friends; he was adamantly opposed to being placed in the at-risk dropout program and being sent to the counselor.

The counselor introduced herself and explained to Tyrone the reason for his referral. Tyrone stated, "Nothin's wrong with me. The problem's the teacher who don't like me cause I'm black. I'll be glad to get out of that honky school. I'd quit now if my parents wouldn't find out about it." Tyrone mostly looked down at the floor or at the picture on the counselor's wall. His failure to look her in the eye concerned the counselor, but she did realize it was a common habit among her African-American clients.

The counselor assessed Tyrone's case. His academic problems qualified him for the dropout program, and he appeared to harbor strong feelings that he was victim of racism in his school. Still, she had to note that not all Tyrone's teachers were Anglo. Could it be that his African-American teachers who had been academically successful had lost perspective of what it meant to be poor and African-American? While the counselor didn't want to imply that racism was not a factor, she hoped to help Tyrone get the situation in perspective.

During Tyrone's first session, the counselor tried to make him feel comfortable with her. She was Anglo and might not understand what it was like to be poor and African-American, but she sought to learn more about him, his friends, and his culture. She realized that establishing rapport was all-important. She informed Tyrone that she wanted him to return for additional counseling. She carefully explained that this was not punishment. She wanted to help him and would not "put him and his race down" as he thought his teachers did. Another decision was to continue individual therapy until she could see whether there were sufficient students in Tyrone's situation to form a small group. Also, she considered future family counseling, since the referral slip mentioned that Tyrone's parents were interested in his work. Yes, she thought, maybe Tyrone's parents could help with this situation.

Some of the counseling needs of Asian-American adolescents may result from the following problems:

1. failure to develop a positive adolescent and Asian-American identity;
2. adverse effects of the "model minority" stereotype;
3. the adolescent's failure to meet cultural expectations for behavior; e.g., restraint of strong feelings and avoidance of outspokenness;
4. conflicts involving family cultural characteristics such as rigidly defined roles;
5. problems with English language proficiency and the Anglo-American inability to understand nonverbal communication;

6. conflicts between Anglo emphasis on "individualism" and the Asian-American commitment to family and the welfare of others;

7. conflicts arising from generational differences between the adolescent and elders;

8. the adolescent's developmental differences, for example, in height and weight;

9. problems associated with the adolescent's social interests expanding from family to the wider community and peers;

10. the adverse effects of racism, prejudice, and discrimination.

Cultural Differences

Living in a democratic society that purports to respect equality of all peoples, Anglo counselors sometimes experience difficulty in appreciating the Asian-American's cultural traditions; e.g., rigidly defined social roles, adherence to family expectations, paternal dominance, sons being of greater value than daughters, and sons having more responsibility and freedom than daughters (Lum, 1986). The problem is growing even more complex due to the acculturation of some members of the younger generation (Kalish & Moriwaki, 1973).

Chinese-Americans often do not readily admit having emotional problems; hence, they underuse mental health services. This tendency can be traced to the culture-based reluctance to reveal information or events that could lower respect for the family. Counselors must deal with the Asian-American belief that problems are to be solved within the family so as not to risk shame. Such beliefs can hinder the therapeutic relationship between counselor and client (Sue & Sue, 1983).

Younger Asian-Americans choosing to hold firm to their cultural beliefs and heritage can also result in problems for clients and counselors. According to Sue and Sue (1983), a growing number of Chinese-American students on college campuses throughout the nation are emphasizing pride in their own heritage and self-identity, just as African-Americans. These students feel that others embracing Anglo standards are selling out. "Banana" is the derogatory term they use to describe a person of Asian ancestry who is "yellow on the outside but white on the inside." To gain the self-respect they feel has been denied them by the majority culture, they have banded together to reverse the negative tendency toward becoming "Americanized." These individuals are openly suspicious of such institutions as counseling services; they are viewed as agents of the establishment. Very few of the more ethnically conscious and militant Asians seek counseling because of its identification with the status quo. When they do, they are usually suspicious and hostile toward the counselor. Before counseling can proceed effectively, the counselor must deal with certain challenges. Sue and Sue (1983) cite the following comments from students:

> First of all . . . I don't believe in psychology. . . . People in psychology are always trying to adjust people to a *sick* society, and what is needed is to overthrow this establishment. . . . I feel the same way about those stupid tests. Cultural bias . . . they aren't applicable to minorities. The only reason I came in here was . . . well, I heard your lecture in Psychology 160 [a lecture on Asian-Americans]. (p. 101)

> Psychologists see the problem inside of people when the problem is in society. Don't you think white society has made all minorities feel inferior and degraded? (p. 102)

Language Problems

Problems due to lack of English-speaking ability can lead to counseling intervention and can interfere with communication during actual counseling sessions. Language problems fail to improve due to the client's allegiance to native languages; however, rather than blame the victims for the situation, the counselor should focus primarily on how to address the language problems.

In a study by Watanabe (1973), it was found that over 50 percent of Asian-Americans failed a "bonehead" English examination, which documents the seriousness of the problem. This language deficiency may result from difficulty with the English language or from conflicts surrounding native languages being spoken in the home and English in the schools. Whatever the reason, adolescents experience problems that can result in difficulties in meeting age-appropriate developmental tasks.

The counselor can help adolescent students with limited English proficiency in several ways. They may arrange for a bilingual translator, either through contacts with the school or with community organizations such as The United Way and the American Red Cross. They may also provide a support system for the adolescent, including teachers and adolescent peers. Finally, they may reduce cultural conflict by helping both the culturally different student and other students to understand cultural variations (Keyes, 1989).

Generational Differences and Other Family Issues

Generational differences between parents and adolescents in the United States reflect the ongoing acculturation process. According to Vontress (1970), many Chinese clients experience a dislike for their own culture, especially in their social life. Such a situation is typified in the following counseling interchange (Sue & Sue, 1983) where the Asian adolescent girl discusses her parents' reluctance toward her dating Caucasians:

Counselor: You seem to prefer dating Caucasians. . . .

Client: Well . . . It's so stupid for my parents to think that they can keep all their customs and values. I really resent being Chinese and having to date all those Chinese guys. They're so passive, and I can make them do almost anything I want. Others [Chinese] are on a big ego trip and expect me to be passive and do whatever they say. Yes . . . I do prefer Caucasians.

Counselor: Is that an alternative open to you?

Client: Yes . . . but my parents would feel hurt . . . they'd probably disown me. They keep on telling me to go out with Chinese guys. A few months ago they got me to go out with this guy—I must have been the first girl he ever dated—I wasn't even polite to him.

Counselor: I guess things were doubly bad. You didn't like the guy and you didn't like your parents pushing him on you.

Client: Well . . . actually I felt a little sorry for him. I don't like to hurt my parents or those [Chinese] guys, but things always work out that way. (p. 100)

The client's last statement reflected some feelings of guilt over her rudeness toward her date. Although she was open and honest, she confused her desire to be independent with her need to reject her parents' attempts to influence her life. During a later session, she was able to express her conflict:

Client: I used to think that I was being independent if I went out with guys that my parents disapproved of. But that isn't really being independent. I just did that to spite them. I guess I should feel guilty if I purposely hurt them, but not if I *really* want to do something for myself.[3]

Although the rejection of Chinese culture is often a developmental phase adequately resolved by most Chinese-Americans, many come to look upon Western personality characteristics as more admirable. Some Chinese-American girls come to expect the boys they date to behave boldly and aggressively in the Western manner. In fact, one study revealed that some Chinese-American college females were quite vehement in their denunciation of their male counterparts as dating partners. They frequently described the Chinese male as immature, inept, and sexually unattractive. Although the males denied the more derogatory accusations about themselves, they tended to agree that they were more inhibited and unassertive than Caucasians (Sue & Sue, 1983). Such differences of opinion and the younger generation's tendency to date people of other cultures can result in considerable turmoil between generations.

Developmental and Other Concerns

Poor self-concepts due to language inadequacies and developing positive personal and cultural identities in a multicultural society may result in potential counseling problems for Asian-American adolescents. It will be the counselor's responsibility to understand the Asian-American culture, understand the implications of poor self-concepts and confused identities, and to plan appropriate counseling intervention.

Other concerns might include the differences in Asian- and Anglo-American expectations regarding competition and achievement. While the Anglo competes for individual recognition, the Asian-American attempts to achieve for the recognition it brings to the family. Also, although many Asian-Americans have excelled in the American school systems, some suffer serious academic and communication problems due to their lack of English proficiency. Another concern is comparing Asian- and Anglo-American achievement scores when Asian-Americans often must work far harder due to their lack of proficiency with English.

Counseling Considerations

Several challenges confront counselors working with Asian-American adolescents. First, these adolescents often feel that family members should be sought for advice and assistance rather than sharing concerns with an outsider. This situation may lead to the counselor having to explain the objectives, procedures, and confidentiality of the counseling process. Second, it is important to understand the Asian traditional

---

[3]From Donald R. Atkinson, George Morten, and Derald Wing Sue, *Counseling American Minorities,* pp. 100–101. Copyright © 1983 Wm. C. Brown Publishers, Dubuque, Iowa. All rights reserved. Reprinted by permission.

commitment to the family and the problems resulting from acculturation, generational differences, and differing peer and family expectations. Third, nonverbal behaviors may be misinterpreted. Asian-Americans' forward and backward leaning indicates feelings; e.g., a forward lean indicates politeness and concern while leaning backward indicates that the listener wants to withdraw from the conversation. Similarly, the Japanese-American, in particular, might express anxiety though silence (Bond & Shirashi, 1974).

Another barrier interfering with counseling Asian-Americans is a tendency not to disclose personal problems. For example, Chinese-American students frequently experience difficulty admitting emotional problems because of the shame it might bring to the family. These students might request help indirectly by referring to academic problems or somatic complaints. The Asian-American's difficulty with disclosure often requires that counselors emphasize the confidentiality of counseling relationships. Many Chinese-American clients are able to open up and express feelings quite directly once they develop trust in the counselor (Sue & Sue, 1983).

Asian students tend to view counseling as a directive, paternalistic, and authoritarian process. Hence, they are more likely to expect the counselor to provide advice and a recommended course of action. Speaking specifically of Chinese-Americans, Leong (1986) concluded that they expected more expertise from the counselor and believed that clients did not need to be as responsible, open, or motivated as counselors. A FOCUS ON RESEARCH 7–5 points out several cultural factors that may prove to be particularly difficult or troublesome for Southeast Asians in counseling situations.

Effective counseling intervention includes making the Asian-American client feel comfortable and relaxed, since many are unaccustomed to counseling techniques and situations. As related by Sue & Sue (1983), Anne W. was quite uncomfortable and anxious during the first interview dealing with vocational counseling. This anxiety seemed related to the ambiguity of the counseling situation. Since Anne appeared confused about the direction of the counselor's comments and questions, the counselor felt that an explanation of vocational counseling would be useful:

 A FOCUS ON RESEARCH 7–5
Issues in Counseling Southeast Asian Students

Southeast Asians accounted for 143,680 of the 342,113 international students attending U. S. institutions of higher education in the 1984–1985 academic year. However, as Fernandez (1988) points out, research on effective multicultural counseling continues to be mea-

ger. Fernandez delineates several aspects of the Anglo-American culture that have the potential to cause culture shock in Southeast Asians. These aspects relate to time orientation, the role of the family, value systems, social behavior, student expectations, and the effects of acculturation. Fernandez suggested that traditional Western counseling theories do not always work with Southeast Asian students.

Source: Fernandez, M. S. (1988). Issues in counseling Southeast Asian students. *Journal of Multicultural Counseling and Development, 16,* 157–166.

Counselor: Let me take some time to explain to you how we usually proceed in vocational counseling. Vocational counseling is an attempt to understand the whole person. Therefore, we are interested in your interests, likes and dislikes, and specific abilities or skills as they relate to different possible vocations. The first interview is usually an attempt to get to know you ... especially your past experiences and re- actions to different courses you've taken, jobs you've worked at, and so forth. Espe- cially important are the hopes and aspirations that you have. If testing seems indicated, as in your case, you'll be asked to complete a battery of tests. After testing we'll sit down and interpret them together. When we arrive at possible vocations, we'll use the vocational library and find out what these jobs entail in terms of background, training, etc.

Client: Oh! I see. . . .

Counselor: That's why we've been exploring your high school experiences. . . . Some- times the hopes and dreams in your younger years can tell us much about your interests.[4]

Counselors must also understand the influence of the family and its impact on student behavior and achievement. Consider the case of Pat H., a 19-year-old Chinese- American prepharmacy major who came for vocational counseling. As the counselor and Pat examined the abasement score on his Edwards Personal Preference Schedule, the following interchange took place (Sue & Sue, 1983):

Counselor: Do you see this score [abasement score]?

Client: Yeah, I blew the scale on that one. . . . What is it? [some anxiety observable]

Counselor: Well, it indicates you tend to be hard on yourself. For example, if you were to do poorly in pharmacy school ... you would blame yourself for the failure. . . .

Client: Yeah, yeah . . . I'm always doing that . . . I feel that . . . it's probably exaggerated.

Counselor: Exaggerated?

Client: I mean . . . being the oldest son.

Counselor: What's it like to be the oldest son?

Client: Well . . . there's a lot of pressure and you can feel immobilized. Maybe this score is why I feel so restless.[5]

As noted by Sue and Sue, this progression marked a major breakthrough in Pat's case and led to an increasingly personalized discussion.

Individual/Group Therapy

Deciding whether to use individual or group therapy with adolescents requires con- sidering the Asian-American's expectation to protect and honor the family's name. With such an expectation, group therapy may be perceived as very threatening. A

---

[4]From Donald R. Atkinson, George Morten, and Derald Wing Sue, *Counseling American Minorities*, p. 105. Copyright © 1983 Wm. C. Brown Publishers, Dubuque, Iowa. All rights reserved. Reprinted by permission.
[5]Ibid., pp. 103–104.

frequent concern of many Chinese-American students is that their friends, and especially their parents, will learn of their counseling sessions (Sue, 1981); therefore, information that could place the adolescent's or family's status in jeopardy is not likely to be disclosed. Chinese students frequently refuse to participate in group counseling; in a group setting, they are usually quiet and withdrawn.

Family Therapy

In view of the Asian-American client's unfamiliarity with family therapy, the first session should be planned so that the client and the family will want to return for future sessions. Many Asian-Americans do not understand the role of a family therapist; they may perceive the therapist as a knowledgeable expert who will guide them through their problem. It follows that they will expect the counselor to be more directive than passive. Being directive does not imply that the counselor must tell family members how to live their lives, but it does involve guiding the family therapy process. The family therapist must convey confidence and should not hesitate to disclose his or her educational background and work experience. Asian-Americans need to feel that their therapist is more powerful than their problems, and that counseling will be accomplished with competence and skill (Ho, 1987).

UP CLOSE AND PERSONAL 7–3
Counseling Rieko Sukuzi

Rieko Sukuzi, age 16, was referred by her teacher for counseling. The teacher had advised Rieko to refer herself, but Rieko thought secretly that counseling was out of the question since she valued her family's wishes to keep problems within the family. Therefore, the teacher had referred her, promising Rieko that her peers would not know and that her family's name and honor would remain unsullied.

The Anglo counselor, 32 years of age, knew she would have to move cautiously with Rieko—ensure confidentiality, build trust, explain the counseling process and the client-counselor relationship, and allay Rieko's fears about shaming the family. During the first session, Rieko was quiet and unwilling to disclose significant information. After the third session, the counselor decided that Rieko's two major problems were her language and her lack of Anglo friends. Specifically, Rieko's loyalty to her

family's wishes and her commitment to excel in all endeavors "turned off" some potential friends, and her problems with English resulted in an inability to communicate with ease. The counselor had to help Rieko believe she was a worthwhile person regardless of whether she had Anglo friends. Also, remedial assistance with the language problems was long overdue, especially since Rieko's language problems required her to study much harder than most of her peers.

The counselor decided that Rieko would enroll in a special English class and that she would continue in counseling on a regular basis to discuss making friends in multicultural situations and to explore ways for her to deal with students who seemed to turn their backs on her. The counselor quickly ruled out both group and family therapy, since Rieko would be very unlikely to disclose information in either situation.

A basic consideration in implementing family therapy with Asian-Americans is to plan counseling therapy in such a manner that all family members will feel free to speak. In family counseling situations, the father, being considered head of the household, might assume the spokesperson role, with other family members for the most part remaining silent.

HISPANIC-AMERICAN ADOLESCENTS

Hispanic-American adolescents' problems, to a great extent resulting from cultural stereotypes and economic conditions, will likely challenge counselors in schools and mental health agencies to understand the Spanish-speaking people, the many variations of Hispanic cultures, and the Hispanic-American's reluctance to forsake traditional cultural values or to adapt to Anglo-American ways.

In considering the problems facing Hispanic-American adolescents, it is important to remember that the Hispanic culture is composed of many individual diverse cultures, making counseling generalizations difficult. Some of the problems that may warrant counseling intervention include the following:

1. failure to develop a positive Hispanic-American identity and a healthy self-concept;
2. adverse effects of stereotypes; e.g., the Hispanic as a lawbreaker, gangmember, or hotblood;
3. the adolescent's commitment to such cultural values as *machismo, dignidad,* and *respeto*, which other cultures may misunderstand or reject;
4. conflicts between Anglo expectations for "self-advancement" and the adolescent's commitment to family over self;
5. failure to comply with traditional Hispanic family expectations: strict family roles, natural superiority of males, women assuming subordinate roles;
7. the adolescent's academic problems;
8. the adolescent's language problems: reluctance to give up Spanish as the mother tongue; reluctance to move out of a Spanish-speaking enclave;
9. the adolescent's developmental differences; for example, in height and weight;
10. the adverse effects of racism and discrimination directed toward Hispanic-Americans.

Cultural Differences

Understanding which cultural differences have the potential for resulting in problems is a prerequisite to effective counseling intervention. A significant problem facing Hispanics is the continuing level of poverty that plagues their culture. Although some improvement can be detected between first- and second-generation Hispanics, two factors continue to contribute to the poverty problem: (1) the increase in the number of female-headed households and (2) the high unemployment rate of some Hispanic-American groups (twice as high as the Anglo-American rate) (Fitzpatrick, 1987).

The high unemployment rate and low socioeconomic status of Hispanic-Americans take a toll on male Hispanics who consider themselves to be heads of the household and the economic providers for the family (Lum, 1986). The effects of living in a household on welfare, where the father is unemployed, or where the wife is the primary breadwinner, have yet to be definitively studied. Adolescents may quickly realize that some cultural expectations (e.g., the father as breadwinner) are simply not realistic given family circumstances.

Several differences between Hispanic and Anglo cultural family perspectives that might lead to conflict and misunderstandings include the Hispanic-American commitment to family over self; the husband/father being the ruler of the household (and the women's traditional acceptance of this situation); and the loyalty to extended family members. If commitment to family is not maintained, the Hispanic-American may experience loss of respect and dignity (Mirandé, 1986).

Language Problems

The Hispanic-American's allegiance to the Spanish language is evident. More than two-thirds of the Hispanic population continue to identify with Spanish and nearly half report Spanish to be spoken in the home (Ruiz, 1981). This loyalty to the mother tongue is understandable; however, being forced to live in Spanish speaking communities for lack of English skills may cause young people to miss many economic and employment opportunities and may reduce their level of acculturation.

The English language problem may also create conflicts during counseling sessions. The Anglo counselor, unable to speak Spanish and perhaps lacking an understanding of the Hispanic-American's allegiance to Spanish, may make matters worse by insisting that the client speak English or by trying to communicate using a smattering of Spanish words.

Generational Differences and Other Family Issues

As with generational differences among other cultural groups, these differences between Hispanic-American adults and the younger generation have implications for counselors working with adolescents. Some writers (Knight & Kagan, 1977; Knight, Kagan, Nelson, & Gumbiner, 1978) have concluded that increasingly younger generations adapt American norms and behavior patterns to a greater degree. Major conflicts arise when younger generations, especially males, acculturate faster than older members of the family (Knight & Kagan, 1977; Knight et al., 1978). A study of Cuban adolescent refugees revealed high rates of mental illness due to ambiguity about role performances, especially regarding dating and expressions of sexuality (Naditch & Morrissey, 1976). Vast differences exist in general values, family roles, and marriage practices between first- and second-generation Puerto Rican immigrants. Due to acculturation, the extended kinship support system, which is a valued cultural characteristic, dissipates with time spent in the predominantly Anglo society (Fitzpatrick, 1987). The implications for counselors of individuals of all ages on the lifespan ring clear: Generational differences may result in problems requiring counseling intervention.

Other issues that may require counseling intervention include differences of opinion between adolescents and their families on such Hispanic traditions as beliefs in spirituality, dignity of the individual, respect for authority, and allegiance to both the immediate and extended families (Garcia-Preto, 1982).

Developmental and Other Concerns

Developing within a lifespan period that does not receive great respect and forging personal and cultural identities in an increasingly complex multicultural society can result in counseling problems. Other developmental factors such as variations in size, stamina, and social maturity have implications for adolescents growing into adulthood. Acutely aware that *machismo* is a cherished cultural trait to all Hispanic males, the adolescent male may feel an even greater need to meet expectations in this domain, whether in convincing a potential girlfriend that he is worthy of her respect or in taking care of the family in a manly and responsible manner.

Young adolescent males and females with a realistic outlook toward life face significant challenges. The male must eventually find gainful employment in a society where Hispanic-American rates of unemployment and poverty run high and where limited education will not allow them to compete in the marketplace. Young Hispanic females probably will witness such social changes as more equality among the sexes and more women joining the workforce, perhaps at higher salaries than the often poorly educated Hispanic males.

Counseling Considerations

The wide diversity in Hispanic-American cultural characteristics complicates a discussion of generic counseling strategies. Counselors must seek knowledge of the specific population with whom they expect to interact. This section focuses on Puerto Ricans living in the United States because they are such a sizeable population.

Cultural concepts that Puerto Rican clients may value include fatalismo, respeto, dignidad, and machismo. *Fatalismo* refers to a sense of a fatalism. *Dignidad* and *respeto* refer to the dignity of the individual and respect of those deserving it. *Machismo*, already discussed elsewhere, refers to the males' superiority (Fitzpatrick, 1987). Understanding these cultural attributes is important when counseling Hispanic-Americans; however, it may be even more important to understand clients as individuals within their respective Hispanic cultures.

When formulating counseling programs, effective multicultural counselors should understand several aspects of the Hispanic culture that influence counseling effectiveness. First, family structure and the attendant sex roles are important counseling considerations. The extended family structure characteristically includes (a) formalized kinship relations such as the *compadrazgo* (godfather) system and (b) loyalty to the family, which takes precedence over loyalty to other social institutions. Anglo counselors, unaccustomed to counseling Hispanic-Americans, might be somewhat surprised at the more rigid and more clearly delineated family member roles (Nieves & Valle, 1982). Consider Maria who has begun to resent her father's absolute authority:

Maria is a nineteen year old female in her second year of college. Her family migrated to the United States from a town outside of San Juan, Puerto Rico three years ago. She is the second of six children; four are females and two are males. All of the children, including the wife and child of the oldest brother, live in the same house with both parents. The family is very traditional. The father is the dominant figure and makes all the major decisions for the family.

Maria began college after her high school graduation. She attended an inner-city school. She is a biology major and is interested in a career as a pharmacist. Although the college placement test indicated a weakness in English, she has performed at an above average level in all her courses.

Maria first came to counseling to discuss her goals and to obtain information for transfer to a senior college. Further interviews resulted in Maria's expressing anger and hostility toward her father. This case exemplifies the authority role of the father and the underlying feelings of conflict held by many females toward the male as a rigid and dominant figure. It also illustrates the support given by the extended family. (Nieves & Valle, 1982, p. 156)

Other factors that have significance for counselors include the Puerto Ricans' poverty status, insecurities about a social identity in the United States, their seemingly defensive and aggressive attitudes, and their extensive repertoire of gestures (Blatt, 1976). Developing an appropriate cultural and adolescent identity can be affected by perceptions of these factors and also by the counselor's reaction toward and respect for valued cultural attributes.

For the most effective counseling intervention, those working with Hispanic-American adolescents must demonstrate four important traits: (1) the ability to listen carefully and offer feedback to the client, (2) the ability to identify and label potential problems, (3) the ability to raise the client's expectations for change, and (4) the ability to describe the attitudes and feelings of the client according to his or her cultural perceptions. A FOCUS ON RESEARCH 7–6 provides concrete suggestions for counseling Puerto Rican students.

Individual/Group Therapy

A decision as to whether to use individual or group therapy must be reached with a solid understanding of the culture, the individual, and the advantages and disadvantages of each counseling modality. School counselors working with Hispanic students have reported group counseling to be particularly effective for developing the students' skills in expressing their feelings in English, stimulating self-respect and pride in the Hispanic culture, and clarifying personal values (Padilla, 1981). Walker and Hamilton (1973) described a successful group encounter that included six African-Americans, four Chicano-Americans, and four-Anglo-Americans. Counseling techniques included teaching listening skills, focusing on feelings, and reinforcing participant's interaction. The counselor may want to begin with individual adolescents and then progress to group therapy after establishing rapport and trust.

Family Therapy

Family therapy offers particular promise with Hispanics because of the high value placed on family and kinship ties. In interviewing or counseling the entire family at one time, one family member can be designated as an adjunct counselor, who also works to achieve family goals (Padilla, 1981). As solutions are determined for family's difficulties, the particular problems of this family member may decrease significantly.

Success has also been reported with group sessions in which three or four families meet jointly for weekly sessions of two hours. Counselors provide information on group dynamics, and families actually try to help one another solve their problems. The counselor then meets separately with each family in an attempt to improve communicational skills for use in the group sessions and in private life (Padilla, 1981). The family can be included in therapy in several ways. Counselors may choose to work with the whole family directly or request specific family members to attend counseling sessions. Or the counselor may work with one family member, who, in turn, works with the family as a group (Christensen, 1977; Padilla, 1981).

Christensen (1989) contends that it is best for the counselor to work with both the youth and the family in counseling Hispanic clients. If such an arrangement is not possible, the counselor should at least meet with the family at some point. Since Hispanics often feel that the family can provide the greatest assistance, involving as many members as possible may result in a cooperative effort to help the client. By involving the family, the counselor also demonstrates awareness that the family can play a therapeutic role, and that each person has something to offer (Christensen, 1989).

 A FOCUS ON RESEARCH 7–6
Counseling Puerto Rican Students

Nieves and Valle (1982) directed their attention toward Puerto Rican family roles and their effects on college students. After an extensive review of the literature, the authors provided detailed descriptions of both male and female roles. They included three excellent case studies to illustrate how college students were affected by traditional family expectations. Finally, Nieves and Valle offered several counseling suggestions:

1. Use active counseling approaches that are concrete, specific, and focused on the student's behalf.

2. Develop an awareness of the Puerto Rican culture.

3. Use approaches that allow for the client's frame of reference as a vehicle for growth.

4. Examine prejudices and attitudes toward Puerto Ricans.

5. Make home visits if possible and make reference to the family during sessions.

6. Call students by their correct names. In Puerto Rico, people are given two last names—the first is that of the family, the second is from the mother. Using the wrong name is insulting, and may raise identity questions.

7. Accept the role of expert; however, work to relinquish the role of authority. Clients must accept responsibility for their lives.

Source: Nieves, W., & Valle, M. (1982). The Puerto Rican family: Conflicting roles for the Puerto Rican college student. *The Journal of Non-White Concerns, 10,* 154–160.

◤ UP CLOSE AND PERSONAL 7–4
Counseling Carlos Suarez

Carlos, age 16, spoke in both English and Spanish as he told his 45-year-old Anglo counselor what had happened. He had been referred by the police department to the counseling organization that worked with delinquent adolescents. Not having had any previous conflicts with the law, Carlos had been picked up with several other boys who had broken into a vacant store and had done several hundred dollars worth of damage. Carlos's parents had been notified, and his father and older married brother had come to the police station. Carlos further explained that he had been released since he had not actually taken part in the crime and because his father had agreed that Carlos would meet with the counselor.

During his first session, Carlos was cooperative. He discussed his academic problems, his poor self-concept, and his lack of Anglo friends. Although the counselor insisted that Carlos accept responsibility for his actions, he did believe that Carlos's friends were to blame for his encounter with the police.

In determining counseling priorities, the counselor decided to meet with Carlos on an individual basis for several sessions and then, if Carlos continued to disclose information, switch to group sessions with other Puerto Rican adolescents with similar problems. The counselor would first attempt to get Carlos to understand his culture better, work to improve Carlos's self-concept, and help him to understand his Hispanic identity. As a second priority, he would attempt to get Carlos to accept responsibility for his schoolwork and for selecting friends.

A POINT OF DEPARTURE

Challenges Confronting Multicultural Counselors of Adolescents

Several challenges await counselors working with adolescents in multicultural settings. First, understanding the adolescent developmental period and each individual culture present the most important challenges. A related challenge is to understand identity formation and self-concept development, both vital during this lifespan period. Third, the adolescent's expanding social world involves a transition from parent-centered surroundings to a peer-centered society, resulting in new ideas about life and living. These developmental changes and the accompanying acculturation may result in generational differences with which counselors may have to contend. Fourth, counselors are continually encouraged to understand the "individual within the culture" and to realize that individuals vary as to backgrounds, needs, and aspirations.

SUMMARY

Counseling culturally different adolescents requires a counselor who is knowledgeable with respect to both the developmental period and the adolescent's cultural background. Knowing when to use individual, group, and family therapy and where to seek additional knowledge about cultural differences are prerequisites to planning and implementing effective counseling. Simply having knowledge, however, is insufficient; it is necessary to appreciate the life circumstances of a culturally different adolescent and to understand why counseling intervention must reflect the client's particular cultural background and developmental period.

Suggested Readings

Change: The Magazine of Higher Learning. (May/June 1988 [Special issue]). A special report, entitled "Hispanics and the Academy," contains nine articles on Hispanic-Americans including discussion of their plights and ambitions in institutions of higher education.

Change: The Magazine of Higher Learning. (November/December 1989). This issue of *Change* features a section, "Asian and Pacific Americans: Behind the Myths." Seven articles and an excellent bibliography are included.

Fernandez, M. S. (1988). Issues in counseling Southeast-Asian students. *Journal of Multicultural Counseling and Development, 16,* 157–166. Maintaining Southeast Asians experience culture shock, Fernandez discusses such issues as time orientation, the role of the family, differing values, and social behaviors.

Folensbee, R. W., Draguns, J. G., & Danish, S. J. (1986). Impact of two types of counselor intervention on Black-American, Puerto Rican, and Anglo-American analogue clients. *Journal of Counseling Psychology, 33,* 446–453. This article focuses on female students to determine the extent to which counseling intervention depends on cultural background.

Manese, J. E., Sedlacek, W. E., & Leong, F. T. L. (1988). Need and perceptions of female and male international undergraduate students. *Journal of Multicultural Counseling and Development, 16,* 24–29. Surveying students from Southeast Asia, the Middle East, Europe, Latin America, and Africa, this study focuses on differences in needs and perceptions of male and female undergraduate international students.

Miller, M. J., Springer, T. P., Milford, G., & Williams, J. (1986). Identifying the counseling needs in Black high school students: A field-tested needs assessment questionnaire. *Journal of Multicultural Counseling and Development, 14,* 60–64. These authors explain the development of a questionnaire designed for African-American students and provide criteria for successful evaluation.

Schwartz, L. J. (1976). Group counseling with disruptive adolescents. In G. S. Belkin (Ed.), *Counseling: Directions in theory and practice.* (pp. 357–361). Dubuque, IA: Kendall/Hunt. This excellent article, which crosses cultural boundaries, examines basic assumptions of group therapy and looks at the didactic-affective approach.

Sowa, C. J., Thomson, M. M., & Bennett, C. T. (1989). Prediction and improvement of academic performance for high-risk Black college students. *Journal of Multicultural Counseling and Development, 17,* 14–22. These researchers concluded that traditional predictors of academic success such as SAT scores do not account for differences in college GPAs as a function of race.

Part III

Understanding and
Counseling the Adult

Continuing with the lifespan perspective, Part III focuses attention on culturally diverse adults. The first chapter in this part describes the cultural characteristics of Native-American, African-American, Asian-American, and Hispanic-American adults; the second chapter offers suggestions for intervening with adults in multicultural settings.

Chapter 8

Social and Cultural Aspects of Adulthood

Questions To Be Explored

1. What is the nature of the adult developmental period? How does this period differ culturally from adolescence and the elderly years?

2. What societal and cultural influences affect adults' lives?

3. What are some unique cultural differences during the adult years? Are generational differences sufficiently significant to warrant the multicultural counselor's attention?

4. What are the effects of cultural differences on adults' lives and thinking?

5. Is it possible to make cultural generalizations without stereotyping cultures? How can we distinguish between reality and stereotypical labels?

6. What are the adulthood years like in the Native-American, African-American, Asian-American, and Hispanic-American cultures? How do they differ from each other and from adulthood in the Anglo-American culture?

7. What challenges confront counselors working with culturally different adults?

8. What are some additional sources of information for counselors working with adults?

INTRODUCTION

In contrast to childhood and adolescence, adulthood was considered for many years to be a time when nothing much was happening developmentally—a "mature" time that was not deemed sufficiently worthy or interesting to warrant serious study. A more contemporary and enlightened view of this developmental period recognizes its importance and appreciates the need to respond appropriately to adult clients' ethnic and cultural backgrounds.

211

THE ADULT YEARS: SOCIETAL AND CULTURAL INFLUENCES

What kind of problems do adults face? How do these problems and challenges differ across cultures? What crises and conflicts characterize the adult years? Do these conflicts vary significantly from one cultural group to another? Are some problems or conflicts unique to specific cultures? Multicultural counselors deal daily with these difficult questions and other issues that are unique to adulthood. Understanding the social and cultural characteristics of the adult years provides a foundation for counseling decisions. Whereas Chapter 3 examined the adult developmental period, this chapter examines the various societal and cultural characteristics of four cultural groups and provides a portrait of the adult years in each culture.

The rich diversity among people with respect to lifespan period, socioeconomic class, geographical location, and other variables prevents professionals from making wholesale generalizations about cultures. There are significant differences, for example, between first-generation adults and second- and third-generation adults with respect to degree of allegiance to cultural customs and traditions. Through acculturation, second- or third-generation cultures typically become more "Americanized." Conflicts may occur when younger generations acculturate rapidly, perhaps repudiating the parental culture, while older generations cling to long-held values and beliefs.

Although extreme caution is necessary in generalizing across cultures, the following statements are considered valid:

- African-Americans have a dialect different from the language of Anglo-Americans. (Hall, 1981; Weber, 1985)
- Native-Americans often appear to be somewhat aloof and lower their voices when they are angry. (Lum, 1986)
- Hispanic-Americans demonstrate a powerful commitment to *dignidad, machismo,* and *respeto*; males are generally considered biologically superior. (Nieves & Valle, 1982)
- Asian-Americans demonstrate extreme loyalty to the family, especially to the father and to older generations. (Sue, 1981)

Although intracultural and individual differences must not be overlooked, it would be expected that individuals of each culture mentioned would agree that the preceding statements are indeed cultural characteristics.

NATIVE-AMERICAN ADULTS

Societal and Cultural Description

Although the early history of the Native-American culture is still somewhat of a mystery in several respects, we have sufficient information to provide a fairly clear picture of the Native-American culture. Their lack of acceptance of the early settlers (and of many contemporary Anglo-Americans) has contributed to an erroneous cultural picture. In today's world of difficulties and instabilities, Native-Americans must struggle to overcome others' images of their past; even worse, they may have to overcome their own negative images. Too often, when the Native-American culture is mentioned, the image brought to mind is of an evil, inferior savage, prone to excessive drinking and violent and erratic behavior. This stereotypical image has led many Native-Americans to view themselves in a negative light. Undoubtedly self-flagellation has contributed to Native Americans' lack of success in the predominantly Anglo society. Poorer-than-average economic achievements and lower social status resulting from such stereotypes in turn have resulted in the culture being referred to as "the culture of poverty" (Wax, 1971). As Richardson (1981) points out,

> the statistics ... indicate that the life of the American Indian is one of hardships, incarcerations, degradations, exploitations and that of a second-class citizen which makes for problems of survival, low self-esteem, and rejection. (p. 216)

Other professionals providing social and cultural descriptions of Native-Americans agree that the Native-American population has more than its proportionate percentage of problems. Lum (1986) contends that

> in contrast to Black and Asian-Americans, Native-Americans represent the minority with needs in the areas of income, education, health, and mental health. There are higher rates of arrest, drinking, and unemployment among Native-Americans than among other ethnic groups. (p. 64)

Such circumstances no doubt contribute to negative stereotypes of all Native-Americans seeking professional counseling. However, as A FOCUS ON RESEARCH 8–1 points out, some Native-Americans have been successful, despite the adversity with which they have had to contend.

Although a wide variety of personality traits, cultural practices, and lifestyles characterize Native-Americans, some of the more general traits include relative passivity and shyness in dealing with professionals, sensitivity to strangers (resulting in soft speech), a tendency to focus on the present, a fatalistic view of life, strong family obligations, noninterference with others, and the avoidance of assertive or aggressive situations (Miller, 1982). Although cultural characteristics, of course, vary from tribe to tribe and may vary with individuals, a broad picture emerges:

1. Happiness is paramount. One must be able to laugh at misery and enjoy life.

2. Sharing is a basic cultural value. Everything belongs to others.

3. Tribe and extended family come first. The elderly family members are accorded great respect.

4. Traditional ways are cherished. The old ways are the proven and the best. Remember the days of youth.

5. The land must be respected. Live with your hands, in harmony with nature, and live as naturally as possible. (Richardson, 1981)

Axelson (1985) describes several other traits that contribute to a cultural portrait. First, individualism, so valued in Anglo-American society, does not hold significant meaning for Native-Americans. In the Native-American culture, individuals may do as they please, but only if their actions are in harmony with nature. Second, the Native-American culture values what a person is rather than what he or she has; thus, the

---

A FOCUS ON RESEARCH 8–1
Native-Americans' Success in Business Ventures

Says one Native-American businessperson, "we never, never give up." Such an attitude has led to considerable successes in business ventures for some Native-Americans. The Navajo Nation produces electronic missile assemblies for General Dynamics; the Choctaws of Mississippi build wire harnesses for Ford Motor Company; the Seminoles in Florida own a 156-room hotel; and the Swinomish Indians of the state of Washington are planning a 60-acre boat basin, an 800-slip marina, and a 3-story office and commercial headquarters. *Newsweek* reports that such aggressive approaches to business were previously unheard of on the reservations. High unemployment, high rates of alcoholism, and poverty-level living conditions have characterized the Native-American people for many decades.

Critics claim that successful business ventures have not helped the entire culture: Unemployment affects 35 percent of some tribes and young people increasingly must leave home to find work. Some critics worry that economic development will threaten the cultural identity of Native-Americans.

Source: Indian tribes, incorporated. (1988, December 5). *Newsweek,* pp. 40–41.

---

accumulation of personal possessions is not emphasized. Third, childrearing practices are characterized by early training in self-sufficiency, always in harmony with the natural habitat. Fourth, respect for the elderly is mandatory; it is they who impart wisdom and acquaint the young with traditions, customs, legends, and myths.

Language

Native-Americans at one time or another have spoken about 2,200 different languages. The difficulty of categorizing these languages into six major families attests to the argument that understanding the communication patterns of this culture requires considerable effort (Banks, 1987).

Although verbal communication is the usual means by which adults interact, nonverbal communication is extremely important also. Only during the last decade have professionals begun to realize the urgent need to understand the "silent language" by which messages are communicated. Rooted deeply in cultural heritage, nonverbal communication must be recognized and appreciated as a cherished cultural tradition (Jensen, 1985). Common nonverbal behaviors of Native-American adults include avoidance of eye contact, listening with an indirect gaze, looking away after initial acknowledgment, and less use of encouraging sounds, such as "uh huh." (Sanders, 1987). Anglo-Americans who tend to look each other in the eye can often be disturbed by clients who indeed are listening, yet looking in another direction.

There is little doubt that considerable diversity characterizes Native-American language. For example, Native-Americans on one reservation in New Mexico avoid the English language entirely, while almost everyone speaks English on another reservation in North Dakota (Vontress, 1976a).

Families

Native-American families, just as individuals of the culture, have widely differing personality traits, cultural practices, and lifestyles. There are, however, several characteristics of families that appear to pertain to large segments of the culture.

First, the culture expects adults to demonstrate strong allegiance to extended family members. Respect for and protection of the elderly result from the Native-American belief that older generations impart wisdom gained from their many years of life experiences. All family members feel an obligation to care for the elderly, and, in return, the elderly assume the task of acquainting the young with the traditions, customs, and myths of the culture (Lum, 1986). Grandparents often assume considerable responsibility for infant and toddler care, and thus continue a relationship of mutual concern with grandchildren throughout the lifespan (Attneave, 1982).

Second, Native-American childrearing practices are characterized by early training in self-sufficiency, with physical development and psychological learning being in harmony with knowledge gained from the natural world. Elderly family members' opinions on childrearing are continually sought and their advice considered with reverence and respect (Axelson, 1985). Families often choose for children to remain at home rather than attend school when an elderly family member is ill, demonstrating the close relationship of family members and the genuine concern for both young and old alike (Sanders, 1987). Other family characteristics that appear to cross tribal lines include the sharing of material goods, encouraging the young to respect individuality, and modeling a tendency toward noninterference.

Adherence to fairly specific sex roles, another widespread family characteristic, has the potential for causing problems. Traditionally, men and boys brought physical strength to the job market, while women and girls worked in the home and cared for children and the elderly. As Native-Americans have moved away from traditional expectations of only men being employed outside the home, women have tended to experience more success than men because of their household skills and ability to nurture children. The few employment opportunities for men and boys often have resulted in dead-end jobs because of their erratic employment patterns, meager educational skills, and lack of successful experiences in coping with a predominantly Anglo-American society (Attneave, 1982).

One study (Rindone, 1988) that explored Native-American students' motivation to succeed in college demonstrated the strong influence of adult family members on the young. The parents had low socioeconomic status and spoke mainly the Navajo language. Despite these factors, the students completed their college degrees, some even extending their studies beyond the baccalaureate. Parents and other adult family members constituted the driving force in these students' desire to succeed. In the view of Herring (1989a), however, Anglo-Americans historically have attempted to weaken or dissolve the Native-American family, this powerful source of cultural strength.

A FOCUS ON RESEARCH 8–2
Dissolution of the Native-American Family

Herring (1989a) implores social and educational institutions to increase their understanding of Native-American families. Maintaining that these families differ significantly from their Anglo-American counterparts, Herring provides a comprehensive description of Native-American family characteristics and summarizes Anglo-American attempts to dissolve Native-American families. Reference is made to the military ventures during the seventeenth and eighteenth centuries, the relocation attempts during the nineteenth century, the Relocation Acts of 1953, and attempts to remove Native-American children from their families and to sterilize young Native-American women. After presenting a disturbing argument that the Native-American family is, indeed, being threatened, Herring addresses the implications of this situation for educational and social counseling.

Source: Herring, R. D. (1989a). The American native family: Dissolution by coercion. *The Journal of Multicultural Counseling and Development, 17,* 4–13.

Unique Challenges Confronting Native-American Adults

Solutions to the several challenges confronting Native-American adults must be sought by both clients and their counselors in a cooperative spirit. Although Native-Americans must accept responsibility for their lives, many of their problems stem from a history of discrimination, prejudice, and broken treaties. Although the reasons for the Native-American's personal and social condition should be recognized and understood, major emphasis should focus on solutions to the obstacles hampering personal and social progress.

Table 8–1   Cultural comparison: Native-American and Anglo-American adults

Native-American Adults	Anglo-American Adults
Value the person—who he or she is	Value the person's material possessions
Show great respect for elders and the aged	Believe the future lies with youth
Have fairly specific sex roles	Stress equality of the sexes
Value loyalty and respect group accomplishments	Respect individual achievements
Share material goods	Stress ownership rather than sharing
Encourage noninterference with others	Interfere as necessary
Tend to be humble	Tend to be competitive
Look backward—toward traditional ways	Look forward—toward the future
Tend to be nonjudgmental toward those of their own culture	Tend to be more critical
Emphasize the mystical	Emphasize the scientific

Source: Adapted from Richardson, E. H. (1981). Cultural and historical perspectives in counseling American Indians. In D. W. Sue, *Counseling the Culturally Different* (pp. 216–255). New York: John Wiley.

Education has always been a controversial issue that basically revolves around the pressures of domination, value conflict, and self-determination. Regardless of these factors, however, the poor academic attainments of Native-Americans have, indeed, been major drawbacks to their progress (Axelson, 1985). Native-Americans continue to have one of the highest dropout rates of any ethnic group at the high school level, regardless of region or tribal affiliation. A recent survey indicated that only 57 percent of Native-American adults had a high school diploma or its equivalent (Sanders, 1987). A second and undoubtedly related problem facing Native-Americans concerns their dismal employment statistics; e.g., under 1 percent have obtained employment in private industry (Axelson, 1985). Third, Native-Americans' language problems undoubtedly affect their progress (Vontress, 1976b).

Perhaps one of the most significant problems for Native Americans, and at least a contributing factor to their other problems, is the destructive stereotypical images that are often perpetuated in literature, in movies, and on television. These stereotypes have the potential for influencing the decisions of counselors and the career and employment aspirations of clients. Both client and counselor must strive to overcome stereotypes that continue to thwart Native-American progress.

Table 8–1 provides a cultural comparison of Native-American and Anglo-American adults. UP CLOSE AND PERSONAL 8–1 looks at a particular Native-American adult.

AFRICAN-AMERICAN ADULTS

Societal and Cultural Description

Because of the relative youth of the African-American population, its growth over the next several decades will outpace that of the Anglo-American population. Thirty-nine percent of African-American adolescents 16 to 21 years of age live below the federally defined poverty level, while approximately 41 percent of those under 16 years of age live below the poverty level (Bell-Scott & McKenry, 1986). The family roots of most African-Americans can be traced to the rural South where they were poorly prepared for urban living. Specifically, their education, the skills they learned, and the society in which they lived left them unable to cope well in an urban setting (Baughman, 1971). However, by no means have African-Americans had a monolithic experience, nor is their culture homogeneous. Within the African-American culture, broad ranges of behavior exist as well as important class and geographical distinctions (Smith, 1981).

A Common Destiny: Blacks and American Society, the report of the Committee on the Status of Black Americans (1989), concluded that African-Americans are arrested, convicted, and imprisoned for criminal offenses at rates much higher than Anglo-Americans. The report contains some startling statistics: African-Americans' representation in prisons is about four times their representation in the general population; compared with the overall population, African-Americans are twice as likely to be victims of robbery, vehicle theft, and aggravated assault, and six or seven times as likely to be victims of homicide (Jaynes & Williams, 1989).

The health problems of the African-American males are so serious that their life expectancy is beginning to decline. Many African-American males are threatened by loss of life due to murder, drug addiction, and AIDS. Between ages 15 and 44, three African-American males die for every Anglo-American male; life expectancy is 68.8 years, six years shorter than for Anglo-American males; homicide is the leading cause of death of African-American males between 15 and 24 (from 1984 to 1986, homicide claimed the lives of 903.6 African-American males per 100,000); and African-American males have AIDS at a rate of 29.9 per 1,000 as opposed to an Anglo rate of 9.7. The prevalence of drugs and violence in the African-American community has reduced the quantity and quality of African-American life (Black males' life expectancy is declining . . . , 1989).

UP CLOSE AND PERSONAL 8–1
John Lonetree—A Native-American Adult

John, age 38, shares traits common to fathers of all cultural backgrounds. His main goals are to provide financial support for his family and to provide a home for 8-year-old Bill, 15-year-old Carl, his wife of 17 years, and his elderly mother. John works at a manufacturing plant and wonders where he could find another job if he were laid off. He realizes the difficulty that job hunting would entail, especially with his limited education, his lack of marketable skills, and his poor English.

Through hard work at the same job for nine years, John's condition belies that of the stereotypical Native-American. John has a job, does not have a drinking problem, has never been in jail, and is not overly self-critical as many Native-Americans are thought to be. The fact that he does not have extensive material possessions is of little concern to him; he thinks people should appreciate him as a person rather than for what he owns. He is aware that he has experienced fewer problems than many of his friends.

John has several family concerns that adults of other cultures often share. First, he sometimes worries about Carl and Bill's educational accomplishments. His sons will need a better education than he has had in order to compete in the predominantly Anglo-American society.

His second concern is with his mother, who is showing signs of advancing age. Although she doesn't make a direct financial contribution to the family, she is an important source of advice and counsel. Also, she takes care of Bill and Carl when they are too ill to attend school. Because of her years, she deserves to be protected and respected. John often goes to her for advice on how to raise the boys.

Although John is fairly content and happy in comparison to many of his friends, he does have several problems. As previously mentioned, he wants Carl and Bill to finish high school. Then, he wants to do something to help those friends who have not been as fortunate as he has. He also would like to rid himself, his family, and his people of the drunken, lazy, uneducated image of Native-Americans that continues to be so demoralizing. Finally, since he often speaks a combination of two languages with his friends, he sometimes experiences communication difficulties when he travels outside his Native-American community.

John has doubts about his future: With his present skills, will he always have a job? If not, what will he do? Will his boys finish high school? What will his family be like when his mother passes away?

◆ A FOCUS ON RESEARCH 8–3
AIDS in Ethnic Minority Males

Ethnic minority males, especially African- and Hispanic-Americans, represent a significant proportion of the AIDS cases in the United States, with these cases linked primarily to homosexual or bisexual behavior and intravenous drug use. Peterson and Marin address the issues of high-risk sexual behavior and attitudes surrounding

AIDS. Problems in developing successful prevention programs include lack of information and difficulties in approaching target groups. The authors conclude that information must be provided in a culturally appropriate manner; cultural values, norms, and attitudes must be integrated into media messages and into the format of counseling interventions; and additional research is needed to address the task of developing culturally sensitive prevention programs.

Source: Peterson, J. L., & Marin, G. (1988). Issues in the prevention of AIDS among Black and Hispanic men. *American Psychologist, 43,* 871–877.

A related problem facing African-Americans is their health-care insurance coverage. Twenty-two percent of African-Americans are not covered by private health insurance or Medicaid. The cumulative effects of health disadvantages and the tendency to avoid medical visits until conditions are serious predispose African-American adults to higher incidences of chronic disability and illness (Jaynes & Williams, 1989). A FOCUS ON RESEARCH 8–3 examines a contemporary health problem facing large numbers of African-American males.

The African-American culture has acquired the reputation for being innately more aggressive than other cultures, especially the Anglo-American culture. While there is no scientific evidence to support the culturally aggressive theory, there are several reasons why other cultures (including some African-Americans, themselves) have accepted it as fact. First, many Anglo-Americans feel that aggression is somehow linked to genetic makeup and have unfairly emphasized the violence of African-Americans. Secondly, many assume that African-Americans have been treated in such a manner that they *should* respond aggressively. They are perceived as being "loaded" with suppressed aggression waiting to be released (Baughman, 1971).

Some African-Americans, either by choice or necessity, have somewhat adopted the social and cultural patterns of the larger society in which they live. Significant cultural adaptation among middle- and upper-class African-Americans often makes these groups barely distinguishable culturally from Anglo-Americans of comparable socioeconomic levels. Some evidence points to an overconforming to middle-class Anglo-American standards in religious observances, dress, sexual behavior, and child-rearing practices. Some cultural adaptation has also occurred among lower-class African-Americans. In the rural South, lower-class African-Americans and lower-class Anglo-Americans both tend to consume inexpensive foods and both tend to focus on the emotional aspects of religious ceremonies (Pinkney, 1975). The contemporary status of African-Americans is further examined in A FOCUS ON RESEARCH 8–4.

A FOCUS ON RESEARCH 8–4
Black and White in America

Newsweek's special report (March 7, 1988), "Black and White in America," recalls the influence of Dr. Martin Luther King, Jr. in integrating classrooms, lunch counters, and public transportation facilities and ultimately in stirring Congress to enact a voting rights measure. The report points out two striking developments of significance to the current status of blacks in America: (1) the emergence of an authentic black middle class—better educated, better paid, and better housed than any other group of blacks, and now so large that its members outnumber the black poor; and (2) the concurrent emergence of an "underclass" resulting from the movement of these comparatively well-off blacks to better neighborhoods.

Source: Black and White in America. (1988, March 7). *Newsweek*, pp. 18–23.

What about this socially disabled nucleus of poor people who compose the underclass? What statistics characterize them?

1. Around 55 percent of the families are headed by females.

2. The rate of pregnancy among black women 15 to 19 years of age is more than twice that of whites.

3. Blacks account for about half of all crimes of violence.

4. The rate of unemployment for black youth is twice that of whites.

5. In 1986, 1 in 3 blacks, compared to 1 in 10 whites, still lived below the poverty level: $11,203 for a family of four.

Language

There are considerable differences between the speech patterns of African-Americans and Anglo-Americans. First, the African-American is more likely to interject comments such as "all right," "make it plain," and "that all right" into conversations, whereas Anglo-Americans are more likely to sit quietly or perhaps smile or nod. To the speaker, these comments are perceived as signs of encouragement. African-Americans do not consider them rude or annoying. Second, African-American speech is rhythmic and allows for considerable verbal creativity. In the consonant-vowel-consonant-vowel pattern, some syllables are held longer than in standard English and are accented differently. Rhythmic speech patterns are learned early by young African-Americans and are reinforced as the child grows into an adolescent (Weber, 1985).

Nonverbal language that is culturally based may play an important role in the counseling relationship. It is essential that the counselor understand this nonverbal language so as not to misinterpret it. For example, the directness of some African-Americans during conversations may be offensive to some counselors and interpreted as hostile. African-American males may choose to "play it cool"; that is, act worldly, unconcerned, and "together." This is usually a strong defense mechanism that allows the client to limit personal involvement, to test the counselor, or to save face in some situations (Smith, 1981).

Counselors working in cross-cultural situations can benefit from an understanding of certain expressions associated with different cultures. For example, Weber (1985) contends that although "rappin" is currently used by many people to mean simply talking, it originally described a dialogue between a man and woman in which the man's intention was to win the admiration of the woman through creative and imaginative statements. Another cultural term is "runnin it down," which simply explains something in great detail. The speaker's responsibility is to recreate an event so vividly for the listener that there is complete agreement and understanding. As a third example, "playing the dozens" is a battle of insults between speakers. The term *dozens* refers to a slavery practice in which "damaged" slaves (those with disabilities) were sold in lots of 12 at discount prices; thus, the term calls attention to negative physical characteristics (Weber, 1985). Such expressions as the three just mentioned often are not understood by majority counselors, or even other minority professionals; however, they have special significance for African-American adults. Unfortunately, although Black English meets all cultural and commonly accepted standards, it is often considered a degraded, substandard form of English (Hall, 1981).

Families

The cultural heritage of the African-American family includes the extended kinship network system that serves as a supportive and therapeutic base. African-American households are more likely than Anglo-American homes to include individuals other than parents and their children. Frequently these individuals are relatives; yet, often the African-American household includes people who are not related to the family. A study of the extended kinship relations in African-American and Anglo-American families found that (a) the former families interacted with relatives more often, (b) they considered a broader range of kin as important, and (c) they were given more assistance in childcare (Smith, 1981). These researchers concluded that "Black families have apparently developed a more pervasive and encompassing structure which meets more needs with more intensity than [the structure] among White families" (Hays & Mendel, 1973, p. 56).

Extended family and kinship networks result in mutual reliance. Needs for financial aid, child care, advice, and emotional support can be met through such familial arrangements. Lum (1986) reports such networks also foster a sense of corporate responsibility. In fact, children and adolescents may be informally "adopted" by grandparents and other close relatives within the extended yet well-defined close-knit system of relationships (Lum, 1986). A FOCUS ON RESEARCH 8–5 examines the role of grandmothers in extended family homes.

The effects of unemployment and underemployment on the African-American male and his family represent a clear problem for the culture. One result of joblessness is family disruption, which also increases murder and robbery rates. Although research does not suggest that the culture is more conducive to crime, the high rates of crime in African-American neighborhoods appear to stem from the linkages between unemployment, economic deprivation, and family disruption in urban African-American communities (Sampson, 1987).

A FOCUS ON RESEARCH 8–5
African-American Grandmothers in Multigenerational Households

In an attempt to describe child development within the context of the extended family, Pearson et al. (1990) reported the frequency of African-American grandmothers' coresidence in households with first-grade children, their patterns of involvement in parenting, and the degree to which family structure and employment affected the grandmothers' parenting involvement. Findings included the following:

1. Of the homes studied, approximately one-third were "extended," with 10 percent of the households including the grandmother.

2. The degree of the grandmothers' parenting involvement differed as a function of family structure, with grandmothers in mother-absent homes being the most likely to be involved.

3. Grandmothers' employment did not moderate their engagement in parenting behaviors.

4. Grandmothers' parenting behavior was substantial and included both authoritarian and nurturing behaviors.

Source: Pearson, J. L., Hunter, A. G., Ensminger, M. E., & Kellam, S. G. (1990). Black grandmothers in multigenerational households: Diversity in family structure and parenting involvement in the Woodlawn community. *Child Development, 61,* 434–442.

Changes in the family since the 1960s include higher divorce rates, decreased marriage rates, increasing numbers of female-headed households, and increasing percentages of children living in single-parent households (Jaynes & Williams, 1989). The issue of increasing concern is the single-parent African-American family. Fifty-two percent of the African-American children in America in 1987 lived in female-headed households, as compared to 37 percent in 1970. Surprisingly, more college-educated African-American women headed households than African-American women who did not finish high school. Also, women who had never married represented the largest number of females heading households. The consequences of the situation become clear when one considers that 68 percent of African-American children in single-parent households are poor (Hill, 1989).

Childrearing techniques and practices in African-American families differ significantly from those of the Anglo-American culture. Parents in African-American families

Table 8–2   Marital status of the African-American population in 1986

| Sex | Population (Thousands) | | | |
	Single	Married	Widowed	Divorced
Male	3,155	4,391	328	626
Female	3,284	4,645	1,301	1,211
Total	6,439	9,036	1,629	1,837

Source: Based on data from U.S. Bureau of the Census, 1988b.

Table 8–3   Interracial married
couples—1970, 1980, and 1987

Racial Mix	1970	1980	1987
Husband black; wife white	41,000	122,000	121,000
Wife black; husband white	24,000	45,000	56,000
Total black-white couples	65,000	167,000	177,000

Source: U.S. Bureau of the Census, 1989.

are generally stricter and more authoritarian in their use of discipline than Anglo-American parents, arising from the historical legacy of socializing children for survival (Bell-Scott & McKenry, 1986). Staples (1976) states that although African-Americans may use more physical punishment, their actions are counterbalanced by expressions of love and affection. Also, African-American parents encourage acceleration of development and early independence training to provide stronger survival skills needed in a highly competitive society (Bell-Scott & McKenry, 1986). In fact, many African-American families strive to increase the likelihood of the children's success by emphasizing high achievement. Acquiring an education is thought to be very important, with both mother and father providing support, encouragement, reinforcement, and modeling of achievement-oriented behaviors (Scanzoni, 1977). According to Hill (1989), to achieve economic parity with families in the Anglo community by the year 2000, African-American families must attain economic self-sufficiency, strengthen and stabilize the family, and develop viable and healthy communities (Hill, 1989).

As Table 8–3 indicates, the number of interracial marriages is continuing to increase in the United States. In fact, interracial marriages in the Western states have reached their highest recorded levels in American history (Tucker & Mitchell-Kernan, 1990). Counselors intervening with interracial couples can benefit from being aware of trends in African-American interracial marriages. A FOCUS ON RESEARCH 8–6 provides interesting information concerning interracial marriages among African-Americans.

Unique Challenges Confronting African-American Adults

African-Americans living in a predominantly Anglo-American society confront many problems. First, the dialect difference will continue to challenge them. While their distinctive dialect is a unique cultural characteristic, some African-Americans are beginning to view it as a handicap to success in a society that demands the use of standard English. Second, African-Americans must address the problem of their negative image. The stereotype of the violent black may be affecting their economic opportunities and social progress. A third challenge to African-Americans is their poor academic showing and low socioeconomic status. Complicating this problem is the fact that many African-Americans who have not succeeded live in environments in which social conditions are often detrimental to self-improvement (Jaynes & Williams, 1989). Held back by discrimination, racism, and unjust treatment for many centuries, African-Americans have simply not had opportunities to achieve their fair

A FOCUS ON RESEARCH 8–6
Interracial Marriages

Tucker and Mitchell-Kernan (1990) directed their efforts toward identifying recent patterns in black-white marriages in the United States. Interracial marriages were barred at one time or another in 40 of the 50 states until the landmark *Loving v. Virginia* Supreme Court decision of 1967 brought an end to such statutes. Still, despite these laws, black-white unions are recorded from the early colonial period.

After offering a brief historical review of interracial marriages, Tucker and Mitchell-

Kernan (1990) turned to trends. Their findings include the following:

1. Current rates of interracial marriage differ dramatically according to both region and gender. Specifically, more interracial marriages occur in the West and more black men marry out of their race than do black women.

2. Interracial couples tend to be younger and are more likely to have been married previously.

3. African-Americans born in the Northeast and North Central regions (and those born in foreign countries) are more likely to be married to nonblacks than African-Americans from other regions in the United States.

Source: Tucker, M. B., & Mitchell-Kernan, C. (1990). New trends in Black-American interracial marriage: The social structural context. *Journal of Marriage and the Family, 52,* 209–218.

share of education and financial gains. Evidence does not support the hypothesis that government support programs or the existence of a culture of poverty contributes to female-headed households, high birth rates of unmarried women, high unemployment of African-American males, and lower academic achievement (Jaynes & Williams, 1989).

Table 8–4   Cultural comparison: African-American and Anglo-American adults

African-American Adults	Anglo-American Adults
Use statements such as "make it plain" to encourage the speaker	Use nods and smiles to encourage the speaker
May not look a speaker in the eye	Make eye contact to indicate attentiveness
Respect unique and rich dialectical differences	Respect standard English
Value the extended family network	Value the immediate family
Tend to be stricter and more authoritarian in childrearing	Tend to be more democratic and less authoritarian in childrearing
Stress cultural pride	Stress individual pride
Believe racism and discrimination must be eliminated rather than compromise cultural traditions	Believe others should adopt Anglo-American traditions and values

Sources: Data compiled from Axelson, 1985; Hall, 1981; Lum, 1986; Pinkney, 1975; Smith, 1981.

◢ **UP CLOSE AND PERSONAL 8–2**
Cynthia Johnson—An African-American Adult

Cynthia Johnson, age 33, considers herself fairly fortunate. She has her husband, William; her sons, Tyrone and Carl; two younger daughters; and the children's grandmother. William has not been laid off recently at the manufacturing plant, and she still has her job as a hospital aide. Although Cynthia knows that William is worried about losing his job, she feels fairly secure about hers. Having William's mother in the house is another positive; she can look after the family when Cynthia is at work.

Cynthia's life is not free of problems, however. Providing for four children is often difficult, especially when William is without work. Furthermore, her own lack of formal education and marketable skills are holding her down. She is also concerned about her lower middle-class neighborhood, which appears to be deteriorating in several areas. Drugs are becoming increasingly visible, the police are being called more frequently, delinquency and vandalism are more rampant, and three cases of AIDS are rumored. Just the other day, she thought she overheard Carl ask Tyrone whether he had smoked pot. Cynthia questions whether her children should be growing up in such an environment. She understands the temptations 10-year-old Carl and 16-year-old Tyrone can experience. Also, she wonders about the safety of her family. She tends not to be aggressive and has always been opposed to guns in the house. However, recent neighborhood events are making her more receptive to William's suggestion of buying a gun for protection. Also, although her two young daughters are not presently on the streets much, they are developing rapidly and will soon be leaving the supposedly safe confines of the home.

Cynthia sometimes thinks of herself, too—her own frustrations and accomplishments. Life should be more than just work and survival, shouldn't it? Is this the way it will always be? Will Carl and Tyrone be around when she grows old? Will she still be healthy? Although Cynthia does not dwell on her concerns, she is somewhat apprehensive about the future.

Table 8–4 offers a cultural comparison of African-American and Anglo-American adults. UP CLOSE AND PERSONAL 8–2 focuses on Cynthia Johnson, one African-American adult.

ASIAN-AMERICAN ADULTS

Societal and Cultural Description

The Asian-Americans and Pacific Islanders in the United States include the Chinese, Pilipino, Japanese, Asian Indian, Korean, Indochinese, Hawaiian, Samoan, and Guamanian cultures (Asian and Pacific Islander data: . . . , 1988). Readers are reminded that grouping a variety of different cultures for purposes of discussion necessitates caution. All groups differ, just as individuals differ within a culture.

As previously mentioned, the Asian-American people have sometimes been referred to as a "model minority" (Suzuki, 1989). Although statistics indicate that many

Asian-Americans have experienced considerable economic and academic success, a comprehensive picture must be considered before reaching conclusions. First, the "model minority" stereotype of economic success does not take into account that the culture has a higher percentage of more than one wage earner per household. Nor does it take into account a significant incidence of poverty. Second, although academic achievements have been impressive, widely differing achievement levels continue to exist among individual Asian-Americans, and language problems constitute a major barrier for many. Third, areas with large Asian-American populations, such as San Francisco and New York, have experienced ghetto problems, unemployment, poverty, health problems, and juvenile delinquency (Sue, 1981).

A widespread cultural belief among Asian-Americans is that discussing unpleasant events will actually cause them to happen. In fact, discussing sickness, mental illness, or death with members of the Chinese culture often constitutes a social taboo. Physical or mental problems also are thought to reflect negatively upon families. In some situations, an entire family might be ostracized if it is learned that one family member has some form of mental illness (Lum, 1986).

Religious rites and ceremonies play a significant role in the lives of many Asian-Americans. Formal religions include Buddhism, Protestantism, and Catholicism. Protestant and Buddhist churches serve specific Asian groups, such as the Japanese, Chinese, Pilipino, Korean, and Vietnamese, while the members of the Catholic Church are generally integrated with other ethnic groups in a geographic parish. The religious values of Asian-Americans tend to be closely intertwined with family obligations and expectations (Lum, 1986).

Language

Despite the notable academic successes of many Asian-Americans, their proficiency levels in English have undoubtedly slowed their progress and cultural assimilation. Table 8–5 indicates group percentages for Asian-Americans experiencing difficulty with English. This language problem is evidenced by the over 50 percent failure rate of Asian-Americans taking a basic English examination and the extent of required

Table 8–5   Asian cultural groups experiencing difficulty with English

Language of Group with Difficulty	Percentage Having Difficulty with English	Percentage Unable to Speak English at All or Well
Chinese	52.5%	28.9%
Pilipino	20.5%	14.1%
Japanese	76.5%	23.4%
Korean	63.3%	45.1%

Source: From *Counseling and Development in a Multicultural Society* by J. A. Axelson. Copyright © 1985 by Wadsworth, Inc. Adapted by permission of Brooks/Cole Publishing Company, Pacific Grove, CA 95950.

noncredit remedial work to overcome language deficiencies before beginning university work. Asian-American students are twice as likely to fail the basic English examination as compared to their Anglo-American counterparts (Sue, 1981).

Understanding also that the Asian-American's language structure changes with differing situations provides counselors with additional cultural insights. Language changes with respect to syntax, word endings, and terminology, depending upon individuals and the nature of relationships. In situations where little is known about another person, anxiety may result from doubt about the style of communication to use; e.g., whether to speak loudly or softly (Shon & Ja, 1982).

Families

The Asian-American family is characterized by unique familial roles and expectations that warrant the counselor's attention. We continue to stress the fact that this culture consists of many different populations shaped by environmental, historical, and social pressures. These groups differ not only among themselves, but also differ in important respects from the broader Anglo-American culture.

Asian-American families are patriarchial in nature, with clearly defined roles for both adults and children. Children are expected to be obedient to parents and elders and, in return, the parents are responsible for the upbringing, education, and support of the child (Kitano, 1974; Lum, 1986). The father's dominant position carries with it tremendous responsibilities. In the eyes of the community, the successes and failures of the family as a whole and of its individual members are rooted in the father's influence. Shon and Ja (1982) describe the father as follows:

> It is expected that he will provide for the economic welfare of his family. The responsibility of providing food, clothing, and shelter rests squarely on his shoulders. He enforces the family rules and is the primary disciplinarian. Because of this, he is frequently seen as somewhat stern, distant, and less approachable than the mother. (p. 212)

The traditional role of the mother is that of the nurturant caretaker of both her husband and children. Until recently, the primary role of women was the care of the family; they were not allowed to engage in the same kinds of work and activities as men. The mother raised the children, cared for her husband, and sometimes interceded with the father on the children's behalf (Shon & Ja, 1982).

Family honor is often maintained through highly developed feelings of obligation, including the avoidance of shame to the family at nearly any cost (Lum, 1986; Shon & Ja, 1982). Lum explains that the family provides a reference point, a source of personal identity and emotional security. Although there have been some changes in values and a trend toward increasing individualism, such concepts as family loyalty, respect and obligation, and harmony and group cooperation all continue to play significant roles in determining family and individual behavior. Shon and Ja point out that the concept of loss of face involves not only the exposure of an individual's actions for all to see, but also the possible withdrawal of the confidence and support of the family, community, or society. Fear of losing face can be a powerful motivating force for conforming to family and societal expectations.

Unique Challenges Confronting Asian-American Adults

Language problems, dismal employment opportunities for unskilled minorities, the "model minority" stereotype, and conflicting familial roles and expectations all create unique challenges for Asian-American adults. First, the language problems detailed by Sue (1981) and the often dismal employment prospects described by Shon and Ja (1982) will undoubtedly continue to lead to frustrations. Second, the "model minority" stereotype of Asian-Americans poses a challenging situation. To reiterate, many Asian-Americans have achieved considerable academic and financial success that should not be understated; however, it is also important to note that many have experienced considerable failure in these same areas (Suzuki, 1989). Third, problems may arise when family roles and expectations conflict with those of the Anglo-American culture. With acculturation, Asian-Americans are placing increasing emphasis on the Anglo ideals of individuality and personal achievement (Lum, 1986). The pedestal on which fathers and sons are placed and the relatively low status of mothers and daughters conflict with traditional Anglo-American thinking. Changes in values and family relationships in the Asian-American culture have the potential for creating a schism between younger and older generations.

Table 8–6 lists examples of the cultural differences between Asian-Americans and Anglo-Americans. UP CLOSE AND PERSONAL 8–3 introduces Han Suzuki, an Asian-American adult.

Table 8–6   Cultural comparison: Asian-American and Anglo-American adults

Asian-American Adults	Anglo-American Adults
Hold that good performance and achievement bring honor to the family	View good performance and achievement as personal accomplishments
Exhibit great respect for ancestors and elders	Respect the living—especially youth
Place family first, individuals second	Place individuals first, family second
Regard the father as leader of the family—the decision-maker	Believe in more equal and shared decision-making
Believe that the son's primary allegiance must be to his own family	Believe that the son's primary allegiance must be to his wife and new family
Regard females as subservient—primarily caretakers	Increasingly, are regarding females as equal to men and deserving of equal respect
Approach problems indirectly and in a discreet manner	Approach problems head-on and openly
Generally consider divorce shameful	Tend to accept divorce as a fact of life, with no "shame" attached

Sources: Data compiled from Axelson, 1985; Lum, 1986; Sue, 1981.

UP CLOSE AND PERSONAL 8–3
Han Sukuzi—An Asian-American Adult

Han, 36 years old, lives in a predominantly Asian-American neighborhood with his wife, 10-year-old Mina, another son and daughter, and the children's elderly grandfather. Han really appreciates Grandfather's presence in his household, especially when his two jobs leave him weary and in need of encouragement. Han's full-time job is with an Anglo-American company; his part-time job is with an Asian-American friend who owns a small and struggling construction company. Although he likes his friend, Han would prefer to have only one job. The extra money is handy, but he has little time to spend with the family.

Han views his role as critical to the welfare of the family. He makes most of the financial and household decisions. Some of his Anglo-American friends question his strong, authoritarian hand, but that's the way it was with his father, and that's the way it should be. Han is not sure he could change, even if he wanted to. What would his wife and children think? What would Grandfather think? Everyone in his family expects him to make all the important decisions.

Han is proud of his daughter Mina. Her part-time library job, her musical gifts, and her recent initiation into the School Honor Society please him. In fact, all his family members are worthy. Only once did Mina's younger brother appear to be a little lax in his behavior at school. Before taking action, Han went to the grandfather to seek his advice. The solution was to approach the problem indirectly and with great tact. The boy did not suffer great shame or embarrassment, but he knew what his father expected him to do.

Han acknowledges that he has problems—his two jobs, uncertainty about whether he should allow his wife to work to supplement his salaries, and his aging father. He is fairly content and is proud of his close-knit family, but today's changing society is likely to change the family too. Han is uncertain about what the future will bring.

HISPANIC-AMERICAN ADULTS

Societal and Cultural Description

Banks (1987) cautioned against labeling Hispanic-Americans as a single cultural group on the basis of their common language. Race and ethnicity figure largely in the diversity among Hispanics. Depending on geographical origin (Mexico, Cuba, Puerto Rico, El Salvador, the Dominican Republic, Colombia, Venezuela, and so on), Hispanics can be Caucasian, Mongoloid, Negroid, or various combinations (Pederson et al., 1989). Recent population data indicate that the Hispanic people numbered 19.4 million in 1988 and will total 29 million by the year 2000 (U.S. Bureau of the Census, 1988b). Geographical origins of the Hispanic population include 62.3 percent from Mexico, 12.7 percent from Puerto Rico, 11.5 percent from Central and South America, 5.3 percent from Cuba, and 8.1 percent from other Spanish-origin groups (U.S. Bureau of the Census, 1988a). In 1988, over half of the Hispanic-American population resided in either California or Texas. (See Figure 1–2, p. 17, for a more detailed breakdown of the states with significant Hispanic populations.)

Hispanic-Americans have experienced considerable difficulty in achieving academic and economic successes in the United States. Whether a result of cultural discrimination, poor English skills, lack of employment skills, or problems of coping in a predominantly Anglo-American society, the Hispanic-American population, generally speaking, has not made gains comparable to those of other minority groups. Consider the following statistics, as reported by the U.S. Bureau of the Census (1988a):

- From 1980 to 1988, the Hispanic-American population increased by 34 percent; that is, by about 5 million people.
- The poverty level of Hispanic families in 1987 was 25.8 percent and had not changed significantly since 1982. About 1.2 million of the 4.6 million Hispanic-American families (or about 25.8 percent) lived below the poverty level in 1987.
- The percentage of Hispanic-American unemployed totaled 8.5 percent in 1988, as compared to 5.8 percent of the non-Hispanic population.
- The percentage of Hispanic-Americans completing high school increased from 44 percent in 1980 to 51 percent in 1988, as compared to non-Hispanic percentages of 68 percent and 78 percent, respectively.
- The percentage of Hispanic-Americans completing four or more years of college

Figure 8–1   Comparison of Hispanic and Non-Hispanic income levels. (Source: U.S. Bureau of the Census, 1988.)

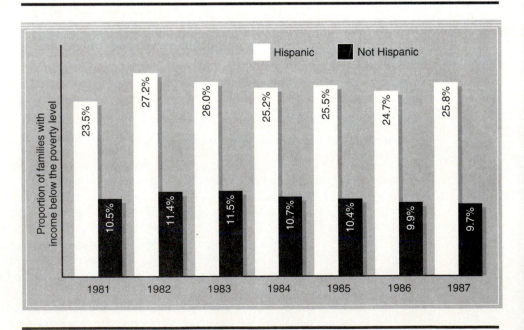

increased from 8 percent in 1980 to 10 percent in 1988, as compared to non-Hispanic percentages of 17 percent and 21 percent, respectively.

Although the education level of Hispanic-Americans is continuing to rise, there is still great need for improvement. Only 51 percent of Hispanics over 25 years of age have completed four years of high school; only 10 percent have completed four or more years of college (U.S. Bureau of the Census, 1988a). In the economic domain, Figure 8-1 illustrates the magnitude of the Hispanic predicament.

As mentioned previously, the Spanish-speaking people are reluctant to forsake their native language. They continue to emphasize *respeto, machismo,* and *dignidad* and persevere in defining rigid family roles. Other cultural characteristics considered to be significant are their love for children, their tendency toward gregariousness, and their hospitality (Christensen, 1989).

Language

Although discrimination cannot be discounted, the reluctance of the Hispanic-American culture to speak the English language also has contributed to their academic and employment problem; in all likelihood this reluctance has also hindered their acculturation.

The language problem is not only a first-generation problem. Many second- and third-generation Hispanics continue to have difficulty with English. Even younger generation Hispanics tend to speak Spanish in the home, or "Hispanicized English." Their limited English-language skills have been debilitating and have contributed to increased discrimination and lack of opportunity. As noted by Brislin (1981), first-generation immigrants are especially vulnerable to discrimination if they do not have language skills enabling them to learn about their legal guaranteed rights.

Families

To avoid generalizations about the entire Hispanic culture, our discussion here will be organized around the three Spanish-speaking groups that are currently most prominent in the United States: Puerto Ricans, Mexicans, and Cubans.

Puerto Ricans. Although there are cultural differences between Puerto Ricans raised in Puerto Rico and those raised in the United States, both groups are distinctly different from the dominant Anglo culture and both suffer disadvantages in the Anglo culture (Christensen, 1989). A deep appreciation of family life characterizes Puerto Ricans, regardless of whether the family is rich or poor. Since the family unit is fundamental, individuals tend to evaluate themselves in relation to other members of the family. A second important characteristic is the notion of male superiority, with the male considered as the unquestioned head of the household. According to Fitzpatrick (1987),

> the man expects to exercise the authority in the family; he feels free to make decisions without consulting his wife; he expects to be obeyed when he gives commands. (p. 71)

Although the role of women is in the process of being redefined, in contrast to the characteristics of cooperation and companionship evident in many Anglo-American families, the woman in the Puerto Rican family still occupies a clearly subordinate role.

Mexicans. In a discussion of Mexican families, regional, generational, and socioeconomic variation makes generalization difficult. The following characteristics for the most part pertain to Mexican-Americans of relatively poor and working-class backgrounds who migrated to the United States over the past three or four decades. First, the nuclear family is embedded in an extended family network with family boundaries encompassing grandparents, uncles, aunts, and cousins. Children who were orphaned or whose parents divorced may be included in households of relatives, along with adults who remained single or who were widowed or divorced. The term *hijo de crianza* refers to someone other than the child's parents raising the child (Christensen, 1989). Second, a degree of interdependence characterizes this supportive network. Family functions such as caretaking, disciplining of the children, problem solving, managing finances, and providing emotional support are shared. Third, the family protects the individual and demands loyalty. Family cohesiveness and respect for parental authority endure throughout an individual's lifetime. Autonomy and individual achievement are not particularly emphasized. Fourth, most families are usually large, consisting of the parents and four, five, or more children. Birth rates are substantially higher than those of Anglo-American families at all socioeconomic levels (Falicov, 1982).

Cubans. The Cuban-American population shares many of the Mexican-American characteristics. The family is also the most important social unit in Cuban life and is characterized by a bond of loyalty. This bond unites both nuclear and extended family members, as well as a network of friends, neighbors, and community members. As in other Hispanic cultures, the man is the leader and provider of the household. If the man is unable to find work, his self-esteem is damaged, and he may lose the respect of his wife and children. This loss of respect is likely to result in marital difficulties, especially if the wife must assume the role of economic provider. Cubans, too, emphasize *machismo.* Also significant is the term *choteo* (meaning humor), which refers to making fun of people, situations, or things. Finally, there is a certain "specialness" that many Cubans feel about themselves and their culture (Bernal, 1982).

Unique Challenges Confronting Hispanic-American Adults

Hispanic-American adults—no longer children or adolescents in developmental transition—have major responsibilities as financial providers, nurturers of the family, or some combination of both. Problems can result from a lack of appropriate social skills for coping in a predominantly Anglo-American society and from discrimination and prejudice. Counselors who understand the complexity of the Hispanic culture and the problems confronting adults will want to keep the following points in mind as they work with their clients:

1. Recommending that the client speak only English may in all fairness be too much to ask, especially of first-generation Hispanics. Nonetheless, clients should be made aware that some proficiency in communicating in the language of the majority culture is prerequisite to obtaining employment and to beginning the acculturation process.

2. Hispanic-Americans must seek to improve their education. They must be encouraged to finish high school and seek entry into college, if they measure up academically. A recent report revealed that only 10.9 percent of Hispanic males and 11.2 percent of Hispanic females aged 25 to 29 had four or more years of college (Blacks and Hispanics trail . . . , 1987).

3. Meeting the challenge with respect to education will allow Hispanic-Americans to improve their employment possibilities. A move away from low-level jobs to positions of greater responsibility will require better education, the ability to speak English fluently, and the determination to fight discrimination by informing people about positive aspects of the Hispanic-American culture and demanding legal guaranteed rights.

Something else to keep in mind is AIDS and its effect on the Hispanic culture, as detailed in A FOCUS ON RESEARCH 8–7.

In Table 8–7 characteristics of the Hispanic-American and Anglo-American cultures are compared. UP CLOSE AND PERSONAL 8–4 presents a portrait of Carla Suarez, a Hispanic-American adult.

A FOCUS ON RESEARCH 8–7
Hispanic-Americans and AIDS

According to *Newsweek* (December 5, 1988), machismo, homophobia, and Roman Catholic sexual taboos (along with poverty and poor education) have resulted in Hispanic Americans being one of the last groups in the United States to take preventive measures against AIDS. Although the Anglo-American and African-American populations account for higher percentages of all AIDS cases, Hispanic-Americans account for a notable 15 percent.

Cultural Group	Percentage of Cases
Anglo	58%
African	26%
Hispanic	15%
Asian or others	1%

Because a large number of Hispanic cases are heterosexual male IV drug users, Hispanic women are eleven times more likely to contract the virus than non-Hispanic women. The Hispanic's reluctance to use condoms poses a major problem. A survey of Chicago's sexually active Hispanics revealed that 80 percent do not want to use prophylactics of any kind.

Source: Waking up to a nightmare: Hispanics confront the growing threat of AIDS. (1988, December 5). *Newsweek*, pp. 24, 29.

Table 8–7   Cultural comparison: Hispanic-American and Anglo-American adults

Hispanic-American Adults	Anglo-American Adults
Come from patriarchial families, with specific and well-defined roles	Come from families that are more egalitarian
Measure confidence and define themselves in terms of the family	Judge themselves by individual standards
Have extended family networks	Have immediate family networks
Value family loyalty and respect authority	Value autonomy and individual achievement
Expect godparents to play an active role in childrearing	Expect godparents to play only a minor role in childrearing
Usually have greater allegiance to Spanish than to English	Generally speak only English

Sources: Data compiled from Christensen, 1989; Fitzpatrick, 1987.

UP CLOSE AND PERSONAL 8–4
Carla Suarez—A Hispanic-American Adult

Carla has just turned 35 and her family life is causing her a lot of concern. Her husband, Oscar, works intermittently as a laborer on various construction crews. Living in a large and growing urban area, Oscar has been fairly lucky; however, he has been out of work for several weeks and his chances of being called back to work in the near future appear to be slim. To make financial ends meet, Oscar and Carla have borrowed a little money from their married son who lives across the street in the predominantly Hispanic-American neighborhood. But what will happen if Oscar is not called back to work soon? How will they make ends meet? Carla suggested that she apply for a job with a company that cleans offices at night, but Oscar is vehemently opposed. So Carla is stuck—she has no other choice but to do what Oscar says. And although the money is sorely needed, she realizes that Oscar's pride is involved—after all, it is the man's responsibility to support the family.

Besides Oscar's layoff, there are other things to worry about: The neighborhood is becoming increasingly dangerous, Ramon is having school problems, Carlos's friends are a bad influence on him, and she can't change Oscar's attitude about her taking a job. In the face of all this, Carla feels powerless. She wants to help her family financially and emotionally, but Oscar makes the decisions. He has the final word on everything, including money and child-rearing. Even though it is she who takes care of the children, Oscar tells her what behaviour is appropriate for them. She sees that some of the younger women in the neighborhood are beginning to question their husbands. A lot of them seem to be much more assertive than she is. She sometimes wonders, What would Oscar's reaction be if I just got the job and went to work?

A POINT OF DEPARTURE

Challenges Confronting Multicultural Counselors of Adults

Learning to understand adults in terms of their developmental stage and their unique cultural characteristics is a formidable challenge for multicultural counselors. Counselors trained in techniques geared toward the Anglo-American culture should base their strategies on knowledge of each culture, taking into account the cultural differences between their clients and themselves. A recognition of the significance of these cultural differences in the counseling intervention is essential. It is the counselor's professional responsibility not to treat all cultures and periods of the lifespan alike.

SUMMARY

Considering a client's problems and tasks with an understanding of his or her developmental period and cultural background is fundamental to successful counseling intervention with multicultural adults. Culturally relevant issues, such as proficiency with English, nonverbal communication customs, family structures, and the struggle to overcome stereotypes, will no doubt come to the counselor's attention. The importance of the adult period on the lifespan continuum will also become clear to the counselor. Adults face challenges that are different from those of any other developmental period. Multicultural counselors, then, must work from a lifespan perspective, understand the culture of each client, understand their own culture in relation to other cultures, and plan appropriate counseling strategies based on their beliefs, understandings, and skills.

Suggested Readings

Dewart, J. (Ed.). (1989). *The state of Black American 1989*. New York: National Urban League. This excellent collection of essays examines the economic and political status of African-Americans. Their children, their church, and their educational opportunities are highlighted.

Fitzpatrick, J. P. (1987). *Puerto Rican Americans* (2nd ed.). Englewood Cliffs, NJ: Prentice-Hall. This book discusses the migration of Puerto Ricans to this country and focuses on the Puerto Rican community and family. Poverty and drug abuse are two of the issues considered.

Hirschfelder, A. B. (1982). *American Indian stereotypes in the world of children: A reader and bibliography*. Metuchen, NJ: Scarecrow Press. Hirschfelder offers a collection of readings focusing on the perception of Native-Americans in American culture and literature.

Jaynes, G. D., & Williams, R. M. (1989). *A common destiny: Blacks and American society*. Washington, DC: National Academic Press. This text from the National Research Council contains the summary and conclusions of a report from the Committee on the Status of African-Americans. Racial attitudes and behaviors, children and families, economics, and schooling are some of the topics examined.

Journal of Counseling and Development. (1990). *68*(4). The March/April 1990 issue considers gender and psychological distress, feminist therapy, the psychotherapy process, and gender issues for the twenty-first century.

McGoldrick, M., Pearce, J. K., & Girodano, J. (Eds.). (1982). *Ethnicity and family therapy*. New York: Guilford. In this collection of readings, the authors explore ethnicity and family therapy.

Peterson, J. L., & Marin, G. (1988). Issues in the prevention of AIDS among Black and Hispanic men. *American Psychologist, 43*, 871–877. Peterson and Marin provide a detailed discussion of high-risk sexual behavior, AIDS attitudes and beliefs, drug use and AIDS, and HIV transmission. They then focus attention on the difficulties in developing successful prevention programs.

Pinkney, A. (1975). *Black Americans*. Englewood Cliffs, NJ: Prentice-Hall. Pinkney examines the African-American culture in depth. Particularly interesting is his discussion of acculturation in middle- and upper-class African-Americans.

Suzuki, B. H. (1989). Asian-American as the "Model Minority": Outdoing Whites? Or media hype? *Change*, *21*(6), 13–19. Debunking the term *model minority* as a shibboleth, Suzuki contends that people use it to absolve themselves of racism. The consequences of the myth can be dangerous to Asian-Americans at all educational and developmental levels.

Chapter 9

Counseling the Adult

Questions To Be Explored

1. What differences can counselors expect when counseling culturally diverse adults?

2. What are the typical stresses and concerns of the adult years? Are some problems more prevalent in particular cultures?

3. What are the problems and concerns of adults in the Native-American, African-American, Asian-American, and Hispanic-American cultures? To what extent do cultural differences, language problems, and marriage and family concerns affect adults in each of the cultures? Do some cultures have problems and concerns that other cultures do not experience?

4. What counseling strategies should counselors employ when counseling culturally diverse adults?

5. How should the counselor decide whether to use individual, group, or family therapy? To what extent does the decision on counseling modality depend on the specific culture?

6. What unique challenges confront counselors working with culturally diverse adults?

7. Where can counselors working with culturally diverse adults find additional information?

INTRODUCTION

Counseling services for adults are based on the premise that all individuals have the capacity for controlled growth and development in psychosocial, vocational, emotional, and other areas; furthermore, that life transitions in adulthood often give rise to conflict. Such conflict may cause individuals to be less effective in coping with daily living. Counselors of adults seek to provide services that maximize the growth and coping abilities of clients and that help them explore these areas of their lives.

DIFFERENCES IN COUNSELING CULTURALLY DIVERSE ADULTS

Adults have reached a stage in development where the most natural means of communication for the majority is speech. Most adult counseling is achieved through direct verbal communication in group or individual sessions. Language problems, both verbal and nonverbal, can be complex and have the potential for reducing counseling effectiveness.

In addition to language problems, counselors also must often contend with the negative consequences of racism and discrimination as well as with problems associated with client's differing world views and structures of reasoning. Finally, as suggested in Chapter 3 on growth and development, developmental tasks and psychosocial crises usually associated with adulthood may cause many adults to seek mental health services.

Typical Concerns and Stresses of the Adult Years

Disruptive events are to be expected in the normal process of adult growth. Such common disruptions as divorce, death of a loved one, relocation, loss of a job, and dual-career marriages are a few common concerns that often lead adults to seek counseling (Janosik, 1984). Increasingly, alcoholism and drug addiction are requiring counseling intervention. Holmes and Rahe (1967) specified life events they believed were particularly stressful for adults. Some of these include the following:

Death of spouse
Divorce
Marital separation
Jail term
Death of close family member
Personal injury or illness
Marriage
Loss of job
Marital reconciliation
Retirement
Change in health of family member
Pregnancy
Sex difficulties
New family member
Change in financial state
Death of close friend

Foreclosure of mortgage or loan
Change in work responsibilities
Departure of son or daughter from
    home
Trouble with in-laws
Wife beginning or stopping work
Beginning or ending school
Trouble with boss
Change in work hours or conditions
Change of residence
Change of school
Change in recreation
Change in social activities
Change in sleeping habits
Change in number of family
    get-togethers

Career change	Change in eating habits
Change in number of arguments with spouse	Vacations
	Minor violations of the law

To prepare for counseling culturally diverse clients, counselors should obtain a list of service organizations and agencies that are prepared to deal with specific situations. Some of these organizations include crisis hotlines, family shelters, rape crisis networks, Sistercare for Abused Women, the Salvation Army, and the Urban League. Counselors can also benefit from community organizations that primarily serve culturally diverse adults and their families.

NATIVE-AMERICAN ADULTS

Counseling Native-American adults requires an understanding of the culture's historical traditions, an appreciation of the effects of centuries of discrimination, and an awareness of such contemporary problems as high suicide rates, low educational levels, and high rates of alcoholism. The influx of civilization fostered by colonialism, government control and regulations, and harassment fueled by racism all contributed to the mental health problems of Native-Americans. With the introduction of alcohol and, more recently, drugs, mental health has become a major concern of many Native-American communities. Despite this concern, counselors working out of community mental health centers agree that Native-Americans tend to underutilize their services, are likely to have higher dropout rates than other minorities, and are less likely to respond to mental health services than other groups. The fact that Native-Americans often feel that mental health services do not meet their unique needs may account for this underutilization. Another factor may be that Native-Americans are likely to distrust non-Native-American counselors with values appreciably different from their own (Trimble & Fleming, 1989).

Major problems and concerns of many contemporary Native-Americans include the following:

1. difficulties in overcoming myths that the culture is evil, savage, and inferior;
2. adverse effects of injustice, discrimination, hardship and degradations;
3. adverse effects of a "culture of poverty"—high unemployment, low socio-economic status;
4. the adult's differing cultural characteristics;
5. high suicide rates and low life expectancy rates associated with the culture;
6. the adult's language problems, including "on reservation" and "off reservation" languages and the majority culture's misunderstanding of nonverbal mannerisms;
7. problems associated with midlife: the affects of aging, marriage crises, psychosocial crises, and developmental tasks;
8. the adult's problems with alcohol or drugs;
9. the adult's poor self-concept and feelings of rejection;
10. the adult's low educational level.

Cultural Differences

We are already familiar with the cultural portrait of the Native-American adult. Typical characteristics include passivity, shyness, a tendency to avoid assertiveness and aggressiveness, reverence for the person rather than possessions, respect for elders and the aged, adherence to fairly specific sex roles, noninterference with others, humility, an inclination to share, and a reluctance to criticize the Native-American culture.

Although many of these characteristics are widespread among Native-Americans, their many intracultural and individual differences must be taken into account. Counselors are admonished not to base intervention on broad cultural or stereotypical generalizations. For example, the Blackfeet tribe of Montana would not like being compared to the Sioux, the Flathead, or the Shoshoni, even though there may be evidence of similar life-styles, values, and problems. Another common mistake is to assume similar characteristics for all Native-American populations in a particular geographical region (Attneave, 1982).

A consideration of cultural differences must also include a recognition of the client's degree of acculturation. The counselor should develop a battery of open-ended questions to obtain information in the areas of education, employment, urbanization, media influence, political participation, religion, language, daily life, and social relations (Trimble & Fleming, 1989).

It is the task of the counselor to help clients accept and value their culture and to assist them with difficult conflicts that can impede personal and social growth. Consider the following example (Axelson, 1985) in which the Anglo counselor helps a Native-American client consider his cultural beliefs about religion:

Client: Where can I start? Take religion, for instance. O.K.? I have a strong traditional Indian background ... and I try to cope with whatever is good in the non-Indian society. But, coming from the Indian way of life, I feel that how I can relate myself to the way of praying to nature is not the same as saying I got to be good and go to church on Sunday and pray to a certain god. How can I relate myself to that way?

Counselor: You're saying that you are religious, that you don't find that the White religion is in harmony with what you are; you find conflict in some practices of the White religion.

Client: I'm not sure that you understood.

Counselor: Would you try to explain to me again?

Client: I know that I feel there is something around me that is good. I can take a piece of rock and say that it was formed from something that I believe in. I can take a tree branch and say that I pray to this tree and feel good. I feel the obligation that is imposing on me to make me go to church; and I don't want to do that.

Counselor: You feel an obligation to go to church and somehow you want to resist the obligation. You're caught in the middle in giving in to it and fighting against it. You'd rather fight against it than do it; somehow you're not quite free to do that.

(Pause)

Client: Do you think I should? . . . go to church?

(Pause)

Counselor: I'm wondering if going to church would help you, like anybody else, since you feel so reluctant. It just doesn't seem to be you.

Client: Eh . . . they tell me I should go to church.

Counselor: Who are "they"?

Client: The people who taught me about their religion. The Catholic Church.

Counselor: You don't want to do this. Somehow I'm puzzled because you don't want to do it; in other words, you feel an obligation to go to church because they told you to. And yet you don't feel a real need inside yourself to go.

(Pause)

Client: I think . . . (Pause) . . . I think the need is there.

Counselor: The need to go to church on Sunday?

Client: Eh . . . I think the need is there because . . . I don't know . . . I don't know what to say. It's kind of confusing now.

Counselor: You sound like you don't understand yourself. It's almost like someone sneaked up and put this need in you.

Client: I think I know what is good and I know that there is something there that is good. You know, why should I go to church on Sunday when I know that there is the same thing outside the church?

Counselor: One thing. You see yourself as a good man. Is that right? And, as a good man, you can recognize good within this Catholic religion and that gives a . . .

Client: I don't know what's good within the Catholic religion.

Counselor: You feel some kind of obligation or attraction to the good that you see there, but not enough obligation to make you feel that you want to go to church, or go to that church. That you can be good by praying before the stone or tree branch. Or by doing whatever you do on Sunday besides going to church.

Client: What do you think I should do?

Counselor: (sighs) . . . What do you want to do?

(Pause)

Counselor: What do you think a good man would do in your situation?

(Pause)

Client: I'm confused. I don't want to talk about it. (pp. 397–399).

Other concerns related to culture are derived from the previously mentioned centuries of racism and discrimination. Many Native-Americans think that the predominantly Anglo society continues to manipulate their life through the Bureau of Indian Affairs. They feel that employment and economic discrimination are not being addressed. Such feelings can, without doubt, affect personal and social growth and can contribute to a high incidence of alcoholism and suicide (Richardson, 1981).

Communication Barriers

Native-Americans' many languages and accompanying communication problems have been documented adequately (Sanders, 1987; Vontress, 1976b). Although language problems need additional study, perceptive counselors will consider the degree to which language interferes with communication and also base assessment and counseling intervention on the premise that communication might be hampered. Nonverbal communication is as important as verbal communication. The Anglo counselor may misinterpret the Native-American tendency to look the other way in speaking and listening situations and the tendency to let conversation lapse for a few moments.

Marriage and Family

It is important to emphasize in any discussion of Native-American family issues that tribal cultures and subcultures vary significantly. In order for clients to develop trust and confidence in the counseling process, counselors working with Native-American families must understand cultural traits associated with particular tribal backgrounds (Attneave, 1982).

Although Native-American families have endured many societal prejudices, these families also can be perceived as survivors and sources of strength to one another. Rather than focusing on the negative aspects of Native-American families, counselors diagnosing problems and planning intervention should recognize their strengths. These strengths are evidenced in the perseverance with which problems are confronted, the large numbers of families living in cities and coping with urban life, the openness to learning and using the social skills of the Anglo culture, and the commitment to keep alive the language, folkways, and values associated with tribal identities (Attneave, 1982).

The sources and symptoms of Native-American marriage and family problems are quite similar to those of families of other cultures. Counseling Native-American adults in marriage and family situations requires an understanding of the adult period of the lifespan (as discussed in Chapter 3), the Native-American culture, and the dynamics of couples and family units (both immediate and extended). Marriage and family therapy also requires an understanding of such Native-American characteristics as nonassertive behavior, sharing, and being in harmony with one another (Attneave, 1982).

Developmental and Other Concerns

Health problems and psychological frustrations commonly associated with middle age may affect Native-Americans earlier in life and may have more severe consequences due to their relatively poor socioeconomic condition. What particular problems might Native-Americans experience? Although there is some controversy over actual numbers (Attneave, 1982), higher rates of alcoholism and lower life expectancies appear to be two problems affecting Native-Americans during the adult years (Richardson, 1981). Native-Americans also may experience problems due to not being able to meet social and civic obligations or to perform satisfactorily in job situations.

Counseling Considerations

Working with Native-American clients presents counselors with numerous challenges: intracultural diversity, lifestyle preferences that vary considerably from one client to another, communication differences, the reluctance of clients to disclose troublesome thoughts, and the shyness of some clients in counseling situations (Trimble & Fleming, 1989; Trimble & Hayes, 1984; Youngman & Sadongei, 1974).

Anglo-American counselors have not traditionally received training in counseling the Native-American population; therefore, they often do not feel the need to discuss the family's Native-American background and culture, to ask questions in a manner that does not cause discomfort, and to utilize cultural information in assessment decisions. When questioned about dissatisfactions with counseling services, Native Americans cited high costs, ambiguous agency procedures, transportation problems, lack of child care, extended waiting periods, impersonal interaction, limited operating hours, and distant locations (Lum, 1986; Miller, 1982).

Counseling Native-American adults requires techniques carefully planned to accommodate their cultural characteristics. Using counseling techniques developed for Anglo clients with only slight modifications does not go far enough. Counseling and psychotherapy often are based on Western values that may be antagonistic to the Native-American's value system. Not only should culturally appropriate counseling be planned, counselors should also be aware of personal characteristics that may offend or confuse the client. Richardson (1981) sounds a cautionary note:

> You may be oriented to be most understanding; however, subtle aspects like the tone of your voice, the manner in which you study the client with your eyes, and innocent little comments may be met with resistance. You must be aware of the fact that suggestions seem like orders to Native-American people when they come from authority. (pp. 231–232)

It is essential that counselors working with Native-American clients be adaptive and flexible in their professional intervention. Equally essential is a commitment to understanding the cultural context and unique cultural characteristics of the clients (Trimble & Fleming, 1989). According to Miller 1982, (a) a counselor's personal identification with the culture of the client is not sufficient for an understanding of the client; (b) a client's personal history contains information that can be useful in promoting positive counseling expectations; (c) counselors should be aware of their own personal biases and stereotypes; and (d) the most important counseling approaches involve empathy, caring, and a sense of importance of the human potential.

Although some counseling strategies are effective for all cultures, Richardson (1981) recommends that Anglo counselors consider the following strategies to enhance the possibility of effective counseling sessions with Native-Americans:

1. *Admit your ignorance.* The counselor may admit not fully understanding the Native-American culture and may request to be corrected if a cultural error is made.
2. *See the positives.* The counselor with a feeling for others appreciates the greatness of the Native-American culture and its many accomplishments.

3. *Help by listening*. The counselor should take the attitude that he or she can help best by listening. The tendency to tell too much and listen too little has blinded Anglo counselors.

4. *Make the client comfortable*. Counselors should have a small, homey, lived-in office. Pictures of American Indians or artifacts (genuine, yet not showy) may put the client more at ease. Rather than sitting side by side, some clients may prefer that the counselor sit behind the desk (to provide a form of separation).

5. *Settle back*. Counselors should not lean toward the client to study him or her. They also should not be upset with long pauses in the conversation. Counselors may want to take short notes and summarize at the end to let the client know they have been listening.

Richardson states further that counselors must give special attention to the manner in which they speak. It is wise to crystallize the client's thinking after he or she has been talking for awhile. In particular,

> do not talk too long, make your sentences short and lucid, do not talk down to the client, and make it clear that your views are only general opinions, not gospel truths or facts. (pp. 241–242)

Individual/Group Therapy

The decision of whether to use individual or group therapy must be based on the individual client and his or her culture. One advantage of group therapy is that clients may share similar problems and frustrations. Disadvantages include Native-American clients' possible reluctance to share personal concerns and also their cultural tendency toward noninterference with others (Lum, 1986). Groups should be effective for Native-Americans who value the concept of sharing. In group interactions, clients can share their joys, achievements, problems, and sorrows, and perhaps improve their lives. Caution must be exercised to avoid the group session lacking genuineness, depth, and commitment. Clients should never feel they are being manipulated. Intervention must be directed in such a manner that Native-American virtues such as mutual respect and consideration are essential components of the group process. Using the group to pressure members who are late or silent will likely jeopardize intervention effectiveness. Also, with Native-American clients, it is doubtful whether heterogeneous grouping will produce desired results (Lewis & Ho, 1989).

It is worth reiterating the following important points with respect to counseling Native-Americans. First, the client is apt to be silent for what may seem like a long time to the Anglo counselor. Secondly, restating or summarizing the client's comments at the end of the session may enhance understanding.

Family Therapy

Trimble and Fleming (1989) maintained that several factors indicate that family therapy is a particularly effective practice with Native-Americans. Extended family members in the community can be called upon to assist the counselor or therapist in meeting goals or changing behavior. A prerequisite to effective family counseling is an understanding of family patterns, peer group relationships, and community relationships.

The Native-American culture emphasizes harmony with nature, endurance of suffering, noninterference with others, and a strong belief that people are inherently good and deserving of respect. Such traits, however, make a family experiencing difficulty reluctant to seek counseling or other professional help. Their fear and mistrust of Anglo-Americans make it difficult for an Anglo family therapist to gain entry into their family system. Family therapists are generally consulted after all other help-seeking attempts have failed. Also, Native-Americans' lack of knowledge as to what a family therapist actually does often makes the first session awkward. To lessen the family's discomfort, the therapist should be cognizant of Native-Americans' central cultural themes and the concepts of communication theory (Ho, 1987).

As previously mentioned, the Native-American attitude toward silence can be extremely frustrating to counselors providing family therapy. This silence may sometimes be used as a safe response to defend against outsiders who are perceived as intruders. However, during the beginning phrases of social contact, silence is also a customary practice among Native-Americans (Ho, 1987).

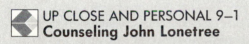

UP CLOSE AND PERSONAL 9–1
Counseling John Lonetree

John Lonetree, age 38, was referred by his medical doctor to a community mental health clinic that provides free counseling to qualified Native-Americans. John had complained of headaches for several months and the doctor had been unable to pinpoint an actual cause.

The 45-year-old Anglo counselor greeted John at the office door and tried to make him feel as comfortable as possible. The counselor sat behind a small desk and requested that John sit across from him. The counselor took special care to let John know that he was fairly unaccustomed to counseling Native-Americans. He also encouraged John to make him aware of any misconceptions he might have about the culture. The counselor avoided looking John in the eye for long periods, and he tried not to seem concerned when John paused for long intervals while speaking. Being off the reservation, John experienced problems with English, which made communication somewhat difficult.

The counselor concluded that John had sev-

eral problems related to his age and the financial and emotional demands placed upon him. First, John was nearly 40; relative to his life expectancy, 40 was "older" than for other cultures. Second, with John's advancing age, his responsibilities seemed to be growing heavier and harder to bear. He was concerned about Carl and Bill and their schoolwork. And then, what he would do if he lost his job? So many people depended on him for financial support. The counselor suggested additional sessions to which John agreed, somewhat to the surprise of the counselor who was aware that Native-Americans often place a high premium on noninterference. Also, because John considered his problems to be family-oriented, the counselor decided that group counseling was inappropriate at this stage. The decision of whether to include John's family would have to wait until the counselor knew more about the family situation.

The close-knit family structure of Native-Americans and their cultural tradition of keeping family matters private may result in few opportunities for family therapy. When the counselor is able to engage the family, he or she should proceed cautiously to allow family members to deal with problems at their own pace. Also, an overbearing or manipulative counselor will almost certainly alienate the Native-American client.

AFRICAN-AMERICAN ADULTS

African-Americans have been dealt severe blows in the course of years of discrimination and racism. Racism continues today: Anglo health practitioners tend to devalue African-American's lives; African-Americans serve longer jail sentences than Anglos for comparable offenses (Reveron, 1982). They also have higher rates of poverty, higher unemployment, and generally lower economic status (Swinton, 1989). One could also point to the disturbing infant mortality rate and the poor general health of many African-American children (Edelman, 1989). Drug abuse among African-Americans is another problem that many feel is out of control (Nobles & Goddard, 1989). Some of the cultural and developmental problems that African-American adults might bring to counseling sessions are as follows:

1. adverse effects of myths and stereotypes regarding the African-American culture;
2. historical and contemporary racism and discrimination; the adult's low self-esteem, confused cultural identity, and feelings of rejection resulting from years of discrimination;
3. the adult's lack of education;
4. the adult's communication problems;
5. the adult's differing cultural characteristics and customs;
6. unequal employment and housing opportunities;
7. underemployment, unemployment, and low socioeconomic status;
8. the increasing number of one-parent and/or female-headed households;
9. the adult's inability to cope with problems associated with adulthood: appearance and personality changes, psychosocial crises, marital discord.

Cultural Differences

First, misunderstandings about the African-American's concept of the immediate/extended family might result in the need for counseling intervention. The African-American head of the household (whether male or female) trying to provide financial and psychological support to both the immediate and extended family is likely to experience stress. When African-American family traditions are viewed with an Anglo frame of reference the counseling process may be undermined. Second, African-American communication patterns are often misunderstood by Anglo professionals. One example, cited previously, is the African-American tendency to interrupt a speaker with certain culture-specific phrases. These are meant to encourage the speaker; they should not be misconstrued as rude (Weber, 1985). Another potential problem, although not a specific cultural difference, is the majority culture's response to African-Americans based on a distorted image of African-Americans. Changing the societal perception that African-Americans are genetically aggressive must be a cross-cultural effort.

Communication Barriers

In working with African-American adults, counselors must be sensitive to their unique style of communicating. First of all, African-Americans tend to be highly verbal. There is a strong oral tradition in the culture; for example, storytelling and folk sermons have served to preserve and express the philosophy of the African-American people (Smith, 1981). This oral tradition has its roots in the slavery era, was refined over the centuries, and is carried on today. Secondly, the use of dialect continues to be disconcerting to some counselors (Warfield & Marion, 1985). Black English tends to omit the *to be* verb in certain situations. For example, one might say "She come" or "He going" instead of "She is coming" or "He is going." Another unique convention is to pronounce the *th* in words such as "the" and "them" as *d* ("de" and "dem"). Similarly, African-Americans speakers tend to use different auxiliary verbs; e.g., "They *be* going" instead of "They *are* going" (Warfield & Marion, 1985).

Marriage and Family

The African-American family is so diverse that some believe the prototypic black family does not exist (Ho, 1987). Maintaining that this diversity results from a complex interplay of factors, Ho suggests that counselors view the family as a social system interacting with a number of other systems. In essence, the African-American family has traditionally been a source of strength, and strong, supportive kinship networks have been reported consistently as a familial characteristic. The informal social network supports the African-American nuclear family by providing economic and social resources needed for survival and upward mobility in an often hostile environment (Guadin & Davis, 1985). Counselors can benefit from understanding the strong education and work achievement orientation of these families, the flexibility of family roles, and the commitment to religious values and church participation (Ho, 1987). It is also important to be aware of recent research findings on marriage and parenthood (Broman, 1988) and the increasing number of female single-parent families (Smith & Smith, 1986).

In A FOCUS ON RESEARCH 9–1 the problem of African-American battered women is examined. There seems to be general agreement among authorities (Aborampah, 1989) that unhealthy conflicts often exist between African-American males and females that may result in the need for counseling. African-American male and female relationships may be affected adversely by the sex ratio imbalance, income inequalities, high unemployment rates, and the double standard that allows African-American males to practice polygamy (Aborampah, 1989). A FOCUS ON RESEARCH 9–2 looks at marriage, parenthood, and African-American satisfaction.

A FOCUS ON RESEARCH 9–1
African-American Battered Women

Although there has been an increasing amount of literature on battered women, the empirical literature on African-American women continues to be sparse in counseling, psychological, social work, and sociological journals. Coley and Beckett's review of empirical literature de-

stroyed the myth that African-American and other minority women are more likely to be victims of spouse abuse. Instead, the review states that "domestic violence crosses racial and socioeconomic boundaries" and that "regardless of race, battered women share the psychological pain of guilt, emotional and economic insecurities, and fear of reprisal from their mates if they seek help" (p. 269).

Source: Coley, S. M., & Beckett, J. O. (1988). Black battered women: A review of empirical literature. *Journal of Counseling and Development, 66,* 266–270.

The increasing prevalence of African-American female-headed households has the potential for increasing caseloads of counselors working with single-parent families. Feelings of loss of personal freedom, poor relationships between men and women, a high rate of unemployment, confusion over priorities, alcoholism, and general powerlessness also suggest increasing caseloads for counselors (Smith & Smith, 1986). The decline of the nuclear family is documented by earlier sexual activity, the increasing number of children born out of wedlock, the increasing number of abortions, the higher divorce rate (an increase of 120 percent in a decade), and the social and economic forces that undermine marital stability. It should be noted that the divorce rate of middle-class African-Americans is not as high as that

A FOCUS ON RESEARCH 9–2
African-American Satisfaction: Marriage and Parenthood

On the basis of data from a national survey, Broman (1988) reported that marital and parental status have an important impact on levels of satisfaction of African-Americans. Data consisted of 2,017 completed interviews of African-Americans adults 18 years and over. Broman offered several conclusions:

1. Blacks who are divorced or separated have lower levels of satisfaction than those who are married.

2. Marital status interacts with age, education, and location of residence to predict life satisfaction. Parental status interacts with education, and marital status with social participation, health problems, and income to predict satisfaction with family life.

Source: Broman, C. L. (1988). Satisfaction among Blacks: The significance of marriage and parenthood. *Journal of Marriage and the Family, 50,* 45–51.

for lower-class African-Americans, since increased incomes and higher educational levels improve the chances of marriage success (Staples, 1987).

What strategies might counselors want to employ in working with either married couples or females heading families? With couples, the counselor might want to see each partner individually or both of them at once. In the case of females heading families, the counselor might want to involve the extended family. Individual family circumstances must be considered in each case in deciding on the appropriate strategy. Margolin (1982) suggested that counselors should explain the process and approaches to be taken at the outset, since marriage and family counseling might be relatively new to many African-Americans. The counselor should clarify (a) procedures, (b) the role of the counselor and his or her qualifications, (c) discomforts or risks, (d) benefits to be expected, and (e) alternatives to counseling that might be of similar benefit. The client(s) should be assured that all questions concerning treatment will be answered and that he or she may withdraw and discontinue participation at any time.

Developmental and Other Concerns

The middle years can be a difficult period to endure. Strength and stamina are decreasing, gray hair and wrinkles are increasing, and the body frame is beginning to stoop (Papalia & Olds, 1989). In A FOCUS ON RESEARCH 9–3, the plight of the adult African-American male is highlighted.

 A FOCUS ON RESEARCH 9–3
African-American Men: An Endangered Species?

The theme being echoed in recent literature has been alarming—"Black men are rapidly becoming an endangered species" (Parham & Davis, 1987, p. 24). Contributors to the counseling literature, however, have been slow to translate societal concerns into strategies for counseling blacks, especially men. Why are black men considered an endangered species?

1. Black men have the lowest life expectancy rates in the nation.

2. Many receive inadequate health care.

3. Alcoholism is one of the leading mental health problems facing the black community.

4. The suicide rate for black men is escalating.

5. Biased and discriminatory educational systems have damaged the self-esteem of black men and have lowered their achievement levels.

6. Facing harsh job markets, black men often enlist in the military.

7. All classes of black men face harsh realities and stressful conditions in looking at their futures.

Source: Parham, T. A., & McDavis, R. J. (1987). Black men, an endangered species: Who's really pulling the trigger? *Journal of Counseling and Development, 66*, 24–27.

African-American adults who feel that past and present racism and discrimination have prevented them from dealing well with psychosocial crises or have hindered their achievement of age-level developmental tasks may be candidates for counseling. Taking stock of one's life, including past accomplishments and the possibilities of attaining future goals (financial, personal, and societal) can be both frustrating and depressing. Also, the perception of how age has affected sexuality significantly influences one's self-image.

Counseling Considerations

Over the past fifteen or twenty years in which African-Americans have been treated in counseling and psychotherapy in increasing numbers, questions have often been raised about appropriate intervention procedures (Jones, 1985). The counselor, seeking to intervene successfully in the lives of African-Americans, may encounter difficult tasks; for example, clients may often feel that their problems have been imposed upon them by a racist society and that support systems have failed to meet their needs (Warfield & Marion, 1985). Smith (1981) maintains that too many counselors do not understand the culture. They tend to remark, "I never notice the color of my client's skin" or "What really counts in counseling is empathy and not the cultural backgrounds of my clients" (p. 161). The question remains as to whether an Anglo therapist can intervene effectively with an African-American client. Perhaps it would be preferable to match counselors and clients whenever possible with respect to race. Some African-Americans may not want to see an Anglo therapist, just as some women may not want to see a male therapist. The client's choice of a therapist usually is indicative of self-perceptions and certain expectations for the counseling relationship. Reviews of diagnostic studies, preference studies, and field studies of individual and group therapy indicate few, if any, important effects of racial similarity in therapy (Jones, 1985; Sattler, 1977). Although client preferences are addressed as an issue in Chapter 12, A FOCUS ON RESEARCH 9–4 looks at a recent study that focused specifically on counselor preferences.

Contending that traditional counseling and therapy models tend to blame the victim, Gunnings and Lipscomb (1986) developed a model, the Systematic Approach to Counseling, for use with African-Americans. The new activist, or action, counseling model goes beyond blaming the victim and calls for action by counselors on behalf of clients. Rather than focusing on the individual's intrapsychic state of behavior, systemic counseling focuses on the environment as a key factor in determining attitudes, values, and behaviors. The steps in Gunnings and Lipscomb's systemic approach include

1. identification of symptoms;
2. exploration of the problem's cause;
3. discussion of problem-solving strategies and techniques;
4. selection of problem-solving strategies and techniques;
5. implementation of selected strategies;
6. evaluation of the effectiveness of the problem-solving process, and
7. expansion of client use of the model in other life areas.

A FOCUS ON RESEARCH 9–4
African-American Preferences for Counselors

Atkinson et al. (1986) asked 128 African-American subjects (42 males and 86 females) to express their preference for counselors relative to eight counselor characteristics: ethnicity, sex, religion, educational background, socioeconomic background, attitudes and values, personality, and age. Their study showed that although African-American subjects preferred an African-American counselor over a non-African-American counselor, other counselor characteristics were deemed more important than the counselor's race and ethnicity. Strong preferences were for better educated, older counselors who had attitudes and personalities similar to the clients. The two strongest preferences—for a counselor who was older and better educated than the client—suggested that the counselor's expertise was an important consideration for African-American clients.

Source: Atkinson, D. R., Furlong, M. J., & Poston, W. C. (1986). Afro-American preferences for counselor characteristics. *Journal of Counseling Psychology, 33,* 326–330.

A major task for the counselor continues to be persuading reluctant African-American males to participate in the counseling session. Larrabee (1986) suggests that it is generally difficult for African-American males to disclose vital information or to perceive the benefits of therapeutic interaction. Males often have the inner compulsion to work out their own difficulties; consequently, they develop fears of intimacy, another barrier to the acceptance of the counseling process. The opinion that seeking counseling is an indication of weakness must be overcome to achieve maximum effectiveness with male clients. Counselors perplexed by difficulties experienced when counseling African-American males can take an affirmation approach that works toward "the resumption of client dignity and personal responsibility through the process of affirming the client's integrity" (p. 28).

African-American females are also subject to mental health problems. Just as with males, many of the problems result from their racial, historical, cultural, and structural position in American society:

- Alcoholism among African-American women has increased dramatically. Related facts include (a) an increase in cirrhosis of the liver among African-American women; (b) a link between alcohol and an increased incidence of crime, child abuse, and unemployment; (c) a stronger interest in treatment for alcohol abuse among African-American men than women; and (d) the likelihood of African-American female heavy drinkers in an urban environment to be household heads, poor, and weekend drinkers.

- The suicide rate among young African-American females is also increasing. Factors affecting the suicide rate include migration, rage and frustration, unemployment, racism, and the breakdown of traditional institutions. The threat of loss of love or of a spouse is often a precipitating event for suicide. Among African-Americans, suicide rates are highest for the young, whereas with Anglos, suicide rates increase with advanced chronological age. (Smith, 1985).

Individual/Group Therapy

Planning intervention for African-American clients requires reaching a decision on whether to use individual or group counseling. Although African-American females are more likely than their mates to initiate or at least be open to therapy as a means of solving relationship problems, counselors are often frustrated by females who express intense dissatisfaction with relationships, but who also resist change or dissolution of the relationship. Such a lack of initiative must be understood in light of the female's situation. Financial insecurity, fear of loneliness, and the fact that African-American women far outnumber African-American men all contribute to the female's reluctance to act (Hines & Boyd-Franklin, 1982). While African-American males might tend to self-disclose freely in group sessions about their lives and perceptions of racism, African-American women in sexually mixed groups may not be as willing to discuss their push for equality and the problems associated with female-headed households.

Family Therapy

Working effectively with African-American families requires that therapists be willing to explore the impact of the social, political, socioeconomic, and broader environmental conditions of families. Although this concept is central to therapy with all families, it is critical in working with African-American inner-city families. The family's environment and community must be considered in the diagnostic process and in the planning of treatment (Hines & Boyd-Franklin, 1982).

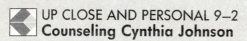

UP CLOSE AND PERSONAL 9–2
Counseling Cynthia Johnson

Cynthia Johnson, age 33, referred herself for counseling through a counseling program operated for the hospital staff. Counselors, either in private practice or employed by community mental health organizations, conducted counseling sessions at the hospital on a regular basis.

During Cynthia's first session, the 38-year-old Anglo female counselor discussed Cynthia's reasons for the self-referral. Speaking in black dialect interspersed with standard English, Cynthia explained that she felt trapped. Her husband tried hard to make a living—his work record was good, he never did time in jail, and he didn't have drinking problems. Still, Cynthia wanted more; she was already over 30 and nothing much was changing in her life. Although she hadn't spoken to her husband about her plans, Cynthia was thinking about beginning school at night. She had a desire for something else—she wanted to improve her life. The counselor listened intently, took notes, and encouraged Cynthia to examine her goals carefully and to consider the impact of her decision on her family. The counselor accepted Cynthia as a client. First, she would meet with her several times individually, then move to a group session (surely there were other women in the hospital with similar concerns), and, finally, depending on Cynthia's progress and her husband's reaction, she might decide to schedule a family session in which other family members could see the reasons for Cynthia's concerns and understand her goals.

Respect is a key to success in engaging the family during a family counseling session. Therapists should openly acknowledge the family's strengths, should avoid professional jargon, and should relate to the family in a direct but supportive manner. Counselors should avoid assuming familiarity with adult family members without asking their permission. A therapist who uses first names prematurely may expect negative reactions. Such concerns are often overlooked by cultures not sensitive to the disrespect that many African-Americans have received (Hines & Boyd-Franklin, 1982).

The literature documenting the use of family therapy with African-American clients has focused primarily on urban African-American families whose lives and survival systems are very different from those of non-African-American middle-class therapists (Block, 1981). Family therapy might not always be the treatment of choice in such situations. Still, individual consideration of African-American clients is recommended. In essence, until there is definitive research suggesting appropriate treatment strategies, the wisest policy continues to be consideration of individual clients and their particular circumstances.

ASIAN-AMERICAN ADULTS

What Asian-American cultural characteristics pose barriers to effective counseling intervention? What problems and concerns will Asian-American adults bring to counseling sessions? Of course, any discussion of counseling Asian-Americans should be considered in terms of individual and intracultural differences among Asian-Americans. Some of their potential counseling problems include the following:

1. acceptance of the model-minority stereotype that "all is well" and that counseling is not needed;
2. adverse effects of historical and contemporary discrimination;
3. the considerable poverty and low socioeconomic status of many Asian-Americans;
4. the adult's belief that discussing physical and mental problems actually causes these problems;
5. the adult's language and communication difficulties;
6. the effects of rigid and authoritarian family structures;
7. conflicts arising from the acculturation of younger generations;
8. the adult's belief that seeking counseling reflects negatively upon the family;
9. the adult's problems associated with midlife: aging and successfully meeting adult tasks and crises;
10. the adult's problems resulting from marriage and family situations; e.g., expecting traditional Asian-American family roles in a majority culture that emphasizes equality.

A review of the literature by Leong (1986) revealed that cultural factors may influence diagnosis and assessment of Asian-Americans in four areas: First, culture has been found to influence the expression of symptoms among Asian-Americans. Second, cultural biases often influence diagnostic evaluations of Asian-American behavior. Third, the use of interpreters has been a concern in the diagnostic evaluation of Asian-Americans. Finally, a fourth area of concern is the influence of cultural factors in evaluating clinical tests.

Cultural Differences

Speaking of the Asian-American culture as a whole, there are apparent cultural differences concerning beliefs about achievement and honor, respect for elders, allegiance to family and designated privileges and responsibilities, and approaches to handling problems (Axelson, 1985; Lum, 1986; Sue, 1981). Perceptive counselors work with their clients in an Asian-American frame of reference; they do not expect them to mold themselves into the Anglo-American cultural system.

With respect to comparing the Japanese-American and Anglo-American cultures, even more fundamental differences come to light. An unquestioned assumption in the Anglo culture is that the "self" or the core of ones's identity is located within the individual. When an Anglo-American refers to "self," he or she is pointing inward—within the physical confines of the body. A related, cherished concept that of individual autonomy. This is in contrast to the Japanese cultural assumption that the "self" is located in an interdependent network of obligations and affections. A word that perhaps has similar psychological meaning for the Japanese as *myself* has for Anglos is *uchi*. This can mean "my" home, "my" school, or any other place to which the individual feels an emotional linkage. While Americans cherish independence and autonomous rights, the Japanese prize interdependence and obligations toward others (Minatoya & Higa, 1988).

Other cultural differences between Asian-Americans and Anglo-Americans include the following:

1. Asian-Americans favor less ambiguity; they tend to prefer structured activities and immediate solutions to practical problems.
2. Asian-Americans tend to be less verbal and more controlled emotionally than Anglo-Americans.
3. Objective tests indicate that Asian-Americans have more personality problems than Anglo-Americans.
4. Culture probably influences the Asian-American expression of symptoms; i.e., the client may view physical illness as more "acceptable" than psychological disturbance, substituting somatic symptoms for psychological ones. (Leong, 1986)

Communication Barriers

The language problems of the Asian-American culture have been sufficiently documented (Axelson, 1985; Brower, 1980; Sue, 1981). These communication barriers have the potential for impeding personal and social growth, economic opportunities, and the counseling relationship. Although Brower (1980) referred specifically to the

Vietnamese, the language barrier of Asian-Americans is so widespread that conclusions apply to other Asian cultures.

Speaking to Vietnamese-Americans, some communicational situations may be so difficult that the counselor must engage the services of an interpreter. In such situations, an older person should be used rather than a young person or a student, since the Vietnamese client has more respect for older authority figures. Second, it may be wise to avoid questions that can be answered with simply a yes. To be polite, clients may respond yes to a question they really do not understand. The counselor should emphasize that a client can say no and still be polite (Brower, 1980).

Verbal mannerisms and nonverbal communication are also vitally important for both counselor and client to understand. First, a loud voice and a warm, hearty greeting are typical of Anglo-American communication. This mode of speech may seem rude to the Vietnamese client and unbefitting a person of authority. Second, a smile in the Anglo culture usually signifies happiness; in the Vietnamese culture it can signify anger, rejection, embarrassment, or other such emotions. Third, while Anglos consider "shifty eyes" or an unwillingness to make eye contact as suspicious, looking someone in the eye is a sign of disrespect or rudeness in the Vietnamese culture (Brower, 1980).

Marriage and Family

Prior to marriage and family counseling with Asian-Americans, Anglo-American counselors must acknowledge the cultural differences between the two cultures and understand familial structures within the Asian frame of reference. It should be readily obvious that Anglo counselors cannot counsel expecting Asian clients to accept equal status of marriage partners, to accept equality of sons and daughters, or to change traditional family structures of authority.

Asian-Americans traditionally have considered divorce a great shame and tragedy, especially for females. Asian-American disapproval of divorce is related to the serious social ostracism involved, which few can afford to experience, even at the risk of an unhappy household. Also, since few Asian-Americans males would consider befriending a woman who previously had been engaged to another man, associating with a divorcée would be even more unlikely. Therefore, the divorce rate among Asian-Americans has been relatively low and continues to be low today (Ho, 1987; Schwertfger, 1982).

Given the changing attitudes and generational differences due to acculturation, how do women's attitudes and behaviors differ in American, Japanese, and cross-cultural marriages? A FOCUS ON RESEARCH 9–5 addresses this question.

Developmental and Other Concerns

The development of a positive self-concept and cultural identity continues to be crucial during all periods of the lifespan. Realizing the developmental significance of a positive self-concept, counselors will be interested in the relationship between self-concept and perceived prejudice among Asian-American clients. Focusing their research on this relationship, Asamen and Berry (1987) concluded that counselors

A FOCUS ON RESEARCH 9–5
Women's Attitudes and Behaviors in American, Japanese, and Cross-Cultural Marriages

Marriages between Japanese and American citizens grew from approximately 55,000 annually in the mid-1950s to approximately 130,000 annually in the 1970s. Minatoya and Higa (1988) administered a questionnaire to 428 women. With respect to the Japanese women married to American men, they reported several interesting findings:

1. The Japanese women were significantly more likely than American women to have people living in their households beyond the nuclear family.

2. Thirty-four percent of the Japanese women in cross-cultural marriages were employed full-time outside the home, 11 percent were employed part-time, and 12 percent were seeking work outside the home.

3. The occupations of the Japanese women included office worker, teacher, scientist, service worker, and manager.

4. Their religions included Buddhist, Protestant, Roman Catholic, Shinto, and several others.

Source: Minatoya, L. Y., & Higa, Y. (1988). Women's attitudes and behaviors in American, Japanese, and cross-cultural marriages. *Journal of Multicultural Counseling and Development, 16,* 45–62.

should address the degree of alienation experienced by minorities. Also, while developing counseling intervention for Asian-Americans, it is important to remember that programs must be culturally appropriate; that is, Asian-Americans include Japanese-Americans, Pilipino-Americans, Korean-Americans, and many other subgroups. Problems that often cross cultural boundaries include the effects of the aging body and the deterioration of mental processes.

Asian-Americans may seek or be referred for help for numerous psychological stresses caused by living in war-torn areas, being separated from relatives, and for having to cope in a nation with a different language that continues to harbor racism and discrimination.

Counseling Considerations

Although Asian-Americans' tendency to underuse counseling facilities has been documented (Tracey, Leong, & Glidden, 1986), this underutilization does not result from less of a need for counseling services. Indeed, Asian-Americans have demonstrated higher-than-normal rates of psychological disturbances (Minatoya & Higa, 1988). Reports of Southeast Asians indicate the immense stigma associated with seeing a therapist and convictions that talking about feelings and emotions is equivalent to "parading in the nude in public" (Folkenberg, 1986. p. 10). Writing specifically of Japanese-American women, Minatoya and Higa (1988) agreed that women tend not to seek professional help and concluded that professional helpgivers were the least preferred source of assistance. Instead, women seek help much more frequently from family, neighbors, co-workers, and friends. In one study of 17 community health centers of the clients who did seek counseling, 52 percent did not return after the first session. For the 48 percent who did return, the average number of counseling sessions was only 2.35. These statistics are typical for urban areas and seem to imply the lack of development of an initial relationship and alliance between counselor and client (Shon & Ja, 1982; Sue & McKinney, 1975).

Counselors should understand why Asian-Americans tend to underutilize mental health services; they should also attempt to convince them that use of such services may be in their best interest. Although Asian-Americans have emotional disturbances, just as the rest of the population, problems brought to counseling centers usually pertain to academics and careers. Talking about problems of this nature is not as threatening to Asian-Americans as disclosing personal and emotional concerns. Counselors working with Asian-Americans who understand their values and motivations will use techniques that encourage clients to be open about personal and family matters (Tracey et al., 1986).

Once the counselor understands the Asian-American culture and its tendency to underutilize counseling services, what strategies are appropriate? Specifically, what should the counselor do or not do? Exum and Lau (1988) have specific suggestions for counselors working with Chinese clients:

1. Counselors working with Chinese-American clients should exhibit considerable involvement by modulating voice tone and by asking questions at appropriate times concerning the client's problems or feelings. Caution should be used, however, because clients may feel that they are being interrogated. It is important that questions be posed with tact and that they not be excessive.

2. The self-confidence of the counselor is important for Chinese-American clients. Self-confidence is demonstrated by voice control and sureness of presentation. Moderate pitch and volume suggests self-confidence to Chinese clients; paraphasing a client's comments often seems unnatural and suggests hesitancy or weakness on the part of the counselor.

3. Because Chinese-American clients expect the counselor to be an expert or a wise person, the counselor needs to project a solid, secure image before he or she can be perceived as trustworthy. Moving about too much may suggest nervousness or insecurity. The counselor should remain relatively still and not gesticulate excessively.

4. Self-disclosing remarks on the part of the counselor and firm speech also help to convey a sense of trustworthiness. Consistent with the clients expectations of nurturance from the counselor, it is also important that the counselor's voice quality and nonverbal behavior be gentle and encouraging yet firm.

5. It is very important that counselors provide a discernible structure to problem solving. Without interpretation and solution, counseling will seem futile to clients and leave them confused.

A FOCUS ON RESEARCH 9–6 examines the counseling preference of Chinese-American college students. As the study described implies, it is imperative to recognize traditional Chinese cultural values and to employ directive counseling techniques. Consider the following directive approach illustrated by Exum and Lau (1988):

A FOCUS ON RESEARCH 9–6
Chinese College Students' Preferences for Counseling Styles

Much of the literature on cross-cultural counseling suggests that traditional, nondirective counseling approaches may be in conflict with the values and life experiences of Asian-American clients. Because of Asian-American cultural orientations, nondirective approaches may even be counterproductive. Also, Asian-American clients assign more credibility to counselors who employ a directive approach than to counselors using nondirective approaches. It follows that Chinese clients expect to assume a passive role and expect the counselor to be more assertive. Exum and Lau sought to determine whether Cantonese-speaking Chinese students responded best to directive or nondirective approaches. Their study, which used a subject pool of adults in the age range of 18 to 32 who had been in the United States an average of 1.8 years, suggested that counselors should use a directive counseling approach.

Source: Exum, H. A., & Lau, E. Y. (1988). Counseling style preference of Chinese college students. *Journal of Multicultural Counseling and Development, 16,* 84–92.

Counselor: What would you like to share with me today?

Client: (sigh) Well, I'm not sure if it's going to help to talk about it.

Counselor: Since you're here, there must be something bothering you. I do believe that talking about it would help.

Client: Maybe the more I talk about it, the worse I'll feel. Maybe I shouldn't talk as much and let time take care of itself.

Counselor: Seems like you're feeling a great pain inside you. Can you tell me more about it? We'll see if we can find some ways to solve the problem.

Client: Yeah, maybe I should do that, since you've seen so many difficult problems before, you might be able to give me some suggestions.

Counselor: Well, since this is something bothering you so much, you might feel even worse if you keep it all inside. I think it's very courageous of you to come to seek counseling. (p. 92)

Axelson (1985) used the following exchange between a career training counselor and a Vietnamese client to illustrate how the language barrier poses a problem:

Counselor: How are things going now that you and your family have settled into your new apartment?

Client: Yes. (Smiles and glances down)

Counselor: Sometimes moving into a strange neighborhood and new home brings problems.

Client: Many things for Kien fix up, work hard ... need stove, one [burner] only work, but cos' so much. Friends [sponsors] help get good price, and get TV.

Counselor: A TV?

Client: Yes, they get good education, get better life. Can no teach English Kim and

Van, school help . . . (pauses) . . . worry abou' Lan. Change so much, go far from Vietnamese way. She have American boy friend. Want be like American. (Smiles, and becomes very quiet, looks at floor, seems embarrassed by what she has said)

Counselor: You seem sad.

Client: (Grins and laughs) My father tell me take care of Lan. My brothers all made dead by soldiers . . . only me left to watch Lan . . . (pauses) . . . our boat ge' Thai pirates. Lan and me make face black, hide in boat . . . no see us! (Laughs and begins to sob quietly) Oh, excuse me.

Counselor: That's o.k. I know it's difficult to talk about those past days and the things that hurt you. And it's a big responsibility to look out for Lan. It's all right to show how you feel to me. I won't take it as being impolite to me and I'll try to help you in any way I can—including listening and caring for how you feel about something that hurts or makes you sad or angry. It's my job to help you with things that are difficult for you.

Client: Oh (faint smile) so many problems wan' to please father; help Kien . . .

Counselor: Yes, that's all important to you. How is Kien's job training going for him?

Client: Kien in Vietnam, big navy officer . . . now nothing . . . feel bad, but training good . . . become computer-electronic man. That good for him, get job, more money, feel better.

Counselor: Yes, that's a good thing for your family.

Client: Thank you.

Counselor: Let's talk now about the work that you want. You said before that you like to sew. That's a skill that you have that you can use right now to add to the family income.

Client: Yes, make clothes for children, mend Kien's shirt.

Counselor: I know. You showed me some of the good work you have done. There's a job that I'd like to see you try at the—store. It will be to alter clothes that customers buy.

Client: Oh . . . speak little English, so har' for me, make others feel bad . . . no way go store . . . can't find . . . where bus? (pp. 415–417)

In working with Southeast Asian clients, counselors can expect understatement; they should realize that modesty, discretion, and self-depreciation do not necessarily reflect a poor self-concept. Discussing family matters calls for considerable discretion; likewise, obtaining sexual information, which may prove difficult. All symptoms exhibited by Southeast Asians should be considered in terms of cultural relevance (Kitano, 1989; Tung, 1985).

With specific reference to Vietnamese-Americans, Brower (1980) offers the following suggestions:

1. Rapport and trust are all-important. Showing concern for the client's family helps; e.g., asking about their welfare.

2. Counseling sessions should have considerable structure, since Vietnamese are accustomed to authoritarian stances.

3. Efforts should be made to break down communicational barriers; this involves an understanding of nonverbal behaviors.

4. The Vietnamese may be unwilling to disclose personal information; they also tend to be very humble.

5. Rigidly defined sex roles include the man being the family ruler.

6. Mental health problems may include accumulated stress from years of war and delayed reactions to dangerous escapes and refugee camps.

Individual/Group Therapy

Leong (1986) suggested a high likelihood of negative outcomes for Asian-Americans participating in group counseling or psychotherapy. Outcomes are likely to be negative due to inherent conflicts between the demands of the group therapy process and the cultural values of Asian-Americans, which include verbal unassertiveness, reluctance to display strong emotion, and unwillingness to disclose problems to strangers. The conflicts may be exacerbated if the counselor is unaware of Asian-American culture-based behavior and expects participation in the Anglo manner. Such pressure may result in the client withdrawing from group counseling.

According to Kitano (1989), sessions with the most potential for positive outcomes are those in which the groups are homogeneous in terms of sex, background, profession, and social class. Goal-oriented sessions are probably more productive than free-floating, process-oriented ones. Clients often look for firm leadership and clear structure. In some instances, participants may need or prefer to speak in their native languages, requiring the services of a translator.

Family Therapy

Family therapy normally focuses on one individual, protects the dignity of the individual, and honors the good name of the family. The therapist's goal while working with this individual is to modify the emotional dynamics of the family through the individual's change. The technique is especially applicable with Asian-Americans because it allows them to define and to clarify family relationships by speaking directly to the therapist instead of, for example, a husband or wife speaking to one another. Detached but interested, intellectual, calm, low-key approaches to problem solving correspond closely to Buddhism's teaching of moderation in behavior, self-discipline, patience, and modesty. Furthermore, teaching the family how to differentiate, clarify values, and resolve family problems coincides with the family's expectation of the therapist as an expert (Ho, 1987). Discussions of feelings or of psychological motives for behavior are uncommon in most Asian-American homes, even second- and third-generation homes. Disturbed behavior is often attributed to lack of will, supernatural causes, or physical illness. Hard work, effort, and developing character are thought to be the most effective means to address most problems (Kitano, 1989).

Special caution is encouraged when husbands and wives are together in therapy. Alert counselors may want to talk with the husband prior to the wife to show respect for Asian custom and tradition. They may also choose to place the husband and wife in different groups to prevent the wife's speaking from being considered an affront to the husband (Intercultural Development Research Association, 1976). Non-Anglo

UP CLOSE AND PERSONAL 9–3
Counseling Han Sukuzi

Han Sukuzi, age 36, was referred by his company's medical doctor to a mental health counseling organization. The doctor wrote to the counselor that Han was experiencing stress. If it hadn't been for the physical examination, I wouldn't have to see that counselor who will probably ask a lot of nosy questions, Han thought.

The 44-year-old Anglo male counselor immediately picked up several cues that did not augur well for the counseling relationship: Han was reluctant to come, he was quiet and withdrawn, and he did not want to discuss personal problems with a stranger. The counselor explained the counseling process, its confidentiality, and the intent. Then, the counselor cautiously encouraged Han to talk (being sure not to give the impression of interrogating or snooping). Although it was difficult at first for

Han to reveal his problems, the counselor was able to reach several conclusions after several sessions: Han was working two jobs and felt uncomfortable about being away from his family. He was worried about his wife seeking a part-time job. Not only would this reflect badly on him, but who would take care of Grandfather? He was also worried about Mina. So far, she had been an excellent daughter and student and had brought much honor to the family, but would she be swayed by her Anglo friends?

The counselor decided to meet with Han individually for several more sessions. A group session would allow Han to see that other men shared similar problems, but Han would without doubt be unwilling to share personal information in a group setting. Also, Han's traditional ways of thinking would undermine the effectiveness of a family session.

counselors, perhaps not fully comprehending the structure of the Asian-American family, who encourage the wife and children to speak for themselves might lose the respect of the family and may seriously impede the counseling relationship.

HISPANIC-AMERICAN ADULTS

Multicultural counselors working with Hispanic-American adults face challenges arising from a variety of situations: Hispanic-Americans' allegiance to the Spanish language and traditions, their low educational levels and lack of job-related skills, and the stereotypes plaguing their culture. Changing women's roles is yet another issue with which counselors often must contend. Although not all Hispanic women are seeking to change their traditional roles, there is an increasing trend among them to seek greater equality. This trend has profound implications for males who have traditionally demanded and received recognition as being biologically superior. Some of the problems that may affect Hispanics as they interact in a predominantly Anglo society are the following:

1. negative effects of the stereotype that all Hispanics are hotbloods, fighters, and drug dealers;

2. the belief that all Hispanic adults, regardless of geographical origin, have the same cultural characteristics;

3. the adult's commitment to long-held traditions of *respeto, machismo,* and *dignidad,* which may slow down the acculturation process;

4. the adult's language problems and communicational barriers;

5. differing cultural characteristics: allegiance to immediate and extended families, large families, patriarchial families, rigidly defined sex roles (in some cases), and belief (in some cases) of the inherent superiority of the male;

6. the adult female's changing role; e.g., increasing numbers of Hispanic-American women working outside the home;

7. the adult's low socioeconomic status;

8. difficulties encountered in achieving equal educational and employment opportunities in the Anglo society;

9. problems associated with midlife: meeting tasks and crises and marriage and family problems.

Cultural Differences

What should multicultural counselors working with Hispanic-Americans know about the Hispanic culture? What makes the culture unique? Several areas, all having implications for counselors and the counseling relationship, can be pinpointed for better understanding:

1. *Language skills and preferences.* Many Hispanic-American people continue to view Spanish as the "mother tongue."

2. *Sex roles and marriage.* Although rigidly defined sex roles in marriage are often assumed to characterize all Hispanic cultures, such is not the case.

3. *Family structure and dynamics.* According to Ruiz (1981), the immediate or nuclear family tends to be relied upon in urban areas, while in rural settings, the extended family structure plays an important role in providing support.

Communication Barriers

The Hispanic-American's allegiance to the mother tongue is understandable, yet it is socially and economically unrealistic. Hispanic-Americans choosing to speak mainly Spanish to some extent explains the high unemployment rates and show acculturation process among Hispanics. Hispanic-Americans continuing to live in Spanish-speaking enclaves do not desire or perceive a need to learn English (Ruiz, 1981).

The following hypothetical case of Francisco, a Mexican-American, illustrates the effects of language barriers in a situation that might confront counselors:

Francisco is a 39-year-old man who is married and raising five children. He is bilingual and bicultural; he usually feels quite comfortable speaking English, but on some topics prefers the Spanish language. . . . Because of particular financial circumstances in his life, he presently has to deal regularly with a city agency in which there is no representative of the Spanish-speaking community. Francisco finds it extremely difficult to assert himself and make his request known in English. As a result, he is experiencing considerable frustration and anxiety, which is beginning to manifest itself in physical symptoms—tension headaches and stomach pains. This anxiety is indirectly creating negative interactions between himself and his family. This negative family interaction is causing Francisco guilt, and he becomes angry at himself and increasingly self-blaming. The situation is getting out of hand, and Francisco decides to see a physician for his physical symptoms. After a medical checkup and ensuing conversation, the physician refers him to a neighborhood counseling agency. (Ponterotto, 1987, p. 310)

As the vignette illustrates, the Hispanic-American's need for counseling services can often be traced to a language barrier. Many times, the Hispanic cannot even gain telephone access to health care because of the few Spanish-speaking operators and bilingual health care providers (Berry & Ojeda, 1985). Verbal interaction, which is crucial to the counseling process, cannot be developed unless the counselor and client understand one another. A counselor who speaks only English, regardless of skill in therapeutic techniques, will no doubt experience frustration developing a counseling relationship with a client who speaks only Spanish.

Marriage and Family

The Hispanic-American population, the fastest-growing ethnic group in the United States, is also one of the most heterogeneous groups (Weiner, 1983). Ruiz (1981) contends that some writers suggest too much similarity among Hispanic-Americans. Not only do they vary widely with respect to their specific subgroups, but also in terms of degree of acculturation. Acculturation is very likely to create stresses that result in problems for families. Counselors must understand the dynamics of acculturation, as well as the tremendous intracultural diversity among the various Hispanic subgroups.

Basically, counselors have a three-fold task when providing marriage and family therapy to Hispanics. First, they must look for valid cross-cultural generalizations and, second, they must consider each culture's unique characteristics. The third task is to consider individual marriage partners and family members to determine the most effective counseling intervention.

Do some Hispanic-American groups have lower rates of marital instability than others? Research suggests that Mexican-Americans tend to experience less marital disruption. A study designed to compare marital instability of several different cultures revealed that (a) stability patterns vary substantially across Hispanic populations, (b) conclusions of earlier research that Mexican-American women enjoy a "stability edge" is supported in both nationwide and regional analyses, and (c) the incidence of marital disruption ranges from very low among Mexican-American, Cuban, and Anglo women to comparatively high among Puerto Ricans and African-Americans (Frisbie, 1986).

Mexican-American families are characterized by cohesion and a strong hierarchical organization, generational interdependence and loyalty to the family, interpersonal involvement, and a tendency for individuals to live in families at every developmental stage. All life cycle events and rituals are family celebrations and affirmations of family unity. It is also important for counselors to recognize that marriage and family rules and expectations are organized around age and sex, since these two factors are the most important determinants of authority (Falicov, 1982).

Developmental and Other Concerns

Building a positive cultural and individual identity and successfully meeting psycho-social crises and developmental tasks challenge Hispanic-American adults. Their progress may be slowed by communication barriers, lack of education, unemployment, and misunderstandings of individual Hispanic cultures. Maintaining allegiance and commitment to Hispanic traditions while living in a predominantly Anglo society can also result in frustrations and the need for counseling intervention.

Other developmental concerns may focus around the aging process—loss of stamina and impaired sexual functioning. The counselor who understands the adult development period can provide better services to the individual adult client. Carefully planning intervention that takes into account developmental characteristics of the adult years and the problems of adult Hispanics is necessary for effective counseling.

Counseling Considerations

It is essential for professionals planning counseling intervention to understand that Hispanics do not consider mental health services a solution to their emotional and family problems (Ho, 1987). The underutilization of these services by Hispanics can be attributed to several factors: (a) language barriers, (b) cultural and social-class differences between therapists and clients, (c) an insufficient number of health facilities, (d) overuse or misuse of such services by physicians, (e) reluctance to recognize the urgency for help, and (f) lack of awareness of the existence of mental health clinics (Acosta, Yamamoto, & Evans, 1982).

Casas (1976) and Ruiz and Casas (1981) identified the behavioral approach as appropriate for many ethnic minority groups, including Mexican-Americans. The behavioral approach has an environmental focus that usually empowers the client to effect change. Such intervention focuses on skill-building and moves away from "blaming the victim," which is inherent in some insight-oriented therapies (Casas & Vasquez, 1989).

When the client and counselor meet for the first time, both bring well-established ideas about how each should act and about the nature of the counselor-client relationship (Cherbosque, 1987). Furthermore, the counseling relationship will be affected by differing opinions of what constitutes appropriate behavior and differing expectations for the counseling intervention (Ka-Wai & Tinsley, 1981). It is important, therefore, to recognize individual differences and to acknowledge the diversity among Hispanic cultures. We will now turn our attention to several specific Hispanic-American populations and offer counseling suggestions for each.

Latino-Americans. Latino-Americans are largely urban dwellers, poor and under-paid, menially employed, uneducated, and fearful of layoffs. Further complicating the situation is the commitment of some Latinos to Spanish as the preferred language at home, at work, and at school (Ruiz & Padilla, 1977). The counselor understanding the importance of *personalismo* to these clients will want to greet them warmly, using his or her first name, rather than a title. The counselor should employ small talk to build rapport and trust and should understand that since Latinos perceive psychological problems as physical problems, sessions should be scheduled promptly. Counseling centers should emphasize a "business-model approach," aggressively pursuing clients who need services. These centers should be staffed with professionals having a knowledge of Latino ethnohistory and culture. The small number of Latino counselors and the somewhat dismal outlook for future Latino counselors calls for the short-range solution of teaching Spanish and Latino culture to non-Latino counselors (Ruiz & Padilla, 1977).

Mexican-Americans. Another Hispanic-American group, Mexican-Americans, deserves individual consideration and counseling intervention based on their ethnohistory and culture. There are several clear-cut distinctions between Mexican-Americans and Anglo-Americans with respect to expectations for counseling. For example, Mexican clients expect more openness from counselors and they prefer more formality from professionals than Anglo-Americans. Also, Mexican-Americans favor counseling that deals with present rather than past events, while Anglo-Americans often prefer psychoanalytic techniques (Cherbosque, 1987).

The following counselor-client dialogue illustrates the client's frustrations in having to deal with several troublesome problems at once:

Counselor: Juan, workers' employment compensation will pay for your lost time, but the health insurance will pay only for the authorized medical treatment that you received for the accident you had at work.

Client: My eyes still don't work so I can see the assembly charts. I get so darn shaky whenever I think about all my money problems, bills, if I can't do the work, what's going to happen to my children. . . .

Counselor: Yeah, I know, it seems like everything is hitting you all at once.

Client: Ha! You know, maybe it sounds crazy or something but there's this woman in my neighborhood who has some things that she gives me and advises me how to feel better. It really helps.

Counselor: I can't really advise you on what type of treatment you should receive. If it helps and you feel better, why not use it? You're also getting the medical help for your visual problem. You're doing the most you can for yourself at this time. (Axelson, 1985, p. 402)

Another consideration for counselors is the Hispanic-American's strong religious beliefs. The following case history of José attests to the powerful role religious beliefs play in the lives of many:

José, a young 35-year-old Spanish-speaking Mexican, came to the clinic complaining of trembling in his hands, sweating, and shortness of breath. He appeared to be a strong and straightforward individual. He stated that his work performance as an upholsterer has been deteriorating for several months. His major conflict focused on his wish to marry his girlfriend and the resulting need to decrease the amount of money he was sending to his parents and younger brothers and sisters in Mexico. He felt he would be committing a crime or a sin if he were to reduce his help to his family. He has sought advice in the mental health clinic because he thought he was going crazy. He had never experienced such sudden onsets of anxiety before. In addition to helping his patient express his feelings and his needs in short-term therapy, the therapist encouraged him to speak to a priest about his fears of committing a sin against his family. José did consult with a priest over several meetings and also completed eight sessions of short-term therapy. His anxiety diminished, his work improved, and he decided to propose marriage to his girlfriend when therapy ended.[1]

Sources of stress for Hispanic-American women include unfavorable conditions of poverty such as substandard housing, depressed social status, limited education, and minimal political influence. Many women are struggling for increased equality and a greater range of personal and vocational options. In seeking such goals, Mexican-American women find themselves in a double bind:

> Not only are they [Mexican-American women] treated as subordinate to men, but they are considered as inferior as a result of their ethnic group membership. Mexican-American women are caught between two worlds—one that tells them to preserve and to abide by traditional customs and another that tells them to conform to the teachings and beliefs of the dominant culture. (Palacios & Franco, 1986, p. 127)

Casas and Vasquez (1989) point to potential problems the Hispanic-American woman confronts as she returns to school. While most women may experience loss of income, change of status, or other adjustments, the Hispanic-American female may experience additional stress resulting from conflicts over commitment to children and her marriage partner. The positive valuation of family and relationships can result in guilt and frustration when study schedules monopolize time. Other stresses may result from negative attitudes of peers and faculty members who doubt the Hispanic-American woman's ability to succeed.

Although directed toward counseling Mexican-American females, several suggestions are equally applicable in intervening with males: (a) Professionals need to identify mental health systems as appropriate sources of help by making personal appearances at meetings and contacting doctors and clerics; (b) they must acquaint themselves with the most recent and effective innovations in counseling; and (c) they must ensure that bilingual informational materials explaining mental health services and how to use them are disseminated (Palacios & Franco, 1986).

Puerto-Ricans. Counseling literature provides several suggestions for planning intervention with Puerto Ricans. First, the vast differences between first- and second-generation Puerto-Ricans deserve recognition in counseling strategies. Second, Puerto Ricans often have problems with American school systems. Parents initially surrender responsibility for their children to the school system because they feel it is a be-

---

[1]From F. X. Acosta, J. Yamamoto, and L. A. Evans, *Effective Psychotherapy for Low-income and Minority Patients,* p. 57. Copyright © 1982 by Plenum Publishing Company. Reprinted by permission of Plenum Publishing Company.

nevolent institution; later, they become suspicious of the schools and are unwilling to cooperate. Third, counselors working with Puerto Rican clients should understand the Spanish-speaking culture and its attitudes toward the family. Fourth, counselors should be sensitive to two problems that are widespread among the Puerto Rican population: drug abuse and depression (Weiner, 1983). One study concluded that death from drug dependence ranked sixth as a cause of death among Puerto Ricans of all ages (Alers, 1978). Also, the high incidence of depression in low-income Puerto Rican women has seen attributed to cultural factors, such as women's subordinate status (Comas-Diaz, 1981).

Individual/Group Therapy

A decision of whether to use individual or group counseling may be difficult due to the tremendous diversity among Hispanic-American groups. The choice of intervention approach with Hispanic-Americans should be based on which therapeutic mode is most beneficial for the individual client and culture. Ponterotto (1987) suggests a multimodal approach in which the individual needs of the client are considered. Socioeconomic status, place of birth, language spoken, and generational level must all be taken into account.

Psychological acculturation (Dillard, 1985) is another important factor in counseling individuals. Research on counseling Mexican-Americans documents the relationship of acculturation to the following: dropout rates, tendency toward self-disclosure, experienced levels of stress, attitudes toward counseling and counselors, willingness to seek professional help, and preference for an ethnically similar counselor (Ponterotto, 1987).

Family Therapy

Although research is limited, some findings indicate that Hispanic-Americans can benefit from family counseling and therapy. The family can be included in several ways: by asking specific family members to join in the counseling process, by working directly with the entire family, or by counseling one member of the family as a consultant who then works with the client or other family members (Christensen, 1977; Padilla, 1981).

As a result of prolonged discrimination against Hispanic-Americans, many clients distrust family therapists of the majority culture. This distrust is further compounded if the Hispanic client lacks proper documents to reside in the United States. Therapists should define their role carefully and attempt to disassociate themselves from immigration connections. The therapist should show respect for the Hispanic culture by addressing the father first. Having an interpreter present might be necessary, since older family members may neither speak nor understand English. Being active, polite, and willing to offer advice, the counselor can develop rapport and trust and become a part of the family emotional process (Padilla, 1981).

Loyalty to family members, both immediate and extended, is important to Hispanics in family counseling situations. Some research suggests that the prevalence of the extended family structure and the importance of family interaction in the daily lives of most Latinos indicate that family approaches will be successful (Ruiz & Padilla, 1977).

◆ **UP CLOSE AND PERSONAL 9–4**
Counseling Carla Suarez

Carla, age 35, referred herself to a neighborhood mental health organization. She has been experiencing frustrations and stresses: her husband's job or the lack of one, the borrowed money, Oscar's objection to her getting a job, problems with her son's progress in school, her inability to initiate change as other women are, her feelings of powerlessness, and her desire to put her husband's authority to the test. She has finally concluded that she should get a job and enroll in night school, despite her husband's protestations. "I want to improve my life," Carla says, "Oscar runs my life—I'm ready for a change."

The Anglo counselor, female and age 34, recognized that Carla needed immediate help and also that she would be receptive to counseling. The counselor had some degree of multi-

cultural expertise and understood some of the problems affecting contemporary Hispanics. She told Carla that although she had a fairly good knowledge of the Hispanic culture, she still might make mistakes. She encouraged Carla to talk more about herself and what she wanted. She also advised her to consider the repercussions of her getting a job and attending school as opposed to how she might feel if she failed to take action. The counselor decided to meet with Carla several times to counsel her as she moved against Oscar's authoritarian demands. Individual therapy would be best for the first few sessions. Then, group therapy might be appropriate, since she knew other Hispanic women in similar situations. Family therapy was not a possibility; Oscar would stifle Carla's ambitions and would monopolize the counseling session.

A POINT OF DEPARTURE

Challenges Confronting Multicultural Counselors of Adults

The counselor intervening with culturally diverse clients has several challenges, each requiring a knowledge of the adult lifespan period:

1. understanding what being an adult member of a particular culture is like;

2. knowing what it means to face particular adult crises and tasks in a predominantly Anglo-American society;

3. understanding that diversity exists within cultures resulting from geographical, socioeconomic, generational, and other individual differences;

4. being motivated to counsel effectively and to learn appropriate techniques for individual cultures; and

5. choosing the best therapeutic mode for the individual client.

Although these challenges at first glance may seem overwhelming, acquiring an understanding of the adult developmental period of the lifespan and gaining first-hand experiences with culturally diverse people are primary steps to providing effective counseling in multicultural situations.

SUMMARY

Counseling Native-American, African-American, Asian-American, and Hispanic-American adults requires understanding the adult development period within the individual cultures. To determine appropriate counseling intervention, such factors as racial and ethnic differences, language and communication barriers, and concerns associated with the adult years must be understood. Particularly challenging to multicultural counselors are class and generational differences and other differences among cultural groups that sometimes may not be so obvious.

Suggested Readings

Attneave, C. L. (1985). Practical counseling with American Indian and Alaska native clients. In P. B. Pedersen (Ed.), *Handbook of cross-cultural counseling and therapy* (pp. 135–140). Westport, CT: Greenwood Press. Attneave examines the history, fundamental assumptions, and future directions of Native-Americans and Alaskan native clients.

Boynton, G. (1987). Cross-cultural family therapy: The escape model. *The American Journal of Family Therapy, 15,* 123–130. This article focuses on problems that may confront family therapists as they attempt to acquire cultural sensitivity and choose appropriate techniques.

Brower, I. C. (1980). Counseling Vietnamese. *The Personnel and Guidance Journal, 58,* 646–652. This excellent reading provides specific information to help the counselor establish rapport, avoid misunderstandings in explicit and implicit communication, and deal with Vietnamese attitudes toward sex roles and family relationships.

Ho, M. L. (1987). *Family therapy with ethnic minorities.* Newbury Park: Sage Publications. Ho examines family therapy with Native-, African-, Asian- and Hispanic-Americans in considerable detail and looks at similarities and differences among ethnic minorities.

Journal of Multicultural Counseling and Development (April 1985, July 1985, and January 1986). These three issues focus on the African-American male. Counseling, developmental, and therapeutic issues are considered.

Kitano, H. H. L. (1989). A model for counseling Asian Americans. In P. B. Pedersen, J. G. Draguns, W. J. Lonner, & J. E. Trimble (Eds.), *Counseling across cultures* (pp. 139–151). Honolulu: University of Hawaii Press. Kitano presents a model for counseling Asian-Americans that takes their diversity into account.

Leong, F. T. L. (1986). Counseling and psychotherapy with Asian-Americans: Review of the literature. *Journal of Counseling Psychology, 33,* 196–206. Leong provides a comprehensive review of the literature and examines many issues crucial to counseling Asian-Americans.

McGoldrick, M., Pearce, J. K., & Giordano, J. (1982). *Ethnicity and family therapy.* New York: Guilford. These authors provide a comprehensive examination of family therapy and ethnicity. Nineteen different cultures are included.

Palacios, M., & Franco, J. N. (1986). Counseling Mexican-American women. *Journal of Multicultural Counseling and Development, 14,* 124–131. Palacios and Franco focus on the cultural characteristics of Mexican-American women. Appropriate counseling techniques for these clients are suggested.

Ponterotto, J. G. (1987). Counseling Mexican-Americans: A multimodal approach. *Journal of Counseling and Development, 65,* 308–312. Ponterotto describes a culturally sensitive therapeutic framework for nonminority and minority counselors working with clients of Mexican-American heritage.

Ruiz, R. A., & Padilla, A. M. (1977). Counseling Latinos. *The Personnel and Guidance Journal, 55,* 401–408. Ruiz and Padilla examine the demographics of Latino clients and offer counseling suggestions.

Trimble, J. E., & Fleming, C. M. (1989). Providing counseling services for Native-American Indians: Client, counselor, and community characteristics. In P. B. Pedersen, J. G. Draguns, W. J. Lonner, & J. E. Trimble (Eds.), *Counseling across cultures* (pp. 177–204). Honolulu: University of Hawaii Press. Trimble and Fleming explore mental health issues, characteristics of both clients and counselors, and counseling styles.

Part IV

Understanding and Counseling the Elderly

The last stage of the lifespan, the elderly years, is examined in Part IV. Following the established format, Chapter 10 provides a cultural portrait of Native-American, African-American, Asian-American, and Hispanic-American elderly people. Chapter 11 then provides readers with strategies for intervening with these clients.

Chapter 10

Social and Cultural Aspects of Aging

Questions To Be Explored

1. What is the nature of the elderly developmental period? How does this period differ from the adult developmental period?

2. How do misconceptions affect the thinking of policy-makers responsible for programs designed for the elderly?

3. Do the minority elderly experience double or even multiple jeopardy?

4. What are some special problems that the minority elderly might experience as a result of their culture/ethnicity and age?

5. What are the elderly years in the Native-American, African-American, Asian-American, and Hispanic-American cultures like?

6. How do the elderly in these minority cultures differ from the elderly in the Anglo-American culture?

7. What challenges confront multicultural counselors working with elderly minorities?

8. What are some additional sources of information for counselors intervening with the minority elderly?

INTRODUCTION

The elderly years represent the culminating developmental period on the lifespan continuum and are receiving increasing attention in both research and applied situations. This well-deserved attention is without doubt long overdue, especially in light of the misconceptions and stereotypes plaguing the elderly. The minority aged, in fact, face greater problems and challenges resulting from being both aged *and* minority. Multicultural counselors preparing to meet the unique challenges facing increasing minority elderly populations will want to understand the social and cultural aspects of aging and what being elderly in each minority culture actually means. To achieve this goal, it is necessary to consider the important intracultural, socioeconomic, geographical, and generational differences among the culturally diverse elderly.

THE MINORITY ELDERLY

Realistically speaking, some may question whether there will be much demand for multicultural counseling of the elderly (Kart, 1985). Do not all of the minority elderly share commonalities that cut across cultural and ethnic lines? While serious study of elderly minorities may lead to conclusions that are generalizable across cultural groups (Kart, 1985; Kent, 1971), demographic data from the American Association of Retired Persons (AARP) listed in Table 10–1 would appear to justify the counselor's training and expertise in working with specific minority elderly populations. Also, predictions of increasing numbers of elderly minorities indicate that multicultural counselors are likely to be called upon to provide counseling intervention with culturally diverse elderly clients over the next several decades.

A Case of Multiple Jeopardy?

Convincing arguments have been presented to suggest that the minority aged experience a case of double jeopardy; that is, they face problems and discrimination from being both aged and minority (Kart, 1985; Jackson, 1970). In comparing the Anglo aged to the minority aged, the U.S. Special Committee on Aging concluded that the latter are not as well educated, have less income, live in poorer quality housing and have less choice about where they live, have a less satisfying quality of life, suffer more illness, and die earlier. Some social scientists contend that the term *triple jeopardy* should be used to represent some members of the minority elderly—those who are poor, as well (Kart, 1985). Being a female may make matters still worse; for example, *quadruple jeopardy* would characterize an African-American woman who is both old and poor.

Table 10–1 Population of elderly minority group members

Culture	Age	Number	Age	Number
Native-American	65+	79,500	85+	6,100
African-American	65+	2.1 mil	85+	157,500
Asian-American	65+	221,500	85+	15,100
Hispanic-American	65+	673,000	85+	45,000

Source: Data compiled from AARP, 1986.

◆ A FOCUS ON RESEARCH 10–1
Double Jeopardy to Health for Older African-Americans?

Ferraro's (1987) study examines health status with the understanding that identification of health indicators is often subjective. Ferraro surveyed 3,042 older adults to determine whether older African-American adults experience dou-

ble jeopardy. The following findings were reported:

1. Although older African-Americans tended to have poorer health than Anglo-Americans, there was no evidence to support the double-jeopardy hypothesis.

2. Optimism about health in elderly people was not evidenced in the entire sample—just among the Anglo-American women.

Source: Ferraro, K. F. (1987). Double jeopardy to health for Black older Americans? *Journal of Gerontology, 42,* 528–533.

---

poverty, income & housing

The income disparities between the Anglo-American elderly and the elderly of other cultures are striking. Consider the following income data for elderly groups in the United States (AARP, 1986):

Anglo-American	$7,408
Native-American	$4,257
African-American	$4,113
Asian-American	$5,551
Hispanic-American	$4,592

These dismally low median incomes indicate that the minority elderly in all probability do experience double (or even triple or quadruple) jeopardy. The wide gap between the Anglo-American annual income (which, itself, can be considered seriously low) and the next highest annual income suggests that minority status and earning power are inextricably linked.

In A FOCUS ON RESEARCH 10–1, another problem—the health status of old people—is considered.

32% Native Am 65 a.older live below poverty line

Stereotyping the Elderly

The study of aging, termed *gerontology* around 1950, is the most recent medical subspecialty to receive widespread recognition (Hendricks & Hendricks, 1981). The lack of knowledge of older people traditionally has plagued this population and has perpetuated misconceptions and stereotypes about them. Older generations have often been portrayed as beset with financial problems, poor health, victimization, and loneliness. Although these situations do often exist and deserve the careful attention of all professionals working with the elderly, it is a serious error to begin counseling intervention with stereotypic beliefs. Stereotypes demonstrate little understanding of individual variation among the elderly and variation across cultures. The following statements reflect stereotypic thinking:

"The elderly are different from the rest of us. They don't have the same desires, concerns, or fears."

"Older people are not sexually active—they're too old to be interested."

"They're unemployed, unproductive, and unfulfilled. How can they feel worthwhile if they don't contribute to society?"

"Special counseling for the elderly? Why? They're too old to have a need for counseling."

Such statements not only demonstrate a lack of knowledge, but also are potentially damaging to the total population of elderly people. Professional decisions and public policy toward the elderly are affected by such misconceptions; and certainly not the least concern, many elderly people, themselves, may actually begin to believe in the stereotypes and base their lives on them.

THE NATIVE-AMERICAN ELDERLY

Societal and Cultural Description

Several facts provide counselors with a clearer understanding of the Native-American elderly:

- The Native-American population is quite young. In 1980, the median age was 23. (Kart, 1985)

- Because of high birth rates and high death rates, the percentage of Native-American elderly in the total elderly population has been relatively low. (Cox, 1984)

- The proportion of elderly people has grown faster in the Native-American population than in other minority groups. Between 1970 and 1980, their numbers increased by 65 percent, a rate twice that of the Anglo-American or African-American elderly. (AARP, 1986)

These facts indicate that although the Native-American population continues to be young relative to the total population, elderly Native-Americans are continuing to grow in numbers. Based on their unique cultural and lifespan characteristics, many are likely to require counseling.

Figure 10–1 indicates states having the greatest concentrations of elderly Native-American populations. The notion that most Native-Americans live on reservations, either because they were forced there by the United States government, or because they lack the motivation and ambition to venture into the predominantly Anglo-American community, is disconfirmed by the following facts:

About one-quarter of Native-American elderly live on American Indian reservations or in Alaskan Native villages. Over half are concentrated in southwestern states of Oklahoma, California, Arizona, New Mexico, and Texas. Of the remainder, most live in states along the Canadian border. (AARP, 1986, unpaged)

Figure 10–1 States with greatest concentrations of elderly Native-Americans (65+ years of age). (Source: AARP, 1986.)

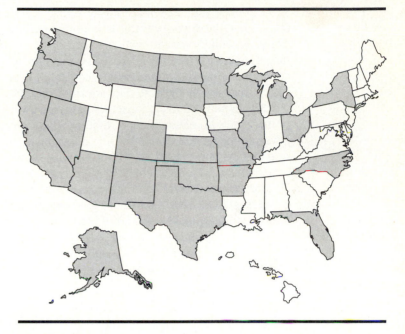

"A state of poverty" probably best describes the socioeconomic condition of the contemporary Native-American elderly. First, unemployment continues to be significantly higher than the national average, with employment opportunities generally being limited to unskilled, semiskilled, and low-wage jobs. About the same number of Native-Americans and Anglo-Americans continue to work after age 65 (12 percent and 13 percent, respectively, but nearly twice as many elderly Native-Americans as older Anglo-Americans (9 percent and 5 percent, respectively) are unemployed and are actively seeking work (AARP, 1986). Considering that the high unemployment rates do not include the large numbers of Native-Americans who have given up looking for work, the situation is even worse. For much of the elderly population, there is no work from which to retire, and old age is simply a continuation of a state of economic deprivation (Kart, 1985). Second, the poverty status resulting from this unemployment is documented in the following dismal statistics: Overall, 32 percent of Native-Americans (versus 13 percent of Anglo-Americans) 65 or older live below the official poverty level. In urban areas, 25 percent of the elderly live in poverty, while in rural areas the proportion tends to be even higher, or 39 percent in 1980 (AARP, 1986).

Closely linked to unemployment and poverty is the lack of education of Native-Americans. Formal educational attainments of Native-Americans lag significantly behind those of their Anglo counterparts. In fact, nearly 12 percent of all Native-American elderly do not have any formal education, and only about 22 percent have high school diplomas. The elderly who were fortunate enough to have received an education almost exclusively attended school systems which, either on or off the reservation, often have been considered poor (AARP, 1986).

Evidence indicates that elderly Native-Americans receive considerable respect (Cox, 1984); however, why this is so remains clouded with uncertainty. Are the Native-American elderly treated with respect because of their age or because of some particular asset? For example, it could be that elderly individuals are respected for their expert skills, power to work magic, control of property rights, or storytelling abilities, rather than simply because they are old (Kart, 1985).

It is imperative that counselors be aware of the often disturbing living conditions of the Native-American elderly. Elderly Native-Americans are being ministered to by government agencies; e.g., the Bureau of Indian Affairs and the Public Health Service. Nonetheless, their health and living conditions remain among the worst in the United States. These programs cannot immunize the Native-American elderly from a lifetime of deprivations such as inadequate nutrition, housing, and health services. Significant changes will be needed for future generations of elderly Native-Americans to witness improvement in their standard of living (Kart, 1985).

Language

It appears that the elderly experience language problems similar to those of Native-American adults; however, evidence does not exist to indicate that they encounter special problems as a result of their age. Native-American elderly persons experience frustration in seeking attention to their health and retirement benefits. Also, as with minority adults, other cultures might misunderstand or misinterpret the elderly Native-American's nonverbal communication style.

Families

As previously mentioned, the elderly receive considerable respect in the Native-American culture. This may be due to their advanced age or to some particular asset they have (Cox, 1984; Kart, 1985). Regardless of the reasons, younger generations seek the opinions of elders and consider their advice with reverence (Axelson, 1985).

Understanding the actual role that the elderly play in Native-American families provides counselors with insights about their problems and the questions they may raise during counseling sessions. First, the extended family continues to play a significant role in family life. Elderly family members provide significant services, such as assisting with the traditional childrearing practices and sex-role identity development (Trimble, Mackey, LaFromboise, & France, 1983). In turn, younger family members respect the symbolic leadership of the elderly and expect them to have an official voice in childrearing (Lum, 1986). Parents defer to the authority of their elders and rarely overrule their decisions regarding the children. Young people seldom ignore the advice or suggestions of their "grandparents," "aunts," and "uncles." Their relationships with the extended family are an important source of strength for the elderly (Red Horse, Lewis, Feit, & Decker, 1978)

It is important for counselors to understand the living arrangements of the Native-American elderly. The AARP (1986) reports that the marital status of the Native-

American elderly closely resembles that of the Anglo-American elderly. Of Native- and Anglo-Americans aged 65 and over, the majority of men are married and the majority of women are widowed. More Native-American women, however, tend to marry in their later years than do Anglo-American women. The following facts pertaining to living arrangements paint a fairly clear picture for professionals working with elderly clients:

- Approximately 96 percent of elderly Native-Americans live in households in the community; others reside in institutions.
- About the same percentage of Native-American elderly as Anglo-American elderly live with family members (66 percent versus 65 percent). For both groups, more men than women live with family members.
- The proportion of Native-American elderly in nursing homes is low. This trend is most apparent among the oldest (85+), with 13 percent of Native-Americans compared to 23 percent of Anglo-Americans living in nursing homes. (AARP, 1986)

Unique Challenges Confronting the Native-American Elderly

Kart's (1985) assertion that "many changes must be made in the situation of American Indians before future generations of elderly Native-Americans can expect a better day" (p. 376) rings true when examining the unique challenges confronting the elderly in this culture. First of all, their deplorable poverty translates into statistics that provide cause for alarm:

- The Indian Health Service figures show average life expectancy at birth for Native-Americans to be eight years less than for Anglo-Americans.
- Major health problems of elderly Native-Americans include tuberculosis, liver and kidney disease, pneumonia, and malnutrition.
- The majority of Native-Americans rarely see a physician. This may be because they live in isolated areas, lack transportation, or depend on ritual folk-healing practices. (AARP, 1986)

A second major challenge is that the relatively small population of elderly Native-Americans is insufficient to attract attention to their plight. Dealing successfully with government agencies, such as the Bureau of Indian Affairs and the Public Health Service, continues to be frustrating, especially for Native-Americans lacking language proficiency and knowledge of their legal rights.

Table 10–2 compares the cultural characteristics of the Native-American and Anglo-American elderly. UP CLOSE AND PERSONAL 10–1 focuses on Wenonah Lonetree.

Table 10–2 Cultural comparison: Native-American and Anglo-American elderly

Native-American Elderly	Anglo-American Elderly
Rely on extended family—receive respect from children and grandchildren	Rely on immediate family—have less authority in family matters
Age 85+ live at home with the family, rather than in nursing homes or institutions	Live in homes away from the immediate family
Are thought to be "needed" in childrearing of their grandchildren	Are considered "meddlesome" in attempting to advise on childrearing of their grandchldren
Rarely visit a doctor, trusting in rituals for healing; also, often live in isolated areas and lack transportation	See physicians more frequently; trust in scientific medicine; transportation less of a problem
"I am elderly—consider the wisdom and experience of my years."	"I am elderly—consider my material possessions."
Believe in the supremacy of nature	Tend to worship a Supreme Being

Sources: Data compiled from AARP, 1986; Cox, 1984; Kart, 1985; Lum, 1986; Richardson, 1981.

 UP CLOSE AND PERSONAL 10–1
Wenonah Lonetree—A Native-American Elderly Woman

Wenonah Lonetree does not doubt she is growing old. She senses it in the way she feels and in the way she is treated by her family and others. Growing old has both rewards and difficulties. She realizes that being 72 is unusual for a person in her Native-American culture; she has already outlived many of her friends. Although Wenonah is financially poor, not having money is nothing new to her. She lives with John, his wife, and the family and contributes whatever she can by helping with the children. In fact, she has assumed virtually all responsibility for childrearing. Carl and Bill have learned that Wenonah's word represents authority—their parents never question her decisions. The family equates Wenonah's years with great wisdom.

Wenonah has the typical problems of the elderly members of the Native-American culture. Her only schooling was a few years on a reservation school and she suffers the usual ailments of the aged. Although her community is not without medical facilities, Wenonah seldom visits the doctor. She has no means of transportation when John and his wife are at work; besides, she places her trust in healing rituals. Finances are also a problem, since living with John and his family off the reservation has lowered her government benefits.

Living with John's family can be both rewarding and frustrating. She likes being close to the children, and her son works conscientiously to provide a good home. Also, telling the boys stories and teaching them about customs and traditions allows her to relive old memories. The troubling aspects are the growing problems of her grandchildren. The school apparently has little regard for Native-American youth, and Carl is talking about joining the Indian League. "That's just not the way to make progress," Wenonah says quietly, yet adamantly.

When Wenonah looks back on her life, she celebrates her accomplishments—her family, her wisdom and knowledge that gains her respect of her family. But the future is uncertain. What will the next few years bring? How much longer will she be able to help John and his family? Will she become sick and need someone to take care of her?

THE AFRICAN-AMERICAN ELDERLY

Societal and Cultural Description

The African-American elderly (65+) population constitutes about 8 percent of the total elderly population. Those states with the greatest African-American elderly populations are indicated in Figure 10–2. Over 59 percent are concentrated in the southeastern states with most of the remainder living in the north central or northeastern regions of the country. Approximately one-fifth of the African-American elderly live in rural areas as compared to one-fourth of the Anglo-American elderly (Kart, 1985).

Three closely related factors influence the quality of life of the African-American elderly: education, employment, and income. Many of the African-American elderly seeking counseling were educated in U.S. school systems when access to equal education was severely limited. Six percent of the African-American elderly do not have any formal education (as compared to 2 percent of the Anglo-American elderly), and only 17 percent managed to complete high school (as compared to 41 percent of elderly Anglo-Americans). Employment, a closely related factor, is about equal for African- and Anglo-Americans; about 13 percent of the over-65 population is employed for both cultures. Income levels tend to be lower for elderly African-Americans than for elderly Anglo-Americans. According to Kart (1985),

> income—or more accurately, the lack of it—is probably the most serious problem faced by aged Blacks in the United States. In 1981 approximately 40 percent of the Black elderly were living in a state of poverty that reduced their capacity to deal effectively with other major concerns, including health, crime, transportation, housing, and nutrition. (p. 366)

Figure 10–2 States with greatest concentrations of elderly African-Americans (65+ years of age). (Source: AARP, 1986.)

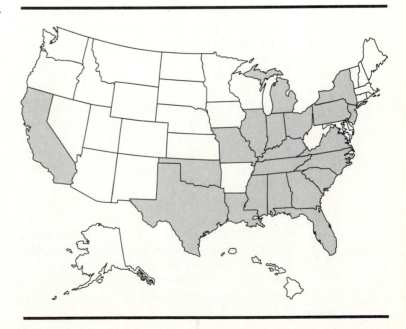

The median income of the African-American elderly is considerably lower than that of the Anglo-American elderly: about $4,113 for African-American men and $2,825 for African-American women, as compared to $7,408 for Anglo men and $3,894 for Anglo women. These dismal income figures result in an unequal poverty status: 32 percent of elderly African-Americans live in poverty (one in three), while 11 percent of older Anglos live in poverty (one in nine). In rural areas, a considerably higher incidence of poverty exists, with nearly half of the African-American elderly living in poverty (AARP, 1986).

Maintaining that the African-American elderly are forgotten Americans and that the elderly years are simply a continuation of their hardships and disadvantages, John E. Jacobs (1988), in his speech to the National Urban League, painted a gloomy picture:

- Most African-American people end their working lifetime without the comfortable pensions and accumulated wealth enjoyed by other elderly groups.
- One out of five older African-Americans lives on an income below 125 percent of the poverty level.
- The African-American elderly are three times as likely to be unemployed, far less likely to own their own homes, and much more likely to live in substandard conditions.

Some feel that elderly African-American women suffer an even worse plight than most culturally diverse elderly people. At least two out of five older African-American women are poor, a rate triple that of Anglo-American women (Jacobs, 1988). Most older African-American women who reside in female-headed families are poor, and their living conditions are often substandard. Generally, African-American women over 65 years of age are in dire financial straits (Jackson, 1982).

Although housing costs consume a substantial portion of African-Americans' income, the money spent does not contribute to their general life satisfaction. In addition, increasing rents and maintenance costs cause additional financial hardships for those with fixed incomes. Elderly African-Americans tend to be clustered in low-income areas in the central districts of cities, and often in apartments crowded with two or three generations (Kart, 1985).

It is not surprising that elderly African-Americans experience more serious health and social problems than their Anglo counterparts (McPherson, Lancaster, and Carroll, 1978). They experience nearly twice as many chronic disabilities as Anglo-Americans, including higher rates of indicators of risk, such as high blood pressure (AARP, 1986). Also, they tend to be hospitalized more frequently and for longer periods of time than Anglo-Americans (Hendricks & Hendricks, 1981).

Religion plays a major role in the lives of many African-American elderly persons. Their pragmatic and family-oriented belief system enables them to cope with the stress of their daily lives. Participation in church-related activities is valued early in life and continues to be important later in life. Historically, the church served as a frame of reference for African-Americans coping with discrimination resulting from their minority position, and it continues to play a key role in their survival and advancement. The church has been one of the few institutions to remain under

African-American control and relatively free from the influence of the majority culture. The church often embraces many different religions including the traditional African-American Protestant denominations, such as Baptist and Methodist, as well as other more fundamentalist groups. African-American religious services tend to be celebrations. Worshipers are inclined to be more demonstrative than Anglo worshipers (Kart, 1985).

Language

The language and speech patterns of the elderly are not significantly different from those of adults. Without doubt, however, the aging process takes its toll on the vocal mechanisms, just as it does on the rest of the body.

The language used in church has relevance for the African-American elderly, and for the congregation as a whole. The congregation responds to the minister with frequent "amens" or "right-ons" to offer encouragement and to indicate agreement. Dialectical differences in language on the part of both minister and congregation have genuine meaning for the African-American elderly. For example, the word *Lawd* might be substituted for *Lord*. The elderly may very well consider "the Lord" as overseer of the "big house" (plantation), while "Lawd" refers to a "friend," who walks and talks with people and who comforts them (Weber, 1985).

Families

Accurate perceptions of the role of the African-American elderly and their contributions to immediate and extended kinship networks contribute to counseling effectiveness. The African-American family has long existed within a well-defined, close-knit system of relationships. Several underlying themes such as respect for the elderly, strong kinship bonds, and pulling together in efforts to achieve common family goals characterize African-American family relationships. For example, corporate responsibility involves a pooling of resources to provide economic and emotional security (Lum, 1986).

The African-American elderly occupy a unique position in the family that differs considerably from the position of Anglo older people. In the African-American family structure, the elderly are often regarded as immediate family members; hence, they are expected to care for the young. Elderly African-American women, in particular, play an important role in this extended family network (Jackson & Wood, 1976).

African-Americans often value elderly family members because of the important role models they provide. For example, they are valued for the following attributes:

1. their accumulation of wisdom, knowledge, and common sense about life;

2. their creative genius in doing so much with so little;

3. their ability to accept aging; and

4. their sense of hope and optimism for a better day. (Dancy, 1977)

The living arrangements of the African-American elderly are important for counselors to know about, especially marriage and family counselors. Among older males, more than twice as many African-Americans as Anglo-Americans are separated or divorced, and the proportion of widowed is higher. This widowed, divorced, or separated status often results in the elderly person sharing a home with a grown child, usually a daughter. Three percent of the African-American elderly (65+) are institutionalized, but the rate of institutionalization among the elderly aged 85+ increases as their need for physical and medical assistance increases (AARP, 1986).

Unique Challenges Confronting the African-American Elderly

Problems posing challenges for elderly African-Americans include the following:

1. The low annual income of elderly African-Americans affects their housing, nutrition, health care, and nearly all aspects of their standard of living.

2. Widowed, separated, or divorced elderly African-Americans who are not accepted into the extended kinship network must live alone and face potentially serious problems. Not being a part of the traditional family is likely to be especially difficult for African-Americans, since they place such a high value on the kinship network.

3. Elderly African-Americans experience more frequent and longer hospitalization stays than the elderly of other cultures (AARP, 1986). Health problems or the fear of health problems may require counseling intervention.

4. The African-American elderly may experience discrimination and unequal treatment on two counts: age and minority status.

Table 10–3 Cultural comparison: African-American and Anglo-American elderly

African-American Elderly	Anglo-American Elderly
Perceive themselves as an integral part of the younger generation's family	Are more likely to live alone, or in a non-family setting, such as an institution
Have lower socioeconomic status (income and housing)	Have higher socioeconomic status; are better able to cope financially
Tend to play a bigger part in rearing of their grandchildren	Have the attitude, "I've raised mine, now you raise yours."
Are more likely to be divorced or separated	Are less likely to be divorced or separated
Require hospitalization more frequently and for longer periods	Have less frequent and shorter hospital stays
May experience both cultural and age discrimination	May experience only age discrimination
Are respected for their wisdom and common sense accumulated over the years	Tend to look to the young for answers
Usually have less formal schooling	Are usually better educated due to enhanced opportunities

Sources: Data compiled from AARP, 1986; Dancy, 1977; Kart, 1985.

UP CLOSE AND PERSONAL 10–2
Eloise Johnson—An African-American Elderly Woman

Eloise, better known as Miss Eloise to her younger friends and Aunt Ellie to her grandchildren, is 73 years old. She moved in with her son William and his family after her husband died. Eloise has worked hard all her life, usually at low-paying jobs with no retirement plans. She lives mostly off her social security, which allows for necessities. Although she cannot contribute financially to William's household, Eloise does take care of the children and helps Cynthia with light housecleaning. She also makes a few extra dollars caring for several children for a neighbor who works. She often cares for nieces and nephews, too, but free of charge, since they are family. Eloise enjoys living with her son and his family. It has proven to be a mutually satisfying relationship and it means a lot to her.

The problems Eloise has are common to many elderly African-Americans. If she didn't have a home with William and Cynthia, she would barely be able to afford a place of her own. Although her health is still fairly good, she worries about falling ill—especially since so many of her friends are in poor health or have died. Another worry, the increasing incidence of crime in the neighborhood, is one that she shares with William. When she grew up, times were difficult for African-Americans, but the problems her grandchildren must face—drugs and AIDS—were not a concern back then.

Eloise has always gone to church and she continues to attend. Her religion has seen her through some difficult times and is still a source of strength for her. William and the family also give her strength. Because of them she has avoided serious financial woes, loneliness, and the fear of growing old alone. In fact, Eloise may be luckier than most old people—she enjoys good health, she has her family close, and she feels needed.

In summary, the African-American elderly are better off now that their culture and age group are receiving increased attention. However, there are still hurdles to overcome in the areas of equal housing, equal access to medical care, and equal opportunities in education and employment.

Table 10–3 compares the African-American and Anglo-American elderly. UP CLOSE AND PERSONAL 10–2 features Eloise Johnson.

THE ASIAN AMERICAN ELDERLY

Societal and Cultural Description

Asian-Americans constitute one of the fastest growing minorities; hence, it is likely that multicultural counselors will increasingly see Asian-American clients of all ages. Between 1965 and 1975, the number of Asian-American elderly increased fourfold. Population estimates indicate that 221,500 Asian-Americans (6 percent) are aged 65 and over, and of this number, 15,000, or 6.7 percent, are aged 85 or over (AARP, 1986). Figure 10–3 indicates where most of the elderly Asian-Americans are concentrated.

Figure 10–3   States with greatest concentrations of elderly Asian-Americans/Pacific Islanders (65+ years of age). (Source: AARP, 1986.)

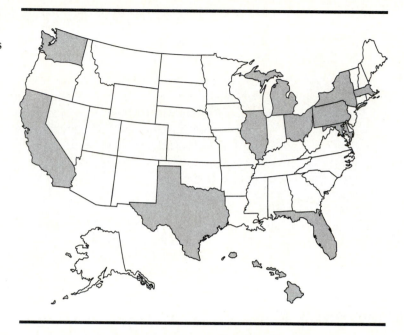

The elderly Asian-American population cannot be adequately understood without considering four factors: (1) their cultural origins and the effects of their early socialization, (2) their history in the United States and Canada, (3) the age-related changes they experience regardless of early learning or ethnicity, and (4) their expectations with regard to old age (Kalish & Moriwaki, 1973).

It is a popular misconception that the Asian-American elderly have no need for assistance. The stereotype holds that Asian-Americans are without pressing problems, that they are cared for within the ethnic group, and that their adjustments to Anglo-American society have been a relatively simple matter (Kalish & Moriwaki, 1973). Although the culture has demonstrated an amazing facility to achieve success in the predominantly Anglo-American world, the culture should not be saddled with such a stereotypic image, especially the elderly. The "model minority" myth serves as a convenient device for justifying Asian-Americans' exclusion from programs related to education, health, housing, and employment. Behind the prosperous shops of the Chinatowns and the Little Tokyos are thousands of disaffiliated old people experiencing poverty and poor health (Kart, 1985). Kim (1973) acknowledges the profound problems of elderly Asian-Americans:

1. Their problems, in many respects, are more intensive and complex than those of the general elderly citizen population.

2. They are excluded by cultural barriers from receiving their rightful benefits.

3. They commit suicide at a rate three times the national average.

4. They are among the people most neglected by programs presumably serving all the elderly.

Although the Asian-American culture still ranks closest to the Anglo-American in education and income as compared to other minority groups, professionals still must remember that most studies have focused on Asian-Americans in general rather than on the elderly in particular. An appropriate perception of the elderly requires knowledge of the culture, the elderly years, and the individual elderly person. As compared to the Anglo-American elderly, the Asian-American elderly fall short in several areas crucial to an individual's well being. First, although the more recent Asian-American immigrants include a large number of well-educated professionals, the percentage of Asian-American elderly lacking formal education continues to be higher than the Anglo-American percentage (13 percent versus 1.6 percent). Of all minority elderly, Asian-Americans have the greatest percentage of high school graduates (26 percent), yet this is still lower than the 41 percent for the Anglo-American elderly. Second, Asian-American elderly people are more likely to continue working past age 65. In fact, even at age 75 and over, approximately 16 percent of all Asian-Americans continue to work. As for unemployment, 8 percent of Asian-Americans are unemployed, as compared to 5 percent of the Anglo-American elderly. The third indicator of the well-being of the elderly is their annual income. Median income for elderly Asian-Americans (65 years or older) is under the amount earned by Anglo-Americans in the same age group: $5,551 versus $7,408 (AARP, 1986). A FOCUS ON RESEARCH 10–2 examines the consequences of poverty in the Chinese-American elderly population.

Most of the elderly in the Asian-American culture continue to receive considerable respect. Old age is equated by many Japanese-Americans with prestige and honor. Respect for elders is evident in the language used when addressing the elderly and behavior such as bowing to them and observing strict rules of etiquette (Palmore,

---

 A FOCUS ON RESEARCH 10–2
Poverty, Problems, and Needs of the Chinese-American Elderly

Chen (1979) interviewed 34 Chinese-Americans in 1972, 25 in 1974, and 22 in 1976 to determine poverty levels, problem areas, unmet needs, cultural and recreational needs, and their perceptions of "filial piety," or sense of obligation or commitment to the family. The Chen study reported the following findings:

1. At least one-third of the respondents lived below the national poverty threshold.

2. The ancient value of "filial piety" appeared to have lost its place in the Chinese-American family.

3. Feelings of isolation were intensified by the infrequency of visits from the few friends and relatives the elderly subjects had.

4. Most people in the study suffered from poor health and malnutrition, poor housing, and a poor physical environment.

5. Lack of knowledge of community resources and the language barrier prevented them from searching for assistance.

Source: Chen, P. N. (1979). A study of Chinese-American elderly residing in hotel rooms. *The Journal of Contemporary Social Work, 60,* 89–95.

1975). In the Japanese-American culture, each generation has a unique title, emphasizing the importance of the role generations play:

Generation	Name
1st	Issei
2nd	Nisei
3rd	Sansei
4th	Yonsei

The values brought to America by first-generation Chinese-Americans are often quite different from the prevailing views of American society. For example, the Chinese society discourages financial independence from parents and the extended family, instead encouraging interdependence. American values of achievement, upward mobility, and competition are at odds with Chinese beliefs. In the Chinese culture, only the elderly maintain control over income, property, and jobs; however, the United States does not recognize such control or power of the elderly (Cox, 1984).

First-generation Asian-American elderly have come to expect a reverence and respect that second and third generations (who have adopted many Anglo-American customs) no longer support. Thus, these Chinese-Americans experience difficulty in attempting to maintain old-world traditions, lifestyles, and status that they were taught to cherish in their homeland (Hsu, 1971).

With reference to intergenerational differences in Japanese-Americans, Osako and Liu (1986) contend that the first-generation (Issei) elderly will be very disappointed in their U.S.-born chldren if they are depending on these children to be responsible for their well-being. The younger generation's upward mobility and their extensive

---

 A FOCUS ON RESEARCH 10–3
Intergenerational Relations among Japanese-Americans

Japanese-Americans frequently experience a widening intergenerational gap as younger generations continue to climb the Anglo social ladder. A study by Osako and Liu (1986) focused on filial piety, social-class variations in kinship interaction, and social isolation of the aged. The authors found that (a) only about one in five elderly Japanese-Americans admitted to being lonely when specifically asked, (b) there were no significant differences between high-mobility and low- or no-mobility groups, and (c) Nisei children had more personal resources than their parents; consequently, the parents had lower prestige in terms of employment. The Nisei, then, are less dependent upon their parents for emotional gratification and material support. Parents must accept their disadvantageous position or jeopardize their rapport with younger generations.

Source: Osako, M. M., & Liu, W. T. (1986). Intergenerational relations and the aged among Japanese-Americans. *Research on Aging, 8,* 128–155.

Table 10–4   A summary of generational differences among Asian-Americans

First Generation	Second Generation	Third Generation
(a) Planned to return to their homeland. Practicing the traditions of the native land was more important than adapting to the foster homeland.	(a) Look to the country of birth for values, attitudes, behavior. Identify more with Anglo cohorts than with elders in their ethnic group.	(a) Often look back for their cultural roots. Attempt to understand themselves in terms of their ethnicity.
(b) Recall from early learning that the elderly are entitled to financial support, personal care, and virtual devotion.	(b) Have not abandoned respect for the elderly, yet sometimes give inappropriate care for a variety of reasons.	(b) Will this generation care for their aged parents to the same extent as past generations cared for the elderly?

Source: Data compiled from Kalish and Moriwaki, 1973.

acculturation may widen the cultural gap between the Issei and the Nisei. While the Issei continue to speak Japanese and deal mostly with fellow Japanese-Americans, the Nisei are English-speaking and work and live in a wider, culturally diverse world. A FOCUS ON RESEARCH 10–3 takes a closer look at generational differences among elderly Japanese-Americans. A summary of generational differences for both Japanese- and Chinese-Americans is provided in Table 10–4.

As do all older Americans, elderly Asian-Americans experience various changes related to advancing age—declining physical strength, increased leisure time, and the imminence of death. In addition, elderly Asian-Americans must adjust to challenges to their established traditions. In short, the difficulties faced by Asian-Americans are also faced by other minorities, and Anglo-Americans as well. Yet many Asian-American difficulties are more acute and arise from a personal history and a present milieu that is unique to their culture (Fujii, 1976).

Language

Available evidence (Chen, 1979; Fujii, 1976; Hendricks & Hendricks, 1981) indicates that language barriers cause considerable problems and frustrations for the Asian-American elderly. Language has undoubtedly played a major role in preventing Asian-Americans from availing themselves of community services and public social and health services. Language difficulties have also hampered their adjustment to the predominantly Anglo-American lifestyle (Fujii, 1976). Since elderly Chinese-Americans have lived most of their lives in predominantly Chinese-speaking communities, language poses a major barrier for them. They may not have the option to improve their living conditions by moving outside their ethnic neighborhoods. They also may not seek medical attention unless their illnesses are extremely severe, or then only visit Chinese-speaking doctors in the neighborhood (Chen, 1979).

The language problem for Asian-American old people is compounded by attitudes and limitations associated with advanced years. Either because of lack of motivation, the difficulty in learning a second language, or the lack of proper professional assistance, it is unlikely that the elderly will undertake any serious effort to improve their language skills. Not having the motivation to improve, or feeling that "it's too late in life to begin such an enormous task," continues to contribute to many Asian-Americans living in substandard housing with inadequate medical attention and nutrition.

Families

Families, both immediate and extended, have traditionally played a significant role in the Asian-American culture and are characterized by specific roles, relationships, and respect for elders (Lum, 1986). Although historically responsibility for the elderly rested on the oldest son, more contemporary expectations do not include the oldest son accepting such responsibility. Elderly family members do, however, expect their children to assist them. In the traditional Japanese and Chinese cultures, the extended family unit functioned as a supportive institution, and all family members shared individual incomes. Although these values carried over to some degree in America, and continue to be appreciated by first-generation Asian-Americans, cultural changes in younger generations indicate that practices toward the elderly might be changing (Hendricks & Hendricks, 1981). It is ironic that at the very time the elderly need stability and adherence to cultural tradition, many younger generation Asian-Americans are beginning to emphasize the values of the traditional Anglo-American society; e.g., financial independence from parents and extended family (Kalish & Moriwaki, 1973). Without doubt, the "Americanization" of Asian-American youth is forcing many older Asian-Americans to compromise their old-world values.

Unique Challenges Confronting Asian-American Elderly

The Asian-American elderly have been erroneously portrayed as a cultural group without need of assistance and as a generation with all of its financial and emotional needs met by the younger generations. Professionals with a knowledge and understanding of the Asian-American elderly clearly understand the fallacy of such thinking. The Asian-American elderly experience challenges unique to their age on the lifespan and to their culture:

1. Elderly Asian-Americans generally distrust social and government agencies; this often results in their being denied services to which they are entitled.
2. Language continues to be a serious problem for elderly Asian-Americans. Being unable to speak effective English results in their being forced to live in neigh-

borhoods where they often receive inappropriate medical care and cannot take advantage of social services.

3. Because of low-paying employment, lack of education, and limited skills, many elderly Asian-Americans live in poverty.

4. An alarmingly high rate of drug use and suicide among older Asian-Americans exists, especially in older men without family or ideological ties to the larger community.

5. Increasing generational differences puts additional stress on the elderly, at a time when they especially need stability.

It is almost paradoxical that an age and a culture with so many problems and challenges can be stereotyped as a "model minority." The elderly are not likely to seek assistance for a variety of reasons: pride, the language barrier, or fear of discrimination outside the Asian-American communities. Furthermore, the Asian-American elderly may be forced to accept rejection of their traditional values as their children and grandchildren assimilate into the majority culture.

Table 10–5 compares elderly Asian-Americans and Anglo-Americans. In UP CLOSE AND PERSONAL 10–3, we meet Grandfather Sukuzi.

Table 10–5   Cultural comparison: Asian-American and Anglo-American elderly

Asian-American Elderly	Anglo-American Elderly
Distrust social and government agencies; hence, often do not receive their fair share of benefits	Trust social and government agencies and receive the benefits to which they are entitled
Lack English language proficiency, intensifying their problems	Experience problems of the elderly, but not intensified by language problems
Expect respect and reverence from younger generations	Expect recognition, yet not the same degree of respect
Encourage younger generations to be interdependent (or financially dependent)	Encourage younger generations to achieve financial independence
Have less formal education, higher unemployment rates, lower incomes	Are better educated, have better jobs and higher incomes
Suffer from poor housing, inadequate health care, and malnutrition	Enjoy better housing, health, and nutrition
Are less likely to live in nursing homes or institutions	Are more likely to live in nursing homes or institutions
Avoid medical doctors—especially English-speaking doctors	Seek the advice of physicians

Sources: Data compiled from Chen, 1979; Fujii, 1976; Kalish and Moriwaki, 1973; Kart, 1985; Lum, 1986.

◀ UP CLOSE AND PERSONAL 10–3
Grandfather Sukuzi—An Asian-American Elderly Man

Eighty-five year old Grandfather Sukuzi continues to live with Han and his wife, their daughters, Mina and Rieko, and the youngest child. He feels very fortunate to live in the same house with his family; some of his elderly friends are not as fortunate and must live either alone or with other elderly people in small apartments. He no longer works outside the home and does very little housework. "Keeping the house is women's work," Grandfather says. Besides, Han's wife, Mina, and Rieko do a very good job in taking care of the house. Grandfather does feel needed, however. He helps the family by giving advice and instructing the children in traditional Japanese customs.

Grandfather's health is generally good, but he does have the usual problems associated with growing old, such as dizziness, aches and pains, and a slight loss of hearing. He is somewhat frail and moves slowly. His forgetfulness worries him. Could it be Alzheimer's disease? He's heard of it, but he doesn't know much about it. Grandfather seldom sees the doctor; in fact, he hasn't been to one in several years. Since Han has the two jobs, Grandfather must go alone, which means he won't understand what the doctor says. He also wonders whether the doctor understands him. Although Grandfather probably could receive government benefits of some kind, he always puts off seeking assistance. "They ask too many questions," he tells Han. Grandfather's pride and lack of language facility are more likely the reasons for his reluctance to apply for benefits.

Although Grandfather has lived in America since he was in his early twenties, his English is still poor. He never attended an American school, and the only English he knows is what he's picked up from talking to others and occasionally watching television. Moreover, living in the Asian-American community has relieved him of undue pressure; everyone knows Japanese.

Although Grandfather is quite content, he does sense some erosion of traditional Japanese values. Of course, the family treats him with great respect, but somehow the younger generations are different now. It's difficult to pinpoint specific examples, but sometimes Han seems to want too much financial independence. And he doesn't seek out Grandfather's advice as much as he once did. Evidence of change is clearer in the neighborhood. Some of his elderly friends seem to be forgotten by their children, who seldom pay them visits.

Grandfather is closest to his grandchildren. He and Rieko speak Japanese at times, and although she isn't fluent, she is making progress, and, of course, Grandfather enjoys teaching her. Strangely enough, it seems that Rieko is more interested in the traditional Japanese culture than her parents are.

What does the future hold for Grandfather? Right now, he is respected and needed by his family. It pleases him that the cultural assimilation of some Asian-Americans is not affecting them to any significant degree. Although he is growing old, his place in the family is secure.

THE HISPANIC-AMERICAN ELDERLY

Societal and Cultural Description

Despite the large and growing Hispanic-American population, meager systematic research has been conducted on elderly Hispanic-Americans. Indeed, research on this cultural group as a whole is made more difficult because of its heterogeneity (Kart, 1985). Attempts to generalize from Cubans in Florida to Puerto Ricans in New York to Mexican-Americans in California are not likely to result in meaningful conclusions. Significant cultural differences, together with stereotypes plaguing the elderly, frequently lead to misunderstandings; hence, counselors must identify specific subgroups and consider the individual within this subgroup.

Although the Hispanic-American population is concentrated largely in the southwestern states of California and Texas, there are clusters in other geographical regions. The various subgroups tend to remain distinct with respect to location. For example, most of the Hispanic-Americans in California and Texas are of Mexican descent, while a majority of the Puerto Ricans live in New York and New Jersey. Figure 10–4 provides a breakdown of the states with large concentrations of Hispanic-American elderly.

What is life like for the Hispanic-American elderly? As with other minority elderly, education, employment, and income play a major role in determining their standard of living and degree of life satisfaction. Of all minority elderly cultures, Hispanic-Americans have the least amount of formal education. Of the 65-and-over group, 16 percent do not have any formal education, and only 19 percent are high school graduates (Barrow & Smith, 1979).

Not surprisingly, this lack of education has consequences that extend to employment and income. Although the percentage of Hispanic-American elderly in the labor

Figure 10–4 States with greatest concentrations of elderly Hispanic-Americans (65 + years of age). (Source: AARP, 1986.)

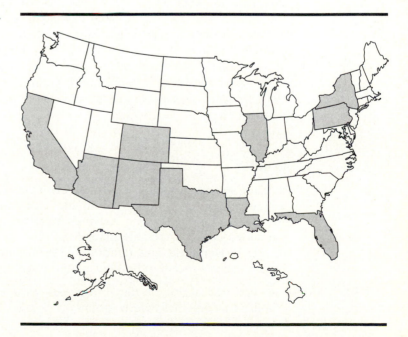

force equals the percentage of Anglo-Americans, unemployment rates for Hispanic-Americans are nearly twice as great (9 percent vs. 5 percent, respectively). Many elderly Hispanic-Americans work as unskilled laborers or farmworkers; they remain in the labor force longer than the Anglo-American elderly. Income levels for Hispanic-American elderly men and women are dismal (Barrow & Smith, 1979).

Low incomes, unemployment, and lack of education without doubt result in poverty for a significant segment of the Hispanic-American community. Poverty rates are higher in rural areas than in urban areas, and more women experience poverty than men. Another factor contributing to the poverty rate is that many of the jobs open to Hispanic-Americans lack retirement plans. Also, some Hispanics enter the United States illegally or do not maintain their status as resident aliens (Barrow & Smith, 1979).

Concern over potential health problems or declining health also characterizes the Hispanic-American elderly. They tend to have more activity limitations and spend more days per year in bed due to illness than other minority cultures (AARP, 1986). In one study of Mexican-American elderly, poor health proved to be a major area of concern, along with financial problems and inadequate transportation (Torres-Gil, 1976).

Language

The low academic achievement of Hispanic-Americans is due, at least in part, to language difficulties. The elderly often speak no English at all; only the Native-American elderly have higher rates of illiteracy (Kart, 1985). As with the Asian-American elderly, many older Hispanic-Americans do not seek the government benefits to which they are entitled due to their inability to communicate in English.

The tendency of Spanish-speaking people to cluster together in neighborhoods in which English is rarely spoken interferes with their acculturation. The convenience of being able to communicate in one's native language also undermines serious efforts toward learning to speak more fluent English. Newspapers and radio and television stations geared specifically toward Hispanic-American audiences contribute to the problem.

Families

Prefacing any discussion of Hispanic-American families, a point made earlier must be emphasized: A description of family life, customs, and traditions depends on the individual culture in question. Although there are similarities among Hispanic-American subgroups, considerable differences make broad generalizations difficult. According to Hendricks and Hendricks (1981), however, several Hispanic-American characteristics do seem to be valid across subgroups:

- Sex and marital data on the Hispanic-American elderly are roughly equivalent to similar data on other elderly groups.

- Hispanic-American females outnumber males; females live somewhat longer, and more often remain widowed or live alone.

- Older Hispanic-American males tend to marry more often or remarry than older males in any other minority group.

- Hispanic-Americans perceive the onset of old age as beginning earlier than do other minority groups.

It appears that the most substantial volume of information on Hispanic-American families pertains to Mexican-Americans. The family meets a variety of emotional and psychological needs of elderly Mexican-Americans. It shields them from isolation by including them within its confines. Living in the family home, the elderly are respected and exert considerable influence in the family's social life (Sotomayor, 1971).

The Mexican-American family is, by tradition, patriarchial. Early on, children are taught that males should have more freedom than females, that males play the dominant role in the family, and that females should subordinate their needs to those of males (Alvirez & Bean, 1976). However, the division of labor in the Mexican-American family often changes as family members grow older. Females tend to play an increasingly active role as they grow older, often to the point that elderly females may become dominant forces in the extended famiy. This, too, may change due to a gradual movement toward a stronger nuclear family in Hispanic-American communities (Maldonado, 1975).

The importance of extended kinship networks among Puerto Rican-Americans can be seen in their effort to provide for the aged or the infirm in their own homes. A strong effort supported by Hispanic-American groups is underway to encourage the government to provide funds to enable family members to care for relatives in the home rather than place them in institutional settings (Fitzpatrick, 1987). In the Puerto Rican extended family network, children are sometimes raised by families other than their own, and family members are assisted in many other ways (Ghali, 1977). However, as with Mexican-Americans, the Puerto Rican-American extended family kinship network may be weakening, which may loosen the familial and social bonds that have provided strong support (Fitzpatrick, 1987).

In short, Hispanic-American customs and practices include a respect for the elderly and a concern for their welfare. Keeping the elderly in the home or at least in the immediate community so younger generations can provide care appears to be the present norm. It may be safely assumed, however, that younger generations will continue to lean toward stronger immediate families, which may leave the elderly in an increasingly precarious situation. Although this trend is not yet firmly established, it is quite possible that Hispanic-American clients will increasingly bring such familial problems to counseling sessions.

Unique Challenges Confronting the Hispanic-American Elderly

Although the Hispanic-American elderly have undoubtedly experienced economic, personal, and social progress, considerable hurdles remain: illiteracy, unemployment, malnutrition, substandard housing, and discrimination. The following five specific areas need immediate attention:

1. raising education and income levels and decreasing the incidence of malnutrition;

2. increasing understanding of the role of the elderly in the family;

3. encouraging proficiency in English so as to allow the elderly to move from Spanish-speaking enclaves;

4. directing attention to the problems of the elderly and ridding them of their stereotypical image; and

5. improving their general health status, which will contribute to their overall well-being.

The extent to which the Hispanic-American elderly improve their lives will depend largely on the effort they put forth to raise their economic status and to improve their ability to speak English. Multicultural counselors working with Hispanic-Americans can contribute significantly to their efforts by understanding both the culture and the elderly period of the lifespan. Although the challenges to both Hispanic-Americans and multicultural counselors are, indeed, formidable, the future might reflect a genuine concern for the minority elderly and set the stage for long overdue changes and accomplishments.

Table 10–6 compares the cultural characteristics of Hispanic-American and Anglo-American elderly people. Papa Rafael Suarez is featured in UP CLOSE AND PERSONAL 10–4.

Table 10–6   Cultural comparison: Hispanic-American and Anglo-American elderly

Hispanic-American Elderly	Anglo-American Elderly
Emphasize the extended family	Rely on the nuclear family
Are cared for in private homes and the community	Are cared for in institutions or nursing homes
Assign a more dominant role to the grandmother as she grows older	Grandparents assume a less important role as they grow older
Have more health problems, are not as well educated, and have lower incomes	Have fewer health problems, are better educated, and have higher incomes
Are more likely to live in poverty conditions	Are less likely to experience poverty
Often do not receive benefits from retirement programs	Are more likely to receive benefits from retirement programs
Have higher rates of illiteracy	Have lower rates of illiteracy
Are less homogeneous culturally	Exhibit individual rather than cultural differences

Sources: Data compiled from Fitzpatrick, 1987; Hendricks and Hendricks, 1981; Kart, 1985; Maldonado, 1975.

> ### ◤ UP CLOSE AND PERSONAL 10–4
> ### ◤ Papa Rafael Suarez—A Hispanic-American Elderly Man
>
> Seventy-five year old Papa Rafael enjoys living close to his family. Having family members nearby means a great deal and provides many satisfying moments. His problems are not unlike those of many of his elderly friends in the predominantly Hispanic-American community. Although the community includes diverse Hispanic cultures, most of the elderly worry about inadequate finances and failing health.
>
> Right now, Papa Rafael's concerns are directed toward his family and their financial condition. His son, Carla's husband, has not worked in several weeks. He is aware that Carla wants to get a job, but in his view, "it just wouldn't be right." Papa Rafael wishes he could help his family financially, but he, himself, is fairly poor. He has a little money saved from when he was employed, but this barely covers his own needs.
>
> There is nothing left over to share with his family. Besides, he thinks, he needs to hold on to every penny now, since the future is uncertain. Aside from his savings, his only other income is the meager government benefits he receives.
>
> Papa Rafael is at a reflective age. He sees a changing Hispanic-American culture and has been known to say, "Too many of our young people are like the Anglos." It shocks him to see how some of the children in the neighborhood treat their parents. Surely, respect for the elderly is not valued as it used to be.
>
> Papa Rafael has the problems all old people experience—problems associated with failing health and family problems. At times, these concerns seem almost too much for him to bear.

A POINT OF DEPARTURE

Challenges Confronting Multicultural Counselors of the Elderly

Counselors working with elderly clients from diverse cultural backgrounds should understand the age period on the lifespan, characteristics unique to specific cultures, and how age-related and cultural factors interrelate. The double, triple, or quadruple jeopardy that some minority people endure is also important to appreciate. A last hurdle is to understand the problems that many minority elderly people experience: failing health, a lowered standard of living, loneliness, and differing cultural expectations of the younger generations. While young minority counselors might find it somewhat difficult to relate to minority clients' perceptions of growing old, the young Anglo-American counselor is doubly challenged to appreciate what it is like being a member of a minority culture *and* being an elderly person.

Multicultural counselors wanting to improve their understanding of culturally diverse elderly clients begin their task at a time when progress toward helping the elderly minority appears truly possible. Research on old age, a lifespan period once virtually ignored, currently receives attention by gerontologists, government agencies, community service agencies, and scholars interested in lifespan development. Likewise, the attention being directed toward differing cultural groups continues to increase as more culturally diverse people enter the United States and as professionals become aware of the unique needs of the various ethnic cultures.

SUMMARY

Although the elderly of all cultures have some characteristics in common, the elderly minority have needs and problems that differ in both scope and magnitude. It is not sufficient for multicultural counselors to view the elderly minority from a young or a middle-aged perspective. An understanding of the age and the culture is mandatory if counseling intervention with these clients is to be successful. It is unreasonable, in the face of their unique needs, to expect them to respond to counseling strategies geared toward middle-class Anglo-Americans.

Suggested Readings

Alvirez, D., & Bean, F. (Eds.). (1976). *Ethnic families in America*. New York, NY: Elsevier Scientific. Alvirez and Bean consider the strengths and problems of culturally diverse families.

American Association of Retired Persons. (1986). *A portrait of older minorities*. Washington, DC: AARP. This excellent publication examines specific populations—their geographical locations, health problems, and financial status.

Brubaker, T. H. (1983). *Family relationships in later life*. Beverly Hills, CA: Sage. As the title implies, this text examines the family relationships of the elderly. Particularly recommended is the reading "The Elderly in Minority Families."

Cox, H. (1984). *Later life: The realities of aging*. Englewood Cliffs, NJ: Prentice-Hall. Cox explores the later years with an emphasis on the changes and problems experienced by the elderly.

Kart, C. S. (1985). *The realities of aging: An introduction to gerontology*. Boston: Allyn and Bacon. Kart details the physical and psychosocial changes associated with aging.

Manuel, R. C. (1982). *Minority aging: Sociological and social psychological issues*. Westport, CT: Greenwood. Manuel's collection of worthy articles focusing on minority aging includes a variety of issues. One article addresses the issue of double jeopardy among African-Americans.

Chapter 11

Counseling the Elderly

Questions To Be Explored

1. What differences can counselors expect when counseling the culturally different elderly?

2. What are some of the typical stresses, concerns, and problems associated with the elderly years?

3. What are the problems and concerns of the elderly in the Native-American, African-American, Asian-American, and Hispanic-American cultures? To what extent do cultural differences, language problems, and marriage and family concerns affect the elderly?

4. What counseling strategies should therapists use when counseling culturally diverse elderly clients?

5. What unique challenges confront counselors working with the culturally diverse elderly?

6. How can individual, group, or family therapy be used when counseling elderly clients?

7. Where can counselors working with culturally diverse elderly clients find additional information?

INTRODUCTION

Although counseling in the United States for the most part has consisted of providing services to youth and adults, indications are clear that the elderly will require a greater share of counseling services in the future. According to census data, approximately 10 percent of the U.S. population presently consists of adults over 65 years of age.

The aging of the baby boom generation, the comparatively low birth rate, and the influx of multicultural groups during recent years probably will cause the proportion of older Americans to increase steadily. It is reasonable to assume that this situation will lead to an increasing demand by the elderly for counseling and psychotherapy (Piggrem & Schmidt, 1982).

It is predicted that by the year 2000, 31.8 million Americans will be over age 65 (Keller & Hughston, 1981), with the 75-plus and 85-plus age groups being the fastest growing in the United States (Butler & Lewis, 1982). The growth in numbers of older Americans and their increasing longevity have created a crisis in this country that is just now receiving widespread attention (Baruth & Robinson, 1987). Although not all culturally diverse groups have the same life expectancies, it is safe to assume that the elderly population as a whole will live to an older average age.

DIFFERENCES IN COUNSELING THE CULTURALLY DIVERSE ELDERLY

Many counselors called upon to work with elderly people may lack the knowledge and skill to work with this population; they may not be psychologically prepared to cope with the reactions of the elderly in counseling situations. The inexperienced counselor may fail to recognize important physiological symptoms of malnutrition or drug abuse (Piggrem & Schmidt, 1982). Counselors working with elderly clients must understand what being elderly means and how the elderly person thinks and feels. As events occur in the life of the elderly that disrupt normal coping strategies, this theme often surfaces:

Client: I don't know. I don't seem to be able to do anything since my son passed away. I just sit and think.

Counselor: He was very important in your life.

Client: He was my life. (Baruth & Robinson, 1987)

Counseling elderly culturally diverse clients also requires professional preparation in dealing with multicultural populations. Counseling the elderly in the Native-American, African-American, Asian-American, and Hispanic-American cultures requires an appreciation of problems resulting from not being granted equal status in the community at large (Vontress, 1976a). Challenges for cross-cultural counseling of the elderly include (a) understanding the specific problems of each individual client; e.g., the generational differences affecting the elderly Asian-American, the extreme poverty of the elderly Native-American; (b) knowing the barriers to effective cross-cultural encounters; and (c) planning counseling techniques and strategies appropriate for each culture.

As with intervention with clients at other stages of the lifespan, counselors working with the elderly are advised to be aware of organizations and agencies that provide services for this particular age group. Some of these include Meals on Wheels, health departments, senior citizen centers, councils on aging, mental health centers, community care organizations, and hospitals with special geriatric services. Counselors and their elderly clients will also benefit from knowing agencies and organizations that cater specifically to the culturally diverse elderly.

A FOCUS ON RESEARCH 11–1
Ethical Dilemmas in Counseling the Elderly

Counselors working with elderly adults often experience ethical dilemmas in planning appropriate strategies. Counselors must adhere to ethical principles of *fidelity* (faithfulness to obligation, trust, and duty); *autonomy* (the right of the client to make choices affecting his or her own life); and *beneficence* (helping clients by preventing harm and by intervening for positive benefit). Questions such as the following must

be answered: What are the counselor's responsibilities and to whom is he or she responsible—the client, the family, the employing institution, the profession, or society? Do counselors have special obligations and considerations in their work with the elderly? Based, in part, on medical and health considerations and a comprehensive intervention model, Fitting (1986) concludes that counselors must increase their knowledge about the elderly population and apply their knowledge in accordance the the AACD *Ethical Principles*.

Source: Fitting, M. D. (1986). Ethical dilemmas in counseling elderly adults. *Journal of Counseling and Development, 64,* 325–327.

A FOCUS ON RESEARCH 11–1 discusses ethical dilemmas that may be encountered when working with the elderly. Some of these dilemmas might revolve around issues such as death and dying. Increasingly, elderly people are considering living wills, a legal precaution in the hope of dying with dignity. Living wills usually describe certain physical conditions that would warrant a specified course of action and list the types of treatment the person wishes to avoid. Two groups, the Society for the Right to Die and Concern for Dying, both located in New York City, have distributed millions of living will forms over the past twenty years. Many right-to-die advocates recommend the use of health-care proxies, documents authorizing another person to make medical decisions on one's behalf in the event of an incapacitating accident or illness. The main shortcoming of the living will is that it does not take effect unless the person is terminally ill. Since state definitions of terminal illness vary, people with debilitating strokes or Alzheimer's disease may not be protected by living will statutes. Sachs (1990) recommends that counselors suggest the following to their elderly clients (or clients at any stage of the lifespan) who may be considering living wills:

- Obtain the proper forms or enlist the help of an attorney.
- Discuss the living will with a proxy or a doctor.
- Be certain the living will reflects precise wishes.
- Inform family members and friends that the documents have been signed.
- Update the documents once a year.

Typical Concerns and Stresses of the Elderly Years

Most people associate the elderly years with declining physical and mental abilities; however, gerontologists have only just begun to comprehend the aging process and

Table 11–1   The effects
of aging

	Age 25	Age 45	Age 65	Age 85
Maximum heart rate	100%	94%	87%	81%
Lung capacity	100%	82%	62%	50%
Cholesterol level	198	221	224	206
Muscle strength	100%	90%	75%	55%
Kidney function	100%	88%	78%	69%

Source: Begley, S., Hager, M., & Murr, A. (1990, March 5). The search for the
Fountain of Youth. *Newsweek*, pp. 44–48.

its effects. Table 11–1 provides a listing of declining functions and capacities at various
ages along the lifespan.

Although the concerns the culturally diverse elderly bring to counseling can be
as broad as the human experience itself, there are a number of problems that are
often the focal point of the client's distress. Keller and Hughston (1981) mention
"feelings of depression, diminished initiative, inadequacy, unrealistic goals, low self-
concept, discouragement, and lack of a sense of belonging" (p. 39). Stereotypes of
aging often underlie these negative feelings and can seriously affect the counseling
process. Although myths surrounding aging were discussed in Chapter 10, it seems
appropriate to take another look at them now. Piggrem and Schmidt (1982) point
out several common stereotypes that are potentially damaging to the elderly:

- The elderly are senile, dependent, impotent, rigid, physically impaired, hard of
  hearing.
- The elderly are eccentric, foolish, disrespected, lacking in common sense.
- The elderly are helpless and need their children or younger people to care for
  them, to lead them around.

It is important for counselors to examine their beliefs and disaffirm misconceptions resulting from stereotypic thinking. Having accomplished this task (which may
prove to be difficult), counselors can then assist elderly clients to rid themselves of
stereotypic images, to understand their aging, and to learn how to manage it more
effectively.

The life events and crises of the elderly represent another area of concern. Crises
may include the death of a spouse, institutionalization, or chronic or terminal illness
(Baruth & Robinson, 1987). Understanding these life events from the elderly client's
viewpoint requires recognizing that stresses and problems vary among individuals
and cultures.

Other problems specific to the elderly include the following:

1. *Confusion over the aging process.* Simply put, the physiology of aging is not
   understood. For example, Levy, Derogatis, Gallagher, and Gatz (1981) have reported nearly 100 reversible disorders that mimic irreversible brain damage related to aging. Although counselors cannot be expected to recognize all the disorders, knowing the symptoms of the most prevalent ones may help many clients.

2. *Drug misuse.* A physician may prescribe drugs for the elderly for specific disorders. If these drugs are taken along with over-the-counter drugs or drugs prescribed for other conditions, the consequences may be damaging. Counselors should learn to recognize situations in which drug misuse may be a factor.

3. *Poor nutrition.* Either due to long-standing poor eating habits, lack of ability to cook, or lack of desire to eat alone, many elderly people do not eat properly. Counselors may be in a prime position to notice signs of malnutrition.

4. *Learned dependency.* Using the term "learned helplessness," Seligman (1973) attributed the dependency of some elderly people to the behavior of family and friends. Although well-intentioned, these people may imply that the elderly are unable to care for themselves. In efforts to be helpful, they may tend to "take over," so that the elderly come to believe they really are helpless.

Although the preceding problems undoubtedly cause stress for the aged, Axelson (1985) provides examples of still other problems of particular relevance for the culturally diverse elderly:

1. *Low socioeconomic status.* According to Jackson (1980), low-income elderly African-Americans are "substantially more likely to report personal problems with insufficient clothing, job opportunities, housing, medical care, education, and monies [than low-income Anglos]." (p. 203)

2. *Problems with family ties.* McAdoo (1978) noted extensive kin involvement among three generations of upwardly mobile African-American families. Some studies document the importance of ethnic family ties, often extending into the third generation (Cohler & Grunebaum, 1981). Others, however, queston whether the extended Hispanic family is a support system in that more than twice as many Hispanics as Anglos over the age of 65 are admitted to state mental hospitals.

3. *Shorter life expectancy.* The life expectancy of Anglo males born in 1980 is 71.4 years; for African-American males, the life expectancy is 64.8. Likewise, Anglo females born in 1980 have a life expectancy of 78.7 years; for African-American females, the life expectancy is 73.8 years.

4. *Psychological aging.* People may feel psychologically old near retirement or when their childrearing responsibilities have diminished. Several studies (Bengston, Kasschau, & Ragen, 1977; Reynolds & Kalish, 1974) revealed that Anglos saw themselves as old at around age 70; African-Americans, at about age 65; and Mexican-Americans, at about 60 years of age. African-Americans believed they would live longer than Anglos, and Mexican-Americans expected fewer remaining years than did either African-Americans or Anglos.

The elderly during the 1990s and beyond will face problems that, in all likelihood, will grow more severe. One such problem is the rapidly rising cost of health care. According to Beck, Hager, Beachy, and Joseph (1990), 9 million people now require long-term health care. While 2 million are now 65 or older, by the year 2030, their number will double. For the nearly 2 million elderly living in nursing homes, costs may average $30,000 per year. Of those needing long-term medical care, more than 7 million live at home or in their communities. Three-fourths of all home care is provided for free by family members and friends.

Alzheimer's disease, another major problem affecting many elderly people, is the fourth leading cause of death for adults and may afflict 14 million people by the year 2050. Approximately 10 percent of people over 65 have a probable diagnosis of Alzheimer's, and 47 percent of those over 85 have the disease. An estimated 10 to 30 percent of Alzheimer's patients have the type that is inherited (Gelman, Hager, & Guade, 1989). Counselors intervening with the elderly benefit from common-sense advice about Alzheimer's disease. Kantrowitz (1989) offers the following:

- Alzheimer's is not a normal part of aging. It is a fatal and, so far, incurable disease.
- Forgetting where the car keys were left is not a sign of Alzheimer's. Forgetting how to use them may be.
- Many disorders have similar symptoms. A person suspected of having Alzheimer's should have a full medical and neurological workup.
- Obtain help from family, friends, and community groups to help cope with the emotional, physical, and financial strain.

THE NATIVE-AMERICAN ELDERLY

The many problems facing the Native-American elderly include their health concerns and low life expectancies, their difficulties in maintaining long-cherished cultural traditions, and their previously mentioned poverty status. More specifically, elderly Native-Americans may be faced with problems such as these:

1. difficulties in overcoming cultural and age-related stereotypical images;
2. double or multiple jeopardy as a result of being elderly and minority;
3. the elderly person's low socioeconomic status;
4. the elderly person's inadequate nutrition and housing;
5. the elderly person's health problems: tuberculosis, diabetes, pneumonia, liver and kidney disease, or high blood pressure, for example;
6. inadequate health services, either due to the elderly person's lack of communication skills or overdependence on folk rituals;
7. the elderly person's low self-esteem and poor self-concept;
8. the effects of aging on the elderly person: changes in physical appearance, general health deterioration, and social/intellectual changes;
9. the elderly person's lack of education;
10. generational differences due to the acculturation of younger Native-Americans.

Cultural Differences

The allegiance of elderly Native-Americans to traditional cultural values and customs (or, perhaps, the lack of opportunity to acculturate) has contributed to their state of despair. Their trust in ritual folk medicine and their general poverty have the potential for impeding the counseling process. The elderly Native-Americans' slow acculturation rate and lack of opportunity in the Anglo society have prevented progress in improving their condition. Perhaps as a result, the elderly minority continue to exhibit cultural characteristics such as shyness and the expectation of extended family support. Overall, the Native-American culture is economically and educationally depressed, which has left many of the elderly population in poverty and poor health (Vontress, 1976a).

Of all cultural groups affected by unemployment, the Native-American is the most hard-hit, both on and off the reservation. As Vontress (1976a) puts it, "the older Indians especially are handicapped in the job market because they are more apt to be sickly, alcoholic, and unable to read, write, or speak English" (p. 133).

Communicational Barriers

Communicating effectively with elderly cultural minorities can be enormously frustrating. Although monocultural Anglo counselors usually communicate fairly well with younger Native-Americans who have at least some bilingual expertise, counselors may have difficulty interacting verbally with elderly Native-Americans. On and off the reservation, many older Native-Americans are unable to speak more than a few words of English; nearly a third of the 96,000 Navajos are functional illiterates. Although communication barriers may not totally block intervention efforts, they constitute obstacles to counseling efforts (Vontress, 1976a).

Health

The majority of elderly Native-Americans rarely visit a physician, primarily because they live in isolated areas and lack transportation or rely on ritual folk healing (AARP, 1986). Differing attitudes about how the body functions is another reason for the health-related problems of Native-Americans. High morbidity rates could be attributed to an indifferent and impersonal attitude concerning the body; it is often viewed as a machine, designed to keep on working until it breaks down (Rainwater, 1970; Vontress, 1976a). In addition to attitude differences, many poor people, especially the elderly, lack the health-care opportunities afforded others. Transportation presents a major problem on reservations, and waiting periods are often interminable. Older Native-Americans hospitalized in understaffed and poorly equipped medical facilities often find themselves more threatened by unsafe conditions than they would have been at home (U. S. Commission on Civil Rights, 1975; Vontress, 1976a).

Marriage and Family

What problems and issues related to marriage and the family might the Native-American elderly bring to counseling sessions? It is reasonable to assume that their problems will not vary significantly from those of the elderly in other cultures. Elderly problems include generational differences, dealing with lowered incomes, dealing with ailing spouses or other family members, coping with grief, experiencing children growing up and leaving the immediate locality, problems with family relations, nutritional problems, and a failure to deal appropriately with growing older. Ho (1987) feels that due to acculturation, counselors working with the elderly in marriage and family situations might increasingly witness problems with parent-child relationships, problems involving grown children, and marriage problems. Esoteric problems involving exotic religious practices or strange customs are not likely to be encountered, since missionaries of all denominations have been at work for several hundred years (Attneave, 1982).

It will be necessary for counselors to perceive the elderly's problems in a proper perspective. The years of discrimination toward their diverse cultures, the misunderstandings due to stereotypes, and, at least in some cases, clients' feelings of despair over the aging process must be appreciated. Also, the essence of the Native-American culture must be understood and accepted as worthwhile (Attneave, 1982).

The Lifespan: Elderly Concerns

During the elderly period of the lifespan, Native-Americans experience three major problem areas: (1) the previously mentioned problems associated with poverty and unemployment; (2) increasing illness and health-related problems; and (3) the usual physical, psychosocial-emotional, and intellectual changes commonly associated with aging. What developmental changes commonly associated with this lifespan period might warrant counseling intervention? Physical changes, such as the aging of the skin or a deteriorating skeletomuscular system, or psychosocial-emotional changes, such as adjusting to poor health, the death of a spouse, or relocation to a reservation for economic reasons, may warrant counseling intervention.

Counselors working with older Native-Americans have a special task of understanding the trials and joys of the elderly period from the Native-American frame of reference. Many problems will require an understanding of the complex relationship between age and cultural background.

Counseling Considerations

Although the literature on counseling the Native-American elderly as a specific population is sketchy at best, counselors can use their existing knowledge of the elderly and their knowledge of the Native-American culture as a basis for formulating appropriate counseling strategies. It is also important for them to understand the centuries of deprivation and discrimination Native-Americans have endured, the current status of the uneducated Native-American elderly trying to live and cope with the stress common in a today's contemporary Anglo society, and the elderly client's hesitation to seek professional counseling from an Anglo professional.

In addition to understanding the culture and the lifespan period, there are other prerequisites to effective counseling of the Native-American elderly. For example, Anglo counselors must build rapport with their elderly clients. Native-American history includes years of broken treaties and promises by Anglos. Native-American clients often must be convinced that Anglo professionals can be trusted to think in terms of Native-American welfare and well-being. Also, counselors must be careful not to let their confusion about the aging process affect the counseling relationship. Finally, they should make sure that the client understands the counselor's role and knows what to expect in the counseling relationship (Piggrem & Schmidt, 1982).

What specifically can counselors do to promote an effective counseling relationship? Several strategies may be considered:

1. Allow adequate time to get acquainted. The atmosphere should be relaxed. Counseling professionals will not want to give the impression that they are uninterested or in a hurry. (Lum, 1986)

2. Allow for pauses and be patient when the client avoids eye contact or appears to just sit and think. (Richardson, 1981)

3. Make clients feel that their age is accepted. Although the counselor might not be aware of the realities of being elderly, communicating a willingness to listen and learn is imperative.

4. Allow a paraprofessional from the client's ethnic background to assist with communication barriers. (Vontress, 1976a)

5. Understand the client's cultural background and elderly status, and the complex relationship between the two.

Individual and Group Therapy

The decision of what type of therapy should be used should be based on individual Native-American client. One approach may be to intervene using individual therapy at first, and then move to a group therapy session. Of course, the individual client's willingness to speak in group sessions must be considered. How willing will elderly Native-Americans be to disclose feelings of grief in group settings? What about concerns over decreasing strength or sexual abilities? Counselors should first explore the elderly Native-American's problems in individual sessions and then come to a decision regarding the feasibility of group therapy.

Family Therapy

Counselors intervening with Native-American families first of all need to be relaxed. Elderly Native-Americans, accustomed to noninterference with others and unaccustomed to counseling procedures, tend to be silent for prolonged periods. Conversational exchanges may be relatively short. This pattern might last throughout an entire session, or perhaps stretch into two sessions. The counselor's actions during the initial session are critical, since the stage is being set for future counseling sessions (Attneave, 1982).

During the initial session with the Native-American elderly, it might be useful to ask open-ended questions designed to elicit family history. Showing genuine interest without being judgmental helps to establish rapport. It allows the elderly and the family members to get to know the therapist and the therapist to get acquainted with the family (Attneave, 1982).

Effective counseling sessions might emphasize the elderly's "place" in the family structure and the counselor's awareness of the respect traditionally accorded the Native-American elderly. The counselor should keep in mind that some elderly clients might not want to disclose personal information with their families present and that some family members might look to the elderly client to act as spokesperson for the family.

▶◣ **UP CLOSE AND PERSONAL 11–1**
Counseling Wenonah Lonetree

Wenonah, age 72, was referred to a free counseling clinic when she went to a government office to try to increase her monthly benefit check. Wenonah's poverty, lack of education, and language problems indicated that she could qualify for counseling assistance. Although Wenonah at first refused to go, her son John convinced her to visit the clinic, especially since he was off work that day and could take her. She was not at all sure, though, that she was doing the right thing.

The 38-year-old female Anglo-American counselor immediately recognized Wenonah's many problems. It was clear that she rarely visited a physician and saw her only role as taking care of the children. The counselor spoke to Wenonah alone, while John waited outside. She began very slowly with Wenonah—not urging her on and not confronting her when she paused or looked the other way during conversations. The counselor made Wenonah feel that her age was respected and that her problems were important and deserving of attention.

The counselor decided that Wenonah's problems were related primarily to language difficulties and poverty. She suggested that Wenonah meet with the agency's language specialist, but Wenonah immediately responded that she did not have transportation back to the clinic. In the meantime, the counselor told Wenonah that she would speak to the government agency to see if Wenonah's benefits could be raised sooner. What about another session? What could be addressed? The counselor pointed to several issues, including Wenonah's feelings about growing old and about how society was changing. The counselor asked Wenonah to return, and she managed to schedule an appointment when John was off work and could take her. In future sessions, she would try to convince Wenonah to see a physician for a checkup.

THE AFRICAN-AMERICAN ELDERLY

Years of prejudice, racism, and discrimination have resulted in a dismal state of affairs for the African-American elderly. Plagued by both cultural and age-related stereotypes, elderly African-Americans generally live in substandard housing and have more health problems and lower incomes than the Anglo elderly population (AARP, 1986). Counselors must first try to understand what it means to be elderly and African-American, and also to be growing old in a predominantly Anglo society that places a premium on youth. Clearly, in the face of such adversity, the problems that the African-American elderly might bring to counseling sessions are many and varied:

1. adverse effects of stereotypes about the culture and elderly status;
2. the possibility of multiple jeopardy;
3. the elderly person's lack of education, lack of a job, and low socioeconomic status;
4. the elderly person's health problems: chronic diseases, functional impairment, high blood pressure; more frequent and longer hospitalizations;
5. the elderly person's cultural differences—traditions and customs;

6. the high divorce/separation rate for African-Americans;

7. the elderly person's poor self-concept and low self-esteem;

8. problems with generational differences due to the acculturation of younger African-Americans;

9. the elderly person's difficulties with developmental tasks and his or her psycho-social crises.

Cultural Differences

Prior to counseling elderly African-Americans, counselors should understand the cultural differences that make the African-American culture unique. They should also examine their own prejudices and stereotypical beliefs about both the culture and the elderly years.

Religion is one cultural aspect that plays a tremendous role in the lives of many elderly African-Americans. The church is considered by many to be the primary institution in the African-American community, second in importance only to the family (Neighbors, Jackson, Bowman, & Gurin 1982; Taylor, 1986). The church has served as a catalyst for civil rights and the elimination of job discrimination. It has also served to promote African-American unity in the face of discrimination and racism.

A second cultural aspect is the importance of the extended family, which emphasizes a sense of corporate responsibility for the economic and emotional security of its members (Lum, 1986). Together, the church and the extended family provide African-Americans with considerable support. However, these forces may also work against the efforts of counselors. With the church and extended family to help them, the African-American elderly might question the need for Anglo counselors, who very well might not understand their unique needs.

Communicational Barriers

The African-American elderly's language patterns need to be understood by the counselor. Although counselors working with these clients may not experience communication barriers as great as when counseling Asian and Hispanic clients, a language problem still may exist. Although older African-Americans who have been speaking English for years may be fluent in English, there are other elderly people who may have attended inferior segregated schools, or perhaps no schools at all. They may be unable to communicate sufficiently well to respond to traditional approaches to counseling. Another potential barrier is the tendency of many African-Americans to engage in a type of stylized deception designed to keep people they do not trust off balance. Two examples include verbalizing loudly the opposite of what they really feel and "playing it cool" to avoid showing true emotions (Vontress, 1976a).

Although counselors and African-American elderly clients speaking English have a common language by which to communicate, counselors also should appreciate the African-American dialect as a unique aspect of the culture. They also must know their clients well enough to be able to recognize when they are hiding emotions.

Health

The seriousness of the elderly African-American's health problems has been sufficiently documented (AARP, 1986; McPherson et al., 1978). First, hospital stays are longer and more frequent than for Anglo-Americans. Second, chronic diseases, functional impairments, and such risk indicators as high blood pressure are more prevalent in the African-American culture (AARP, 1986). Effective counselors, placing health problems in proper perspective, recognize that being ill, poor, and living in substandard housing can result in problems requiring counseling intervention as well as medical attention.

Marriage and Family

Understanding the African-American family entails viewing the institution as a social system interacting with other systems, realizing its historical significance, and perceiving it in light of social-political conditions (Billingsley, 1968). African-American families are extremely diverse from a socioeconomic standpoint. It is a misconception that all such families are low-income groups (Ho, 1987).

Several aspects of African-American family life may result in the need for counseling intervention. One example is the orientation toward kinship bonds, resulting in a wide array of uncles, aunts, "big mamas," boyfriends, older brothers and sisters, deacons, preachers, and others frequenting the African-American home. The increasing number of three-generational families may result in "boundary" or responsibility problems involving the elderly. A second aspect is the African-American's strong religious orientation. Consider the following family dialogue that illustrates the powerful influence of the church:

Therapist: (to Ms. K.) Do you understand why your children worry about you?

Ms. K: No.

Therapist: Find out from them now.

Ms. K: Why? Do you think I'm gonna die?

Cynthia: The way daddy be hitting on you.

Ms. K: Ray don't hit on me.

Karen: When he fought you that time.

Ms. K: John, you think I'm gonna die?

John: The way you two get in serious arguments sometimes (pause)—someone might get injured.

Ms. K: Nobody gets serious injuries. You know the Bible says everybody is gonna die but they come back, John.

John: I know.

Ms. K: Then you all don't have anything to worry about. Jehovah tells you that you're not supposed to worry about anything like that 'cause he'll take care of his people and we'll live right back here on this earth . . . if you be good. Dying is something to get out of all this agony now. (Hines & Boyd-Franklin, 1982, p. 97)

Clearly, the children's valid concerns for Ms. K's safety are being blocked by her religious beliefs. Counselors confronted with such situations are in a better position to intervene successfully if they understand the traditional role of the church and the influence it exerts today.

The Lifespan: Elderly Concerns

Knowing what it is like to be African-American in a predominantly Anglo society and understanding the trials associated with this lifespan stage benefit counselors planning intervention. Perceiving one's life as being nearly over with the feeling that one has lived his or her entire life in a racist society poses barriers to the counseling process. The double jeopardy of being both African-American and elderly without doubt creates problems that may be resistant to helping efforts (Kart, 1985; Jackson, 1970). Perceptive counselors consider each individual situation, and then further consider the complexity of being both African-American and elderly.

Counseling Considerations

As with other stages of human development, counselors working with the African-American elderly should be aware of the body of knowledge pertaining to the elderly developmental period in the African-American culture. However, research and scholarly opinion on counseling the African-American elderly, in particular, is without doubt scarce. Counselors must synthesize their understanding of the culture with their knowledge of the lifespan period to form a basis for counseling decisions.

Most the the techniques used in counseling adults also apply to the elderly. The roles most appropriate to counselors of adults will serve the elderly well. What steps, then, can counselors take to improve the likelihood of a positive counselor-client relationship? First, rapport must be established by convincing the client that the counselor appreciates what it is like to be old—the health-related concerns, the financial problems, the loneliness, the expectations of family and the church. Although the elderly client may think, You're too young and too white to know my problems and to know how I feel, the counselor can still try to gain the client's confidence by demonstrating a "feel" for the various aspects of the elderly years.

Individual and Group Therapy

Whether to use individual or group therapy is another professional decision facing the counselor. The first several sessions should focus mainly on individual therapy directed toward building rapport and letting the client know what to expect from a counseling relationship; however, if there are other clients with similar problems (and, in all likelihood, there will be such clients), group therapy might be feasible. Group therapy for the African-American elderly is most beneficial when several clients have problems in common, either with their culture, their age, or with the racism and discrimination they are subjected to.

Family Therapy

Family therapy may be particularly appropriate for elderly African-American clients in certain situations. Consider the following example of a "boundary" problem in which the therapist worked with three generations:

> A ten year boy was brought for treatment because of stealing. The first session was attended by the parents and their two children. Both parents appeared bewildered and unsure of their parenting skills with the children. When it was learned that the grandmother had the primary responsibility for child care, she was asked to join the family sessions. It became apparent that the grandmother ran the household. She had her way of handling the children, and the parents had theirs.
>
> The therapist's goal was to form a working alliance between the parents and the grandmother so that the children were no longer given conflicting messages. This was accomplished by having a number of joint meetings with the parents and the grandmother to discuss family rules, division of labor, and childcare policies. Disputes and differences of opinions were discussed. Later, the children were included in sessions in order to clarify the boundaries of the family. (Hines & Boyd-Franklin, 1982, p. 92)

What are some other problems the African-American elderly might bring to counseling sessions? Possibilities include parent-care relationship problems, problems with adult children, intermarriages, and divorces or remarriages. And, of course, there are the problems specific to aging; e.g., grief and growing old in a society that favors youth. In summary, counselors need to understand the elderly period on the lifespan, the problems experienced by elderly African-Americans, and the strategies employed in family therapy. A FOCUS ON RESEARCH 11–2 describes a counseling tool for use with the elderly.

 A FOCUS ON RESEARCH 11–2
Guided Autobiography: A Counseling Tool for Older Adults

Malde (1988) describes the Guided Autobiography, a course of therapy based on the life review concept, and evaluates its impact on self-concept, time comprehension, and perceived life purpose. Life review refers to the process evaluating one's life—one's goals, accomplishments, failures, and regrets. Malde suggests that counselors who are contemplating using the Guided Autobiography with older clients determine first whether the client has the required writing skills or whether other means of recording should be used; for example, a tape recorder. Although Guided Autobiography can be a rewarding experience for many, Malde cautions that it also could result in feelings of guilt and depression.

Source: Malde, S. (1988). Guided autobiography: A counseling tool for older adults. *Journal of Counseling and Development, 66,* 290–293.

UP CLOSE AND PERSONAL 11–2
Counseling Eloise Johnson

Eloise, age 73, visited her community medical doctor for stomach pains and was referred to a community mental health counselor. She decided to keep her appointment mainly because the agency was near her son's home. The 34-year-old Anglo female counselor recognized that Eloise had a few problems, but, generally speaking, she was in much better shape than most of the other elderly African-American clients. Although Eloise was poor, she was better off financially than many African-American women, her health was relatively good, and she felt needed by her grandchildren, nieces, and nephews. The counselor decided that the best strategy for this first session was to gain Eloise's confidence and learn more about her. Conversation focused on Eloise's life, her age, and her family and church. At the end of the session, Eloise concluded that the counselor was, indeed, interested, and that she knew a little about what being an elderly African-American woman was like.

The counselor reached several conclusions during this first session. Although Eloise did not have any serious problems, she did feel that she lacked control over her life. There was the possibility of financial problems and the neighborhood was becoming more dangerous. The counselor decided to meet with Eloise again on an individual basis, and then maybe a group session could be arranged. Also, the supportiveness of Eloise's family suggested to the counselor that a family session might benefit Eloise.

THE ASIAN-AMERICAN ELDERLY

The "model minority" stereotype of the Asian-American culture as not needing service organizations or financial assistance has consequences for Asian-Americans of all ages, including the elderly. Consider this myth: Elderly Asian-Americans do not need help because they have achieved economic success and the younger generation takes care of them. Without doubt, Asian-American accomplishments have been dramatic, especially considering discrimination and language barriers. However, counselors must see through the myth of a culture not in need and understand that elderly Asian-Americans do, indeed, have problems requiring counseling and other forms of assistance. Some of the common problems elderly Asian-Americans clients might bring to counseling sessions including the following:

1. adverse effects of stereotypes;
2. being both Asian and elderly—the possibility of double or multiple jeopardy;
3. discrimination and injustices due to the elderly person's age and culture;
4. the elderly person's culture differences and characteristics;
5. the elderly person's poor English skills;
6. the elderly person's distrust of social and government agencies;
7. the lack of education, low income, unemployment, and poor housing that characterize many elderly in the culture;

8. the elderly person's reluctance to disclose personal information;
9. the elderly person's poor health;
10. problems with developmental tasks and psychosocial crises of the elderly person.

Cultural Differences

What cultural differences have implications for counselors of elderly Asian-Americans? First of all, Asian-Americans are hesitant about seeking the help of English-speaking professionals, either due to mistrust or language barriers. Also, many elderly Asian-Americans believe that younger generations should care for them, rather than professionals of another culture. The fact that they continue to live in predominantly Asian enclaves inhibits their acculturation and reinforces their determination to cling to old-world values (Kalish & Moriwaki, 1973).

As mentioned previously, the Asian-American elderly experience considerable frustration and stress from the stereotypic portrayal of all Asian-Americans as highly successful. A more realistic view is supported by the White House Conference on Aging (1972):

> The Asian-American elderly are severely handicapped by the myth that pervades society and permeates the policy decisions of agencies and govenmental entities ... that Asian-Americans do not have any problems, that Asian-Americans are able to take care of their own, and that Asian-American aged do not need or desire aid in any form. (Cited in Kart, 1985, p. 376)

The prevalence of poverty, unemployment, and low incomes take a considerable toll on the elderly. Counselors must work to eliminate stereotypic images of elderly Asian-Americans by realistically assessing their socioeconomical levels.

Counselors are better equipped to help elderly Asian-Americans when they appreciate the racism and discrimination the culture has traditionally experienced. Many elderly Asian-Americans recall their elders discussing their rude awakening to discrimination upon entering the United States. The Chinese, for example, were forced to hard labor in gold mines and in railroad construction, suffering rallying cries such as "The Chinese must go!" (Banks, 1987).

Communication Barriers

Many elderly Asian-Americans have never learned English. The language barrier intensifies problems of loneliness, ill-health, poverty, and their deep sense of hopelessness (Chen, 1979). Elderly people with little knowledge of English cannot read labels, street signs, newspapers, or the signs of stores. As immigrants "they felt 'imprisoned' and considered themselves as 'deaf, dumb, and blind,' or 'crippled' by their language problem" (Wu, 1975, p. 272).

The implications of such language problems for counselors are innumerable. Communication barriers may impede the counseling process, or prevent counseling from taking place at all. An inability to communicate may also lower self-esteem and retard the development of a positive cultural identity. Elderly Asian-Americans may come to doubt their worthiness as contributing members of society.

Counselors working with elderly Asian-Americans have a threefold challenge: First, they must get the client to come for counseling sessions; second, they must work to break down communication barriers; and third, they must convince the client to disclose personal information. Counselors who rely heavily on nonverbal communication might be frustrated in attempting to interpret interactions, especially with Japanese-Americans who are noted for their dependence on an elaborate yet subtle systems of nonverbal communication (Vontress, 1976a).

Health

A persistent problem plaguing attempts to determine the Asian-American's health status is the lack of systematically kept records with specific ethnic classifications. Research by Yu (1986) suggests that Chinese-Americans are relatively healthier than Anglo-Americans. Also, age-specific death rates for all causes of death are lower for Chinese than for the Anglo population. Such findings, however, should not be taken to imply that the Asian-American culture is without health problems. Asian-Americans do, indeed, have major health-related concerns; e.g., certain types of cancers, hypertension, and tuberculosis (AARP, 1986). The elderly are especially vulnerable to hypertension, with some reports suggesting that over 40 percent of all persons aged 65 and over experience this ailment to some degree (Liu, 1986).

Another issue related to health is that elderly Asian-Americans often fail to receive health benefits and services to which they are entitled due to language or cultural barriers (Kim, 1973). Research suggests that not all Asian-Americans are cared for by younger generations or ethnic community facilities to the extent that was once believed. In fact, many elderly Asian-Americans live alone or with nonrelatives. Elderly Asian-Americans' distrust of Western medicine also contributes to their reluctance to use available services (Liu, 1986).

The implications of these issues are clear to counseling professionals. Counselors may have to encourage elderly Asian-Americans to take advantage of services, they may need to provide a convincing argument that counseling professionals can be trusted, and they may need to overcome the reluctance of Asian-Americans to reveal the family's personal problems and secrets.

Marriage and Family

An understanding of traditional customs regarding marriage and family in the Asian-American culture sheds light on contemporary problems experienced by the elderly in the culture. While one such custom, arranged marriages, is disappearing (Ho, 1987; Shon & Ja, 1982), the choice of a marriage partner is heavily influenced by families on both sides. Marriage does not mark the beginning of a new family but rather the continuation of the male line. The wife becomes absorbed into her husband's family as a person of lower status. In the nuclear family, fairly rigid role expectations prevailed traditionally, with each family member being accorded privileges in line with his or her position (Shon & Ja, 1982).

Today's Asian-American younger generations, experiencing economic and social mobility in Anglo society, are moving away from more traditional cultural concepts. Their new ways of thinking and behaving no doubt frustrate their elders, and may cause them considerable stress. Not only are the elderly experiencing the changes of growing old; at the same time they are witnessing a devaluation of traditional Asian customs. They may feel they are being displaced as rulers of the family and traditional spokespersons in family matters.

Dysfunction within family systems often hits the elderly hardest. They are the ones who can least cope with change in their cultures. Attempting to adhere to traditional methods of family problem solving, such as reliance on hierarchial authority, male domination, and separation of material and emotional giving, the family in cultural transition frequently cannot adapt to the necessary change. One family member's inability to adapt may lead to dysfunction in the entire family (Shon & Ja, 1982).

The implications for counselors of the Asian-American elderly are clear. Marriage and family counselors understanding traditional Asian customs recognize the effects generational differences can have on elderly people's self-esteem.

The Lifespan: Elderly Concerns

Asian-Americans face the same changes that all older people face, regardless of geographical location, culture, or ethnicity. These include the possible reduction of vitality and energy, some decrease in memory and intellectual functioning, more time for leisure, the loss of significant others due to death, and increased physical discomforts and pain. At the same time, clients functioning in the elderly lifespan period are faced with changing values, new lifestyles, and aggressive challenges to established authority (Kalish & Moriwaki, 1973). Counselors planning intervention procedures should take these age-related factors into account. They also have the responsibility to avoid basing counseling decisions on myths and erroneous beliefs.

Counseling Considerations

The problems Asian-American clients most often bring to counseling sessions center around differing intergenerational expectations and the elderly's expectation that their kin and younger generations will care for them. Culturally diverse groups frequently experience a widening gap between generations as the young move up the social and economic ladder (Osako & Liu, 1986). When younger generations attain middle-class or higher status, the elderly often are subjected to conflict and strain. Will they continue to be cared for? Will they receive the same respect? What will happen when they are no longer able to care for themselves? It is imperative to understand the history of Asian family loyalty and allegiances; also, to understand the elderly's problem as younger generations rapidly acculturate. Realistically speaking, the elderly client probably has multiple problems that may be interrelated and perhaps made more severe by the double or multiple jeopardy often associated with the elderly years (Kart, 1985).

Counselors are often at a loss to explain why Chinese-Americans do not participate more actively in counseling sessions. Sue and Sue (1983) maintain that Anglo
counselors are likely to interpret the undemonstrative demeanor of Asian-Americans
as the result of repressed emotional conflicts. They remind professionals that behaving openly with strangers can be quite difficult for Asian-Americans. To overcome
this potential impediment to counseling progress, counselors should (a) show respect
for elderly clients and their culture, (b) establish a trusting atmosphere and develop
rapport, (c) understand that the elderly Asian-American might be hesitant to disclose
personal problems, and (d) explain the counseling process to the client, including
the concept of confidentiality. These strategies may encourage Asian-American participation and self-disclosure.

Individual and Group Therapy

The decision of whether to use individual or group therapy should be based on a
consideration of the individual Asian-American client. Individual therapy might be
the most effective technique, unless the client is willing to disclose personal information in a group session. Reluctance to reveal personal information may stem from
the Asian-American client's fear of shaming or degrading the family. Even in an
individual counseling situation, the Asian-American male will be hesitant to reveal
information that could reflect negatively on his family or on his performance in
meeting his responsibilities to the family.

Family Therapy

The decision to enter treatment is not an easy one for many Asian-Americans. Elderly
Asian-Americans, in particular, might be reluctant to admit their need for counseling.
They also are more apt to be totally unfamiliar with what counseling is all about
(Shon & Ja, 1982).

It is important for the counselor to know what the client expects of him or her.
The Asian-American family (especially the parents) will view the counselor as a knowledgeable expert who will guide family behavior in the proper course. During the
first session, the counselor must take an active role, rather than wait for the family
to initiate interaction. A passive initial approach on the counselor's part is quite often
interpreted as due to lack of knowledge or skill (Shon & Ja, 1982).

Counselors, of course, are well aware of the importance of communication in
any counseling endeavor; thus, they may find communication with Asian-Americans
difficult and frustrating. The elderly Asian-American's reluctance to speak could be
due to lack of facility with English or an unwillingness to disclose personal information. In any event, the counselor can try to develop a trusting and comfortable
alliance with the family, especially the elderly, to whom other family members will
look for direction. The family may want to know something about the therapist, so
the counselor should be willing and prepared to share personal information (Shon
& Ja, 1982).

Also to be considered during family therapy is the powerful Asian belief that the
father is head of the household and spokesperson for the family. This belief may
cause other family members to remain silent. Certainly, family members would be
unlikely to disagree with the father under any circumstances. It is important for
counselors to recognize this family dynamic in evaluating their clients' behavior.

▶ UP CLOSE AND PERSONAL 11–3
Counseling Grandfather Sukuzi

Grandfather, 85 years old, finally decided to visit the doctor because of his worsening dizziness, his fading hearing, and his forgetfulness. Han took a half day off from work and drove Grandfather to the doctor. The doctor diagnosed the dizziness as due to an ear infection, for which he prescribed an antibiotic. The mild hearing loss was nothing to worry about—it was common to people Grandfather's age. The doctor did refer Grandfather to a counselor, however, to discuss his fears that the family was becoming too Americanized.

The 43-year-old Anglo male counselor experienced considerable difficulty with Grandfather Sukuzi. He could hardly speak English, he was reluctant to talk about himself or his family, and he seemed to be waiting for the counselor to do something so he could finally leave. Obviously, Grandfather was extremely uncomfortable. Little could be done, the counselor thought, during this first session, except to try to build trust. He would show Grandfather that he was interested in him, and assure him that the counseling relationship would remain confidential.

The counselor decided on at least two or three more sessions with Grandfather Sukuzi to try to build rapport and to give Grandfather a chance to disclose significant personal information. Group therapy was out of the question, since Grandfather would not want to share his concerns in a group setting. Family therapy was impossible, too, since Grandfather would do all the talking for the family. In this case, the counselor thought, progress will be slow. Not only was there a communication barrier, his client would not always have transportation, and the chance of Grandfather revealing personal information was remote.

THE HISPANIC-AMERICAN ELDERLY

Counselors confront several obstacles in planning professional intervention for elderly Hispanic-American clients. First, the vast intracultural diversity among Hispanic-Americans challenges multicultural counselors to understand the unique cultural characteristics of specific subgroups. Second, questions surrounding the problems and crises of the elderly years further complicate the counseling process. Third, the intensity of the elderly Hispanic's problems can be psychologically overwhelming to the counselor, as well as to the client. Aging, grief from loss, and relationship problems are common and may lead to crises if individuals do not have sufficient coping skills to deal with them (Casas & Vasquez, 1989). Specific problems that Hispanic-American elderly clients may bring to counseling sessions include the following:

1. the elderly person's inability to overcome stereotypes;
2. being both Hispanic and elderly—the possibility of double or multiple jeopardy;
3. the vast intracultural differences that make generalizations difficult;
4. problems associated with urban life—poverty and crime;
5. the elderly person's low socioeconomic status, lack of education, lack of a job, low standard of living, or unmet basic needs;

6. the elderly person's possible illegal immigrant status;

7. the health-related problems of the elderly person: chronic ailments, frequent bouts with illnesses, lack of transportaton to obtain medical services;

8. the elderly person's developmental problems and psychosocial crises;

9. the elderly person's allegiance to Spanish, hampering improvement in English;

10. the patriarchial nature of the Hispanic-American family and the inability to accommodate change.

Cultural Differences

It is not difficult to imagine the counseling implications of a commitment to such cultural traditions as allegiance to Spanish, a patriarchial family structure, and the belief that males are biologically superior to females. Continuing to emphasize cultural values that run counter to values of the majority culture leave many Hispanic-Americans in need of counseling services. Counselors may be faced with planning intervention for an elderly client who does not understand that a son or daughter wants equal opportunity in the home and in the workplace. Acculturation of the younger generations and their awareness of the benefits that economic and social mobility bring may leave the elderly client shocked or angered by a perceived rejection of traditional Hispanic beliefs.

Counselors working with elderly Hispanic-Americans also must be prepared to confront fairly dismal situations. Not many in this population have graduated from high school; some lack any formal education at all (Kart, 1985). Conditions of extreme poverty are not unusual. Neither is working long after retirement age and habitual poor health. To further complicate the counseling process, counselors not fluent in Spanish will probably have to deal with communication barriers resulting from the client's inability to speak English.

Other obstacles facing elderly Hispanic-Americans and their counselors are racism and discrimination—both ageism and cultural discrimination. Young or even middle-aged Anglo counselors need to gain an understanding of what it means to be elderly and Hispanic. Language and communication problems; the perceived erosion of traditional Hispanic values; being stereotyped and plagued by cultural myths; and discrimination in housing, employment, and other areas all have the potential for taking a serious psychological toll on the elderly and for presenting their counselors with significant challenges.

Communication Barriers

We have already detailed the considerable communication barriers that add to the difficulties in counseling elderly Hispanics. Many of these clients have lived most of their lives in the United States unable to speak English. Further complicating the language problem are the many distinctions between the Puerto Rican, Mexican, and Cuban-American cultures (Vontress, 1976a).

It is important that counselors understand that the language problem of the elderly has been perpetuated by their decision to live in predominantly Spanish-speaking communities (Kart, 1985). Their reluctance to learn English has without doubt contributed to their lack of success in the predominantly Anglo culture. Furthermore, the Hispanic-American, recognizing the implications of the language problem, might be reluctant to seek counseling. Other troublesome communication barriers include the negative feelings of older Hispanic-American clients toward younger and well-educated Anglo counselors who might not understand the older Hispanic's cultural traditions (Vontress, 1976a).

Health

The seriousness of the Hispanic-American's health status has been adequately documented (AARP, 1986; Kart, 1985; Torres-Gil, 1976) and has implications for counseling, particularly for counseling intervention with the elderly. Of all Hispanics aged 65 and over and living in the community (rather than in nursing homes), 85 percent report at least one chronic illness and 45 percent report some limitation in performing day-to-day activities (AARP, 1986). The health situation is further complicated by elderly Hispanics working past retirement age, their low annual incomes, and the poverty conditions many live in. Solutions to Hispanic health problems depend on improved health services, better nutrition, and better education (Barrow & Smith, 1979). Lack of transportation, financial difficulties, and language problems all relate to health issues. The total situation, in all its complexity, must be addressed by the counselor in order to effect meaningful change.

Marriage and Family

Intracultural differences make generalizations about Hispanic-American marriage and family practices difficult. Most research on Hispanic cultures focuses on a specific population, with the expectation that findings may cross cultural lines. Although such assumptions may be valid for certain characteristics, intracultural differences must always be reflected in counseling decisions.

What marriage and family problems might the elderly Hispanic-American experience? First, and probably foremost, are the problems resulting from increasing acculturation. Speaking specifically of Mexican-Americans, traditional family life revolved around prescribed roles for men and women. For example, when a young bride went to live with her new husband, the working out of the relationship of mother-in-law and daughter-in-law was vital to the success of the marriage. By tradition, the daughter-in-law had the same responsibilities and obligations as a daughter. In essence, she performed her domestic duties under the supervision of her mother-in-law. Today, even if they only temporariy live with the husband's family, most young women no longer tolerate this role (Falicov, 1982).

Cultural traditions of Puerto Rican families also affect marriage and family relationships. The moving away from spiritual values, respect for authority, and rigid family structures by younger generations has the potential for creating dysfunctions. Still other problems can result from racism, traditional and contemporary sex roles, the increasing number of female-headed households, and the increasing number of female breadwinners in two-parent households (Garcia-Preto, 1982).

Other situations causing stress for elderly Hispanics may include problems of social isolation, lack of knowledge about social and community resources, and the differing expectations of the home and social institutions. If these problems impair the elderly person's or the family's ability to cope, then the therapist may assume the role of "social intermediary" between client and community. Counselors may also choose to use members of the clergy, the extended family, or neighbors to help the client (Garcia-Preto, 1982).

The Lifespan: Elderly Concerns

Counselors should make every effort to understand what it is like to face the double jeopardy of being both Hispanic and elderly. Havighurst (1979), describes the plight of elderly Hispanics trying to adjust to retirement and reduced income. He or she probably cannot afford to retire or does not have a job from which to retire, and does not have much income to be reduced! In Erikson's (1980) integrity vs. despair stage, the person faces the crisis of coping with the difficulties of advancing years. Such a crisis constitutes an even greater challenge for the Hispanic who is poor, uneducated, beset by racism and discrimination, and who is generally the recipient of few life satisfactions. Also contributing to the Hispanics' dismal situation are the problems usually associated with the elderly period of the lifespan: loss of stamina, changes in physical appearance, and sometimes the loss of sensory perceptions.

As with other cultures and stages of the lifespan, counselors should consider the effects of being elderly, the effects of being a member of a particular culture, the vast complex relationship between age and culture, and the various intracultural and individual differences among their clients.

Counseling Considerations

Two basic considerations crucial to the success of counseling the elderly Hispanic-American are (1) understanding what problems and issues might be raised during intervention and (2) understanding what counselor techniques and strategies may enhance the counseling relationship. The following discussion centers on specific steps the counselor can take to increase the likelihood of gaining the client's confidence, building rapport, and getting the client to disclose information freely.

Counselors working with elderly Hispanic-Americans must first of all let their clients know that they understand and accept the traditional Hispanic familial structure. The client must be confident that the counselor does not harbor negative feelings about the culture or subscribe to damaging stereotypes. Second, the counselor must be aware of the client's commitment to Spanish and understand why it has persisted as such an important cultural characteristic. Third, the counselor should appreciate the possible reluctance of the client to take a young Anglo counselor seriously, especially a female counselor. Fourth, the counselor must work to build trust and encourage disclosure of relevant personal information. Fifth, planning appropriately for communication barriers will be all-important. If the Anglo counselor has the need for an interpreter, it will be best to use a co-counselor or paraprofessional rather than the client's child, neighbor, or friend. Finally, the Hispanic-

American client's needs for respect, privacy, and dignity must not be overlooked. It is especially important to consider these needs in counseling elderly Hispanics (Vontress, 1976a).

Individual and Group Therapy

As always, the counselor's decision on whether to use individual or group therapy should be based on the individual, the specific culture, and the reasons for counseling. Several generalizations, however, may be noted in dealing with Hispanic-Americans. Elderly Hispanics, although not generally accustomed to disclosing significant information that may reflect poorly on the family, might be willing to discuss problems associated with aging in a group session. However, the elderly's lack of experience with group counseling would probably call for special effort on the part of the counselor to explain the group process.

Family Therapy

Counseling Hispanic-Americans requires addressing their cultural and individual backgrounds, behavioral characteristics, and, of course, their problems. Counselors working with elderly Hispanic-Americans will note some unifying cultural concepts, such as familism, personalism, a sense of hierarchy, spirituality, and fatalism (Ho, 1987). Also, counselors can benefit from an understanding of traditional family structures, extended family ties, and the changes that contemporary society is making in these areas.

What, then, do research and scholarly opinion offer for counselors working with Hispanics? With respect to family therapy with Puerto Ricans, Garcia-Preto (1982) has the following suggestions:

1. The counselor should speak Spanish, if possible, if communication in English presents a problem.
2. The counselor should make the family comfortable by providing a warm and personal setting.
3. Puerto Ricans are likely to respond to a therapist who is active, personal, and respectful of the family's structure and boundaries.
4. Asking the family when the problems began, what types of solutions they have tried, and what their expectations are for change may help the counselor acquire information on family history and assess the role of socioeconomic status in the situation.

The plight of an elderly Mexican was documented by Falicov (1982):

An elderly lady, Mrs. R, was referred to a mental health center by a priest. She had been seeing him because she was depressed and irritable and had been losing weight. Mrs. R was in an isolated situation within the ethnic neighborhood. She had migrated from Mexico eight years before to live with her two sons and an older single daughter who spoke no English and did not work. Among other questions, the therapist asked, "Are you losing weight because you have lost your appetite?" Mrs. R quipped, "No, I've lost my teeth, not my appetite! That's what irks me!" Indeed, Mrs. R had almost no teeth left in her mouth. Apparently, her conversations with the priest (an American who had learned to speak Spanish during a South American mission) had centered on emotional losses she had suffered recently as the cause of her "anxious depression" without considering the practical issues. As an undocumented immigrant, Mrs. R had no medical insurance, did not know any dentists, and had no financial resources. It was necessary for the therapist to help find dental care for Mrs. R. Finally, a university dental school clinic agreed to have her seen by supervised practicum students. This required a long trip to another part of the city to an institution that had no Spanish-speaking personnel. Mrs. R also needed reassurance that her undocumented legal status would not result in any consequences for her sons.

The next step was to enlist the cooperation of a bilingual neighbor, Rose, to accompany Mrs. R to her appointment at the dental clinic. Rose was willing to do it. To reciprocate (and with only a hint on the therapist's part), Mrs. R began to do some baby-sitting for Rose's young baby. (p. 155)

In all likelihood, the patriarchial nature of the Hispanic family will dictate that only the father or husband will speak for the family. The possibility of the wife or children disagreeing with the head of the household is remote. Although there are some indications that Hispanic females are becoming more outspoken, they cannot be expected to disclose much personal information during the course of a family session.

◤ UP CLOSE AND PERSONAL 11—4
Counseling Papa Rafael Suarez

Papa Rafael, 75 years old, referred himself to a community health organization for counseling. Although the counselor was surprised that a 75-year-old man with English problems had referred himself, the 48-year-old Anglo male counselor was eager to talk with him. Since he had come of his own volition, surely Rafael would be willing to discuss his problems and disclose his feelings.

During the first session, the counselor explained the counseling process, assured confidentiality, and sought to establish trust and rapport. The client's problems became clear: financial difficulties and his son's unemployment; his own meager government benefits; growing old poor; and concern that his family, like many others, might abandon traditional Hispanic beliefs. Rafael saw a solution to the family's financial woes, but it was not a satisfactory solution in his view. Carla could take a job to make ends meet, but Carla working could also lead to "the downfall of the family." Women in his family had not worked; they had stayed home to care for the children. Who would cook? Take care of the children? Clean the house? And what if Carla started developing "Anglo" notions? The counselor understood how Rafael felt. Finances were a problem, and so was the threat of loss of traditional values. Upon assessing the situation, the counselor decided that he wanted to see Rafael again. Perhaps a group session would be appropriate, since there were other elderly clients who were having similar difficulties. Since Rafael's problem involved the family, a family session might be in order. Meeting with Rafael, Oscar, and Carla to discuss their financial situation and possible solutions was an idea worth exploring.

Several counseling considerations that apply to all Hispanic groups are pointed out by Ho (1987):

1. Because of the counselor's position of authority, family members might consider it impolite or inappropriate to disagree with him or her during the counseling session.

2. To maintain a good working relationship with the Hispanic family, especially with the father, the counselor's communicative style should be businesslike and non-confrontational.

3. Hispanics consider the exertion of personal power to be threatening, disrespectful, and Western; hence, it is likely to alienate them.

A POINT OF DEPARTURE

Challenges Confronting Multicultural Counselors of the Elderly

Relatively few counselors have adequate training and counseling skills to deal with the problems of the elderly in a multicultural context; however, specific steps can be taken to correct this situation. The elimination of stereotypic thinking continues to be a major task for counselors working with culturally diverse elderly clients. Moreover, it is imperative that counselors approach the elderly with the view that they very well may be socially integrated and well adjusted within the context of their own cultural value system. Counselors are challenged to consider the uniqueness of each client and each family, taking into account generation differences, ethnic background, socioeconomic status, and geographic location (Axelson, 1985).

SUMMARY

Counselors working with culturally diverse elderly clients need to understand the personal and social problems facing this age group: poor nutrition, drug abuse, suicide, generational differences and other marital and family concerns, loneliness, language barriers, poverty, and the threat of health problems such as Alzheimer's disease. Understanding the age period, the cultural group, and the complex relationship between them provides a sound foundation for counseling intervention. Since few professionals have been trained to work with the culturally diverse elderly, counselors are challenged to improve their skills by carefully reviewing the pertinent literature and by seeking first-hand experiences with culturally diverse elderly clients.

Suggested Readings

Casas, J. M., & Vasquez, M. J. T. (1989). Counseling the Hispanic client: A theoretical and applied perspective (3rd ed.). In P. B. Pedersen, J. G. Draguns, W. J. Lonner, & J. E. Trimble (Eds.), *Counseling across cultures* (pp. 153–175). Honolulu: University of Hawaii Press. Casas and Vasquez provide a framework for counseling Hispanic-American clients by discussing the counselor, the client, and the counseling process.

Fitting, M. D. (1986). Ethical dilemmas in counseling elderly adults. *Journal of Counseling and Development, 64,* 325–327. Fitting presents a case-study approach using a critical-evaluative model as a means of analyzing and resolving ethical dilemmas.

Herr, J. J., & Weakland, J. H. (1979). *Counseling elders and their families.* New York: Springer. An excellent counseling text that examines practical techniques for applied gerontology. Family problem solving is discussed and detailed case studies included.

Piggrem, G. W., & Schmidt, L. D. (1982). Counseling the elderly. *Counseling and Human Development, 14*(10), 1–12. Piggrem and Schmidt discuss counseling fundamentals and explore special areas of concern, including the problem of stereotypes.

Seligman, M. (1975). *Helplessness on depression, development, and death.* San Francisco, CA: W. H. Freeman. Seligman examines theories of anxiety and depression—conditions that characterize many elderly adults.

Vontress, C. E. (1976). Counseling middle-aged and aging cultural minorities. *Personnel and Guidance Journal, 55,* 132–135. Vontress looks at problems likely to confront the elderly; for example unemployment, failing health, and loneliness.

Part V

Professional Issues

Part V consists of Chapter 12 and the Epilogue. Chapter 12 explores a variety of issues of interest to scholars, practicing professionals, and students. These include approaches to multicultural counseling, the relevance of a lifespan perspective, research directions, ethics, stereotyping, and the effects of diversity on professional intervention, among others. The Epilogue provides readers with a look at future directions multicultural counseling may take.

Chapter 12

Issues in
Multicultural Counseling

Questions To Be Explored

1. What issues will confront multicultural counselors in the 1990s and beyond?

2. Why must counselors be aware of the complex relationship between culture, counseling, and the client's developmental stage?

3. How do the client's cultural differences affect counseling intervention?

4. What ethical and legal standards must be adhered to when counseling culturally diverse clients?

5. How much cultural similarity can therapists assume in counseling culturally different clients?

6. What research issues remain to be resolved? Should practicing counselors engage in research?

7. What additional sources of information are available in seeking more information on the issues confronting multicultural counselors?

MULTICULTURAL COUNSELING IN THE YEARS TO COME

Counselors of the 1990s and beyond will continue to intervene with increasing numbers of culturally diverse clients with unique racial, ethnic, and cultural backgrounds. Without doubt, some of their problems will be specific to their particular culture, while other problems and frustrations will cross cultural boundaries. Specific issues that will continue to apply to nearly all cultures include the influence of cultural diversity on counseling intervention, ethical and legal concerns, lifespan and developmental aspects, and issues specific to individual cultures. This chapter examines selected issues relevant to multicultural counseling and shows how these issues impact the counseling process as well as the counseling profession.

Basic Questions/Issues Confronting Multicultural Counselors

According to Brislin (1981), three basic questions for multicultural counselors are the following:

1. What happens to people when they interact with others from different cultures?
2. Can a common language of fundamental concepts be developed to facilitate communication among people interested in different types of multicultural experiences?
3. Can the advantages of multicultural interaction be better and more accurately specified?

As previously suggested, the events experienced during multicultural intervention may take a variety of forms, each having the potential for promoting or hindering the counseling outcome. The stresses and strains of multicultural interaction may result in conflict. This is evidenced in everyday situations in the workplace, in schools, and in neighborhoods where people from different cultures coexist. Counseling outcomes may actually be negative in some cases, which may result in additional stress for culturally different clients. Other outcomes may result in improved relationships among people of varying cultural backgrounds in the long term, but without any immediate positive benefits that can be attributed to counseling (Brislin, 1981). In any event, how the counselor and client perceive their multicultural relationship and their perception of the actual outcome of the intervention warrants consideration.

Multicultural Understandings: Is There a Need for Multicultural Counseling Perspectives?

At least one writer (Lloyd, 1987) has questioned whether multicultural counseling should be a part of counselor education programs. Lloyd contended that although multicultural counseling has the support of such affirmative action groups as the NCATE (National Council for Accreditation of Teacher Education) and the CACREP (Council for Accreditation of Counseling and Related Education Programs), a lingering concern is whether it might be better for counselors to de-emphasize culture-based characteristics. Contending that all individuals within similar cultures are unique, Lloyd cautioned that counselors need to avoid stereotypes and cultural misunderstandings about their clients:

> An approach to multicultural counseling that emphasizes the differences between groups and attempts to teach simplistic views of cultural traits, characteristics, and beliefs does not seem to be the type of instruction that should be part of teacher education or counselor education. (p. 167)

Other writers do not agree with Lloyd's belief that specific training for multicultural counseling is unnecessary. Hood and Arceneaux (1987) point out that individuals within a culture are not always representative of their cultural group. In fact, many individual differences exist that may affect the outcome of counseling. In response to Lloyd's suggestion that multicultural education courses would be better eliminated from counselor training programs, Hood and Arceneaux suggest that such courses

A FOCUS ON RESEARCH 12–1
A Reply to Lloyd

Das and Littrell (1989), focusing on the issues raised by Lloyd, reached the following conclusions concerning the worth of multicultural counseling:

- Knowledge of the cultural backgrounds of clients should help rather than hinder counselors in better understanding clients and their problems, because problems often stem from the sociocultural environment in which clients live. (p. 13)

Source: Das, A. K., & Littrell, J. M. (1989). Multicultural education for counseling: A reply to Lloyd. *Counselor Education and Supervision, 29,* 7–15.

- Students should recognize the strong set of Western assumptions that permeate counseling theories and techniques. (p. 13)
- Students should recognize that traditional communication and counseling skills may need modification, depending on the counseling context. (p. 14)

The authors suggested that counselor educators provide numerous opportunities for students to intervene with culturally diverse clients to explore how culture influences clients' world views, to expand sensitivity to others, and to broaden the students' repertoire of counseling skills.

---

are designed to replace false stereotypes with accurate information. As a third point, training in multicultural counseling increases counselors' sensitivity and awareness of cultural diversity. Still another viewpoint is offered in A FOCUS ON RESEARCH 12–1.

The steadily increasing number of culturally different clients seeking counseling and psychotherapy further documents the need for professionals trained in multicultural techniques. Also, the increase in the number of counselor education programs recognizing the need for multicultural courses is evidence of the strong professional move toward training counselors to work with clients in multicultural settings.

Stereotyping

Stereotyping represents the tendency of a person or group to generalize behavioral characteristics on the basis of race, sex, or religion. The potential for damaged relationships is clear when one considers negative stereotypes referring to low mentality, welfare freeloading, and pathological behavior. Stereotypes can be used to justify one's beliefs that various cultures or ethnic groups have inferior or defective mental abilities (Lum, 1986). The outcome of counseling intervention with African-Americans is likely to suffer if the counselor subscribes to the notion that all African-Americans are lazy and stupid. Similarly, Asian-Americans may be stereotyped as sneaky, shy, or good with numbers but poor with words (Atkinson, Morten, & Sue, 1989).

Counselors working in multicultural settings can easily recognize the implications of basing intervention and assessment on erroneous assumptions. Majority-culture counselors may have difficulty adjusting to a counseling relationship with a minority client; or, failing to recognize the client as an individual, the counselor may assume cultural characteristics that do not apply. The counselor may also profess "color blindness" and avoid discussing differences. Or the counselor may be so overly concerned with differences that the client cannot fail to perceive some degree of stereotyping on the counselor's part (Atkinson, Morten, & Sue, 1989).

Locus of Responsibility

An issue facing culturally different clients and their counselors is where blame should be placed for the minority person's plight. For example, should low-income African-Americans blame themselves for their high unemployment and poverty, or is the society that allows discrimination at fault? Must Native-Americans blame themselves for their alarmingly high school dropout rates and widespread alcoholism? In essence, should the victim or the society be blamed? Sue (1978b) explains that those with a person-centered orientation tend to emphasize the individual's motivation, values, feelings, and goals. Success or failure is attributed to an individual's skills or inadequacies; thus, there is a powerful relationship between ability and effort and the attainment of success in society. Conversely, the system-blame view holds that success or failure depends largely on the social and economic system rather than on personal attributes. A Western outlook generally holds individuals responsible for their problems; minorities are often labeled deviant in both thought and behavior. This person-centered philosophy has dominated counseling and has resulted in the responsibility for change being placed on the individual rather than on the larger society (Sue, 1981).

This issue relates directly to the concept of world views as discussed in Chapter 2. Either Sue's (1978c) theories of internal-external locus of control or the Scale to Assess World Views (SAWV) proposed by Ibrahim and Kahn (1984) may be used by counselors to better understand how clients perceive life and the sociocultural environment. In attempting to gain understanding, however, counselors are admonished not to allow their Anglo middle-class backgrounds (if, indeed, such a background applies) to serve as a basis for blaming the victim for not taking a more assertive stand to change life events.

ISSUE: HOW CAN A CLIENT'S CULTURAL DIVERSITY AFFECT INTERVENTION?

Counselors' perceptions of culturally diverse clients undoubtedly affect intervention strategies. During the 1990s counselors will be focusing attention on several different models of cultural deficiency/difference, a host of conflicting opinions regarding counseling approaches, and the effects of verbal and nonverbal communication between counselor and client.

Models of Cultural Deficiency/Difference

The study of differences in intelligence as a function of race has sometimes been flawed with inaccurate scientific data or faulty analysis. This situation has resulted in some researchers contributing, knowingly or unknowingly, to racism and stereotyping. Thomas and Sullen (1972) in their text *Racism and Psychiatry* cite examples of African-Americans being characterized as prone to anxiety, content with subservience, faithful and happy-go-lucky, and as having a smaller brain than Anglo-Americans. Sue (1981) reports that G. Stanley Hall, often referred to as "the father of child study," described Africans, Indians, and Chinese as members of races that were "incomplete" developmentally. Such flawed thinking can be detected in some of the models suggested to explain minority differences. The issue, however, has far greater implications than whether minorities are categorized according to the *genetic deficient model,* the *cultural deficit model,* or the *culturally different model.* For example, counselors believing that low intelligence and strong athletic ability characterize African-Americans, or that Asian-Americans are by nature mathematically oriented, may plan intervention with a biased perception of the client.

The Genetic Deficient Model. This model holds that the culturally different are genetically inferior. Scholarly opinion offered around the turn of the century argued for the genetic intellectual superiority of whites and the genetic inferiority of the "lower races." Writers portrayed minority cultures as lacking desirable attributes and as being uneducable (Sue, 1981). Frighteningly, these opinions continue to be voiced. The works of Jensen (1969) and Shockley (1972) contend that genetic inheritance plays a significant role in the determination of intelligence. Believing that "weak genes" in the African-American population lowers overall intelligence, Shockley (1972) recommended that low IQ people be sterilized so as not to bear low IQ children.

The Cultural Deficit Model. In the cultural deficit model, social scientists described the culturally different as "deprived" or "disadvantaged" on the basis that they demonstrated behavior at variance with middle-class values, language systems, and customs. From a class perspective, middle-class Anglo-Americans assumed that other cultures did not seek to advance themselves because of a cultural deficit (Draguns, 1989). Thus, rather than attributing undesirable differences to genetics, blame was shifted to cultural lifestyles or values. The term *cultural deprivation* was popularized in Frank Riessman's (1962) book, *The Culturally Deprived Child.* The term was used to indicate that some groups perform poorly academically because they lack the advantages of middle-class culture; hence, they are culturally deprived (Sue, 1981).

Both the genetic deficient and the cultural deficit models failed to address the implicit cultural biases that shaped these negative perceptions and inhibited the understanding of the role of sociopolitical forces (Jenkins, 1982). Both have been refuted and largely superseded by the culturally different model (Draguns, 1989; Sue, 1981).

The Culturally Different Model. The culturally different model holds that people with culturally diverse backgrounds have unique strengths, values, customs, and traditions that can serve as a basis for enriching the overall counseling process. Researchers have begun to establish an information base documenting that cultural differences are not deficiencies and that they can be built upon as counseling progresses. For counselors to provide the most effective professional intervention, deliberate attempts must be made to capitalize on differences as resources rather than disregarding them, or viewing them as deficits to be eliminated.

Proponents of the culturally different model still believe that all culturally different people, regardless of lifespan period, need to be aware of mainstream cultural values and knowledge. A degree of cultural compatibility is attained as counselors and clients increasingly develop an awareness of each other's cultural differences. The situation for culturally different clients is probably more difficult than for their counselors, especially since clients are faced with interacting in a number of different cultures. In any event, culturally different people should not be condemned for their language or culture; rather, they should be encouraged to retain and build upon their differences whenever possible (Sleeter & Grant, 1988).

Etic-Emic Approaches to the Study of Culture

Two basic approaches to multicultural study and related research are the *emic* and the *etic*. Draguns (1976) offers the following definitions:

> Emic refers to the viewing of data in terms indigenous or unique to the culture in question, and etic, to viewing them in light of categories and concepts external to the culture but universal in their applicability. (p. 2)

In other words, in the etic approach cultures are examined in terms of similarities and dissimilarities with other cultures. In essence, the focus of the cultural study is external in nature. By contrast, the emic approach makes comparisons within the cultural system in question by looking at the culture, itself, rather than making external comparisons (Lee, 1984). In an emic approach, counselors could study Native-Americans through first-hand experiences with members of the culture. Counselors taking an etic approach would compare Native-American characteristics, values, and customs with those of other cultures. Regardless of the approach, students should be cautious of theories and studies that fail to take into account individual differences among people (Peterson & Nisenholz, 1987).

According to Draguns (1989), it is probably impossible to conduct counseling based purely on etic or emic approaches. Counseling that ignores multicultural differences demonstrates cultural insensitivity; yet counselors should not focus exclusively on cultural differences. The most effective approach will probably be a combination of both etic and emic; however, the exact combination is yet to be determined.

Autoplastic and Alloplastic Approaches

People of all cultures adapt to their environmental situations—by changing themselves, in an *autoplastic* approach; by changing the environment, in an *alloplastic* approach; or by combining the two approaches. The question has been raised concerning the extent to which multicultural psychotherapy and counseling lean toward changing the individual as opposed to helping the client change the environment. Traditionally, counseling has been directed at the socially and culturally deviant, with the goal of changing client behavior to be more conforming with the norms of the dominant majority group. The situation becomes more complex when counselors consider multicultural situations. Does the counselor prepare the client to change external reality or help the client accommodate to that reality? The increasingly pluralistic society of the 1990s expands the client's options as to the nature of his or her relationships, reference groups, and ethnic and cultural identities. However, this issue continues to be crucial to multicultural counselors who must reach decisions on whether to foster assimilation or to encourage self-development (Draguns, 1981).

The autoplastic-alloplastic distinction has the potential for creating controversy. How much should the client be helped to accept or to change a situation? One has to consider the role of culture in this regard. While Latin-Americans traditionally are socialized to accept and endure life gracefully, North Americans are taught to confront obstacles and, if possible, remove them. Traditionally, the Anglo-American counselor's mandate has been to reorganize and improve the client's personal resources rather than to prepare the client to change the social structure (Draguns, 1989). What then should the counselor do when the client's attainment of goals is blocked by racism or discrimination? Draguns maintained that "correcting the traditionally autoplastic bias in counseling, especially with culturally different clients, is to be welcomed" (p. 15); however, he cautioned that deliberate attempts must be made to prevent the pendulum from swinging too far in the other direction.

Existentialist Approaches

Although counseling usually draws upon psychological theories, the existentialist approach to counseling emphasizes philosophical concepts. Vontress (1988) applied well-known principles of existentialist philosophy to people across cultures. In this global and holistic view, the therapeutic ingredient is the existential encounter, itself. Developing an "I-thou" relationship allows for an exploration of questions that are critical to the client's existence. A FOCUS ON RESEARCH 12–2 takes a closer look at Vontress's existentialist approach.

Ibrahim (1985) contends that existential philosophy enhances multicultural counseling because it respects and recognizes cultural differences as it organizes human experiences in ways that reflect universal concerns of humankind. The counselor's willingness to explore his or her own world view and that of the client is vital to all effective counseling; it is even more important when the counselor and client are from different cultural groups (Casas & Vasquez, 1989).

Communication: Verbal and Nonverbal Language

The outcome of any psychological intervention depends ultimately on the degree to which counselors and clients understand each other. A heightened awareness of the

A FOCUS ON RESEARCH 12–2
An Existentialist Approach to Multicultural Counseling

Vontress (1988) first defines relevant terms, such as existentialism, culture, and multicultural counseling. In contrast to such systematic

Source: Vontress, C. E. (1988). An existentialist approach to cross-cultural counseling. *Journal of Multicultural Counseling and Development, 16*, 73–83.

approaches as behavioral counseling and rational-emotive counseling, existentialist counseling views human beings from a holistic perspective. Vontress explains his existentialist approach with reference to the counselor-client relationship, the diagnosis, and intervention choices.

communication issue is justly deserved, considering that most counselors come from Anglo middle-class backgrounds and are likely to experience difficulty communicating with some clients with culturally different backgrounds (Sue, 1981).

Simply understanding the client's spoken language may not be enough, however. There are other variables that enter into the picture. First, communication styles (both verbal and nonverbal) must be understood. We have already mentioned the Native-American tendency to avoid eye contact, the tendency of some African-Americans to "play it cool" and act "together," the Asian-American confusion as to whether to speak loudly or softly due to contrasting cultural expectations, and the Hispanic-American tendency to maintain allegiance to the mother tongue. Second, the communication issue is further complicated when counselors consider the lifespan period and generation of their clients. The language culturally different children learn in American schools is quite different from the language of the teenage dropout dealing drugs on the street. Moreover, children and adolescents both might differ from adult and elderly clients with respect to language. Older clients are more likely to feel a sense of obligation to remain faithful to their native tongue.

Although all aspects of communication style are in play during a counseling session, some are likely to be more salient than others depending on the individual and the culture. It might be very important with some clients to consider which topics are appropriate to discuss, tone of voice, or taking turns in conversation. Even the arrangement of chairs in the counselor's office could affect a client's response to interaction (Thomas & Althen, 1989).

The complex issue of maintaining effective communication between counselor and client does not allow for broad generalizations. For example, the decision as to whether to seek an interpreter, to speak the client's native language (if the counselor is fluent in the client's language), or to use a respected third-party to assist with communication depends on the individual client, the nature of the client's problems, the extent of the language barrier, and how the client perceives the communication problem.

ISSUE: WHAT ETHICAL AND LEGAL STANDARDS SHOULD GUIDE COUNSELORS?

Counselors have an obligation to abide by the ethical standards discussed in Chapter 2 and to respect other ethical standards subscribed to by the AACD (American Association for Counseling and Development) and the APA (American Psychological Association).

Ethics Associated with Multicultural Counseling

How should Anglo middle-class counselors relate to culturally different clients with differing traditions, values, and customs? How can counselors really know their clients' values and mental health needs? According to Pederson (1988),

> [it is] the ethical responsibility of counselors and therapists to know their clients' cultural values, and the public responsibility of professionals to meet the culturally different mental health needs within a pluralistic society. (p. 80)

The ethical responsibility is not only to understand the differing cultural orientations and values of clients, however. The counselor also is ethically bound to examine cultural biases and stereotypes that plague the culturally different. By gaining knowledge about cultural differences and assessing personal feelings toward the culturally different, the counselor reaches a level of awareness that values are culture-specific rather than right or wrong. That is, it is not for the Anglo middle-class counselor to judge, whether or not values esteemed by those of other cultures are "correct."

LaFromboise and Foster (1989) pointed to several issues related to ethics in multicultural counseling. First, with respect to professional self-regulation, an increasing number of psychologists are contending that the APA ethical guidelines do not adequately reflect racial, cultural, intracultural, socioeconomic, and gender differences. In fact, some areas of ethical decision-making relative to culturally different clients are, for the most part, unexplored. Second, with respect to research, there is debate over the relevance of social science research with culturally different populations and the inseparability of political from ethical issues when working with culturally diverse clients. A third issue concerns ethics of counseling, itself, taking into account, for example, differing beliefs regarding moral behavior and the right of clients to psyhological treatment, regardless of race, culture, or gender.

As Goldman (1986) affirms, there is a growing body of literature on ethical and legal concerns related to counseling. Although few standards of the professional organizations were established with respect to culturally diverse clients in particular, all ethical standards pertaining to the counseling profession and to research involving human subjects apply also to culturally diverse populations. Still, sound judgment must be exercised in selecting research designs. Some questionnaires, for example, appropriate for Anglo-American subjects, may be considered immoral by subjects of other cultures.

Clearly, the many ethical and legal dilemmas surrounding the counseling profession are too complex to summarize here. It is apparent, however, that additional research is warranted to determine the effect of the differing perceptions of ethical matters of majority counselors and their culturally diverse clients. In A FOCUS ON RESEARCH 12–3, the hard choices inherent in ethical decision making are acknowledged.

Writing of future directions in multicultural ethics, LaFromboise and Foster (1989) cite several thoughtful recommendations:

> Rather than trying to resolve ethical dilemmas by reasoning alone, psychologists should seek resolution of ethical dilemmas in the context of dialogue with the community or a balancing of facts and values. (Hillerbrand, 1987)

> [Consider] a more relational view of ethics or a move from a discourse of power of the majority to a new form of dialectical inquiry. (Ivey, 1987)

> [Consider] an ethics promoting the maintenance of relationships, rather than adherence to abstractions in the form of ethical rules. (Noddings, 1984)

> Problems can be viewed in more than one way with people alternating perspectives with different permutations of justice—a reasoned process of relativism. (Gilligan, 1987)

Ethical decisions in counseling relationships become more complex when working with culturally diverse clients who have differing world views and unique perspectives on their lives and sociocultural environments. For counselors to meet the ethical challenges of multicultural counseling, LaFromboise and Foster (1989) rec-

---

 A FOCUS ON RESEARCH 12–3
Controversial Ethical Issues

Perceiving the counselor as a moral agent, Stadler (1986) concerns herself with the moral dimension with which professionals must deal. What is the nature of the moral life? To whom can the counselor turn for guidance in resolving ethical dilemmas? Seeking to answer these and other questions involving ethics, Stadler suggests a four-step decision-making model. Integrating the AACD *Ethical Standards* into the model she proposes, Stadler outlines four steps counselors can take to fulfill clinical responsibilities:

1. Identify competing moral principles.

2. Implement moral reasoning strategy:

   a. secure additional information;
   b. identify special circumstances;
   c. rank moral principles; and
   d. consult with colleagues.

3. Prepare for action:
   a. identify hoped-for outcomes;
   b. brainstorm actions to achieve outcomes;
   c. evaluate effects of actions;
   d. identify competing values;
   e. choose a course of action; and
   f. test the action.

4. Take action
   a. strengthen ego;
   b. identify concrete steps necessary to take action;
   c. act; and
   d. evaluate.

Source: Stadler, H. A. (1986). Making hard choices: Clarifying controversial ethical issues. *Counseling and Human Development, 19*(1), 1–12.

ommend (a) comprehensive training that requires the development of culturally sensitive moral reasoning and (b) modeling of culturally sensitive moral reasoning in the workplace by practitioners, including involvement of community and professional organizations.

Counseling and the Law

As previously mentioned, the absence of a specific body of law and the paucity of court cases pertaining to counseling have resulted in confusion and anxiety concerning the legal boundaries in which counselors practice (Wittmer & Loesch, 1986). What legal concerns confront counselors working with culturally diverse clients? The legal issue of greatest concern for all counselors is professional liability. Charges may include defamation of character, sexual harassment, negligence, misrepresentation of professional service, or battery. A second important legal concern for counselors is privileged communication, a legal concept that protects counselors from having to disclose information they have obtained through counselor-client interactions. The privileged communication concept does not apply when the counselor (a) is acting in a court-appointed capacity, (b) believes the client intends suicide, or (c) is being sued by the client (Wittmer & Loesch, 1986).

ISSUE: DO NOT ALL CLIENTS HAVE SIMILAR BASIC NEEDS AND PROBLEMS?

Professionals counseling culturally different clients have undoubtedly heard questions such as these: Don't clients in all cultures have basically the same needs? Why can't the same techniques be used with all clients? Or questions may arise along these lines: Can an Anglo middle-class counselor effectively counsel a lower-class African-American pregnant teenager? How about an elderly Asian-American? Or a young Hispanic defending his honor and family name? This issue of whether a counselor of one culture can counsel clients of another culture has not been resolved to all counselors' satisfaction.

Whether all clients have basically similar interests and needs continues to be an issue challenging multicultural counselors. The contention that cultural considerations have no place in counseling since human needs and dilemmas cross cultural boundaries, and Lloyd's (1987) contention that what multicultural counselors do not know may actually help them, contradict two basic premises of multicultural counseling. These are (1) that individuals have unique cultural and ethnic differences that deserve consideration in counseling situations and (2) that these ethnic and cultural differences have the potential for affecting the outcome of the counseling process.

The Issue of "Sameness"

According to Smith (1981), the following statement is not uncommon: "I never notice the color of my clients' skin." Or, as a slight variation, "What really counts in counseling is empathy and not the cultural backgrounds of my clients" (p. 161). These statements represent the myth of sameness, a belief holding that all clients are essentially alike. Although the importance of empathy in the counseling process should not be downplayed, counselors should have insight into cultural characteristics and into their own attitudes regarding their clients' cultural backgrounds. Cultural factors influence and often determine how counselors define the needs of their clients. Culture also affects how the counselor perceives his or her role in the counseling process. The stage is set for conflict and misunderstandings when people from one culture expect those from others to think the way they do. To say that minority groups are no different from the majority group or from other minority groups demonstrates a lack of understanding of cultural and individual differences (Hall, 1981).

Can Counselors Effectively Counsel Clients of Differing Cultures?

Schmedinghoff (1977) raises the question, Does the counselor have to share the cultural, racial, and class backgrounds of his or her clients to be effective? The issue of whether counselors can effectively counsel clients of differing cultures has been debated for at least a decade. It is an issue that has yet to be resolved. According to Abramowitz and Murray (1983), "conclusions [run] the gamut from negative through inconclusive to positive" (p. 243). Consider the following findings:

1. In a study by Atkinson et al. (1986), the majority of African-American subjects preferred an ethnically similar counselor over an ethnically dissimilar counselor; however, stronger preferences were exhibited for counselors who were better educated than the subjects, who had similar attitudes, and who had similar personality traits.

2. In a study by Ponterotto, Atkinson, and Hinkston (1988), the majority of African-American subjects considered similarity of attitude to be more important than ethnic similarity.

3. Atkinson (1983) found support for an African-American preference for African-American counselors over Anglo-American counselors.

4. Bernstein, Wade, and Hofmann (1987) reported that both African- and Anglo-American urban university students tended to prefer African-American counselors, regardless of the problem for which counseling was sought.

5. Sanchez and Atkinson (1983) concluded that Mexican-American subjects' preference for racially similar counselors varied, depending on their degree of cultural commitment.

The issue of ethnic group preferences in counseling is further explored in A FOCUS ON RESEARCH 12–4.

In many cases, research findings on the counselor preference issue have been inconclusive. Attempts by researchers to substantiate a particular viewpoint may, in some cases, have contributed to contradictory findings. Future research designs need to address other variables, such as the counselor's prior counseling experiences (Atkinson, 1983). The client's sense of racial identity, social class, and intragroup differences also deserve consideration (Draguns, 1989).

A FOCUS ON RESEARCH 12–4
Ethnic Group Preferences for Counselor Characteristics

Atkinson, Poston, Furlong, and Mercado (1989) used a questionnaire to determine ethnic group preferences for counselor characteristics. The subject pool consisted of Asian-Americans, Mexican-Americans, and Anglo-Americans at two state universities on the West Coast. Findings included the following:

Source: Atkinson, D. R., Poston, W. C., Furlong, M. J., & Mercado, P. (1989). Ethnic group preferences for counselor characteristics. *Journal of Counseling Psychology, 36,* 68–72.

1. For the groups surveyed, ethnicity played a small role in client preferences for counselor characteristics.

2. Preference for an ethnically similar counselor was sometimes less important than preferences for other counselor characteristics.

3. Educational level and attitudes of counselors figured strongly in counsel preferences.

The authors recommended that more attention be given to matching clients and counselors with similar interests and attitudes.

Helms (1984) studied extensively the question of the effects of race on counseling and proposed an interactional stage model for investigating cross- and same-race counseling processes. The model is based on the premise that, regardless of race, people experience a staged process of developing racial consciousness, with the final stage being an acceptance of race as a positive attribute.

Lifespan Differences

The fairly recent attention to lifespan development and the recognition of characteristics associated with each stage have resulted in more appropriate assessment and intervention. Counselors have long recognized that children differ from adults, but only recently have there been serious attempts to provide developmentally appropriate counseling and psychotherapy for adolescents and the elderly. The need for additional scholarly research on counseling and on the lifespan continuum becomes clear in light of the critical differences between lifespan stages and the myriad changes occurring during each stage. Complications arise from the fact that various cultures differ in their perception of lifespan stages. The stages recognized by Anglo-Americans may not correspond to those recognized by other cultural groups.

Intracultural, Generational, Geographical, and Socioeconomic Differences

As mentioned several times in previous chapters, the tremendous diversity among culturally diverse clients makes generalizations difficult. Any number of examples can be offered to provide evidence that culture or ethnicity alone should not be the sole determining factor in reaching professional decisions. For example, there are considerable differences between relatively uneducated, lower-class African-Americans living in the central districts of cities and highly educated, middle-class African-

Americans residing in suburbs. Similarly, differences between first-generation Asian-Americans and later generations may be substantial. Differences may also occur as a function of geographic region of residency. For example, Hispanic-Americans residing in Texas may exhibit characteristics different from those of New York- or Florida-based Hispanics. Counseling professionals should have the knowledge and skill to intervene with individuals within a given culture, recognizing intracultural and individual differences as significant variables in planning appropriate intervention.

ISSUE: WHAT RESEARCH CONCERNS WILL BE RELEVANT IN THE FUTURE?

It goes without saying that counselors should stay abreast of research developments in the field; furthermore, they should conduct research of their own. In reality, however, the majority of counseling practitioners do not participate actively in research endeavors, nor do they always keep up with the latest developments reported in the literature. Clearly, a paucity of quality research poses a problem for multicultural counselors (Goldman, 1986). This section examines some of the research issues that are likely to confront multicultural counselors in the 1990s and beyond.

The Multicultural Counseling Process

What research issues are particularly relevant to the multicultural counseling process? What areas must be considered to provide a more enlightened perspective on counseling culturally different clients? Although research goals and methodologies in the various areas of counseling may be similar, a prerequisite to all research endeavors in a multicultural context is the understanding and acceptance that cultural differences significantly affect outcomes. Also, it must be understood that ethical standards and legal aspects relevant to the counseling profession also apply to research endeavors in multicultural situations.

Assessment

The counselor's goal in assessment is to minimize ethnocentrism and maximize culturally appropriate information. Assessment in counseling and psychotherapy includes interviewing, observing, testing, and analyzing data. A basic question is the extent to which cultural diversity affects assessment. Will a characteristic representative of a specific culture be mistakenly perceived and assessed using Anglo-American middle-class standards? Two important issues in multicultural assessment are (1) whether psychological constructs or concepts are universally valid and (2) the effects of misdiagnosis due to lack of recognition of culture-based factors. Lonner and Sundburg (1985) pose these questions with respect to multicultural assessment:

1. What level and type of assessment is indicated?
2. Which tests are most useful and why?
3. What are the ethical and legal responsibilities associated with multicultural assessment?

![icon] A FOCUS ON RESEARCH 12–5
Issues in Testing and Assessment in Multicultural Counseling

Lonner (1985) considered a number of major issues associated with testing and assessment across cultural or ethnic boundaries. He describes his discussion as "intended for counselors unfamiliar with multicultural methodological problems or the major problems hindering more effective assessment during multicultural

counseling and psychotherapy" (p. 599). Levels of equivalence, nonverbal communication, expectations and beliefs, client-counselor similarities, test biases, and response styles were some of the concerns Lonner addressed. The Minnesota Multiphasic Personality Inventory (MMPI), the Thematic Apperception Test (TAT), and the Peabody Picture Vocabulary Test were all examined with respect to their usefulness in a multicultural context.

Source: Lonner, W. J. (1985). Issues in testing and assessment in cross-cultural counseling. *The Counselling Psychologist, 13,* 599–614.

Another issue facing multicultural counselors is whether testing instruments are culturally appropriate. Are multicultural groups being assessed with instruments designed for middle-class Anglo clients? A FOCUS ON RESEARCH 12–5 takes a brief look at the testing controversy.

Lonner and Ibrahim (1989) maintained that without appropriate assessment strategies, counseling professionals are unable to diagnose problems, unable to develop appropriate goals, and unable to assess the outcomes of intervention. Initial client assessment (e.g., in terms of world view), clinical judgments, standardized and nonstandardized assessment, and the outcomes of counseling evaluation are assessment factors that warrant attention. Simply put, the assessment issue has three broad foci: (1) assessing the client's world views, beliefs, and assumptions; (2) understanding the client's cultural or ethnic group; and (3) using a combination of approaches to understand the nature of the problem.

Research Techniques and Outcomes

Whether counselors employ comparative group research designs, field studies, single-subject studies, or case studies, cultural differences should be taken into account. An important cultural consideration that may have bearing on gathering research data is the possibility of a communication problem (verbal or nonverbal) between researcher and subject. For example, the researcher may construe the Native-American tendency to gaze into space as indicative of boredom, or he or she may not understand an Asian-American's shyness or tendency not to disclose personal information. Or the Hispanic-American's valuing of family over self may be misinterpreted in a variety of ways. Although these represent only selected examples, the point is clear that researchers of one culture may make erroneous judgments with respect to the behavior of culturally different subjects.

Multicultural Counseling and the Lifespan Continuum

Research undoubtedly needs to be directed toward the relationships between multicultural counseling interactions and the client's lifespan stage. These intricate relationships can only be understood by directing research toward (a) the multicultural aspects of the counseling relationship, (b) the actual counselor-client interactions, and (c) the counselor's perception of the client's lifespan stage. Specifically, attention needs to be focused toward the actual effects of culture and the client's developmental period in the multicultural counseling endeavor.

Counselor and Client Cultural Matchups

As stated earlier in this chapter, there is still confusion surrounding the preferences of clients for counselors with certain attributes. Undoubtedly, this controversial topic warrants research. The implications are obvious for community health service personnel, college counseling center personnel, or for counselors working in multicultural settings. Pedersen (1988) reports that several research reviews (Abramowitz & Murray, 1983; Atkinson, 1985; Atkinson & Schein, 1986) have yielded differing opinions regarding the effects of race on psychotherapy. Research by Carkhuff and Pierce (1967), Mitchell (1970), Stanges and Riccio (1970), and LeVine and Campbell (1972) would seem to indicate that counselors and clients should be culturally matched. On the other hand, studies by Gamboa, Tosi, and Riccio (1976), Parloff, Waskow, and Wolfe (1978), Atkinson (1983), and Atkinson, Poston, Furlong, and Mercado (1989) would seem to indicate that counselors and clients do not need to be matched culturally. In fact, the Gamboa, Tosi, and Riccio study concluded that clients actually preferred culturally different counselors. It is an understatement to contend that conclusions regarding counselor-client matchups are difficult to reach and that this issue deserves closer examination.

Research Directions, Tasks, and Challenges

The ultimate determination of counseling effectiveness depends largely on a credible research base. For this base to accrue, studies must seek to synthesize knowledge of culturally diverse clients and knowledge of lifespan differences. According to Pedersen (1988), four research directions will lead to greater multicultural awareness:

1. Research needs to advance approaches to culture and counseling beyond the diffuse and incomplete theoretical basis presently available.
2. Research efforts should identify variables that will explain what has happened, interpret what is happening, and predict what will happen with respect to people, ideas, and cultures.
3. Research needs to identify criteria of expertise for the education and training of professionals counseling in multicultural situations.
4. Research needs to inform counselors of means of providing services based on new counseling theories and new training so that counseling and psychotherapy services can be more equitably distributed among the multicultural society.

   Atkinson (1985) recommends specific directions for research involving the issue of race and ethnicity in the counseling profession:

1. Research on client use and preference for counselor race or ethnicity should focus on within-group differences.

2. Studies need to assess the effect of race and ethnicity on use, diagnosis, and treatment in college counseling settings.

3. Experimental studies need to be conducted to determine the effect of race and ethnicity on diagnosis, treatment, and counseling outcome.

4. Research should examine the relationship between therapist prejudice and differential diagnosis, process, treatment, and outcome.

It is important to note that resolution of research issues will depend on collaborative efforts of scholars and counseling professionals. Practical solutions to counseling dilemmas can emerge only through such collaboration.

Multicultural Counseling Needs

Pedersen (1988) called for improvement in several areas of multicultural counseling:

1. More attention needs to be placed on cultural variables to increase the effectiveness of counseling efforts, to accommodate ethical issues, and to accurately measure counselor competency in multicultural situations.

2. Our understanding of the multicultural dimensions within all counseling situations needs to be increased.

3. Multicultural training needs to be integrated into the core of the counselor education curriculum.

4. More multicultural studies need to be included in professional journals of counseling and psychotherapy.

5. Counseling strategies need to reflect cultural differences to a greater extent.

A POINT OF DEPARTURE

In the coming years, counselors will be faced with unresolved issues and unanswered questions. At least in some cases, this situation will affect the outcome of multicultural counseling and psychotherapy. Let us now take a look at some of the challenges confronting multicultural counselors and consider the options open to counselors in meeting these challenges.

Challenges Confronting Multicultural Counselors

How can multicultural counselors respond to the various unresolved issued in the field? What research priorities should counselors pursue? How can cultural approaches and lifespan approaches be integrated so as to enhance counseling interventions?

Multicultural counselors wanting to better understand how culture, counseling and psychotherapy, and the lifespan approach are interrelated should consider the following recommendations:

1. Seek actively to recognize basic issues pertaining to multicultural situations.
2. Allow for multicultural encounters with clients of all cultures, at all stages of the lifespan.
3. Keep abreast of research studies in journals devoted to counseling and development in multicultural settings.
4. Design and implement your own research studies with culturally different clients.
5. Understand your own cultural background and commit yourself to appreciating cultural differences rather than making value judgments with respect to diversity.

If attention is focused in a methodical and deliberate manner on issues in need of resolution, the effectiveness of the counseling process is likely to increase, even if the issues are not immediately resolved.

SUMMARY

Multicultural counselors in the 1990s will need to (a) provide a rationale for multicultural counseling; (b) deal with the problems of labeling and stereotyping and their adverse effects on clients; (c) consider lifespan issues; (d) assess the effects of cultural diversity on counseling intervention; (e) deal with the issue of "sameness"; (f) recognize the ethical and legal dimensions of counseling; and (g) respond to the need for research based on culture, counseling, and lifespan development. The zeal with which counselors and researchers tackle these tasks will greatly influence counseling efforts in multicultural situations.

Suggested Readings

Atkinson, D. R., Poston, W. C., Furlong, M. J., & Mercado, P. (1989). Ethnic group preferences for counselor characteristics. *Journal of Counseling Psychology, 36,* 68–72. These researchers surveyed Asian-Americans, Mexican–Americans, and Caucasian-Americans to determine ethnic group preferences for counselor characteristics.

Counselor Education and Supervision. (1987). *26*(3). In a format using a stimulus paper, reaction papers, and response papers, this special issue examines various controversial topics concerning multicultural education, such as whether multicultural counseling belongs in counselor education programs.

Das, A. K., & Littrell, J. M. (1989). Multicultural education for counseling: A reply to Lloyd. *Counselor Education and Supervision, 29,* 7–15). Das and Littrell respond to three important points raised by Lloyd in his article questioning the need for multicultural counseling.

Helms, J. E. (1984). Toward a theoretical explanation of the effects of race on counseling: A Black and White model. *The Counseling Psychologist, 12,* 153–164. Helms proposes an interactional stagewise model whereby people accept their race as a positive aspect of their lives.

LaFromboise, T. D., & Foster, S. L. (1989). Ethics in multicultural counseling. In P. B. Pedersen, J. G. Draguns, J. Lonner, & J. E. Trimble (Eds.), *Counseling across cultures* (3rd ed.) (pp. 115–136). Honolulu: University of Hawaii Press. LaFromboise and Foster examine ethical issues in such areas as professional self-regulation, research, and counseling.

Lee, D. J. (1984). Counseling and culture: Some issues. *The Personnel and Guidance Journal, 62,* 592–597. Lee examines several issues related to multicultural counseling including the emic-etic distinction, the sociology of knowledge, and contemporary aspects of counseling.

Pedersen, P. (1988). *A handbook for developing multicultural awareness.* Alexandria, VA: American Association for Counseling and Development. Although all of Pedersen's contemporary text is recommended, Chapter 5 in particular examines research issues related to multicultural counseling.

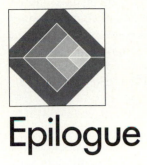

Epilogue

INTRODUCTION

Increased knowledge of cultural diversity and lifespan development and improved understanding of how they are interrelated contribute to better relationships between clients and counselors and to outcomes that are more favorable. The goal of this epilogue is to tie together some of the recurrent themes of the preceding chapters. We will consider the current status of multicultural counseling and related aspects such as lifespan development, individual and intracultural differences among clients, an apparent surge of racism, and the dangers of basing counseling decisions on stereotypes and generalizations.

MULTICULTURAL COUNSELING AND PSYCHOTHERAPY

Its Beginning

Although assigning a "beginning" for multicultural counseling and psychotherapy is difficult, descriptions of the difficulties experienced when counseling African-Americans began to appear in the counseling literature at the start of the 1950s (Jackson, 1987). The growing interest in multicultural counseling over the past several decades is evidenced in the increasing numbers of multicultural studies and in the acceptance of this subspecialty in professional circles. As the United States continues to become ever more diverse culturally, counselors in public agencies, schools, and in private practice will no doubt be challenged to provide effective counseling intervention. Yet many counselors may have been trained in traditional counselor education programs in which assessment and intervention techniques were based on middle-class Anglo standards and expectations.

A Rationale

The rationale for multicultural counseling is clear: Rather than expecting the culturally diverse client to adapt to the counselor's cultural expectations and intervention strategies, multicultural counseling proposes that counselors base intervention on the client's individual, intracultural, gender, socioeconomic, geographical, generational, and lifespan differences. Without doubt, this text has proposed and demonstrated that culturally diverse clients need individual consideration that takes into account both cultural differences and lifespan stage.

Lingering Questions

Although multicultural counseling has continued to gain acceptance in most quarters, some writers (Lloyd, 1987, for one), continue to fuel the debate over whether multicultural training belongs in the counselor education curriculum. Others (Hood & Arceneaux, 1987) vigorously support the subspeciality and raise questions designed to improve the effectiveness of counseling across cultures. As mentioned in A FOCUS ON RESEARCH 12–1, Das and Littrell (1989), in their case for multicultural counseling, suggested that knowledge of cultural backgrounds should help rather than hinder counseling efforts, and that traditional counseling methods might need modification. Multicultural counseling actually benefits from questions regarding its worth. Such questions open the door to dialogue and reflection, adding new perspectives toward counseling culturally diverse clients.

Growing Acceptance: Present and Future

Lee (1989a) maintained that the initial struggles in the field of multicultural counseling have been "fought and won" (p. 165). Considerable other evidence suggests that multicultural counseling is coming of age, and points toward an overall acceptance and a bright future: the growth of the Association of Multicultural Counseling and Development (AMCD) (Lee, 1989a); the *Journal of Multicultural Counseling and Development* (and other prestigious journals listed in the Appendix) the growing numbers of multicultural counseling textbooks; the various conferences and seminars addressing multicultural concerns and issues; the appearance of new college courses designed to enhance the counselor's knowledge and skills; and indications that several universities may soon offer masters degrees or even doctorates in multicultural counseling (Jackson, 1987).

PEOPLE AND THEIR DIVERSITY

To say that American society is growing more diverse is an understatement. Not only is the size of the minority population continuing to increase, we are also seeing an increasing variety of cultures at all stages of the lifespan. From a historical viewpoint, the culturally different have been the recipients of cruel and inhumane treatment. Much has been written about the enormous problems immigrants were faced with upon entering the United States. Consider, too, the unjust treatment of Native-Americans by white settlers. It is difficult to even guess at how many were enslaved or killed. Racism and discrimination continue to exist today, impeding the progress of

African-Americans, Asian-Americans, and Hispanic-Americans, as well as Native-American groups.

Despite the grimness of the historical record, the 1990s can be a time for recognition and acceptance of cultural diversity. Factors that may contribute to such recognition include efforts being directed at youth (e.g., multicultural education courses in elementary and secondary schools); the multicultural emphasis of the National Council for Accreditation of Teacher Education and the Council for Accreditation of Counseling and Related Educational Programs; increasing evidence that the nation actually benefits from cultural diversity; and growing numbers of organizations working to instill cultural pride.

Realities: Racism, Injustice, and Discrimination

As mentioned before, racism and bigotry continue to plague minority groups in the United States. In the fall of 1989, *Newsweek* reported that racial incidents had occurred at 250 colleges since the fall of 1986 (Lessons from bigotry 101 . . . , 1989). Although overt acts of violence and hatred, such as those of the Ku Klux Klan, are not as visible as they were in the past, the more covert forms of racism are currently widespread and continue to affect minorities' progress and well-being. Counselors of all cultures will have to deal with problems resulting from these realities; they will also have to sort through personal biases and long-held misconceptions with respect to race and ethnicity.

AN INCREASING KNOWLEDGE BASE: CULTURAL DIVERSITY AND LIFESPAN

Recognition of Cultural Diversity

The professional literature of the past several decades will increase counselors' knowledge of cultural diversity. More than ever before, counselors have access to objective information describing Native-American, African-American, Asian-American, and Hispanic-American cultural groups. No longer should counseling intervention be based on innaccurate generalizations about culturally different clients. Through personal interaction with minorities and through careful review of pertinent journals, books, and other sources of information, counselors can gain valuable insight into the unique problems of their culturally diverse clients. The Native-American concept of sharing, the African-American unique dialect and extended family, the Asian-American concept of generational and family relationships, and the Hispanic-American *machismo* and commitment to Spanish can provide an accurate basis for counseling intervention. Equally important is the understanding that individuals may vary in the degree to which they represent their culture. Culturally diverse clients vary according to generation, socioeconomic status, geographic location, and other variables.

Knowledge of Human Growth and Development

Counselors can also benefit from the increasing knowledge of lifespan development. No longer should counselors plan assessment and intervention without first considering the client's lifespan period and its unique characteristics, crises, and tasks. For example, the adolescent's view of the role of the family may be quite different from the elderly person's view, or the child's view. The intricate relationship between culture and development can be seen in the generational differences between some younger and older Asian-Americans. Although the work of some developmentalists, e.g., Erikson, Havighurst, and Piaget, may be culturally specific and based on Anglo and middle-class norms, the growing body of developmental literature is providing a sound foundation for counseling across cultures and developmental periods.

Using the Knowledge Base to Enhance Counseling Effectiveness

The benefits of counseling intervention based on lifespan development are numerous. Counselors are better able to plan appropriate strategies if they understand, for example, the minority child's problems growing up in a society that often discriminates against culture and age; the adolescent's need to reconcile peer pressure and family expectations; the adult's frustrations in coping with economic, educational, and employment discrimination; and the multiple jeopardy often faced daily by many minority elderly people.

RESPONDING TO INDIVIDUAL AND CULTURAL DIVERSITY

Differences

Classifying a client by culture or ethnicity actually may say very little about the person. Each client should be considered on an individual basis, with the recognition that intracultural differences and gender, lifespan, generational, socioeconomic, and geographical factors are all relevant in determining the client's uniqueness. Saying someone is an African-American may be true, but it is not enough of a basis on which to plan assessment and intervention. The unemployed African-American male who never finished high school has problems very different from those of the college-educated African-American male working in middle management. Along the same lines, Hispanic culture requires that counselors consider individual populations and individual clients. The Puerto Rican-American living in New York is apt to be quite unlike the Mexican-American residing in southern Texas.

Avoiding Stereotypes and Generalizations

Stereotypes and generalizations have the potential for severely damaging counseling relationships and the outcome of intervention. It should be obvious that all minorities are *not* underachievers, all adolescents are *not* sexually promiscuous, and all elderly people are *not* helpless. However, stereotypic thinking continues to persist, even in people who are well educated and who pride themselves on their logic and reason. The mass media contribute to the problem, albeit for the most part unintentionally. Were one to consider only newspaper and television accounts, it might seem reasonable to assume that most African-Americans were on welfare or were dealing in drugs. In a *Newsweek* report, Raybon (1989) sums up the situation facing minorities. Too often cultural stereotypes and generalizations turn into "truisms"; too often they become the basis for professional decisions affecting personal lives.

Stereotypes and generalizations are not only cultural, they also surround the various lifespan periods. To characterize all children as worry-free, all adolescents as troublemakers, all adults as prone to midlife crises, or all old people as helpless and senile is an affront to individuals all along the lifespan continuum. The expectation that a client will demonstrate certain adverse behaviors due to age may even foster those behaviors.

What steps should be taken to reduce stereotyping and generalization with respect to age groups? First, counselors should learn more about lifespan development and the unique problems of each stage. By so doing, the necessity of basing counseling decisions on accurate and objective information is likely to become clear. Second, counselors should seek first-hand experiences with people along the lifespan continuum. Third, counselors should strive to recognize the severe consequences for their clients of age-related stereotypic thinking.

SEEKING HELP IN A MULTICULTURAL SOCIETY

Tendencies Not to Seek Professional Help

Counselors intervening in multicultural situations should recognize that in some cultures there is a tendency to seek assistance from the immediate and extended family rather than from professionals. Although there are logical reasons for this tendency, counselors are still faced with the need to explain the counseling process and its confidentiality, and to gear the first session to increase the likelihood of clients returning for additional sessions. Some cultural groups may avoid professional help due to a reliance on folk rituals. Others may be reluctant to disclose confidential matters to outsiders. Language and communication difficulties and transportation problems may also be factors. Although it is important for the counselor to be aware of a client's reluctance to seek counseling help, it is even more important to understand the cultural basis for the reluctance. With this understanding, the counselor is better able to foster receptivity to the counseling process and willingness to disclose significant personal information.

Sources of Mental Health Services

Counselors might encounter culturally diverse clients in community mental health agencies, hospitals, schools, or in private practice. Clients might seek counseling because of problems and frustrations associated with acculturation, racism and discrimination, or family relationships. Regardless of the problem or the counseling setting, counselors understanding multicultural groups will be more likely to objectively and accurately address the client's needs.

THE FUTURE: A TIME FOR RESPONSIVE ACTION

Multicultural counseling, lifespan development, and an understanding of the relationship between culture and development have progressed to a point where counseling professionals can take positive action to help culturally diverse clients. To encourage such action, efforts should be directed toward training culturally effective counselors and promoting an enhanced understanding of cultural diversity and lifespan development.

Training Culturally Effective Counselors

Counselors relying solely on strategies traditionally designed for middle-class Anglo adult clients are at a disadvantage in working with culturally diverse clients. The increasing likelihood that counselors will intervene in multicultural situations underscores the need for culturally effective counselors who understand the client's cultural background and who employ strategies that reflect cultural characteristics and expectations. responsive counselor education programs in the 1990s and beyond will take into account the increasing cultural diversity in the United States by providing training and experiences designed to impart the knowledge and skills necessary for effective counseling in multicultural settings.

Recognizing the Relationship between Culture and Lifespan Development

Responsive action also calls for counselor education programs that will assist counselors in recognizing the relationshp between cultural diversity and lifespan development. As previously stated, the elderly Asian-American has unique problems that the African-American child or adolescent has not encountered, or may never encounter. Intervention needs to be based on accurate knowledge of both the client's culture and lifespan period, and, of course, the client's many individual differences.

SUMMARY

Multicultural counseling is beginning to come into its own. Increasing numbers of professionals are recognizing the need to consider a client's cultural background and valued cultural traditions and expectations. Continued advances in the area of lifespan growth and development are enhancing counselors' understanding of the client's developmental period. In the 1990s and beyond, professionals no doubt will be better able to provide counseling services that are culturally and developmentally appropriate. It is hoped, in the years ahead, that the needs and problems culturally diverse clients bring to counseling sessions will increasingly receive the kind of attention they demand.

Appendix

Selected Journals Recommended for Multicultural Counselors

Journal of Multicultural Counseling and Development

Published four times per year by the American Association for Counseling and Development (5999 Stevenson Ave., Alexandria, VA 22304), this journal usually contains six or seven articles and focuses on research, theory, or program application pertinent to multicultural and ethnic minority issues in all areas of counseling and human development.

Counselor Education and Supervision

Published quarterly by the American Association for Counseling and Development, this journal is concerned with matters relevant to the preparation and supervision of counselors in agency or school settings. Multicultural counseling considerations are examined in occasional theme issues, such as that of March 1987 (vol. 26, no. 2).

Journal of Clinical Psychology

Published bimonthly by Clinical Psychology Publishing Company (4 Conant Square, Brandon, VT 05733), this journal directs attention to issues relevant to the clinician. Multicultural studies are occasionally included.

The School Counselor

Published five times per year, *The School Counselor* is another publication of the American Association for Counseling and Development. It focuses primarily on secondary school issues and is geared toward the fields of guidance and counseling.

American Psychologist

Published monthly by the American Psychological Association (1400 North Uhle St., Arlington, VA 22201), this journal focuses on all aspects of counseling and occasionally examines multicultural issues and concerns.

Child Development

Published six times per year by the Journals Division of the University of Chicago Press (57205 Woodland Ave., Chicago, IL 60637), *Child Development* focuses on the development of children of all cultures. Periodically, the journal specifically addresses development in multicultural children; for example, the April 1990 issue features the development of minority children.

Journal of Black Studies

Published four times annually by Sage Publications (2111 West Hillcrest Dr., Newbury Park, CA 91320), this journal discusses and analyzes issues related to people of African descent. Although counseling and development are not usually addressed specifically, this publication does provide a comprehensive examination of the black culture.

Journal of Counseling and Development

Published ten times per year, this journal is also a publication of the American Association for Counseling and Development. It focuses on a broad range of topics for a readership composed of counselors, counseling psychologists, and student personnel specialists. Articles occasionally deal with multicultural issues and concerns. Gender issues are highlighted in the March/April 1990 issue (vol. 68, no. 4).

Journal of Counseling Psychology

Published quarterly by the American Psychological Association, this journal publishes articles reporting the results of empirical studies related to the various counseling areas.

Counseling and Human Development

Published nine times per year, *Counseling and Human Development* examines counseling issues in the context of human development. Published by Love Publishing Company (1777 South Bellaire St., Denver, CO 80222), the journal usually includes a featured article, more extensive than the rest.

Journal of Cross-Cultural Psychology

Published four times annually by Sage Publications, this journal publishes cross-cultural research reports exclusively. The main emphasis is on individual differences and variation among cultures.

Elementary School Guidance and Counseling

Published four times per year by the American School Counselor Association Division of the AACD, this journal examines the role of elementary, middle school, and junior high school counselors. Multicultural issues related to children are frequently addressed.

The Counseling Psychologist

Published quarterly by Sage Publications, this journal is the official publication of the Division of Counseling Psychology of the American Psychological Association. Each issue focuses on a specific theme of importance to the theory, research, and practice of counseling psychology. Special issues on aging (vol. 12, no. 2) and on cross-cultural counseling (vol. 13, no. 4) should be of interest to multicultural counselors.

Daedalus

Published quarterly by the American Academy of Arts and Sciences (136 Irving Street, Cambridge, MA 02138), *Daedalus* includes scholarly articles on contemporary topics of interest. Counselors intervening along the lifespan with culturally diverse clients will be especially interested in the issues on gender (Fall 1987), on aging (Winter 1986), and on cultural diversity (Spring 1981).

Harvard Education Review

The *Harvard Education Review* (Gutman Library, Suite 349, 6 Appian Way, Cambridge, MA 02138–3752), published in February, May, August, and November, features research and opinion in the field of education. Occasionally, articles have particular relevance for multicultural counselors. The August 1988 issue, for example, includes articles on race and the effects of racism on American education. The concerns of African-Americans, Asian-Americans, Latino-Americans, and Native-Americans are discussed.

Phi Delta Kappan

Phi Delta Kappan is published monthly, except in July and August, by Phi Delta Kappa, Inc. (Eighth and Union, P.O. Box 789, Bloomington, IN 47402). The magazine covers a broad range of educational issues. Cultural diversity is featured in the November 1988 issue; in the April 1990 issue, there are several articles on racism.

Teachers College Record

Published quarterly, *Teachers College Record* (Columbia University, 522 West 120 St., New York, NY 10027) focuses primarily on topics pertaining to education. The Spring 1990 issue (vol. 91, no. 2) includes an article on race and ethnicity with respect to teacher education curricula.

Journal of American Indian Education

Published three times per year by the Center for Indian Education (College of Education, Arizona State University, Tempe, AZ 85287–1311), this journal, as its name implies, is devoted to topics related to American Indian education.

The Gerontologist

Published bimonthly by The Gerontological Society of America, *The Gerontologist* (Department 5018, Washington, DC 2001–5018) addresses concerns of the elderly of all cultures. Problems affecting minority cultures in particular are sometimes included.

Journal of Gerontology

Also published bimonthly by the Gerontological Society of America, the *Journal of Gerontology* (1411 K St. NW, Suite 300, Washington, DC 20005) publishes studies in which a variety of theoretical and methodological approaches are employed.

References

Abel, T. (1956). A model for delivery of mental health services to Spanish-speaking minorities. *American Journal of Orthopsychiatry*, *44*, 584–595.

Aborampah, O. M. (1989). Black male-female relationships: Some observations. *Journal of Black Studies*, *19*, 320–342.

Abramowitz, W. I., & Murray, J. (1983). Race effects in psychotherapy. In J. Murray & P. R. Abramson (Eds.), *Bias in psychotherapy* (pp. 215–255). New York: Praeger.

Acosta, F. X., Yamamoto, J., & Evans, L. A. (1982). *Effective psychotherapy for low-income and minority patients*. New York: Plenum.

Agrawal, P. (1978). A cross-cultural study of self-image: Indian, American, Australian, and Irish adolescents. *Journal of Youth and Adolescence*, *7*, 107–116.

Alers, J. O. (1978). *Puerto Ricans and health findings from New York City*. New York: Fordham University Press.

Alvirez, D., & Bean, F. (1976). The Mexican-American family. In C. Mindel & R. Haberstein (Eds.), *Ethnic families in America*. New York: Elsevier Scientific.

American Association for Counseling and Development. (April 1988). *Ethical standards*. Alexandria, VA: American Association for Counseling and Development.

American Association of Retired Persons. (1986). *A portrait of older minorities*. Long Beach, CA: AARP.

America's first . . . (1989). *Census and You*, *24*(3), 1.

Appleton, N. (1983). *Cultural pluralism in America*. New York: Longman.

Aries, P. (1962). *Centuries of childhood*. (R. Baldick, Trans.). New York: Alfred A. Knopf.

Arredondo-Dowd, P. M., & Gonsalves, J. (1980). Preparing culturally effective counselors. *The Personnel and Guidance Journal*, *58*, 657–661.

Asamen, J. K., & Berry, G. L. (1987). Self-concept, alienation, and perceived prejudice: Implications for counseling Asian-Americans. *Journal of Multicultural Counseling and Development*, *15*, 146–160.

Asian and Pacific Islander data: '80 census still producing riches. (1988). *Census and You*, *23*, 3.

Atkinson, D. R. (1983). Ethnic similarity in counseling psychology: A review of the research. *The Counseling Psychologist*, *11*, 79–92.

Atkinson, D. R. (1985). A meta-review of research on cross-cultural counseling and psychotherapy. *Journal of Multicultural Counseling and Development*, *13*, 138–153.

Atkinson, D. R., Furlong, M. J., & Poston, W. C. (1986). Afro-American preference for counselor characteristics. *Journal of Counseling Psychology*, *33*, 326–330.

Atkinson, D. R., & Gim, R. H. (1989). Asian-American cultural identity and attitudes toward mental health services. *Journal of Counseling Psychology*, *36*, 209–212.

Atkinson, D. R., Maruyama, M., & Matsui, S. (1978). The effects of counselor race and counseling approach on Asian Americans' perceptions of counselor credibility and utility. *Journal of Counseling Psychology*, *25*, 76–83.

Atkinson, D. R., Morten, G., & Sue, D. W. (1989). *Counseling American minorities: A cross-cultural perspective* (3rd ed.). Dubuque, IA: Wm. C. Brown.

Atkinson, D. R., Poston, W. C., Furlong, M. J., & Mercado, P. (1989). Ethnic group preferences for counselor characteristics. *Journal of Counseling Psychology*, *36*, 68–72.

Atkinson, D. R., & Schein, S. (1986). Similarity in counseling. *The Counseling Psychologist, 14,* 319–354.

Attneave, C. (1982). American Indians and Alaska native families: Emigrants in the homeland. In M. McGoldrick, J. H. Pearce, & J. Giordano (Eds.), *Ethnicity and family therapy* (pp. 55–83). New York: Guilford.

Aubrey, R. F. (1977). Historical development of guidance and counseling and implications for the future. *Personnel and Guidance Journal, 55,* 288–295.

Axelson, J. A. (1985). *Counseling and development in a multicultural society.* Monterey, CA: Brooks/Cole.

Bakan, D. (1971). Adolescence in America: From idea to social fact. *Daedalus, 100,* 979–996.

Banks, J. A. (1981). *Multiethnic education: Theory and practice.* Boston: Allyn and Bacon.

Banks, J. A. (1987). *Teaching strategies for ethnic studies* (4th ed.). Boston: Allyn and Bacon.

Baratz, S., & Baratz, J. (1970). Early childhood intervention: The social sciences base of institutional racism. *Harvard Educational Review, 40,* 29–50.

Barnett, R. C., & Baruch, G. K. (1978). Women in the middle years: A critique of research and theory. *Psychology of Women Quarterly, 3*(2), 187–197.

Barrow, G., & Smith, P. (1979). *Aging, ageism, and society.* St. Paul, MN: West.

Baruth, L. G., & Robinson, E. H. (1987). *An introduction to the counseling profession.* Englewood Cliffs, NJ: Prentice-Hall.

Basch, C. E., & Kersch, T. B. (1986). Adolescent perceptions of stressful life events. *Health Education, 17,* 4–7.

Battes, V. A. (1982). Theory related to specific issues: Modern racism—a TA perspective. *Transactional Analysis Journal, 12,* 207–209.

Baughman, E. E. (1971). *Black Americans.* New York: Academic.

Beale, A. V. (1986). A cross-cultural dyadic encounter. *Journal of Multicultural Counseling and Development, 14,* 73–76.

Beck, M., Hager, M., Beachy, L., & Joseph, N. (1990, March 12). Be nice to your kids. *Newsweek,* pp. 72–75.

Begley, S., Hager, M., & Murr, A. (1990, March 5). The search for the Fountain of Youth. *Newsweek,* pp. 44–48.

Bell-Scott, P., & McKenry, P. C. (1986). Black adolescents and their families. In G. K. Leigh & G. W. Peterson (Eds.), *Adolescents in Families* (pp. 410–432). Cincinnati, OH: South-Western.

Bengston, V. L., Kasschau, P. L., & Ragen, P. K. (1977). The impact of social structure on aging individuals. In J. E. Birren & K. W. Schale (Eds.), *Handbook of the psychology of aging.* New York: Van Nostrand Reinhold.

Bennett, C. I. (1986). *Comprehensive multicultural education: Theory and practice.* Boston: Allyn and Bacon.

Berman, J. (1979). Counseling skills used by black and white male and female counselors. *Journal of Counseling Psychology, 26,* 81–84.

Bernal, G. (1982). Cuban families. In M. McGoldrick, J. H. Pearce, & J. Giordano (Eds.), *Ethnicity and family therapy* (pp. 187–207). New York: Guilford.

Bernstein, B. L., Wade, P. D., & Hofmann, B. (1987). Students' race and preferences for counselor's race, sex, age and experience. *Journal of Multicultural Counseling and Development, 15,* 60–70.

Berry, E., & Ojeda, M. (1985). Hispanic women and health care: *Intercultural communication: A reader* (pp. 180–186). Belmont, CA: Wadsworth.

Biehler, R. F., & Snowman, J. (1990). *Psychology applied to teaching* (6th ed.). Boston: Houghton Mifflin.

Billingsley, A. (1968). *Black families in white America.* Englewood Cliffs, NJ: Prentice-Hall.

Black and White in America. (1988, March 7). *Newsweek,* pp. 18–23.

Black male's life expectancy is declining.... (1989, June 6). *The Charlotte Observer,* p. 8A.

Black population is growing.... (1988, June). *Census and You, 23*(6), 3–4.

Blacks and Hispanics trail Whites in college-going rate, study finds. (1987, December 16). *The Chronicle of Higher Education,* p. A25.

Blatt, I. (1976) Counseling the Puerto Rican client:

Special considerations. In G. S. Belkin (Ed.), *Counseling: Directions in theory and practice* (pp. 291–298). Dubuque, IA: Kendall/Hunt.

Block, C. B. (1981). Black Americans and the cross-cultural counseling and psychotherapy experience. In A. J. Marsella & P. B. Pedersen (Eds.), *Cross-cultural counseling and psychotherapy* (pp. 177–194). Elmsford, NY: Pergamon.

Bond, M. H., & Shirashi, N. (1974). The effect of body lean and status of an interviewer on the nonverbal behavior of Japanese interviewees. *International Journal of Psychology, 9*(2), 117–128.

Boykin, A. W. (1982). Task variability and the performance of black and white schoolchildren. *Journal of Black Studies, 12,* 469–485.

Bradley, L. R., & Stewart, M. A. (1982). The relationship between self-concept and personality development in Black college students: A developmental approach. *Journal of Non-White Concerns in Personnel and Guidance, 4,* 114–125.

Brandell, J. R. (1988). Treatment of the biracial child: Theoretical and clinical issues. *Journal of Counseling and Development, 16,* 176–187.

Brislin, R. W. (1981). *Cross-cultural encounters.* Elmsford, NY: Pergamon.

Broman, C. L. (1988). Satisfaction among Blacks: The significance of marriage and parenthood. *Journal of Marriage and the family, 50,* 45–51.

Brower, I. C. (1980). Counseling Vietnamese. *The Personnel and Guidance Journal, 58,* 646–652.

Brown, J. L. (1987), Hunger in the United States. *Scientific American, 256*(2), 37–41.

Brubaker, T. H. (1983). *Family relationships in later life.* Beverly Hills, CA: Sage.

Butler, R. N. (1974). Successful aging. *Mental Hygiene, 58,* 6–12.

Butler, R. N. (1975). *Why survive? Being old in America.* New York: Harper and Row.

Butler, R. N. (1987). Ageism. In G. L. Maddox (Ed.), *The encyclopedia of aging* (pp. 22–23). New York: Springer.

Butler, R. N., & Lewis, M. I. (1982). *Aging and mental health* (3rd. ed.). St. Louis, MO: Mosby.

Carkhuff, R. R., & Pierce, R. (1967). Differentiated effects of therapist race and social class upon patient depth of self-exploration in the initial clinical interview. *Journal of Consulting Psychology, 31,* 632–634.

Carter, T. P. (1968). Negative self-concepts of Mexican-American students. *School and Society, 96,* 217–219.

Casas, J. M. (1976). Applicability of a behavioral model in serving the mental health needs of the Mexican American. In M. R. Miranda (Ed.), *Psychotherapy with the Spanish speaking: Issues in research and service delivery* (pp. 61–65). Los Angeles: Spanish-Speaking Mental Health Center.

Casas, J. M. (1985). A reflection on the status of racial/ethnic minority research. *The Counseling Psychologist, 13,* 581–598.

Casas, J. M., & Vasquez, M. J. T. (1989). Counseling the Hispanic client: A theoretical and applied perspective. In P. B. Pedersen, J. G. Draguns, J. Lonner, & J. E. Trimble (Eds.), *Counseling across cultures* (3rd ed.) (pp. 153–175). Honolulu: University of Hawaii Press.

Cayleff, S. E. (1986). Ethical issues in counseling gender, race and culturally distinct groups. *Journal of Counseling and Development, 64,* 345–347.

Chen, P. N. (1979). A study of Chinese-American elderly residing in hotel rooms. *Social Casework: The Journal of Contemporary Social Work, 60,* 89–95.

Cherbosque, J. (1987). Differences between Mexican and American clients in expectations about psychological counseling. *Journal of Multicultural Counseling and Development, 15,* 110–114.

Children's Defense Fund. (1987). *A children's defense budget: An analysis of the FY '87 federal budget and children.* Washington, DC: Author.

Christensen, E. W. (1977). When counseling Puerto Ricans. *Personnel and Guidance Journal, 55,* 412–415.

Christensen, E. W. (1989). Counseling Puerto Ricans: Some cultural considerations. In D. R. Atkinson, G. Morten, & D. W. Sue (Eds.), *Counseling American minorities* (3rd. ed.) (pp. 205–212). Dubuque, IA: Wm. C. Brown.

Clark-Johnson, G. (1988). Black children. *Teaching Exceptional Children, 20,* 46–47.

Closing the education gap for Hispanics: State aims to forestall a divided society. (1987, September 16). *The Chronicle of Higher Education,* p. 1.

Closing the gap for U.S. Hispanic youth. (1988). Report from the 1988 Aspen Institute Conference on Hispanic Americans and the Business Community. Washington, DC: The Hispanic Policy Development Project.

Cohler, B. J., & Grunebaum, H. U. (1981). *Mothers, grandmothers and daughters: Personality and socialization within three-generation families.* New York: Wiley-Interscience.

Coladarci, T. (1983). High-school dropouts among Native-Americans. *Journal of American Indian Education, 23,* 15–21.

Colburn, D., & Melillo, W. (1987, June 16). Hispanics: A forgotten health population. *Washington Post,* p. 16.

Cole, S. M., Thomas, A. R., & Lee, C. C. (1988). School counselor and school psychologist: Partners in minority family outreach. *Journal of Multicultural Counseling and Development, 16,* 110–116.

Coley, S. M., & Beckett, J. O. (1988). Black battered women: A review of empirical literature. *Journal of Counseling and Development, 66,* 266–270.

Comas-Diaz, L. (1981). Effects of cognitive and behavioral group treatment of the depressive symptomatology of Puerto Rican women. *Journal of Consulting and Clinical Psychology, 49,* 627–632.

Comer, J. P. (1988). Establishing a positive racial identity. *Parents, 63*(3), 167.

Conger, J. J. (1977). *Adolescence and youth* (2nd ed.). New York: Harper & Row.

Cook, D. A., & Helms, J. E. (1988). Visible racial/ethnic group supervisees' satisfaction with cross-cultural supervision as predicted by relationship characteristics. *Journal of Counseling Psychology, 35,* 268–274.

Cook, J. A. (1983). The hydra-headed nature of prejudice: Research perspectives concerning cross-cultural counseling with elementary aged children. *Elementary School Guidance and Counseling, 17,* 294–300.

Copeland, E. J. (1982). Minority populations and traditional counseling programs: Some alternatives. *Counselor Education and Supervision, 21,* 187–193.

Corvin, S. A., & Wiggins, F. (1989). An antiracism training model for White professionals. *Journal of Multicultural Counseling and Development, 17,* 105–114.

Cox, H. (1984). *Later life: The realities of aging.* Englewood Cliffs, NJ: Prentice-Hall.

Dancy, J. (1977). *The black elderly: A guide for practitioners.* Ann Arbor, MI: University of Michigan-Wayne State University.

Danish, S. J. (1981). Life-span human development and intervention: A necessary link. *The Counseling Psychologist, 9,* 40–43.

Das, A. K., & Littrell, J. M. (1989). Multicultural education for counseling: A reply to Lloyd. *Counselor Education and Supervision, 29,* 7–15.

Dauphinais, P. A., LaFromboise, T., & Rowe, W. (1980). Perceived problems and sources of help for American Indian students. *Counselor Education and Supervision, 19,* 37–44.

Davis, F. J. (1978). *Minority-dominant relations: A sociological analysis.* Arlington Heights, IL: AHM Publishing.

Demos, J., & Demos, V. (1969). Adolescence in historical perspective. *Journal of Marriage and the Family, 31,* 632–638.

Devereux, G. (1951). Three technical problems in psychotherapy of Plains Indians. *American Journal of Psychotherapy, 5,* 411–423.

Devereux, G. (1953). Cultural factors in psychoanalytic therapy. *Journal of the American Psychoanalytic Association, 1*(4), 629–635.

Dillard, J. L. (1972). *Black English: Its history and usage in the United States.* New York: Random House.

Dillard, J. M. (1985). *Multicultural counseling* (rev. ed.). Chicago: Nelson-Hall.

Divoky, D. (1988). The model minority goes to school. *Phi Delta Kappan, 70,* 219–222.

Dorris, M. A. (1981). The grass still grows, the rivers still flow: Contemporary Native-Americans. *Daedalus, 110*(2), 43–69.

Draguns, J. G. (1976). Counseling across cultures: Common themes and distinct approaches. In

P. B. Pedersen, W. J. Lonner, & J. G. Draguns (Eds.), *Counseling across cultures* (pp. 3–23). Honolulu: The University of Hawaii Press.

Draguns, J. G. (1981). Cross-cultural counseling and psychotherapy: History, issues, current status. In A. J. Marsella & P. B. Pedersen (Eds.), *Cross-Cultural Counseling and Psychotherapy* (pp. 3–27). Elmsford, NY: Pergamon.

Draguns, J. G. (1989). Dilemmas and choices in cross-cultural counseling: The universal versus the culturally distinctive. In P. B. Pedersen, J. G. Draguns, J. Lonner, & J. E. Trimble (Eds.), *Counseling across cultures* (3rd ed.) (pp. 1–21). Honolulu: University of Hawaii Press.

DuBois, D. L., & Hirsch, B. J. (1990). School and neighborhood friendship patterns of Blacks and Whites in early adolescence. *Child Development, 61,* 524–536.

Edelman, M. W. (1989). Black children in America. In J. Dewart (Ed.), *The state of Black America* (pp. 63–76). New York: National Urban League.

Edwards, D. E., & Edwards, M. E. (1989). American Indians: Working with individuals and groups. In D. R. Atkinson, G. Morten, & D. W. Sue (Eds.), *Counseling American minorities: A cross-cultural perspective* (3rd. ed.) (pp. 72–84). Dubuque, IA: Wm. C. Brown.

Elderly and AIDS—forgotten patients? *Modern Maturity.* (1988, June/July), p. 17.

Elkind, D. (1984). Erik Erikson's eight stages of man. In H. E. Fitzgerald & M. G. Walveren (Eds.), *Human Development 84/85* (pp. 11–18). Guilford, CT: Dushkin.

Erikson, E. (1950). *Childhood and society.* New York: Norton.

Erikson, E. (1968). *Identity: Youth and crisis.* New York: Norton.

Erikson, E. (1980). *Identity and the life cycle.* New York: Norton.

Everett, F., Proctor, N., & Cartmell, B. (1989). Providing psychological services to American Indian children and families. In D. R. Atkinson, G. Morten, & D. W. Sue (Eds.), *Counseling American minorities* (pp. 53–71). Dubuque, IA: Wm. C. Brown.

Exum, H. A., & Lau, E. Y. (1988). Counseling style

preference of Chinese college students. *Journal of Multicultural Counseling and Development, 16,* 84–92.

Falicov, C. J. (1982). Mexican families. In M. McGoldrick, H. H. Pearce, & J. Giordano (Eds.), *Ethnicity and family therapy* (pp. 134–163). New York: Guilford.

Fernandez, J. P. (1981). *Racism and sexism in corporate life.* Lexington, MA: D. C. Heath.

Fernandez, M. S. (1988). Issues in counseling Southeast Asian students. *Journal of Multicultural Counseling and Development, 16,* 157–166.

Ferraro, K. F. (1987). Double jeopardy to health for Black older Americans. *Journal of Gerontology, 42,* 528–533.

First, J. M. (1988). Immigrant students in U.S. public schools: Challenges with solutions. *Phi Delta Kappan, 70,* 205–210.

Fitting, M. D. (1986). Ethical dilemmas in counseling elderly adults. *Journal of Counseling and Development, 64,* 325–327.

Fitzpatrick, J. P. (1987). *Puerto Rican Americans: The meaning of migration to the mainland* (2nd ed.). Englewood Cliffs, NJ: Prentice-Hall.

Fletcher, J. D. (1983). What problems do American Indians have with English? *Journal of American Indian Education, 23,* 1–12.

Folkenberg, J. (1986). Mental health of Southeast Asians. *ADAMHA News, 12*(1), 10–11.

Frisbie, W. P. (1986). Variation in patterns of marital instability among Hispanics. *Journal of Marriage and the Family, 48,* 99–106.

Fu, V. R., Korslund, M. K., & Hinkle, D. E. (1980). Ethnic self-concept during middle childhood. *Journal of Psychology, 105,* 99–105.

Fujii, S. M. (1976). Elderly Asian Americans and use of public services. *Social Casework, 57,* 202–207.

Gamboa, A. M., Tosi, D. J., & Riccio, A. C. (1976). Race and counselor climate in the counselor preference of delinquent girls. *Journal of Counseling Psychology, 23,* 160–162.

Garcia-Preto, N. (1982). Puerto Rican families. In M. McGoldrick, J. K. Pearce, & J. Giordano (Eds.), *Ethnicity and family therapy* (pp. 164–186). New York: Guilford.

Gatz, M. (1989). Clinical psychology and aging. *The Psychology of Aging.* Washington, DC: American Psychological Association.

Gelman, D., Hager, M., & Guade, V. (1989, December 18). The brain killer. *Newsweek,* pp. 54–56.

Gibbs, J. T. (1973). Black students–White university: Different expectations. *Personnel and Guidance Journal, 51,* 463–469.

Gibson, J. T. (1978). *Growing up: A study of children.* Reading, MA: Addison-Wesley.

Gill, W. (1990). African-American: What's in a name? *Educational Leadership, 48*(1), 85.

Gilligan, C. (1987). Moral orientation and moral development. In E. F. Kittany & D. T. Meyers (Eds.), *Women and moral theory* (pp. 19–33). Totowa, NJ: Rowman and Littlefield.

Glazer, N., & Moynihan, D. P. (1970). *Beyond the melting pot: The Negroes, Puerto Ricans, Jews, Italians, and Irish of New York city* (2nd ed.). Cambridge, MA: The MIT Press.

Gold, M., & Petronio, R. J. (1980). Delinquent behavior in adolescence. In J. Adelson (Ed.), *Handbook of adolescent psychology* (pp. 495–535). New York: John Wiley.

Goldman, L. (1986). Research and evaluation. In M. D. Lewis, R. L. Hayes, & J. A. Lewis (Eds.), *An introduction to the counseling process* (pp. 278–300). Itasca, IL: F. E. Peacock.

Gollnick, D. M., & Chinn, P. C. (1990). *Multicultural education in a pluralistic society* (3rd. ed.). Columbus, OH: Merrill.

Gonzalez, E. (1989). Hispanics bring "corazon" and "sensibilidad," *Momentum, 20*(1), 10–13.

Gordon, M. M. (1964). *Assimilation in American life.* New York: Oxford University Press.

Gordon, M. M. (1978). *Human nature, class, and ethnicity.* New York: Oxford University Press.

Grambs, J. D. (1981). Teaching about ethnicity and the immigrant experience. *Education Digest, 47*(4), 39–42.

Grant, A. F., & Grant, A. (1982). Children under stress: What every counselor should know. *Journal of Non-White Concerns in Personnel and Guidance, 11,* 17–23.

Grant, C. A., & Sleeter, C. E. (1986, April). Race, class

and gender in educational research: An argument for integrative analysis. Paper presented at the meeting of the American Educational Research Association, San Francisco, CA.

Graubard, S. R. (1976). Preface to the issue "Adulthood." *Daedalus, 105,* v–viii.

Green, J. W. (1982). *Cultural awareness in the human services.* Englewood Cliffs, NJ: Prentice-Hall.

Guadin, J. M., & Davis, K. B. (1985). Social network of black and white rural families: A research report, *Journal of Marriage and the Family, 47,* 115–121.

Gunnings, T. S., & Lipscomb, W. D. (1986). Psychotherapy for Black men: A systematic approach. *Journal of Multicultural Counseling and Development, 14,* 17–24.

Gutierrez, J., & Sameroff, A. (1990). Determinants of complexity in Mexican-American and Anglo-American mothers' conceptions of child development. *Child Development, 61,* 384–394.

Hale-Benson, J. E. (1986). *Black children: Their roots, culture, and learning styles.* Baltimore, MD: The Johns Hopkins University Press.

Hall, E. T. (1981). *Beyond culture.* Garden City, NY: Anchor.

Harrison, D. K. (1975). Race as a counselor-client variable in counseling and psychotherapy: A review of the research. *Counseling Psychologist, 5,* 124–133.

Hartman, J. S., & Askounis, A. C. (1989). Asian-American students: Are they really a "model minority"? *The School Counselor, 37,* 109–111.

Havighurst, R. J. (1970). Minority subcultures and the law of effect. *American Psychologist, 25,* 313–322.

Havighurst, R. J. (1972). *Developmental tasks and education* (3rd ed.). New York: McKay.

Havighurst, R. J. (1979). *Developmental tasks and education* (4th ed.). New York: Longman.

Hays, W. C., & Mendel, C. H. (1973). Extended kinship relations in Black and white families. *Journal of Marriage and the Family, 35,* 51–56.

Helms, J. E. (1984). Toward a theoretical explanation of the effects of race on counseling: A Black and White model. *The Counseling Psychologist, 12,* 153–164.

Hendricks, J., & Hendricks, C. D. (1981). *Aging in mass society: Myths and realities.* Cambridge, MA: Winthrop.

Hernandez, H. (1989). *Multicultural education—A teacher's guide to content and practice.* Columbus, OH: Merrill.

Herring, R. D. (1989a). The American Native family: Dissolution by coercion. *Journal of Multicultural Counseling and Development, 17,* 4–13.

Herring, R. D. (1989b). Counseling Native-American children: Implications for elementary school counselors. *Elementary School Guidance and Counseling, 23,* 272–281.

Hill, R. (1989). Critical issues for Black families by the year 2000. In J. Dewart (Ed.), *The state of Black America 1989* (pp. 41–61). New York: National Urban League.

Hillerbrand, E. (1987). Philosophical tensions influencing psychology and social action. *American Psychologist, 42,* 111–118.

Hines, P. M., & Boyd-Franklin, N. (1982). Black families. In M. McGoldrick, J. K. Pearce, & J. Giordano (Eds.), *Ethnicity and family therapy* (pp. 84–107). New York: Guilford.

Ho, M. K. (1987). *Family therapy with ethnic minorities.* Newbury Park, CA: Sage.

Hodge, J. L. (1975). Domination and the will in Western thought and culture. In J. L. Hodge, D. K. Struckmann, & L. D. Trost (Eds.), *Cultural bases of racism and group oppression* (pp. 9–48). Berkeley, CA: Two Riders.

Hodge, J. L., Struckman, D. K., & Trost, L. D. (1975). *Cultural bases of racism and group oppression.* Berkeley, CA: Two Riders.

Holland, S. H. (1987). Positive primary education for young Black males. *The Education Digest, 53*(3), 56–58.

Holmes, T., & Rahe, R. (1967). The social readjustment rating scale. *Journal of Psychosomatic Research, 11,* 213–218.

Hood, A. B., & Arceneaux, C. (1987). Multicultural counseling: Will what you don't know help you? *Counselor Education and Supervision, 26,* 173–175.

Hsu, F. L. K. (1971). *The challenge of the American dream: The Chinese in the United States.* Belmont, CA: Wadsworth.

Huang, L. J. (1976). The Chinese American family. In C. H. Mindel & W. Haberstein (Eds.), *Ethnic families in America: Patterns and variations* (pp. 124–147). New York: Elsevier.

Ibrahim, F. A. (1985). Effective cross-cultural counseling and psychotherapy: A framework. *The Counseling Psychologist, 13,* 625–638.

Ibrahim, F. A., & Arrendondo, P. M. (1986). Ethical standards for cross-cultural counseling: Counselor preparation, practice, and research. *Journal of Counseling and Development, 64,* 349–352.

Ibrahim, F. A., & Kahn, H. (1984). Scale to assess world views (SAWV). Typescript. University of Connecticut, Storrs.

Ibrahim, F. A., & Kahn, H. (1987). Assessment of world views. *Psychological Reports, 60,* 163–176.

Indian tribes, incorporated. (1988, December 8). *Newsweek,* pp. 40–41.

Inouye, D. K. (1988). Children's mental health issues. *American Psychologist, 43,* 813–816.

Intercultural Development Research Association. (1976). *Handbook for teachers of Vietnamese students.* San Antonio, TX: Author.

Isen, H. G. (1983). Assessing the Black child. *Journal of Non-White Concerns, 11,* 47–58.

Ishii, S. (1973). Characteristics of Japanese nonverbal communicative behavior. *Journal of the Communication Association of the Pacific,* pp. 2, 3.

Ivey, A. E. (1986). *Developmental therapy: Theory into practice.* San Francisco: Jossey-Bass.

Ivey, A. E. (1987). Cultural intentionality: The core of effective helping. *Counselor Education and Supervision, 25,* 168–172.

Ivey, A. E., & Authier, J. (1978). *Microcounseling: Innovations in interviewing training.* Springfield, IL: Charles Thomas.

Ivey, A. E., Ivey, M. B., & Simek-Downing, L. (1986). *Counseling and psychotherapy: Integrating skills, theory and practice.* Englewood Cliffs, NJ: Prentice-Hall.

Ivey, A. E., Ivey, M. B., & Simek-Downing, L. (1987). *Counseling and psychotherapy* (2nd. ed.). Englewood Cliffs, NJ: Prentice-Hall.

Jackson, J. (1970). Aged Negroes: Their cultural departures from statistical and rural-urban differences. *Gerontologist, 10,* 140–145.

Jackson, J. (1980). *Minorities and aging.* Belmont, CA: Wadsworth.

Jackson, J. (1982). The Black elderly: Reassessing the plight of older Black women. *The Black Scholar, 13*(1), 2–4.

Jackson, M., & Wood, J. (1976). *Aging in America, No. 5: Implications for the black aged.* Washington, DC: National Council on Aging.

Jackson, M. C. (1987). Cross-cultural counseling at the crossroads: A dialogue with Clemmont E. Vontress. *Journal of Counseling and Development, 66,* 20–23.

Jacobs, J. E. (1988). Ageism: Forgotten Americans. *Vital Speeches of the Day, 54*(11), 332–335.

Janosik, E. H. (Ed.). (1984). *Crisis counseling: A contemporary approach.* Belmont, CA: Wadsworth.

Jaynes, G. D., & Williams, R. M. (1989). *A common destiny: Blacks and American society.* Washington, DC: National Academic Press.

Jenkins, A. H. (1982). *The psychology of the Afro-Americans: A humanistic approach.* Elmsford, NY: Pergamon.

Jensen, A. (1969). How much can we boost IQ and school achievement? *Harvard Educational Review, 39,* 1–123.

Jensen, J. V. (1985). Perspective on nonverbal intercultural communiction. In L. A. Samovar & R. E. Porter (Eds.), *Intercultural communication: A reader* (4th ed.) (pp. 256–272). Belmont, CA: Wadsworth.

Johnson, S. D. (1987). Knowing that versus knowing how: Toward achieving expertise through multicultural training for counseling. *The Counseling Psychologist, 15,* 320–331.

Johnson, S. D. (1990). Toward clarifying *culture, race,* and *ethnicity* in the context of multicultural counseling. *Journal of Multicultural Counseling and Development, 18,* 41–50.

Jones, E. E. (1985). Psychotherapy and counseling with Black clients. In P. B. Pedersen (Ed.), *Handbook of cross-cultural counseling and therapy* (pp. 173–179). Westport, CT: Greenwood.

Kalish, R., & Moriwaki, S. (1973). The world of the elderly Asian American. *Journal of Social Issues, 29,* 187–209.

Kantrowitz, B. (1989, December 18). Trapped inside her own world. *Newsweek,* pp. 56–58.

Kart, C. S. (1985). *The realities of aging: An introduction to gerontology.* Boston: Allyn and Bacon.

Katz, J. H. (1985). The sociopolitical nature of counseling. *Counseling Psychologist, 13,* 615–624.

Ka-Wai, Y. R., & Tinsley, R. (1981). International and American expectancies about counseling. *Journal of Counseling Psychology, 28,* 66–69.

Keller, J. F., & Hughston, G. A. (1981). *Counseling the elderly: A systems approach.* New York: Harper and Row.

Kent, D. (1971). Changing welfare to serve minority. In *Minority aged in America* (pp. 73–91). Ann Arbor, MI: Institute of Gerontology.

Kessen, W. (1979). The American child and other cultural inventions. *American Psychologist, 34,* 815–820.

Keyes, K. L. (1989). The counselor's role in helping students with limited English proficiency. *The School Counselor, 37,* 144–148.

Kiev, A. (1964). *Magic, faith, & healing.* Glencoe, IL: Free Press.

Kim, B. (1973). Asian-Americans: No model minority. *Social Casework, 18,* 44–53.

Kitano, H. H. L. (1974). *Race relations.* Englewood Cliffs, NJ: Prentice-Hall.

Kitano, H. H. L. (1981). Counseling and psychotherapy with Japanese-Americans. In A. J. Marsella & P. B. Pedersen (Eds.), *Cross-cultural counseling and psychotherapy* (pp. 228–242). Elmsford, NY: Pergamon.

Kitano, H. H. L. (1989). A model for counseling Asian-Americans. In P. B. Pedersen, J. G. Draguns, J. Lonner, & J. E. Trimble (Eds.), *Counseling across cultures* (3rd ed.) (pp. 139–151). Honolulu: University of Hawaii Press.

Klovekorn, M. R., Madera M., & Nardone, S. (1974). Counseling the Cuban child. *Elementary School Guidance and Counseling, 8,* 255–260.

Kluckhohn, C. (1951). Values and value orientation in a theory of action. In T. Parsons & E. A. Shields

(Eds.), *Toward a general theory of action* (pp. 338–433). Cambridge, MA: Harvard University Press.

Kluckhohn, C. (1956). Toward a comparison of value-emphases in different cultures. In L. D. White (Ed.), *The state of the social sciences* (pp. 116–132). Chicago: University of Chicago Press.

Kluckhohn, F. R., & Strodtbeck, F. L. (1961). *Variations in value orientation*. Evanston, IL: Row, Patterson.

Knight, G. P., & Kagan, S. (1977). Acculturation of prosocial and competitive behaviors among second- and third-generation Mexican-American children. *Journal of Cross-Cultural Psychology, 8,* 273–284.

Knight, G. P., Kagan, S., Nelson, W., & Gumbiner, J. (1978). Acculturation of second- and third-generation Mexican-American children: Field dependence, locus of control, self-esteem, and school achievement. *Journal of Cross-Cultural Psychology, 9,* 87–98.

Kostelnik, M. J., Stein, L. C., Whiren, A. P., & Soderman, A. K. (1988). *Guiding children's social development*. Monterey, CA: Brooks/Cole.

Kuczen, B. (1982). *Childhood stress: Don't let your child become a victim*. New York: Delacorte.

LaFrance, M., & Mayo, C. (1978). Cultural aspects of nonverbal communication: A review essay. *International Journal of Intercultural Relations, 2,* 71–89.

LaFromboise, T. D., & Foster, S. L. (1989). Ethics in multicultural counseling. In P. B. Pedersen, J. G. Draguns, J. Lonner, & J. E. Trimble (Eds.), *Counseling across cultures* (3rd ed.) (pp. 115–136). Honolulu: University of Hawaii Press.

Lamarine, R. J. (1987). Self-esteem, health locus of control, and health attitudes among Native-American children. *Journal of School Health, 57,* 371–373.

Larrabee, M. J. (1986). Helping reluctant Black males: An affirmation approach. *Journal of Multicultural Counseling and Development, 14,* 25–38.

Lazarus, P. J. (1982). Counseling the Native-American child: A question of values. *Elementary School Guidance and Counseling, 17,* 83–88.

Lee, C. C. (1982). The school counselor and the Black child: Critical roles and functions. *Journal of Non-White Concerns, 10,* 94–101.

Lee, C. C. (1989a). AMCD: The next generation. *Journal of Multicultural Counseling and Development, 17,* 165–170.

Lee, C. C. (1989b). Editorial: Who speaks for multicultural counseling? *Journal of Multicultural Counseling and Development, 17,* 2–3.

Lee, C. C., & Lindsey, C. R. (1985). Black consciousness development: A group counseling model for Black elementary school students. *Elementary School Guidance & Counseling, 19,* 228–236.

Lee, D. J. (1984). Counseling and culture: Some issues. *The Personnel and Guidance Journal, 62,* 592–597.

Lefley, H. P. (1989). Counseling refugees: The North American experience. In P. B. Pedersen, J. G. Draguns, J. Lonner, & J. E. Trimble (Eds.), *Counseling across cultures* (3rd ed.) (pp. 243–266). Honolulu: University of Hawaii Press.

Lefrancois, G. R. (1981). *Adolescents* (2nd ed.). Belmont, CA: Wadsworth.

Leong, F. T. L. (1986). Counseling and psychotherapy with Asian-Americans: Review of the literature. *Journal of Counseling Psychology, 33,* 196–206.

Lessons from bigotry 101. . . . (1989, September 25). *Newsweek*, pp. 48–49.

Leung, K., & Drasgow, F. (1986). Relationship between self-esteem and delinquent behavior in three ethnic groups. *Journal of Cross-Cultural Psychology, 17,* 151–166.

Levine, R., & Campbell, D. (1972). *Ethnocentrism: Theories of conflict, ethnic attitudes and group behavior*. New York: John Wiley.

Levine, E. S., & Padilla, A. M. (1980). *Crossing cultures in therapy: Pluralistic counseling for the Hispanic*. Monterey, CA: Brooks-Cole.

Levy, S. M., Derogatis, L. R., Gallagher, D., & Gatz, M. (1981). Intervention with older adults and evaluation of outcome. In L. W. Poon (Ed.), *Aging in the 1980's: Psychological issues* (pp. 41–61). Washington, DC: American Psychological Association.

Lewis, R. C., & Ho, M. K. (1975). Social work with Native-Americans. *Social Work, 20,* 379–382.

Lewis, R. G., & Ho, M. K. (1989). Social work with Native Americans. In D. R. Atkinson, G. Morten, & D. W. Sue (Eds.), *Counseling American minorities* (3rd ed.) (pp. 65–72). Dubuque, IA: Wm. C. Brown.

Light, H. K., & Martin, R. E. (1986). American Indian families. *Journal of American Indian Education, 26*(1), 1–5.

Liu, W. T. (1986). Health services for Asian elderly. *Research on Aging, 8,* 156–175.

Locke, D. C. (1989). Fostering the self-esteem of African-American children. *Elementary School Guidance and Counseling, 23,* 254–259.

Lloyd, A. P. (1987). Multicultural counseling: Does it belong in the counselor education program? *Counselor Education and Supervision, 26,* 164–167.

Lloyd, M. A. (1985). *Adolescents.* New York: Harper and Row.

Lonner, W. J. (1985). Issues in testing and assessment in cross-cultural counseling. *The Counseling Psychologist, 13,* 599–614.

Lonner, W. J., & Ibrahim, F. A. (1989). Assessment in cross-cultural counseling. In P. B. Pedersen, J. G. Draguns, J. Lonner, & J. E. Trimble (Eds.), *Counseling across cultures* (3rd ed.) (pp. 299–333). Honolulu: University of Hawaii Press.

Lonner, W. J., & Sundberg, N. D. (1985). Assessment in cross-cultural counseling and therapy. In P. B. Pedersen (Ed.), *Handbook of cross-cultural counseling and therapy* (pp. 173–179). Westport, CT: Greenwood.

Lum, D. (1986). *Social work practice and people of color: A process-stage approach.* Monterey, CA: Brooks/Cole.

McAdoo, H. P. (1978). Factors related to stability in upward mobile Black families. *Journal of Marriage and the Family, 40,* 761–776.

McConahay, J. B., Hardee, B. B., & Battes, V. (1981). Has racism declined in America? *Journal of Conflict Resolution, 25,* 563–579.

McCormick, T. E. (1984). Multiculturalism: Some principles and issues. *Theory into Practice, 23,* 93–97.

McCubbin, M. J., & Patterson, J. M. (1986). Adolescent stress, coping, and adaptation: A normative family perspective. In G. K. Leigh & G. W. Peterson (Eds.), *Adolescents in families* (pp. 256–276). Cincinnati, OH: South-Western.

McFadden, J. (1976). Stylistic dimensions of counseling Blacks. *Journal of Non-White Concerns, 5,* 23–28.

McNatt, R. (1984, January). The first annual economic outlook for Black America. *Black Enterprise,* pp. 28–30.

McPherson, J. R., Lancaster, D. R., & Carroll, J. C. (1978). Stature change with aging in Black-Americans. *Journal of Gerontology, 33,* 20–25.

Madsen, W. (1973). *The Mexican-Americans of South Texas* (2nd ed.). New York: Holt, Rinehart & Winston.

Maes, W. R., & Rinaldi, J. R. (1974). Counseling the Chicano child. *Elementary School Guidance and Counseling, 8,* 279–284.

Maier, H. W. (1969), *Three theories of child development* (rev. ed.). New York: Harper & Row.

Malde, S. (1988). Guided autobiography: A counseling tool for older adults. *Journal of Counseling and Development, 66,* 290–293.

Maldonado, D. (1975). The Chicano aged. *Social Work, 56,* 213–216.

Margolin, G. (1982). Ethical and legal considerations in marital and family therapy. *American Psychologist, 37,* 788–801.

Maruyama, M. (1978). Psychotopology and its applications to cross-disciplinary, cross-professional, and cross-cultural communication. In R. E. Holloman & S. A. Arutlunow (Eds.), *Perspectives on ethnicity* (pp. 23–75). The Hague: Mouton.

Maslow, A. H. (1968). *Toward a psychology of being* (2nd ed.). Princeton, NJ: Van Nostrand.

Mboya, M. M. (1986). Black adolescents: A descriptive study of their self-concepts and academic achievement. *Adolescence, 21,* 689–696.

Mendelberg, H. E. (1986). Identity conflict in Mexican-American adolescents. *Adolescence, 21,* 215–224.

Miller, N. B. (1982). Social work services to urban Indians. In J. W. Green (Ed.), *Cultural awareness in the human services* (pp. 157–183). Englewood Cliffs, NJ: Prentice-Hall.

Minatoya, L. Y., & Higa, Y. (1988). Women's attitudes and behaviors in American, Japanese, and cross-cultural marriages. *Journal of Multicultural Counseling and Development, 16,* 45–62.

Mindel, H. C., & Habenstein, R. W. (1981). Family lifestyles of America's ethnic minorities: An introduction. In C. H. Mindel & R. W. Habenstein (Eds.), *Ethnic families in America: Patterns and variations* (pp. 1–13). New York: Elsevier.

Mio, J. S. (1989). Experiential involvement as an adjunct to teaching cultural sensitivity. *Journal of Multicultural Counseling and Development, 17,* 38–46.

Mirandé, A. (1986). Adolescence and Chicano families. In G. K. Leigh & G. W. Peterson (Eds.), *Adolescents in families* (pp. 433–455). Cincinnati, OH: South-Western.

Mitchell, H. (1970). The Black experience in higher education. *The Counseling Psychologist, 2,* 30–36.

Mitchum, N. T. (1989). Increasing self-esteem in Native-American children. *Elementary School Guidance and Counseling, 23,* 266–271.

Montagu, A. (1974). *Man's most dangerous myth: The fallacy of race.* New York: Oxford University Press.

Morrow, R. D. (1989). Southeast-Asian parental involvement: Can it be a reality? *Elementary School Guidance and Counseling, 23,* 289–297.

Munroe, R. L., & Munroe, R. H. (1975). *Cross-cultural human development.* Monterey, CA: Brooks/Cole.

Naditch, M. P., & Morrissey, R. F. (1976). Role stress, personality, and psychopathology in a group of immigrant adolescents. *Journal of Abnormal Psychology, 85,* 113–118.

National Black Child Development Institute, Inc. (1986). *1986 NBCDI annual report.* Washington, DC: Author.

Neighbors, H., Jackson, J., Bowman, P., & Gurin, G. (1982). Stress, coping, and black mental health: Preliminary findings from a national study. *Prevention in Human Services, 2,* 5–29.

Neimeyer, G. J., & Fukuyama, M. (1984). Exploring the content and structure of cross-cultural attitudes. *Counselor Education and Supervision, 23,* 214–224.

The new whiz kids: Why Asian-Americans are doing so well, and what it costs them. (1987, August 31). *Time,* pp. 42–51.

Nieves, W., & Valle, M. (1982). The Puerto Rican family: Conflicting roles for the Puerto Rican college student. *Journal of Non-White Concerns in Personnel and Guidance, 4,* 154–160.

Nobles, W. W., & Goddard, L. L. (1989). Drugs in the African-American community: A clear and present danger. In J. Dewart (Ed.), *The state of Black America 1989* (pp. 161–181). Washington, DC: National Urban League.

Noddings, N. (1984). *Caring: A feminine approach to ethics and moral education.* Berkeley: University of California Press.

Offer, D., Ostriv, E., & Howard, K. I. (1977). The self-image of adolescents: A study of four cultures. *Journal of Youth and Adolescence, 6,* 265–280.

Ogbu, J. U. (1978). *Minority education and caste.* New York: Academic.

Ohlsen, M. M. (1983), *Introduction to counseling.* Itasca, IL: F. E. Peacock.

Olsen, L. (1988). Crossing the schoolhouse border: Immigrant children in California. *Phi Delta Kappan, 70,* 211–218.

Olvera-Ezzell, N., Power, T. G., & Cousins, J. H. (1990). Maternal socialization of children's eating habits: Strategies used by obese Mexican-American mothers. *Child Development, 61,* 395–400.

Omizo, M. M., & Omizo, S. A. (1989). Counseling Hawaiian children. *Elementary School Guidance and Counseling, 23,* 282–288.

Orr, E. W. (1987). *Twice as less: Black English and the performance of Black students in mathematics and science.* New York: Norton.

Ortiz, C. G., & Nuttall, E. V. (1987). Adolescent pregnancy: Effects of family support, education, and religion on the decision to carry or terminate among Puerto Rican teenagers. *Adolescence, 22,* 897–917.

Osako, M. M., & Liu, W. T. (1986). Intergenerational relations and the aged among Japanese-Americans. *Research on Aging, 8,* 128–155.

Padilla, A. M. (1981). Pluralistic counseling and psychotherapy for Hispanic Americans. In A. J. Marsella & P. B. Pedersen (Eds.), *Cross-Cultural Counseling and Psychotherapy* (pp. 195–227). Elmsford, NY: Pergamon.

Palacios, M., & Franco, J. N. (1986). Counseling Mexican-American women. *Journal of Multicultural Counseling and Development, 14,* 124–131.

Palmore, E. (1975). What can the USA learn from Japan about aging? *The Gerontologist, 15,* 64–67.

Pang, V. O., Mizokawa, D. T., Morishima, J. K., & Olstad, R. G. (1985). Self-concepts of Japanese-American children. *Journal of Cross-Cultural Psychology, 16,* 99–109.

Papalia, D. E., & Olds, S. W. (1987). *A child's world.* New York: McGraw-Hill.

Papalia, D. E., & Olds, S. W. (1989). *Human development.* New York: McGraw-Hill.

Parham, T. A., & McDavis, R. J. (1987). Black men, an endangered species: Who's really pulling the trigger? *Journal of Counseling and Development, 66,* 24–27.

Parloff, M. B., Waskow, I. E., & Wolfe, B. E. (1978). Research on therapist variables in relation to process and outcome. In S. Garfield & A. Bergin (Eds.), *Handbook of psychotherapy and behavior change* (pp. 233–282). New York: John Wiley.

Pearson, J. L., Hunter, A. G., Ensminger, M. E., & Kellam, S. G. (1990). Black grandmothers in multigenerational households: Diversity in family structure and parenting involvement in the Woodlawn community. *Child Development, 61,* 434–442.

Pedersen, P. B. (1978). Four dimensions of cross-cultural skill in counselor training. *The Personnel and Guidance Journal, 56,* 480–484.

Pedersen, P. B. (1987). Ten frequent assumptions of cultural bias in counseling. *Journal of Multicultural Counseling and Development, 15,* 16–24.

Pedersen, P. B. (1988). *A handbook for developing multicultural awareness.* Alexandria, VA: American Association of Counseling and Development.

Pedersen, P. B. (1990). The constructs of complexity and balance in multicultural counseling theory and practice. *Journal of Counseling and Development, 68,* 550–554.

Pedersen, P. B., Draguns, J. G., Lonner, J., & Trimble, J. E. (1989). *Counseling across cultures* (3rd ed.). Honolulu: University of Hawaii Press.

Pedersen, P. B., Fukuyama, M., & Heath, A. (1989). Client, counselor, and contextual variables in multicultural counseling. In P. B. Pedersen, J. G. Draguns, J. Lonner, & J. E. Trimble (Eds.), *Counseling across cultures* (3rd ed.) (pp. 23–52). Honolulu: University of Hawaii Press.

Pedersen, P. B., & Marsella, A. (1982). The ethical crisis for cross-cultural counseling and therapy. *Professional Therapy, 13,* 492–500.

Perry, J. L., & Locke, D. C. (1985). Career development of Black men: Implications for school guidance services. *Journal of Multicultural Counseling and Development, 13,* 106–118.

Peterson, J. L., & Marin, G. (1988). Issues in the prevention of AIDS among Black and Hispanic men. *American Psychologist, 43,* 871–877.

Peterson, J. V., & Nisenholz, B. (1987). *Orientation to counseling.* Boston: Allyn and Bacon.

Peterson, M. R., Rose, C. L., & McGee, R. I. (1985). A cross-cultural health study of Japanese and Caucasian elders in Hawaii. *International Journal of Aging and Human Development, 21,* 267–279.

Piggrem, G. W., & Schmidt, L. D. (1982). Counseling the elderly. *Counseling and Human Development, 14*(10), 1–12.

Pinkney, A. (1975). *Black Americans.* Englewood Cliffs, NJ: Prentice-Hall.

Plantz, M. C., Hubbell, R., Barrett, B. J., & Dobrec, A. (1989). Indian child welfare: A status report. *Children Today, 18*(1), 24–29.

Ponterotto, J. G. (1986). A content analysis of the *Journal of Multicultural Counseling and Development. Journal of Multicultural Counseling and Development, 14,* 98–107.

Ponterotto, J. G. (1987). Counseling Mexican-Americans: A multimodal approach. *Journal of Multicultural Counseling and Development, 65,* 308–312.

Ponterotto, J. G. (1988). Racial consciousness development among white counselor trainees: A stage model. *Journal of Multicultural Counseling and Development, 16,* 146–156.

Ponterotto, J. G., Atkinson, D. R., & Hinkston, J. H. (1988). Afro-American preferences for counselor characteristics: A replication and extension. *Journal of Counseling Psychology, 35,* 175–182.

Ponterotto, J. G., & Casas, J. M. (1987). In search of multicultural competence within counselor education programs. *Journal of Counseling and Development, 65,* 430–434.

Ponterotto, J. G., & Sabnani, H. B. (1989). "Classics" in multicultural counseling: A systematic five-year content analysis. *Journal of Multicultural Counseling and Development, 17,* 23–37.

Porter, R. E., & Samovar, L. A. (1985). Approaching intercultural communication. In L. A. Samovar & R. E. Porter (Eds.), *Intercultural communication: A reader* (pp. 15–30). Belmont, CA: Wadsworth.

Pregnancy + alcohol = problems. (1989, July 31). *Newsweek,* p. 57.

Prince, R. H. (1976). Psychotherapy as the manipulation of endogenous healing mechanisms: A transcultural survey. *Transcultural Psychiatric Research Review, 13,* 115–134.

Proshansky, H., & Newton, P. (1968). The nature and meaning of Negro self-identity. In M. Deutsch, I. Katz, & A. R. Jensen (Eds.), *Social class, race, and psychological development* (pp. 178–218). New York: Holt, Rinehart & Winston.

Rainwater, L. (1970). *Behind ghetto walls: Black family life in a federal slum.* Chicago: Aldine.

Raybon, P. (1989, October 2). A case of "severe bias." *Newsweek,* p. 11.

Red Horse, J. G., Lewis, R., Feit, M., & Decker, J. (1978). Family behavior of urban American Indians. *Social Casework, 59,* 57–72.

Reed, S. (1984). Stress: What makes kids vulnerable? *Instructor, 93,* 28–32.

Reglin, G. L., & Adams, D. R. (1990). Why Asian-American high school students have higher grade point averages and SAT scores than other high school students. *The High School Journal, 73,* 143–149.

Reveron, D. (1982). Racism. *APA Monitor, 13,* 7.

Reynolds, D. K., & Kalish, R. A. (1974). Anticipation of futurity as a function of ethnicity and age. *Journal of Gerontology, 29,* 224–231.

Richardson, E. H. (1981). Cultural and historical perspectives in counseling Indians. In D. W. Sue, *Counseling the culturally different* (pp. 216–255). New York: John Wiley.

Riessman, F. (1962). *The culturally deprived child.* New York: Harper & Row.

Rogers, D. (1982). *The adult years: An introduction to aging.* Englewood Cliffs, NJ: Prentice-Hall.

Rosenberg, M. (1979). *Conceiving the self.* New York: Basic Books.

Rotenberg, K. J., & Cranwell, F. R. (1989). Self-concepts in American Indian and White children. *Journal of Cross-Cultural Psychology, 29,* 39–53.

Rotheram-Borus, M. J., & Phinney, J. S. (1990). Patterns of social expectations among Black and Mexican-American children. *Child Development, 6,* 542–556.

Rotter, J. (1975). Some problems and misconceptions related to the construct of internal versus external control of reinforcement. *Journal of Consulting and Clinical Psychology, 43,* 56–67.

Rubin, R. H. (1977). *Family structure and peer-group affiliation as related to attitudes about male-female relations among black youth.* San Francisco: R & E Associates.

Ruiz, R. A. (1981). Cultural and historical perspectives in counseling Hispanics. In D. W. Sue, *Counseling the culturally different.* (pp. 186–215). New York: John Wiley.

Ruiz, R. A., & Casas, J. M. (1981). Culturally relevant behavioristic counseling for Chicano college students. In P. B. Pedersen, J. G. Draguns, W. J. Lonner, & J. E. Trimble (Eds.), *Counseling across cultures* (2nd ed.) (pp. 181–202). Honolulu: University of Hawaii Press.

Ruiz, R. A., & Padilla, A. M. (1977). Counseling Latinos. *Personnel and Guidance Journal, 55,* 401–408.

Sachs, A. (1990, March 19). To my family, my physician, my lawyer and all others whom it may concern. *Time,* p. 68.

Saeki, C., & Borow, H. (1985). Counseling and psychotherapy: East and West. In P. B. Pedersen (Ed.), *Handbook of cross-cultural counseling and therapy* (pp. 223–229). Westport, CT: Greenwood.

Samovar, L. A., & Porter, R. E. (Eds.). (1985). *Intercultural communication: A reader* (4th ed.). Belmont, CA: Wadsworth.

Sampson, R. J. (1987). Urban Black violence: The effect of male joblessness and family disruption. *The American Journal of Sociology, 93,* 348–382.

Sanchez, A. R., & Atkinson, D. R. (1983). Mexican-American cultural commitment, preference for counselor ethnicity and willingness to use counseling. *Journal of Counseling Psychology, 30,* 215–220.

Sanders, D. (1987). Cultural conflicts: An important factor in the academic failures of American Indian students. *Journal of Multicultural Counseling and Development, 15,* 81–90.

Santrock, J. W. (1989). *Life-span development* (3rd ed.). Dubuque, IA: Wm. C. Brown.

Santrock, J. W. (1990). *Adolescence* (4th ed.). Dubuque, IA: Wm. C. Brown.

Satir, V. (1967). *Conjoint family therapy* (2nd ed.). Palo Alto, CA: Science & Behavior Books.

Sattler, J. M. (1977). The effects of therapist-client racial similarity. In A. S. Gurman & A. M. Razin (Eds.), *Effective psychotherapy: A handbook of research* (pp. 252–290). Elmsford, NY: Pergamon.

Scanzoni, J. (1977). *The Black family in modern society.* Chicago: University of Chicago Press.

Schiamberg, L. B. (1986). A family systems perspective to adolescent alienation. In G. K. Leigh, & G. W. Peterson (Eds.), *Adolescents in families* (pp. 277–307). Cincinnati, OH: South-Western.

Schmedinghoff, G. J. (1977). Counseling the Black student in higher education. Is it a racial, socioeconomic, or human question? *Journal of College Student Personnel, 18,* 472–477.

Schwertfger, M. (1982). Interethnic marriage and divorce in Hawaii. In G. Crester & J. Leon (Eds.), *Intermarriage in the United States* (pp. 119–135). New York: Haworth Press.

Sebring, D. L. (1985). Considerations in counseling interracial children. *Journal of Non-White Concerns in Personnel and Guidance, 13,* 3–9.

Seligman, M. (1975). *Helplessness on depression, development, and death.* San Francisco: W. H. Freeman.

Shockley, W. (1972). *Journal of Criminal Law and Criminology, 7,* 530–543.

Shon, S. P., & Ja, D. Y. (1982). Asian families. In M. McGoldbrick, J. K. Pearce, & J. Giordano (Eds.), *Ethnicity and family therapy* (pp. 208–228). New York: Guilford.

Simmons, R. G., Brown, L., Bush, D. M., & Blyth, D. A. (1978). Self-esteem and achievement in black and white adolescents. *Social Problems, 26*(1), 86–89.

Sire, J. W. (1976). *The universe next door.* Downers Grove, IL: Intervarsity.

Sleeter, C. E., & Grant, C. A. (1988). *Making choices for multicultural education: Five approaches to race, class, and gender.* Columbus, OH: Merrill.

Smart, M. S., & Smart, R. C. (1982). *Children: Development and relationships* (rev. ed.). New York: Macmillan.

Smith, E. J. (1981). Cultural and historical perspectives in counseling Blacks. In D. W. Sue, *Counseling the culturally different* (pp. 141–185). New York: John Wiley.

Smith, E. J. (1985). Counseling Black women. In P. B. Pedersen (Ed.). *Handbook of cross-cultural counseling and therapy* (pp. 181–187). Westport, CT: Greenwood.

Smith, E. J., & Smith, P. M. (1986). The Black female single-parent family condition. *Journal of Black Studies, 17,* 125–134.

Smith, G. S., Barnes, E., & Scales, A. (1974). Counseling the Black child. *Elementary School Guidance and Counseling, 8,* 245–253.

So, A. Y. (1987). Hispanic teachers and the labeling of Hispanic students. *The High School Journal, 71,* 5–8.

Sotomayor, M. (1971). Mexican-American interaction with social systems. *Social Casework, 52,* 321.

Stadler, H. A. (1986). Making hard choices: Clarifying controversial ethical issues. *Counseling and Human Development, 19*(1), 1–12.

Stanges, B., & Riccio, A. (1970). A counselee preference for counselors: Some implications for counselor education. *Counselor Education and Supervision, 10,* 39–46.

Staples, R. (1976). The Black American family. In C. H. Mindel & R. W. Habenstein (Eds.), *Ethnic families in America* (pp. 217–245). New York: Elsevier.

Staples, R. (1987). Social structure and Black family life: An analysis of current trends. *Journal of Black Studies, 17,* 267–286.

Stevenson, H. W., Chen, C., & Uttal, D. H. (1990). Beliefs and achievement: A study of Black, White and Hispanic children. *Child Development, 61,* 508–523.

Sue, D. W. (1975). Asian-Americans: Social-psychological forces affecting lifestyles. In S. Picou & R. Campbell (Eds.), *Career behavior of special groups.* Columbus, OH: Merrill.

Sue, D. W. (1978a). Counseling across cultures. *The Personnel and Guidance Journal, 56,* 451.

Sue, D. W. (1978b). Eliminating cultural oppression in counseling: Toward a general theory. *Journal of Counseling Psychology, 25,* 419–428.

Sue, D. W. (1978c). World views and counseling. *Personnel and Guidance Journal, 56,* 458–462.

Sue, D. W. (1981). *Counseling the culturally different.* New York: John Wiley.

Sue, D. W. (1989). Ethnic identity: The impact of two cultures on the psychological development of Asians in America. In D. R. Atkinson, G. Morten, & D. W. Sue (Eds.), *Counseling American minorities: A cross-cultural perspective* (3rd ed.) (pp. 103–115). Dubuque, IA: Wm. C. Brown.

Sue, D. W., Bernier, J. E., Durran, A., Feinberg, L., Pedersen, P. B., Smith, E. J., & Vasquez-Nuttail, E. (1982). Position paper: Cross-cultural counseling competencies. *The Counseling Psychologist, 10*(2) 45–52.

Sue, D. W., & Kirk, B. A. (1972). Psychological characteristics of Chinese-American college students. *Journal of Counseling Psychology, 6,* 471–478.

Sue, D. W., & Kirk, B. A. (1973). Differential characteristics of Japanese-American and Chinese-American college students. *Journal of Counseling Psychology, 20,* 142–148.

Sue, D. W., & Sue, S. (1983). Counseling Chinese-Americans. In D. R. Atkinson, G. Morten, & D. W. Sue (Eds.), *Counseling American minorities: A cross-cultural perspective* (2nd ed.) (pp. 97–106). Dubuque, IA: Wm. C. Brown.

Sue, S., & McKinney, H. (1975). Asian Americans in the community mental health care system. *American Journal of Orthopsychiatry, 45,* 111–118.

Sue, S., & Zane, N. (1987). The role of cultural and cultural techniques in psychotherapy. *American Psychologist, 42,* 37–45.

Suzuki, B. H. (1989). Asian-American as the "Model Minority": Outdoing Whites? Or media hype? *Change, 21*(6), 13–19.

Swensen, I., Erickson, D., Ehlinger, E., Swaney, S., & Carlson, G. (1986). Birth weight, Apgar scores, labor and delivery complications and prenatal characteristics of Southeast Asian adolescents and older mothers. *Adolescence, 21,* 711–722.

Swinton, D. H. (1989). Economic status of Black Americans. In J. Dewart (Ed.), *The state of Black America 1989* (pp. 9–39). New York: National Urban League.

Tanfer, K., & Horn, M. C. (1985). Contraceptive use, pregnancy, and fertility patterns among single women in their 20's. *Family Planning Perspectives, 17*(1), 10–19.

Taylor, R. J. (1986). Religious participation among elderly Blacks. *The Gerontologist, 26,* 630–636.

Tein-Hyatt, J. L. (1986–1987). Self-perceptions of aging across cultures: Myth or reality? *International Journal of Aging and Human Development, 24,* 129–146.

Tempest, P. (1987). The physical, environmental, and intellectual profile of the fifth grade Navajo. *Journal of American Indian Education, 26*(3), 29–40.

Terrell, F., Terrell, S. L., & Taylor, J. (1988). The self-concept level of Black adolescents with and without African names. *Psychology in the Schools, 25,* 65–70.

Thomas, K., & Althen, G. (1989). Counseling foreign students. In P. B. Pedersen, J. G. Draguns, J. Lonner, & J. E. Trimble (Eds.), *Counseling across cultures* (3rd ed.) (pp. 205–241). Honolulu: University of Hawaii Press.

Thomas, A., & Sullen, S. (1972). *Racism and psychiatry.* New York: Brunner/Mazel.

Thompson, C. L., & Rudolph, L. B. (1988). *Counseling children* (2nd ed.). Monterey, CA: Brooks/Cole.

Thornburg, H. (1982). *Development in adolescence.* Monterey, CA: Brooks/Cole.

Thurman, P. J., Martin, D., & Martin, M. (1985). An assessment of attempted suicides among adolescent Cherokee Indians. *Journal of Multicultural Counseling and Development, 13,* 176–182.

Torres-Gil, F. (1976). *Political behavior: A study of political attitudes and political participation among older Mexican Americans.* Unpublished doctoral dissertation, Brandeis University, Waltham, MA.

Tracey, T. J., Leong, F. T. L., & Glidden, C. (1986). Help seeking and problem solving among Asian-Americans. *Journal of Counseling Psychology, 33,* 331–336.

Trimble, J. E., & Fleming, C. M. (1989). Providing counseling services for Native American Indians:

Client, counselor, and community characteristics. In P. B. Pedersen, J. G. Draguns, J. Lonner, J. & J. E. Trimble (Eds.), *Counseling across cultures* (3rd ed.) (pp. 177–204). Honolulu: University of Hawaii Press.

Trimble, J. E., & Hayes, S. A. (1984). Mental health intervention in the psychological contexts of American Indian communities. In W. A. O'Conner & B. Lubin (Eds.), *Ecological models: Applications to clinical and community health* (pp. 293–321). New York: John Wiley.

Trimble, J. E., Mackey, D. H., LaFromboise, T. D., & France, G. A. (1983). American Indians, psychology, and curriculum development. In J. C. Chunn, P. J. Dunston, & F. Ross-Sheriff (Eds.), *Mental health and people of color: Curriculum development and change* (pp. 43–64). Washington, DC: Howard University Press.

Tucker, B., & Huerta, C. (1987). A study of developmental tasks as perceived by young adult Mexican-American females. *Lifelong Learning: An Omnibus of Practice and Research, 10*(4), 4–7.

Tucker, M. B., & Mitchell-Kernan, C. (1990). New trends in Black-American interracial marriage: The social structural context. *Journal of Marriage and the Family, 52,* 209–218.

Tung, T. M. (1985). Psychiatric care for Southeast Asians: How different is different? In T. Owan (Ed.), *Southeast Asian mental health: Treatment, prevention, services, training, and research* (pp. 5–40). Washington, DC: National Institute of Mental Health.

Turner, J. S., & Helms, D. B. (1983). *Lifespan development* (2nd ed.). New York: Holt, Rinehart & Winston.

U. S. Bureau of the Census. (1980). *Census of the population, Vol. 1: General population characteristics,* PC 80-1-B. Washington, DC: U.S. Government Printing Office.

U. S. Bureau of the Census. (1986). Current population reports, Series P-25, No. 985. *Estimates of the population of the United States, by age, sex, and race: 1980–1985.* Washington, DC: U. S. Government Printing Office.

U. S. Bureau of the Census. (1988a). Current population reports, Series P-20, No. 431. *The Hispanic population of the United States: March 1988.* Washington, DC: U. S. Government Printing Office.

U. S. Bureau of the Census. (1988b). *Statistical abstracts of the United States: 1988* (108th ed.). Washington, DC: U. S. Government Printing Office.

U. S. Bureau of the Census. (1989). *Statistical Abstracts of the United States: 1989* (109th ed.). Washington, DC: U. S. Government Printing Office.

U. S. Commission on Civil Rights. (1975). *The Navajo nation: An American colony.* Washington, DC: Author.

Valero-Figueira, E. (1988). Hispanic children. *Teaching Exceptional Children, 20,* 47–49.

Vontress, C. E. (1970). Counseling Blacks. *Personnel and Guidance Journal, 48,* 713–719.

Vontress, C. E. (1971). *Counseling Negroes.* Boston: Houghton-Mifflin.

Vontress, C. E. (1976a). Counseling middle-aged and aging cultural minorities. *Personnel and Guidance Journal, 55,* 132–135.

Vontress, C. E. (1976b). Counseling the racial and ethnic minorities. In G. S. Belkin (Ed.), *Counseling: Directions in theory and practice* (pp. 277–290). Belmont, CA: Wadsworth.

Vontress, C. E. (1986). Social and cultural foundations. In M. D. Lewis, R. L. Hayes, & J. A. Lewis (Eds.), *An introduction to the counseling profession* (pp. 215–250). Itasca, IL: F. E. Peacock.

Vontress, C. E. (1988). An existential approach to cross-cultural counseling. *Journal of Multicultural Counseling and Development, 16,* 73–83.

Waking up to a nightmare: Hispanics confront the growing threat of AIDS. (1988, December 8). *Newsweek,* pp. 24, 29.

Walker, J. L. (1988). Young American Indian children. *Teaching Exceptional Children, 20,* 50–51.

Walker, J. R., & Hamilton, L. S. (1973). A Chicano/Black/White encounter. *The Personnel and Guidance Journal, 51,* 471–477.

Walter, J., & Miles, J. H. (1982). Black students' perceptions of counseling appropriateness: A preliminary study. *Journal of Non-White Concerns in Personnel and Guidance, 4,* 133–142.

Wardle, F. (1987). Are you sensitive to interracial children's special identity needs? *Young Children, 42*(2), 53–59.

Warfield, J. L., & Marion, R. L. (1985). Counseling the Black male. *Journal of Non-White Concerns, 13,* 54–71.

Watanabe, C. (1973). Self-expression and the Asian-American experience. *Personnel and Guidance Journal, 51,* 390–396.

Wax, M. L. (1971). *American Indians: Unity and diversity.* Englewood Cliffs, NJ: Prentice-Hall.

Weber, S. N. (1985). The need to be: The socio-cultural significance of Black language. In L. A. Samovar & R. E. Porter (Eds.), *Intercultural communication: A reader* (4th ed.) (pp. 244–253). Belmont, CA: Wadsworth.

Weiner, R. S. (1983). Utilizing the Hispanic family as a strategy in adjustment counseling. *Journal of Non-White Concerns, 11,* 133–137.

Werner, E. E. (1979). *Cross-cultural child development: A view from the planet Earth.* Monterey, CA: Brooks/Cole.

Werner, E. E. (1988). A cross-cultural perspective on infancy. *Journal of Cross-Cultural Psychology, 19,* 96–113.

West, B. E. (1983). The new arrivals from Southeast Asia: Getting to know them. *Childhood Education, 60,* 84–89.

Whitbourne, S. K. (1986). *Adult development* (2nd ed.). New York: Praeger.

White House Conference on Aging. (1972). *The Asian-American elderly.* Washington, DC: U. S. Government Printing Office.

Wittmer, J. P., & Loesch, L. C. (1986). Professional orientation. In M. D. Lewis, R. L. Hayes, & J. A. Lewis (Eds.), *An introduction to the counseling profession* (pp. 301–330). Itasca, IL: F. E. Peacock.

Wrenn, G. C. (1962). The culturally encapsulated counselor. *Harvard Educational Review, 32,* 444–449.

Wrenn, G. C. (1985). Afterward: The culturally encapsulated counselor revisited. In P. B. Pedersen (Ed.), *Handbook of cross-cultural counseling and therapy* (pp. 323–329). Westport, CT: Greenwood Press.

Wu, F. Y. T. (1975). Mandarin-speaking aged Chinese in the Los Angeles area. *The Gerontologist, 15,* 271–275.

Yao, E. L. (1985). Adjustment needs of Asian-American immigrant children. *Elementary School Guidance and Counseling, 19,* 223–227.

Yao, E. L. (1988). Working effectively with Asian immigrant parents. *Phi Delta Kappan, 70,* 223–225.

Yee, L. L. (1988). Asian children. *Teaching Exceptional Children, 20,* 49–50.

Young, R. L., Chamley, J. D., & Withers, C. (1990). Minority faculty representation and hiring practices in counselor education programs, *Counselor Education and Supervision, 29,* 148–154.

Young-Eisendrath, P. (1985). Making use of human development theories in counseling. *Counseling and Human Development, 17*(5), 1–12.

Youngman, G., & Sadongei, M. (1983). Counseling the American Indian child. In D. R. Atkinson, G. Morten, & D. W. Sue (Eds.), *Counseling American minorities: A cross-cultural perspective* (pp. 73–76). Dubuque, IA: Wm. C. Brown.

Yu, E. S. H. (1986). Health of the Chinese elderly in America. *Research on Aging, 8,* 84–109.

Yussen, S. R., & Santrock, J. W. (1982). *Child development: An introduction.* Dubuque, IA: Wm. C. Brown.

Author Index

Subject Index